Business Dynamics in Information Technology

Petter Gottschalk
Norwegian School of Management, Norway

IDEA GROUP PUBLISHING
Hershey • London • Melbourne • Singapore

Acquisitions Editor: Kristin Klinger
Development Editor: Kristin Roth
Senior Managing Editor: Jennifer Neidig
Managing Editor: Sara Reed
Assistant Managing Editor: Sharon Berger
Copy Editor: Killian Piraro
Typesetter: Amanda Appicello
Cover Design: Lisa Tosheff
Printed at: Yurchak Printing Inc.

Published in the United States of America by
          Idea Group Publishing (an imprint of Idea Group Inc.)
          701 E. Chocolate Avenue, Suite 200
          Hershey PA 17033-1240
          Tel: 717-533-8845
          Fax: 717-533-8661
          E-mail: cust@idea-group.com
          Web site: http://www.idea-group.com

and in the United Kingdom by
          Idea Group Publishing (an imprint of Idea Group Inc.)
          3 Henrietta Street
          Covent Garden
          London WC2E 8LU
          Tel: 44 20 7240 0856
          Fax: 44 20 7379 0609
          Web site: http://www.eurospanonline.com

                    Library of Congress Cataloging-in-Publication Data

Gottschalk, Petter, 1950-
  Business dynamics in information technology / Petter Gottschalk.
      p. cm.
  Summary: "This book presents business-technology alignment processes, interaction processes, and decision making processes, in order to help the reader study information technology from a dynamic, rather than a static, perspective. By introducing two simple tools from system dynamic modeling - causal loops and reference modes - the dynamic perspective will become important to both students and practitioners"--Provided by publisher.
  Includes bibliographical references and index.
  ISBN 978-1-59904-429-3 (hardcover) -- ISBN 1-59904-430-7 (softcover) -- ISBN 978-1-59904-431-6 (ebook)
  1. Information technology--Management. 2. Information resources management. 3. Industrial management--Technological innovations. 4. Electronic commerce. I. Title.
  HD30.2.G672 2007
  658.4'038--dc22
                    2006033761
British Cataloguing in Publication Data
A Cataloguing in Publication record for this book is available from the British Library.

All work contributed to this book is new, previously-unpublished material. The views expressed in this book are those of the authors, but not necessarily of the publisher.

Business Dynamics in Information Technology

Table of Contents

Forewords

Interactions between organizational performance and information technology create dynamics over time. Some of these dynamics are counterintuitive and surprising to management. Some of these dynamics have a spiraling effect of information technology that can cause not only exponential growth and prosperity, but also decline and collapse. Understanding the dynamics is essential to successful information technology management.

In my own research, I have found several factors in the work practice that can cause new information systems to fail rather than succeed. One factor is territory guarding between different value areas and between operational organization structures. Another factor is legal obstacles. Territory guarding between different initiatives for organizational development in combination with legal obstacles is also decreasing the possibility to develop information technology systems that are useful to the workplace. Instead of implemented IT systems, development work has often resulted in visions on paper.

According to the sociotechnical tradition, system development should not only be focused on the technology but also take into account organizational and human needs. It is important that information technology affects the work place in such a way that it will contribute to a thought-through and planned development of the work practice. System and work practice must be studied together.

Toward the end of this book, dynamics of police investigation performance is presented as an example of organizational dynamics. Decisions made by the police are often based on information from IT systems. My research shows that important work practice knowledge is filtered out by the IT systems. Information technology people usually have a great influence on the decisions taken concerning the development of IT systems, which means that there often is much focus on technical questions. The technical demands, rather than the core activity, form the central issues.

This is what makes this book so important. Only by increased insight into the use of information technology in supporting organizational activity over time will management be able to make smarter decisions. Understanding how executives themselves influence and are part of the dynamics will further enhance the chances of success.

From action research it becomes clear that conflicts easily arise among employees who have a floor perspective and those who have a managerial perspective. Employees who have a floor perspective must dare to get into conflicts with management. In a large number of interviews that were carried out throughout Sweden, police officers pointed out factors that are negative influences on their working performance. Based on these interviews I compiled a list over the mentioned factors and divided them into nine categories. The first category was discontent of present management—the way the organization is run and work practice follow-ups.

Management has a lot to learn from this book, to avoid IT systems contributing to a counterproductive work practice, and to enable information technology to create successful business dynamics.

Stefan Holgersson, PhD
Police Officer, Stockholm Police, Sweden

* * *

In this book, Petter Gottschalk gives a rich analysis and description of the role of IT in business dynamics, derived from both his wealth of experience as an IT and corporate executive in several organizations as well as his academic research and teaching position, which enable reflection on and the incorporation of current scientific insights in the field.

The book attempts to give answers to questions such as what makes information technology management successful in business, how one can avoid failures of the application of IT in business, and how can we apply systems methodology, and more specifically system dynamics, in the understanding of such issues.

The book examines step-by-step, logically and exhaustively, a wide variety of relevant processes and elements that are put in a strategic, systems, and governance perspective. However, not only an exhaustive analysis is made. Without an integrating approach it is hardly comprehensible to grasp the elements and their interactions in such a way that the reader is able to apply those in his own management or business environment. It is here that Petter Gottschalk has introduced a systems approach, which interlinks these elements.

A red thread through the book is the concept of systems thinking, whereby simultaneous stimuli and processes unroll and show certain different behaviors depending on the system structure and the role of IT in the management of organizations. This integrative and descriptive systems approach proclaims a novel way to management sciences in information technology applied in business dynamics. Business dynamics in information technology can now be seen as one of the major fields of the application of system dynamics.

System dynamics is used as a methodology for analyzing, describing, and understanding systems behavior, and the book succeeds in classifying different settings that cause different outcomes, explaining the role of stakeholders in obtaining more successful outcomes and survival strategies of businesses. The different facets and dynamic interactions described in this book are extremely useful for management information professionals, general management and business schools, and universities that teach information technology-related management sciences and skills.

System dynamics was founded in the early 1960s by Jay W. Forrester of the MIT Sloan School of Management, with the establishment of the MIT System Dynamics Group, which is still leading in the field. At that time, he began applying what he had learned about technical systems to everyday kinds of systems, such as several societal systems. The difference to other approaches of studying complex systems is the use of feedback loops and conceptual tools, which assist in the final formal mathematical modeling. Since then, system dynamics has been applied for the purpose of understanding the behavior of complex systems in disciplines such as demographics, environmental sciences, and economics. Although the book does not explain the actual formal mathematical modeling, it gives a valuable step up for the first phases one has to go through before the actual mathematical modeling for making simulations and studying behavior, robustness, tactics, and the like.

I take this opportunity to share some of my own experience. From the year at the System Dynamics Group at Dartmouth College in the U.S., where I had the pleasure to work with Petter Gottschalk on several projects in which system dynamics was applied, I remember the discussions we had with one of the prominent advocates of system dynamics, Dana Meadows, who sadly has passed away. At that time, the late seventies, the implications of the introduction of information technology in society was hardly felt or understood. However, we developed a strong notion that IT would have a tremendous impact on society and would lead to trend shifts that were hard to predict. At that time, mainly linear models and regression techniques were *en vogue*. With the compilation of this book, I am delighted to see how much technology and systems understanding have been developed since then.

The book represents another milestone in the application of system dynamics in such an important and relatively new field as business dynamics in information technology. Although I have been involved in the scientific research and application of system dynamics only a short period of time, and my professional focus has moved into business development of high-tech companies and research projects in life sciences, I still feel the richness of the system dynamics experience, which I still apply in my profession in basically the same way as described in this book—namely, in terms of causal loops and reference modes.

Though not mainly in information technology, I do frequently apply system dynamics thinking in the identification, selection, and development of new technologies that are suitable for further development into high-tech business enterprises. My work concerns combinations of various high-quality technologies that lead to solutions for which market demand exists. In my consulting and business development work I find that the complexity of factors and their interactions play a role that is nicely suited for system dynamics modeling.

With the step-by-step and comprehensive approach presented in this book and the cases that illustrate the systems approach, I recommend the book for information technology managers, researchers, policy makers, and system dynamics professionals alike.

Rob Tweehuysen
Tweehuysen BV, the Netherlands
www.tweehuysen.nl

Preface

Emerging business models, value configurations, and information technologies interact over time to create competitive advantage. Modern information technology has to be studied, understood, and applied along the time dimension of months and years, where changes are the rule. Such changes created by interactions between business elements and resources are very well suited for system dynamics modeling. System dynamics models represent a framework for understanding both successful and unsuccessful IT management over time. Systems dynamics simulations provide insights into the important interactions between IT investments and firm performance over time.

So many organizations fail in their applications of modern information technology. An important reason for such failure is the lack of understanding of relationships between corporate management and IT management. Relationships between corporate and IT management are not static. Rather, they evolve over time, creating growth or decline in firm performance. The objective of this book is to integrate systems dynamics modeling and IT management to provide a framework for understanding relationships and interactions between business and technology over time.

The most important consequence of this approach to the topic of IT management is that our understanding shifts from event-oriented and sequential management thinking to feedback-oriented and parallel management thinking. The event-oriented thinking is illustrated in Figure 1. Here management discovers a gap between current and desired business situation, leading to decisions, actions, and results.

The feedback-oriented thinking is illustrated in Figure 2. Here management decision-making is part of the business dynamics.

These two thinking styles can lead to very different business behavior over time. Just as an example, Figure 3 illustrates the event approach, while Figure 4 illustrates the feedback-oriented approach.

There are several reasons for the different behaviors in Figure 4 compared to Figure 3. One reason is the way we understand resources that close the gap between desired and current business situation. In event-oriented thinking, management might calculate needed resources as a consequence of the size of the gap, leading to lower resource consumption as the gap decreases, as illustrated in the planning sequence in Figure 1.

In feedback-oriented thinking, resource consumption is determined not only by the gap, but also by business performance. Hence, there are two oppos-

Figure 1. Event-oriented and sequential management thinking

```
┌──────────────────────────┐                              ┌──────────────┐
│ Current Business Situation│                              │  Resources   │
└──────────────────────────┘                              └──────────────┘
            │                                                     │
            ▼                                                     ▼
     ┌────────────┐      ┌────────────┐                    ┌──────────┐   ┌──────────┐
     │    Gap     │─────▶│  Decisions │                    │ Actions  │──▶│ Results  │
     └────────────┘      └────────────┘                    └──────────┘   └──────────┘
            ▲
┌──────────────────────────┐
│ Desired Business Situation│
└──────────────────────────┘
```

Figure 2. Feedback-oriented and parallel management thinking

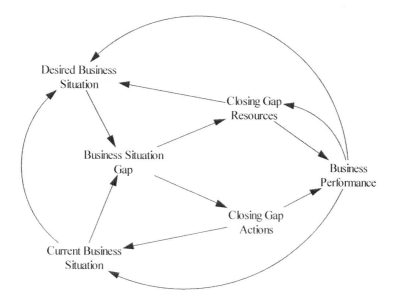

ing mechanisms over time. First, when the gap goes down, then closing gap resources go down. Second, when business performance goes up, then closing gap resources go up, as illustrated in Figure 2.

Business Dynamics in Information Technology is the title of this book. Causal loop diagrams as illustrated in Figure 2 and reference modes as illustrated

Figure 3. Event-oriented business performance management

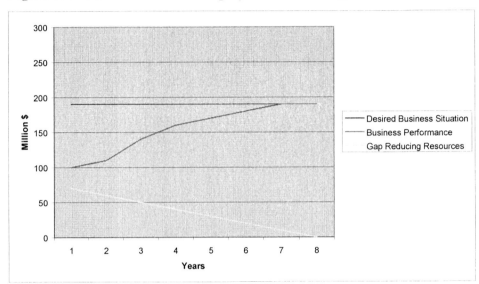

Figure 4. Feedback-oriented business performance management

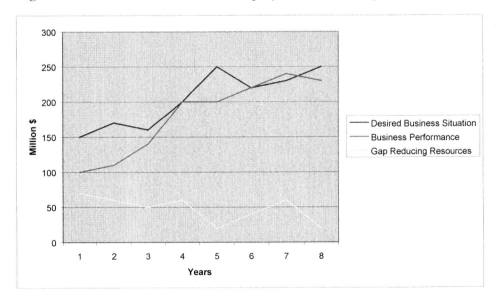

in Figures 3 and 4 will be explained and repeatedly applied throughout this book.

This is a textbook that will be useful to all business schools where management information systems (MIS) courses and decision support systems (DSS) courses, as well as system dynamics, are taught. The book will probably be most useful to graduate students. In addition, managers in charge of IT governance, IT strategy, and IT services will find this book useful in their work.

Theories of the firm, value configurations of the firm, strategic thinking, management roles, technology management, system dynamics, modeling, and simulation are some of the scholarly values of this book. The book makes a significant contribution to the discipline by presenting and applying the dynamic perspective in IT management in organizations.

The integration of system dynamics and IT management is exemplified throughout this book. System dynamics is a modeling technique to represent feedback structures that cause developments to change over time. Information technology management is concerned with applications of IT in terms of information systems that improve and sustain firm performance.

When system dynamics and IT management are integrated, then IT management impacts itself in feedback structures. IT management is not just a one-way practice of making decisions and running systems. Both decisions and operating procedures influence the way users and management perceive IT performance, and both users and management will react to it. Their reaction will in turn influence IT management. That is how IT management impacts itself in feedback structures.

Introduction To Chapters

The overall structure of this book has three parts that represent main messages for the reader:

- *Business-technology alignment processes* are concerned with mutual alignment between business and technology over time. Alignment is the topic in the first chapter about value configurations and there is a later chapter on corporate strategic management. Alignment is related to strategy.

- *Business-technology interaction processes* are concerned with dynamic behavior in system dynamics. This is the topic in many chapters, especially in chapters on the dynamics of e-business, knowledge management, and outsourcing. Interaction is related to system dynamics.

- *Business-technology decision processes* are concerned with decision rights and decision makers in IT governance in the third chapter, as well as the roles of the chief information officer (CIO) and the chief executive officer (CEO) for successful use of IT over time in the eighth chapter. Decision is related to governance.

These three process perspectives are all discussed in most of the book. However, to make it simpler for the reader, each chapter is assigned to one of these processes in Figure 5. But the book is not organized according to these processes, as illustrated by business-technology alignment processes found in chapters 1 and 7. Rather, the book is organized according to IT management topics after two theoretical chapters on resources and dynamics.

Figure 5. Book chapters according to their focus on business-technology alignment, decision, and interaction processes

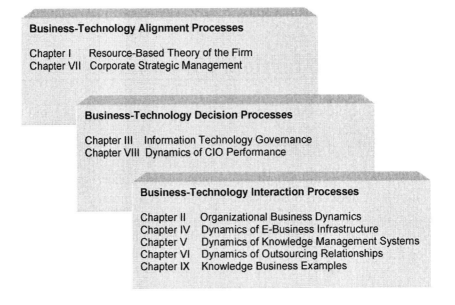

This book starts by presenting the resource-based theory of the firm in Chapter I. An important business-technology alignment process is the alignment of value configuration, information systems, and IT resources. A value configuration of value shop has very different primary activities from value chains and value networks.

In Chapter I we define the IT resource, which enables the firm to improve and sustain its performance.

Next, the system dynamics perspective is introduced in terms of organizational business dynamics in Chapter II. Here we introduce system dynamics modeling. However, as this book is no textbook on system dynamics, the more complicated parts of modeling—such as stock-and-flow diagrams and parameters for simulation—are left out. Rather, this book focuses on the beginning and the end of the modeling processes, the causal loop diagram and the simulated behavior, which we call reference mode.

Information technology governance has emerged as an important discipline to improve information technology performance in organizations. Information technology governance is concerned with decision rights, resource mobilization, and alignment. The areas for IT governance have been categorized into IT principles, IT infrastructures, IT architectures, IT applications, and IT investments. In Chapter III, we take a dynamic look at these decision areas.

In the following three chapters, important topics in MIS are discussed in terms of their dynamic properties. In Chapter IV, dynamics of e-business infrastructure illustrates the contingent approach to infrastructure services depending on an e-business model. As the chosen e-business model increases its number of IT infrastructure services, the e-business model capability improves.

Next, the dynamics of knowledge management systems in Chapter V presents the stages of growth model for knowledge management technology and discusses technology stage dynamics. For example, as the organization has implemented advanced expert systems at a higher stage, it might be necessary to return to a lower stage to create the information resources needed to apply such systems more effectively.

Then in Chapter VI, one more important IT management topic is presented and discussed as a dynamic phenomenon. The chapter is concerned with IT outsourcing relationships. We have learned that relationships both deteriorate and improve, depending on a variety of factors. When the influence of these factors and the interactions between these factors are studied over time, we find yet another interesting example of business dynamics in IT.

The selection of IT management topics is not random. Rather, the selected topics emerge as important to most organizations toward 2010. The selected IT management topics are IT governance, e-business, knowledge management, and outsourcing.

In Chapter VII, we returned to the firm perspective as introduced in Chapter I. While Chapter I had an organizational focus on resources and value configurations, Chapter VII is focused on the role of management in strategy development and implementation. The resource-based theory is further development in terms of resource-based strategy. Again, business dynamics in IT management is illustrated by causal loop diagramming and reference mode behavior.

Chapter VIII presents the CIO, who is responsible for the IT function in the organization. The perspective of business dynamics incorporates CIO influence and performance in causal relations, together with the performance of the CEO.

So far, all chapters have studied dynamics of IT management. In Chapter IX, two organization examples illustrate knowledge business performance. Here, IT management is a factor, but not the only one. The first example of law firms as knowledge-intensive businesses presents knowledge categories and knowledge levels. The next example of police investigations as part of law enforcement presents knowledge work in investigation value shop.

Finally, in Chapter X, dual MIS topics are presented. First, knowledge management systems and e-business are linked in a dynamic perspective. Next, knowledge management systems and IT outsourcing are linked in a dynamic perspective. These two examples should further illustrate business dynamics in IT. Not only is IT over time interacting with business and firm performance, but there are also dynamic relationships within different aspects of IT.

The material put together in this book serves the purpose of helping the reader study IT from a dynamic, rather than from a static, perspective. By introducing two simple tools from system dynamic modeling—causal loops and reference modes—the dynamic perspective might become the most important to both students and practitioners in the future.

Petter Gottschalk
Oslo, Norway, January 2006
petter.gottschalk@bi.no

Chapter I

Resource-Based Theory of the Firm

In this book, we apply the resource-based theory of the firm that has established itself as an important perspective in strategic management. According to the resource-based theory of the firm, performance differences across firms can be attributed to the variance in the firms" strategic resources and capabilities. Resources that are valuable, unique, and difficult to imitate can provide the basis for firms' competitive advantages (Garud & Kumaraswamy, 2005)

In order to explore the usefulness of the resource-based theory for information technology resources, it is necessary to explicitly recognize the characteristics and attributes of resources that lead them to become strategically important. Although firms possess many resources, only a few of these have the potential to lead the firm to a position of sustained competitive advantage (Wade & Hulland, 2004). In this chapter we will see what separates regular resources from those that confer a sustainable strategic benefit.

Resources are employed in the production of goods and services, which occurs in the firm's value configuration. The value configuration is the way a particular organization conducts its business. There are three alternative value configurations—the value chain, the value shop, and the value network—as we shall see later in this chapter. To comprehend the value that IT provides to organizations, we must understand their value configurations (Stabell & Fjeldstad, 1998).

To some readers, this first chapter might seem too theoretical and possibly put them off. Hopefully, this will not happen. It is important to cover the material included here before going on to the other chapters. What is most important to remember from this chapter when moving on to the rest of the book are (1) strategic resources that influence the success of IT management, and (2) value configurations that introduce a contingent approach to IT management.

Organizational Resources

The central tenet in resource-based theory is that unique organizational resources of both tangible and intangible nature are the real source of competitive advantage. With resource-based theory, organizations are viewed as a collection of resources that are heterogeneously distributed within and across industries. Accordingly, what makes the performance of an organization distinctive is the unique blend of the resources it possesses. A firm's resources include not only its physical assets, such as plant and location, but also its competencies. The ability to leverage distinctive internal and external competencies relative to environmental situations ultimately affects the performance of the business.

Exploring competencies in the context of the management of information technology is a relatively recent development in the evolution of the information systems discipline. The importance of developing competencies that allow organizations to successfully take advantage of information in their specific context has been noted. The concept of competence in the information systems literature is predominantly focused upon individual competence in the form of IT skill sets, rather than treated as an organizational construct. The focus has been on the technology supply side and individuals' skills, emphasizing the requirement for IT professionals to have not just technical skills but also business and interpersonal skills. More recently, being a change agent has been proposed as a skill for IT professionals. The implication of this literature stream is that equipping IT specialists with additional skills can solve the problem of lacking benefits from IT. The inference is that the inability to deliver value from information arises from shortcomings in the IT function and among IT professionals (Peppard, Lambert, & Edwards, 2000).

Conversely, when the IT function is able to deliver value from the information resource, the firm will improve its performance and gain competitive advantage. In turn, competitive advantages produce positive returns. According to Hitt et al. (2001), most of the few empirical tests of the resource-based theory that have been conducted have supported positive, direct effects of resources.

The essence of the resource-based theory of the firm lies in its emphasis on the internal resources available to the firm, rather than on the external opportunities and threats dictated by industry conditions. Firms are considered to be highly heterogeneous, and the bundles of resources available to each firm are different. This is both because firms have different initial resource endowments and because managerial decisions affect resource accumulation and the direction of firm growth as well as resource utilization (Løwendahl, 2000).

The resource-based theory of the firm holds that, in order to generate sustainable competitive advantage, a resource must provide economic value and must be presently scarce, difficult to imitate, nonsubstitutable, and not readily obtainable in factor markets. This theory rests on two key points. First, that resources are the determinants of firm performance and second, that resources must be rare, valuable, difficult to imitate and nonsubstitutable by other rare resources. When the latter occurs, a competitive advantage has been created. Resources can simultaneously be characterized as valuable, rare, nonsubstitutable, and inimitable. To the extent that an organization"s physical assets, infrastructure, and workforce satisfy these criteria, they qualify as resources. A firm"s performance depends fundamentally on its ability to have a distinctive, sustainable competitive advantage, which derives from the possession of firm-specific resources (Priem & Butler, 2001).

The resource-based theory is a useful perspective in strategic management. Research on the competitive implications of such firm resources as knowledge, learning, culture, teamwork, and human capital, was given a significant boost by resource-based theory—a theory that indicated it was these kinds of resources that were most likely to be sources of sustainable competitive advantage for firms (Barney, 2001).

Firms' resource endowments, particularly intangible resources, are difficult to change except over the long term. For example, although human resources may be mobile to some extent, capabilities may not be valuable for all firms or even for their competitors. Some capabilities are based on firm-specific knowledge, and others are valuable when integrated with additional individual capabilities and specific firm resources. Therefore, intangible resources are more likely than tangible resources to produce a competitive advantage. In particular, intangible firm-specific resources such as knowledge allow firms to add value to incoming factors of production (Hitt, Bierman, Shumizu, & Kochhar, 2001).

Resource-based theory attributes advantage in an industry to a firm's control over bundles of unique material—human, organizational, and local resources and skills that enable unique value-creating strategies. A firm's resources are said to be a source of competitive advantage to the degree that they are scarce, specialized, appropriable, valuable, rare, and difficult to imitate or substitute.

Capabilities and Resources

A fundamental idea in resource-based theory is that a firm must continually enhance its resources and capabilities to take advantage of changing conditions. Optimal growth involves a balance between the exploitation of existing resource positions and the development of new resource positions. Thus, a firm would be expected to develop new resources after its existing resource base has been fully utilized. Building new resource positions is important if the firm is to achieve sustained growth. When unused productive resources are coupled with changing managerial knowledge, unique opportunities for growth are created (Pettus, 2001).

The term "resource" is derived from the Latin word "resurgere", which has the meaning "to rise" and implies an aid or expedient for reaching an end. A resource implies a potential means to achieve an end, or as something that can be used to create value. The first strategy textbooks outlining a holistic perspective focused on how resources needed to be allocated or deployed to earn rents. The interest in the term was for a long time linked to the efficiency of resource allocation, but this focus has later been expanded to issues such as resource accumulation, resource stocks, and resource flows (Haanaes, 1997).

Firms develop firm-specific resources and then renew these to respond to shifts in the business environment. Firms develop dynamic capabilities to adapt to changing environments. According to Pettus (2001), the term "dynamic" refers to the capacity to renew resource positions to achieve congruence with changing environmental conditions. A "capability" refers to the key role of strategic management in appropriately adapting, integrating, and reconfiguring internal and external organizational skills, resources, and functional capabilities to match the requirements of a changing environment. If firms are to develop dynamic capabilities, learning is crucial. Change is costly; therefore, the ability of firms to make necessary adjustments depends upon their ability to scan the environment to evaluate markets and competitors and to quickly accomplish reconfiguration and transformation ahead of competition. However, history matters. Thus, opportunities for growth will involve dynamic capabilities closely related to existing capabilities. As such, opportunities will be most effective when they are close to previous resource use.

According to Johnson and Scholes (2002), successful strategies are dependent on the organization having the strategic capability to perform at the level that is required for success. So the first reason why an understanding of strategic capability is important is concerned with whether an organization's strategies continue to fit the environment in which the organization is operating and the opportunities and threats that exist. Many of the issues of strategy development are concerned with changing strategic capability better to fit a changing environment. Understanding strategic capability is also important from another perspective. The organization's capability may be the leading edge of strategic developments, in the sense that new opportunities may be created by stretching and exploiting the organization's capability either in ways competitors find difficult to match, or in genuinely new directions, or both. This requires organizations to be innovative in the way they develop and exploit their capability. In this perspective, strategic capability is about providing products or services to customers who are valued, or might be valued in the future. An understanding of what customers value is the starting point. The discussion then moves to whether an organization has the resources to provide products and services that meet these customer requirements.

A resource is anything that could be thought of as a strength or weakness of a given firm. More formally, a firm's resources at a given time can be defined as those (tangible and intangible) assets that are tied to the firm over a substantial period of time. Examples of resources are brand names, in-house knowledge of technology, employment of skilled personnel, trade contracts, machinery, efficient procedures, capital, and so forth. According to the economic school, resources include human capital, structural capital, relational capital, and financial capital. Priem and Butler (2001) find it problematic that virtually anything associated with a firm can be a resource, because this notion suggests that prescriptions for dealing in certain ways with certain categories of resources might be operationally valid, whereas other categories of resources might be inherently difficult for practitioners to measure and manipulate. One example of a resource that might be difficult to measure and manipulate is tacit knowledge. Some have argued for tacit knowledge—that understanding gained from experience sometimes cannot be expressed to another person and is unknown to oneself—as a source of competitive advantage. Another example is the chief executive officer (CEO) resource. Prescriptions have been made to top managers of poorly performing firms that they are the cause of the problem and should think about voluntarily exiting the firm. This is a case where viewing a CEO as a resource would have more prescriptive implications for boards of directors than for the CEO.

Heijden (2001) measured IT core capabilities for electronic commerce. Capabilities include organization-specific routines, processes, skills, and resources. They need to be built through learning processes and cannot be readily bought. Heijden listed a total of nine core capabilities for the IS function: IS/IT governance, business systems thinking, relationship building, designing technical architecture, making technology work, informed buying, contract facilitation, contract monitoring, and vendor development.

Strategic Resources

Barney (2002) discussed how value, rarity, organization, and other characteristics might be brought together into a single framework to understand the return potential associated with exploiting any of a firm's resources and capabilities. The framework consists of the following five steps:

1. If a resource or capability controlled by a firm is *not valuable*, that resource will not enable a firm to choose or implement strategies that exploit environmental opportunities or neutralize environmental threats. Organizing to exploit this resource will increase a firm's costs or decrease its revenues. These types of resources are weaknesses. Firms will either

have to fix these weaknesses or avoid using them when choosing and implementing strategies. If firms do exploit these kinds of resources and capabilities, they can expect to put themselves at a competitive disadvantage compared to firms that either do not possess these nonvaluable resources or do not use them in conceiving and implementing strategies. Firms at a competitive disadvantage are likely to earn below-normal economic profits.

2.   If a resource or capability is *valuable but not rare*, exploiting this resource in conceiving and implementing strategies will generate competitive parity and normal economic performance. Exploiting these valuable-but-not-rare resources will generally not create above-normal economic performance for a firm, but failure to exploit them can put a firm at a competitive disadvantage. In this sense, valuable-but-not-rare resources can be thought of as organizational strengths.

3.   If a resource or capability is *valuable and rare but not costly to imitate*, exploiting this resource will generate a temporary competitive advantage for a firm and above-normal economic profits. A firm that exploits this kind of resource is, in an important sense, gaining a first-mover advantage, because it is the first firm that is able to exploit a particular resource. However, once competing firms observe this competitive advantage, they will be able to acquire or develop the resources needed to implement this strategy through direct duplication or substitution at no cost disadvantage compared to the first-moving firm. Over time, any competitive advantage that the first mover obtained would be competed away as other firms imitate the resources needed to compete. However, between the time a firm gains a competitive advantage by exploiting a valuable and rare but imitable resource or capability, and the time that competitive advantage is competed away through imitation, the first-moving firm can earn above-normal economic performance. Consequently, this type of resource or capability can be thought of as an organizational strength and distinctive competence.

4.   If a resource is *valuable, rare, and costly to imitate*, exploiting this resource will generate a sustained competitive advantage and above-normal economic profits. In this case, competing firms face a significant cost disadvantage in imitating a successful firm's resources and capabilities, and thus cannot imitate this firm's strategies. This advantage may reflect the unique history of the successful firm, causal ambiguity about which resources to imitate, or the socially complex nature of these resources

and capabilities. In any case, attempts to compete away the advantages of firms that exploit these resources will not generate above-normal or even normal performance for imitating firms. Even if these firms were able to acquire or develop the resources and capabilities in question, the very high costs of doing so would put them at a competitive disadvantage compared to the firm that already possessed the valuable, rare, and costly to imitate resources. These kinds of resources and capabilities are organizational strengths and sustainable distinctive competencies.

5.   The question of organization operates as an adjustment factor in the framework. If a firm with a resource that is *valuable, rare, and costly to imitate, is disorganized,* some of its potential above-normal return could be lost. If the firm completely fails to organize itself to take advantage of this resource, it could actually lead the firm that has the potential for above-normal performance to earn normal or even below-normal performance.

Barney (2001) discussed how value and rarity of resources might be determined. *Value* is a question of conditions under which resources will and will not be valuable. Models of the competitive environment within which a firm competes can determine value. Such models fall into two large categories: (1) efforts to use structure-conduct-performance-based models to specify conditions under which different firm resources will be valuable, and (2) efforts to determine the value of firm resources that apply other models derived from industrial organization models of perfect and imperfect competition. As an example of resource value determination, Barney discusses the ability of cost leadership strategy to generate sustained competitive advantage. Several firm attributes may be associated with cost leadership, such as volume-derived economies of scale, cumulative volume-derived learning curve economies, and policy choices. These firm attributes can be shown to generate economic value in at least some market settings. The logic used to demonstrate the value of these attributes is a market structure logic that is consistent with traditional microeconomics. After identifying the conditions under which cost leadership can generate economic value, it is possible to turn to the conditions under which cost leadership can be a source of competitive advantage (i.e., rare) and sustained competitive advantage (i.e., rare and costly to imitate).

The resource-based theory postulates that some resources will have a higher value for one firm than for other firms. The reasons why the value of resources may be firm-specific are multiple and include (Haanaes, 1997): the experience of working together as a team, the firm possessing superior knowledge about its resources, the bundling of the resources, and the existence of cospecialized or complementary assets. The value of a given resource may change over time as the market conditions change, such as in terms of technology, customer preferences, or industry structure. Thus, it is often argued that firms need to maintain a dynamic, as opposed to static, evaluation of the value of different resources.

Rarity is a question of how many competing firms possess a particular valuable resource. If only one competing firm possesses a particular valuable resource, then that firm can gain a competitive advantage, that is, it can improve its efficiency and effectiveness in ways that competing firms cannot. One example of this form of testable assertion is mentioned by Barney (2001). The example is concerned with organizational culture as a source of competitive advantage. If only one competing firm possesses a valuable organizational culture (where the value of that culture is determined in ways that are exogenous to the firm), then that firm can gain a competitive advantage, that is, it can improve its efficiency and effectiveness in ways that competing firms cannot. Both these assertions are testable. If a firm uniquely possesses a valuable resource and cannot improve its efficiency and effectiveness in ways that generate competitive advantages, then these assertions are contradicted. One could test these assertions by measuring the extent to which a firm uniquely possesses valuable resources, such as valuable organizational culture, measuring the activities that different firms engage in to improve their efficiency and effectiveness, and then seeing if there are some activities a firm with the unique culture engages in to improve its effectiveness and efficiency—activities not engaged in by other competing firms. In general, the rarity of a resource is present as long as the number of firms that possess a particular valuable resource is less than the number of firms needed to generate perfect competition dynamics. Of course, there are difficult measurement problems associated with testing assertions of this form. Barney (2001) points out that additional research work is needed to complete the parameterization of the concept of rarity. Efficient firms can sustain their competitive advantage only if their resources can neither be extended freely nor imitated by other firms. Hence, in order for resources to have the potential to generate rents, they must be rare. Valuable, but common, resources cannot by themselves represent sources of competitive advantage because competitors can access them. Nobody needs to pay extra for obtaining a resource that is not held in limited supply.

In addition to value and rarity, inimitability has to be determined. Inimitability can be determined through barriers to imitation and replication. The extent of barriers and impediments against direct and indirect imitation determine the extent of inimitability. One effective barrier to imitation is that competitors fail to understand the firm's sources of advantage. The lack of understanding can be caused by tacitness, complexity, and specificity, which form bases for competitive advantage (Haanaes, 1997). Several authors have categorized resources. A common categorization is tangibles versus intangibles. Tangibles are relatively clearly defined and easy to identify. Tangible resources include plants, technology, land, and geographical location, access to raw materials, capital, equipment, and legal resources. Tangible resources tend to be property-based and may also include databases, licenses, patents, registered designs and trademarks, as well as other property rights that are easily bought and sold. Intangibles are more difficult to define and also to study empirically. Intangible resources encompass skills, knowledge, organizational capital, relationships, capabilities, and human capital, as well as brands, company and product reputation, networks, competencies, perceptions of quality, and the ability to manage change. Intangible resources are generally less easy to transfer than tangible resources, as the value of an intangible resource is difficult to measure.

Based on this discussion, we might add to the framework by Barney (2002) four more steps:

6. If our firm with a resource that is *valuable, rare, costly to imitate, and organized is easy to substitute*, some of its potential above-normal return could be lost. If a competing firm is able to do the same task as our firm by applying a different resource which can substitute our resource for the same task, it could actually lead our firm that has the potential for above-normal performance to earn normal or even below-normal performance.

7. If our firm with a resource that is *valuable, rare, costly to imitate, organized and difficult to substitute is easy to move*, then again we might be in trouble in terms of not gaining sustained competitive advantage. In this case, a resource might leave the firm and join a competing firm.

8. If our firm with a resource that is *valuable, rare, costly to imitate, organized, difficult to substitute and difficult to move, is difficult to combine*, then some potential benefits from the resource is lost. This is because

many resources are of little value except when they are combined with other resources.

9.   If our firm with a resource that is *valuable, rare, costly to imitate, organized, difficult to substitute, difficult to move and easy to combine is difficult to transfer*, then we might have difficulty in transferring to clients the value that they are paying for. Here we make a distinction between moving (undesired action) and transferring (desired action).

Slack Resources

Ang (1993) studied the etiology of IT outsourcing. Any analysis of outsourcing will typically incorporate the effects of managerial discretionary power on substantive administrative choices. Inclusion of managerial-behavioral factors to understanding outsourcing is consistent with the view of managerial choices to be the primary link between an organization and its environment. The importance of managerial discretion in the operations of the firm has been widely acknowledged in organization theory. In general, the separation of ownership from control of the firm gives rise to problems of controlling managerial behavior. It can be emphasized that when ownership is thinly spread over a large number of shareholders in a firm, control lies in the hands of the managers who themselves own only a tiny fraction of the firm's equity. These circumstances permit managers a greater discretion and decision latitude over substantive domains such as resource allocation, administrative choices, and product market selection.

Organizations with abundant slack tend to induce greater managerial discretion. Slack is defined as the difference between total resources and total necessary payments. It refers to the excess that remains once a firm has paid its various internal and external constituencies to maintain their cooperation. Slack can further be defined as a cushion of excess resources available in an organization that will either solve many organization problems or facilitate the pursuit of goals outside the realm of those dictated by optimization principles. An organization's slack reflects its ability to adapt to unknown or uncertain future changes in its environment. Accordingly, uncommitted or transferable slack resources would expand the array of options available to management. Instead of distributing slack resources back to shareholders, managers tend to retain and invest slack resources in new employees, new equipment, and other assets to promote asset capitalization. One primary reason for retaining earnings within the organization is that increased asset capitalization, the primary indicator of firm size, enhances the social prominence, public prestige, and political power of senior executives.

Investments in IT represent a major approach to asset capitalization in organizations. Information technology may symbolize firm growth, advancement, and progress. Because investments in IT can promote social prominence and public prestige, managers are induced to utilize slack resources to internalize IS services. Inducements toward investments in in-house IS services are further reinforced by well-publicized case studies that demonstrate the competitive advantage and new business opportunities afforded by IT. The above reasoning suggests that managers may exhibit a penchant for building up internal IT resources such as IS employees, equipment, and computer capacity when organizations possess slack resources. In contrast, when slack resources are low, managers tend to conserve resources in response to the anxiety provoked by loss of financial resources. Anxiety is provoked because the loss of financial resources is often attributed to managerial incompetence and organizational ineffectiveness. As a result, leaders are more likely to be blamed and replaced when financial performance is poor. In response to the anxiety provoked by loss of financial resources, decision makers have been observed to reduce costs through downsizing the company by selling off physical assets and laying off workers.

Companies may even sell IT assets at inflated rates to external service providers to generate short-term financial slack. The companies then reimburse the service provider by paying higher annual fees for a long-term outsourcing contract lasting eight to ten years. In other words, long-term facilities management contracts can be drawn where the service providers agree to purchase corporate assets, such as computer equipment, at prices substantially higher than the market value, and to provide capital to the company by purchasing stock from the company. Arrangements such as these permit companies to maintain capital, defer losses on the disposition of assets, and at the same time, show an increase in financial value on the balance sheet. But, because these arrangements also involve companies paying higher fees over the life of the contract, company financial statements are thus artificially inflated and do not reflect the true financial picture of the institution.

According to Ang (1993), when slack resources are low, we would expect firms to downsize internal IS services by selling off IT assets and reducing IS personnel and occupancy expenses—in effect, outsourcing IS services. Thus, we would expect that firms are less likely to outsource when slack resources are high and more likely to outsource when slack resources are low.

Besides managerial discretion over slack resources, top management's perception of the criticality of IT may differ. According to the dependence-avoidance perspective of the firm, organizations will avoid compromising their autonomy, particularly when the resource is vital for the organization's survival. The strength of an organization's aversion to loss of autonomy is thus a function of the criticality of the resource. The organization will proactively struggle to avoid external dependency, that is, outsourcing, regardless of efficiency considerations as long as it depends on IT for survival. The value of IT for competitive advantage intensifies the pressure on firms to internalize sophisticated IS services to avoid leakage of competitive information.

Although it is generally accepted that IT is critical for information-intensive firms, not all members of top management teams attach the same degree of criticality to IT. Perceptions of the CIOs and CEOs of IT importance tend to be misaligned. While CIOs recognize IT as vital to an organization's strategy, CEOs with little background in IT tend to regard IS services as back-room operations, an expense to be controlled rather than a strategic investment to be capitalized. Generally, CEOs' perceptions of IT criticality are as important as, if not more important than, those of the CIOs' with respect to IS sourcing decisions because IS investments represent a significant financial outlay for corporations. Sometimes management policies and direction of IT use are dictated by the CEOs' psychological involvement and participation in IS. Thus, we would expect that the greater the perceived criticality of IT to the firm, the less likely the firm will outsource its IS services (Ang, 1993).

Firm Boundaries

For many years researchers have sought to better understand why companies adopt different modes of governance. The resource-based view of the firm focuses on the opportunity for gain from transactions. A technology's potential for rendering a sustained competitive advantage will influence governance modes for external technology sourcing. The fundamental tenets of a resource-based perspective suggest a positive relationship between the perceived opportunity for sustainable advantage and the probability that a company will source technology with an acquisition from external sources (Steensma & Corley, 2001).

Sourcing technology from outside the organization changes company boundary between the firm that desires the know-how (the sourcing firm), and the firm that has the technology (the source firm). Managers must assess the governance alternatives for procuring desired technological know-how. According to classical decision theory, strategic decisions such as these entail a trade-off between risk and expected return, where risk is conceptualized as the variance of the probability distribution of the gains and losses of a particular alternative.

Steensma and Corley (2001) investigated organizational context as a moderator of theories on firm boundaries for technology sourcing. They found that the resource-based rationale, grounded on the opportunity to develop sustainable advantages, plays a larger role in explaining firm boundaries when a firm has lower levels of recoverable slack and a risk-seeking orientation than when a firm has higher slack and risk aversion. Organizational slack is defined as an organization's excess resources, while firm risk orientation is defined as expected outcome uncertainty.

Activity-Based Theory of the Firm

The resource-based theory of the firm grew out of efforts to explain the growth of firms. Although its origins lay primarily in economics, researchers in strategy have developed the resource-based theory. The main attraction of the resource-based theory is that it focuses on explaining why firms are different and its effect on profitability. The main tenets of the resource-based theory are that firms differ in their resource endowments, that these differences are persistent, and that firm-level performance differentials can be explained by analyzing a firm's resource position. Differences in resources are seen to lead to nonreplicable efficiency rents.

Sheehan (2002) discussed comparing and contrasting the resource-based theory with the activity-based theory, and his discussion is presented in the following. The activity-based theory conceives the firm as a bundle of activities, while the resource-based theory conceives the firm as a bundle of resources. The resource-based theory focuses on explaining why firms create more value than others by examining differences in resource stocks. However, the resource-based theory places little or no emphasis on resource flows. The role of the production function in transforming inputs into end products (other than having the latent ability to transform) is underconceptualized in the resource-based theory. On the other hand, the activity-based theory focuses on flows of resources in activities. It emphasizes the impact of the firm's production function on creating value, while placing little attention on differences in stocks of resources. It is implicitly assumed that all necessary inputs (resources) can be acquired from the market.

The goal of strategy formulation in the resource-based theory is to identify and increase those resources that allow a firm to gain and sustain superior rents. Firms owning strategic resources are predicted to earn superior rents, while firms possessing no or few strategic resources are thought to earn industry-average rents or below-average rents. The goal of strategy formulation in the activity-based theory is to identify and explore drivers that allow a firm to gain and sustain superior rents. Drivers are a central concept in the activity-based theory. To be considered drivers, firm-level factors must meet three criteria: They are structural factors at the level of activities, they are more or less controllable by management, and they impact the cost and/or differentiation position of the firm. The definition of drivers is primarily based on what drivers do. Drivers are abstract, relative, and relational properties of activities. For example, the scale of an activity is a driver, as the size of the activity relative to competitors may represent a competitive advantage.

The analytical focus of the resource-based theory is potentially narrower than that of the activity-based theory. While the activity-based theory takes the firm's entire activity set as its unit of analysis, the resource-based theory focuses on individual resources or bundles of resources. Having a narrower focus means that the resource-based theory may not take into account the negative impact of resources, how a resource's value may change as the environment changes, or the role of non-core resources in achieving competitive advantage.

The activity-based and resource-based theories are similar, as they both attempt to explain how firms attain superior positions through factors that increase firm differentiation or lower firm cost. While drivers and resources share a common goal of achieving and sustaining superior positions, the manner by which they are seen to reach a profitable position is different. With the resource-based theory, it is the possession or control of strategic resources that allow a firm to gain a profitable position. On the other hand, drivers within the activity-based theory are not unique to the firm. They are generic, structural factors, which are available to all firms in the industry, in the sense that they are conceptualized as properties of the firm's activities. A firm gains a profitable position by configuring its activities using drivers. It is this position that a firm may own, but only if it is difficult for rivals to copy the firm's configuration.

The sustainability of superior positions created by configuring drivers or owning resources is based on barriers to imitation. The sustainability of competitive advantage as per the activity-based theory is through barriers to imitation at the activity level. If the firm has a competitive advantage, as long as competitors are unable to copy the way activities are performed and configured through the drivers, the firm should be able to achieve above-average earnings over an extended period. The sustainability of superior profitability in the resource-based theory is through barriers to imitation of resources and immobility of resources. If resources are easily copied or substituted, then the sustainability of the position is suspect.

Sheehan (2002) concludes his discussion by finding similarities between the resource-based theory and the activity-based theory. Resources in the resource-based theory are similar to drivers in the activity-based theory, as both are based on earning efficiency rents. Furthermore, capabilities in the resource-based theory are similar to activities in the activity-based theory, as both imply action.

Information Technology Resources

The resource-based view started to appear in IT research one decade ago. Now IT resources can be compared to one another and, perhaps more importantly, can be compared with non-IT resources. Thus, the resource-based view promotes cross-functional studies through comparisons with other firm resources.

In the beginning of resource-based studies of IT resources, IT was divided into three assets, which together with processes contribute to business value. These three IT assets were labeled human assets (e.g., technical skills, business understanding, problem-solving orientation), technology assets (e.g., physical IT assets, technical platforms, databases, architectures, standards), and relationship assets (e.g., partnerships with other divisions, client relationships, top management sponsorship, shared risk and responsibility). IT processes were defined as planning ability, cost-effective operations and support, and fast delivery. This categorization was later modified to include IT infrastructure, human IT resources, and IT-enabled intangibles.

Wade and Hulland (2004) presented a typology of IT resources, where the IT resources held by a firm can be sorted into three types of processes: inside-out, outside-in, and spanning. Inside-out resources are deployed from inside the firm in response to market requirements and opportunities, and tend to be internally focused. In contrast, outside-in resources are externally oriented, placing an emphasis on anticipated market requirements, creating durable customer relationships, and understanding competitors. Finally, spanning resources, which involve both internal and external analysis, are needed to integrate the firm's inside-out and outside-in resources.

Inside-out resources include IS infrastructure, IS technical skills, IS development, and cost-effective IS operations:

- **IT infrastructure:** Many components of the IT infrastructure (such as off-the-shelf computer hardware and software) convey no particular strategic benefit due to lack of rarity, ease of imitation, and ready mobility. Thus, the types of IT infrastructure of importance are either proprietary or complex and hard to imitate. Despite research attempts to focus on theinimitable aspects of IT infrastructure, the IT infrastructure resource has generally not been found to be a source of sustained competitive advantage for firms.

- **IT technical skills:** IT technical skills are a result of the appropriate, updated technology skills, relating to both systems hardware and software that are held by the IS/IT employees of a firm. Such skills do not include only current technical knowledge, but also the ability to deploy, use, and manage that knowledge. Thus, this resource is focused on technical skills that are advanced, complex, and therefore difficult to imitate. Although the relative mobility of IS/IT personnel tends to be high, some IS skills cannot be easily transferred, such as corporate-level knowledge assets and technology integration skills, and thus these resources can become a source of sustained competitive advantage.

- **IT development:** IT development refers to the capability to develop or experiment with new technologies, as well as a general level of alertness to emerging technologies and trends that allow a firm to quickly take advantage of new advances. Thus, IT development includes capabilities associated with managing a systems development life-cycle that is capable of supporting competitive advantage, and should therefore lead to superior firm performance.

- **Cost-effective IT operations:** This resource encompasses the ability to provide efficient and cost-effective IS operations on an ongoing basis. Firms with greater efficiency can develop a long-term competitive advantage by using this capability to reduce costs and develop a cost leadership position in their industry. In the context of IS operations, the ability to avoid large, persistent cost overruns, unnecessary downtime, and system failure is likely to be an important precursor to superior performance. Furthermore, the ability to develop and manage IT systems of appropriate quality that function effectively can be expected to have a positive impact on performance.

Outside-in resources include external relationship management and market responsiveness:

- **External relationship management:** This resource represents the firm's ability to manage linkages between the IT function and stakeholders outside the firm. It can manifest itself as an ability to work with suppliers to develop appropriate systems and infrastructure requirements for the firm, to manage relationships with outsourcing partners, or to manage customer relationships by providing solutions, support, and/or customer service. Many large IT departments rely on external partners for a significant portion of their work. The ability to work with and manage these relationships is an important organizational resource leading to competitive advantage and superior firm performance.

- **Market responsiveness:** Market responsiveness involves both the collection of information from sources external to the firm, as well as the dissemination of a firm's market intelligence across departments and the organization's response to that learning. It includes the abilities to develop and manage projects rapidly and to react quickly to changes in market conditions. A key aspect of market responsiveness is strategic flexibility, which allows the organization to undertake strategic change when necessary.

Spanning resources include IS-business partnerships, IS planning and change management:

- **IS-business partnerships:** This capability represents the processes of integration and alignment between the IS function and other functional areas or departments of the firm. The importance of IS alignment, particularly with business strategy, has been well documented. This resource has variously been referred to as synergy, assimilation, and partnerships. All of these studies recognize the importance of building relationships internally within the firm among the IS function and other areas or departments. Such relationships help to span the traditional gaps that exist between functions and departments, resulting in superior competitive position and firm performance. An element of this resource is the support for collaboration within the firm.

- **IS planning and change management:** The capability to plan, manage, and use appropriate technology architectures and standards also helps to span these gaps. Key aspects of this resource include the ability to anticipate future changes and growth, to choose platforms (including hardware, network, and software standards) that can accommodate this change, and to effectively manage the resulting technology change and growth. This resource has been defined variously in previous research as "understanding the business case," "problem solving orientation," and "capacity to manage IT change." It includes the ability of IS managers to understand how technologies can and should be used, as well as how to motivate and manage IS personnel through the change process.

In order to explore the usefulness of the resource-based theory for IT resources, it is necessary to explicitly recognize the characteristics and attributes of resources that lead them to become strategically important. Although firms possess many resources, only a few of these have the potential to lead the firm to a position of sustained competitive advantage. What is it, then, that separates regular resources form those that confer a sustainable strategic benefit?

According to Wade and Hulland (2004), resource-based theorists have approached this question by identifying sets of resource attributes that might conceptually influence a firm's competitive position. Under this view, only resources exhibiting all of these attributes can lead to a sustained competitive advantage for the firm. We have already mentioned Barney's (2001) attributes of value, rareness, inimitability, nonsubstitutability, combination, and exploration.

In addition, an important seventh attribute is immobility. Once a firm establishes a competitive advantage through the strategic use of resources, competitors will likely attempt to amass comparable resources in order to share in the advantage. A primary source of resources is factor markets. If firms are able to acquire the resources necessary to imitate a rival's advantage, the rival's advantage will be short-lived. Thus, a requirement for sustained competitive advantage is that resources be imperfectly mobile or nontradable.

To govern IT resources efficiently and effectively, it is necessary to understand the strategic attributes of each resource. In Figure 1.1, the table shows an example of how strategic IT resources can be identified. The scale from 1 (little extent) to 5 (great extent) is applied.

In this example, we see that IT infrastructure is the IT resource with the greatest potential to lead to sustained competitive advantage, which would contradict that the IT infrastructure resource has generally not been found to be a source of sustained competitive advantage for firms. On the other hand, cost-effective IT operations have the least potential.

Wade and Hulland (2004) suggest that some of the resources create competitive advantage, while others sustain that advantage. A distinction is made between resources that help the firm attain a competitive advantage and those that help the firm to sustain the advantage. These two types of resource attributes can be thought of as, respectively, ex ante and ex post limits to competition.

Ex ante limits to competition suggest that prior to any firm's establishing a superior resource position, there must be limited competition for that posi-

Figure 1.1. IT resources in terms of strategic importance based on attributes

Attributes Resources	Valuable	Rare	Exploitable	Inimitable	Non-substitutable	Combinable	Immobile	TOTAL
IT infrastructure	4	2	5	5	2	5	4	27
IT technical skills	4	2	3	3	4	4	3	23
IT development	4	3	3	3	4	3	2	22
Cost-effective IT operations	4	2	3	2	4	3	1	19

tion. If any firm wishing to do so can acquire and deploy resources to achieve the position, it cannot by definition be superior. Attributes in this category include value, rarity, and appropriability.

Ex post limits to competition mean that subsequent to a firm's gaining a superior position and earning rents, there must be forces that limit competition for those rents. Attributes in this category include imitability, substitutability, and mobility.

Damianides (2005) applied a different approach to identify resources. He defined the following naturally grouped processes of IT resources: plan and organize, acquire and implement, deliver and support, and monitor and evaluate. He also developed an IT governance checklist, listing questions to ask to uncover IT issues, questions to ask to find out how management addresses the IT issues, and questions to self-assess IT governance practices.

Characteristics of Value Configurations

To comprehend the value that information technology provides to organizations, we must first understand the way a particular organization conducts business and how information systems affect the performance of various component activities within the organization. Understanding how firms differ is a central challenge for both theory and practice of management. For a long time, Porter's (1985) value chain was the only value configuration known to managers. Stabell and Fjeldstad (1998) have identified two alternative value configurations. A value shop schedules activities and applies resources in a fashion that is dimensioned and appropriate to the need's of the client's problem, while a value chain performs a fixed set of activities that enables it to produce a standard product in large numbers. Examples of value shops are professional service firms, as found in medicine, law, architecture, and engineering. A value network links clients or customers who are or wish to be interdependent. Examples of value networks are telephone companies, retail banks, and insurance companies.

A value configuration describes how value is created in a company for its customers. A value configuration shows how the most important business processes function to create value for customers. A value configuration represents the way a particular organization conducts business.

Figure 1.2. Examples of IS/IT in the value chain

Infrastructure: Use of corporate intranet for internal communications				
Human resources: Use of corporate intranet for competence building				
Technology: Computer-Aided Design (CAD)				
Procurement: Use of electronic marketplaces				
Inbound logistics: Electronic Data Interchange (EDI)	**Production**: Computer Integrated Manufacturing (CIM)	**Outbound logistics**: Web-based order-tracking system	**Marketing and sales**: Customer Relationship Management (CRM)	**Service**: System for local troubleshooting

The Organization as Value Chain

The best-known value configuration is the value chain. In the value chain, value is created through efficient production of goods and services based on a variety of resources. The company is perceived as a series or chain of activities. Primary activities in the value chain include inbound logistics, production, outbound logistics, marketing and sales, and service. Support activities include infrastructure, human resources, technology development, and procurement. Attention is on performing these activities in the chain in efficient and effective ways. In Figure 1.2, examples of IS/IT are assigned to primary and support activities. This figure can be used to describe the current IS/IT situation in the organization, as it illustrates the extent of coverage of IS/IT for each activity.

The knowledge intensity of systems in the different activities can be illustrated by different shading, where dark shading indicates high knowledge intensity. In this example, it is assumed that the most knowledge-intensive activities are computer-aided design and customer relationship management.

The Organization as Value Shop

Value cannot only be created in value chains. Value can also be created in two alternative value configurations: value shop and value network (Stabell

& Fjeldstad, 1998). In the value shop, activities are scheduled and resources are applied in a fashion that is dimensioned and appropriate to the needs of the client's problem, while a value chain performs a fixed set of activities that enables it to produce a standard product in large numbers. The value shop is a company that creates value by solving unique problems for customers and clients. Knowledge is the most important resource, and reputation is critical to firm success.

While typical examples of value chains are manufacturing industries such as paper and car production, typical examples of value shops are law firms and medical hospitals. Often, such companies are called professional service firms or knowledge-intensive service firms. Just as the medical hospital is a way to practice medicine, the law firm provides a standard format for delivering complex legal services. Many features of its style—specialization, teamwork, continuous monitoring on behalf of clients (patients), and representation in many forums—have been emulated in other vehicles for delivering professional services (Galanter & Palay, 1991).

Knowledge-intensive service firms are typical value shops. Sheehan (2002) defines knowledge-intensive service firms as entities that sell problem-solving services, where the solution chosen by the expert is based on real-time feedback from the client. Clients retain knowledge-intensive service firms to reduce their uncertainty. Clients hire knowledge-intensive service firms precisely because the client believes the firm knows something that the client does not and believes it is necessary to solve their problems.

While expertise plays a role in all firms, its role is distinctive in knowledge-intensive service firms. Expert, often professional, knowledge is at the core of the service provided by the type of firm.

Knowledge-intensive service firms not only sell a problem-solving service, but equally a problem-finding, problem-defining, solution-execution, and monitoring service. Problem finding is often a key for acquiring new clients. Once the client is acquired and their problem is defined, not all problems will be solved by the firm. Rather, the firm may only clarify that there is no problem (i.e., the patient does not have a heart condition) or that the problem should be referred to another specialist (i.e., the patient needs a heart specialist). If a problem is treated within the firm, then the firm needs to follow up the implementation to assure that the problem in fact has been solved (i.e., is the patient's heart now working properly?). This follows from the fact that there is often uncertainty in both problem diagnosis and problem resolution.

Sheehan (2002) has created a typology of knowledge-intensive service firms consisting of the following three types. First, knowledge-intensive search firms search for opportunities. The amount of value they create depends on the size of the finding or discovery, where size is measured by quality rather than quantity. Examples of search firms include petroleum and mineral exploration, drug discovery in the pharmaceutical industry, and research in the biotechnology industry. Second, knowledge-intensive diagnosis firms create value by clarifying problems. Once the problem has been identified, the suggested remedy usually follows directly. Examples of diagnosis firms include doctors, surgeons, psychotherapists, veterinarians, lawyers, auditors and tax accountants, and software support. Finally, knowledge-intensive design firms create value by conceiving new ways of constructing material or immaterial artifacts. Examples of design firms include architecture, advertising, research and development, engineering design, and strategy consulting.

Knowledge-intensive service firms create value through problem acquisition and definition, alternative generation and selection, implementation of an alternative, and follow up to see if the solution selected resolves the problem. To reflect this process, Stabell and Fjeldstad (1998) have outlined the value configuration of a value shop.

A value shop is characterized by five primary activities: problem finding and acquisition, problem solving, choice, execution, and control and evaluation, as illustrated in Figure 1.3. Problem finding and acquisition involves working with the customer to determine the exact nature of the problem or need. It involves deciding on the overall plan of approaching the problem. Problem solving is the actual generation of ideas and action (or treatment) plans.

Choice represents the decision of choosing among alternatives. While it is the least important primary activity of the value shop in terms of time and effort, it is also the most important in terms of customer value. Execution represents communicating, organizing, and implementing the decision, or performing the treatment. Control and evaluation activities involve monitoring and measurement of how well the solution solved the original problem or met the original need.

This may feed back into the first activity, problem finding and acquisition, for two reasons. First, if the proposed solution is inadequate or did not work, it feeds back into learning why it was inadequate and begins the problem-solving phase anew. Second, if the problem solution was successful, the firm might enlarge the scope of the problem-solving process to solve a bigger problem related to or dependent upon the first problem being solved.

Figure 1.3. Examples of IS/IT in the value shop

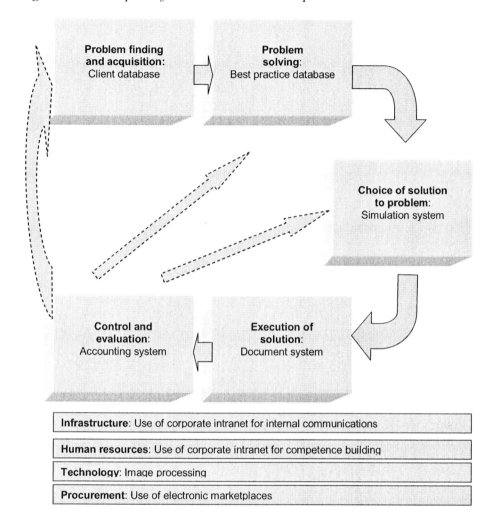

Figure 1.3 can be used to identify current IS/IT in the organization. We let a law firm serve as example in Figure 1.4. Within each of the five activities, there are many tasks in a law firm. For each task, there may be IS/IT support. For example, problem solving may consist of the two tasks of case analysis and reference search. Lawyers will be eager to discuss the case and to search more information on similar cases. A system for case-based reasoning may be installed, where the current case can be compared to similar cases handled by the law firm. Also, intelligent search engines with thesauri may be available in the law firm to find relevant information on the Internet and in legal databases.

Figure 1.4. Examples of IS/IT in the value shop

Activities	Tasks	IS/IT
Problem finding and acquisition	Register client information	Financial system
	Register case information	Case database
Problem solving	Do case analysis	Case-based reasoning
	Do reference search	
		Library search engine
Choice	Evaluate alternatives	Case-based reasoning
	Make recommendation to client	
		Office systems
Execution	Participate at meetings	Office systems
	Revise recommendation	Office systems
Control and evaluation	Register recommendation	Case database
	Check client satisfaction	Financial system

Knowledge-intensive service firms are typical value shops, and such firms depend on reputation for success, as reputation is a key driver of firm value creation. Reputation is a relational concept, in the sense that firms are judged by their stakeholders relative to their competitors. Reputation is what is generally said or believed about an entity by someone, it is the net perception of a firm held by stakeholders judged relative to other firms. According to Sheehan (2002), there are four conditions that must be present for reputation to work. Firstly, rents earned from maintaining a good reputation must be greater than not. Secondly, there must be a minimum of contact among stakeholders to allow for the changes in reputation to be communicated. Thirdly, there needs to be a possibility of repeat business. And lastly, there must be some uncertainty regarding the firm's type and/or behavior.

Reputation is related to the asymmetry of information, which is a typical feature of knowledge intensive service firms. Asymmetry is present when clients believe the firm knows something that the clients do not and believe it is necessary to know to solve their problems.

Reputation can be classified as a strategic resource in knowledge-intensive firms. To be a strategic resource, it has to be valuable, rare, costly to imitate, and possible to organize. Reputation is valuable, as it increases the value received by the client. Reputation is rare, as by definition only a few firms can be considered best in the industry. Reputation is costly to imitate, as it is difficult to build a reputation in the short term. Reputation is possible to organize in the general sense of controllability, which implies that a firm can be organized to take advantage of reputation as a resource.

The Organization as Value Network

The third and final value configuration is the value network. A value network is a company that creates value by connecting clients and customers that are, or want to be, dependent on each other. These companies distribute information, money, products, and services. While activities in both value chains and value shops are done sequentially, activities in value networks occur in parallel. The number and combination of customers and access points in the network are important value drivers in the value network. More customers and more connections create higher value to customers.

Stabell and Fjeldstad (1998) suggest that managing a value network can be compared to managing a club. The mediating firm admits members that complement each other, and in some cases exclude those that don't. The firm establishes, monitors, and terminates direct or indirect relationships among members. Supplier-customer relationships may exist among the members of the club, but to the mediating firm they are all customers.

Examples of value networks include telecommunication companies, financial institutions such as banks and insurance companies, and stockbrokers. Value networks perform three activities (see Figure 1.5):

- Development of customer network through marketing and recruiting of new customers, to enable increased value for both existing customers and new customers.
- Development of new services and improvement in existing services.
- Development of infrastructure so that customer services can be provided more efficiently and effectively.

The current IS/IT situation in a value network will mainly be described through the infrastructure that typically will consist of information technology. In addition, many of the new services may be information systems that will be used by customers in their communication and business transactions

Figure 1.5. Examples of IS/IT in the value network

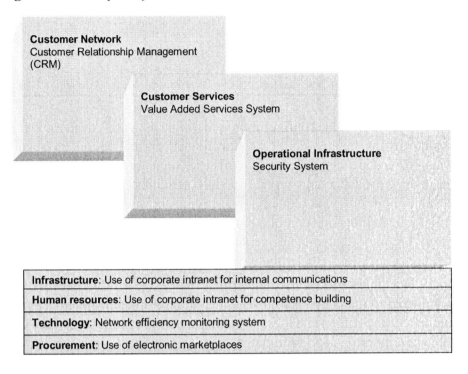

with other customers. The knowledge component will mainly be found in the services of a value network, as information systems are made available to customers to exchange relevant information.

Comparison of Value Configurations

Value chain, value shop and value network are alternative value configurations that impact the use of information technology in the company, as illustrated in Figure 1.6. While the role of IT is to make production more efficient in a value chain, IT creates added value in the value shop, while IT in the form of infrastructure is the main value in the value network. Some companies have more than one value configuration, but most companies have one dominating configuration.

Figure 1.6. Characteristics of value configurations

Characteristics	Value Chain	Value Shop	Value Network
Value creation	Transformation of input to output	Solving clients and customers problems	Connecting clients and customers to each other
Work form	Sequential production	Integrated and cyclical problem solving	Monitored and simultaneous connections
Information systems	Making production more efficient	Adding value to the knowledge work	Main value by use of IT infrastructure
Example	Paper factory	Law firm	Telecom company

In the long term, business organizations can choose to change their value configurations. A bank, for example can be a value shop when it focuses on converting inputs to outputs. The value resides in the output and once you have the output, you can remove the production organization. This removal does not impact the value of the output. The value shop is a solution provider. It's somebody who solves problems. The input is a problem. The output is a solution to the problem. A bank that does this would view itself as a financial service operator, a financial advisor that also has the ability to provide the money. But what it would do is identify client problems, address those problems, select a solution together with the client, and help to implement it. It would have stringent quality controls. As part of it's offering, it would probably supply the client with some cash as a loan or accept some of the client's cash for investment (Chatzkel, 2002).

Or, the bank can be a value network, which is basically the logic of the marketplace. The bank would define its role as a conduit between people who do not have money and those people who do have money. What the bank does is arrange the flow of cash between them. The bank will attract people with money to make deposits and investments. The bank will also attract people without money to take out loans. As a value network, the bank will connect people with opposite financial needs. The network consists of people with different financial needs. Over time, persons in the network may change status from money needer to money provider, and vice versa (Chatzkel, 2002).

Both as a value shop and as a value network, the business organization can be identified as a bank. But it would have completely different consequences for what it will focus on doing well, what it will focus on doing itself, versus what it would not want to do itself. This provides a kind of strategic systems logic. It asks, "Which strategic system in terms of value configuration are we going to operate in?" Choosing an appropriate value configuration is a long-term decision with long-term consequences.

References

Ang, S. (1993). *The etiology of information systems outsourcing.* Unpublished doctoral dissertation, University of Minnesota.

Barney, J. B. (2001). Is the resourced-based "view" a useful perspective for strategic management research? Yes. *Academy of Management Review, 26*(1), 41-56.

Barney, J. B. (2002). *Gaining and sustaining competitive advantage.* Upper Saddle River, NJ: Prentice Hall.

Chatzkel, J. (2002). A conversation with Göran Roos. *Journal of Intellectual Capital, 3*(2), 96-117.

Collis, D. J., & Montgomery, C. A. (1997). *Corporate strategy: Resources and the scope of the firm.* Chicago: McGraw-Hill.

Damianides, M. (2005). Sarbanse-Oxley and IT governance: New guidance on IT control and compliance. *Information Systems Management, 22*(1), 77-85.

Galanter, M., & Palay, T. (1991). *Tournament of lawyers: The transformation of the big law firms.* Chicago: University of Chicago Press.

Garud, R., & Kumaraswamy, A. (2005). Vicious and virtuous circles in the management of knowledge: The case of Infosys Technologies. *MIS Quarterly, 29*(1), 9-33.

Johnson, G., & Scholes, K. (2002). *Exploring corporate strategy.* Harlow: Financial Times/Prentice Hall.

Haanes, K. B. (1997). *Managing resource mobilization: Case studies of Dynal, Fiat Auto Poland and Alcatel Telecom Norway.* Unpublished doctoral dissertation, Copenhagen Business School, Copenhagen, Denmark.

Heijden, H. V. D. (2001). Measuring IT core capabilities for electronic commerce. *Journal of Information Technology, 16,* 13-22.

Hitt, M. A., Bierman, L., Shumizu, K., & Kochhar, R. (2001). Direct and moderating effects of human capital on strategy and performance in professional service firms: A resource-based perspective. *Academy of Management Journal, 44*(1), 13-28.

Løwendahl, B. R. (2000). *Strategic management of professional service firms* (2nd ed.). Copenhagen, Denmark: Copenhagen Business School Press.

Maister, D. H. (1993). *Managing the professional service firm*. New York: Free Press.

Peppard, J., Lambert, R., & Edwards, C. (2000). Whose job is it anyway? Organizational information competencies for value creation. *Information Systems Journal, 10*(4), 291-322.

Pettus, M. L. (2001). The resourced-based view as a development growth process: Evidence from the deregulated trucking industry. *Academy of Management Journal, 44*(4), 878-896.

Porter, M. E. (1985). *Competitive advantage: Creating and sustaining competitive Performance.* New York: Free Press.

Priem, R. L., & Butler, J. E. (2001). Is the resourced-based "view" a useful perspective for strategic management research? *Academy of Management Review, 26*(1), 22-40.

Sheehan, N. T. (2002). *Reputation as a driver in knowledge-intensive service firms.* Unpublished doctoral dissertation, Norwegian School of Management, Sandvika.

Stabell, C. B., & Fjeldstad , Ø. D. (1998). Configuring value for competitive advantage: On chains, shops, and networks. *Strategic Management Journal, 19,* 413-437.

Steensma, H. K., & Corley, K. G. (2001). Organizational context as moderator of theories on firm boundaries for technology sourcing. *Academy of Management Journal, 44*(2), 271-291.

Wade, M., & Hulland, J. (2004). The resource-based view and information systems research: Review, extension, and suggestions for future research. *MIS Quarterly, 28*(1), 107-142.

Zack, M. H. (1999). Developing a knowledge strategy. *California Management Review, 41*(3), 125-145.

Chapter II

Organizational Business Dynamics

It was Sterman's (2000) book entitled *Business Dynamics: Systems Thinking and Modeling for a Complex World* that introduced the term "business dynamics." Business dynamics is concerned with learning in and about complex systems. Effective decision-making by growing dynamic complexity requires executives to become systems thinkers—to expand the boundaries of their mental models and develop ways to understand how the structure of complex systems creates behavior.

In the context of system dynamics, a system might be a manufacturing company, a consulting firm, a government organization, an industry, or some other part of the real world that has cause-and-effect relationships to be understood for decision-making. While in the context of system dynamics an information system has a different meaning, a system here is a set of organizational relationships to be explored as different system structures create different system behaviors.

While the structure of a system can be illustrated by a causal loop diagram, the behavior of a system can be illustrated by a reference mode, as was illustrated in the preface. This will be further explained and explored in this chapter.

Dynamic Business Performance

Business dynamics can be understood as the evolution of one single business as well as the evolution of businesses in an industry or in a region. In the latter meaning, OECD (2004) studied business dynamics in terms of the creation of new businesses and the decline or market exit of less productive firms.

The creation and growth of new firms and the decline or market exit of old firms are often regarded as key to business dynamism and economic growth in OECD economies. New firms are thought to be especially innovative and to play an important role as job creators. Based on these ideas, policy makers often believe that institutions, which foster firm entry, may ultimately enhance the overall economic performance of their country (OECD, 2004).

According to OECD (2004), it is frequently reported in the firm demographics literature that most new firms do not survive for long. Chances of survival are especially low for firms that start small, as they usually do. Two-year survival rates for firms born in 1998 do confirm that there is a high risk of newly created firms being forced to exit the market rapidly. Survival rates correspond to the number of firms of the same cohort that have survived a given number of years as a percentage of all firms that entered the same year with them. In Europe, between 12 and 38 percent of all new firms had failed already after the first two years, as the survival rates varied roughly between 62 and 88 percent.

Firm survival can also be assessed on the basis of hazard rates, which correspond to the conditional probability of leaving the market after a certain life span. These are calculated as the share of exiting firms in the number of survivors of the same cohort as of the previous year. While survival rates decline with firm age by construction, *a priori* there is nothing that precludes hazard rates from being comparable at different durations. One- and two-year hazard rates reveal that while entry rates tend to be higher in services than in manufacturing, the risk that these new firms have to exit the market early in life is higher in services, as well (OECD, 2004).

Similar to the study by OECD (2004) is the study by Callejón and Segarra (1999) on business dynamics and efficiency in industries and regions in Spain. They studied business dynamics in terms of firm births and deaths. According to their approach, new firms are seen more as users of innovations than producers of innovations. The results showed that both entry and exit rates contribute positively to the growth of total factor productivity in industries and in regions.

Business dynamics as the evolution of one single organization is the perspective of Sterman (2000). He argues that effective decision-making and learning in a world of growing dynamic complexity requires us to become systems thinkers—to expand the boundaries of our mental models and develop tools to understand how the structure of complex systems creates their behavior. To make the firm survive and avoid being part of the hazard rate, management needs the skills required to develop systems thinking capabilities, create an effective learning process in dynamically complex systems, and use system dynamics in organizations to address important problems.

Managers seeking to solve a problem sometimes make it worse. Executive policies may create unanticipated side effects. Attempts to stabilize the system may destabilize it. Executive decisions may provoke reactions by others seeking to restore the balance. Such phenomena are called the counterintuitive behavior of social systems. These unexpected dynamics often lead to policy resistance, the tendency for interventions to be delayed, diluted, or defeated by the response of the system to the intervention itself (Sterman, 2000).

The Internet is a classic example of business dynamics in information technology. The Internet was probably the biggest technological revolution of the latter half of the twentieth century, but:

Remember the heady days of the dot.com go-go years, when every company had to have an Internet strategy? The dogma that sparked this search for new business models (or were they muddles?) was that the "Internet changes everything." If you are in the business of book retailing or you're running a travel agency, this doctrine may still hold water, but in the cold light of day, how big an impact has the Internet had on the business design? (McCullagh, 2003, p. 10)

Without doubt, e-mail has drastically reduced the time it takes to send a message or file, and the Web has enabled new e-business models. But, as system dynamics modeling can so nicely visualize and simulate, the interactions between business performance and information technology applications can over time create all kinds of business dynamics, from exponential growth to decline and collapse.

There are all kinds of dynamics in organizations and between organizations. An interesting example is power dynamics within top management. Power dynamics highlight interest conflicts and competition within top management.

A primary cause of interest conflicts and competition among top executives lies in their desire for power and career advancement. Senior executives are ambitious individuals who have high needs for power and achievement. As they move up the corporate hierarchy, their desire to become CEO and "run their own show" becomes even stronger. The extraordinary prestige and material benefits associated with the CEO title provide further incentives for senior executives to challenge the CEO of their company and to participate in a power tournament in the firm's internal labor market (Shen & Cannella, 2002).

In addition, the external labor market generally evaluates executives' talent on the basis of the performance of their employing firms. When firm performance suffers, so does each senior executive's reputation and value in the external labor market. Senior executives thus, even if not direct power contenders themselves, have incentives to monitor the CEO's leadership and join others in taking action against the CEO when they perceive him or her to be less than capable. This is an example of power dynamics, where the interest conflicts and competition between a CEO and other senior executives put the CEO at risk of power contests with senior executives followed by dismissal and inside succession (Shen & Cannella, 2002).

Causal Loop Diagramming

Much of the art of system dynamics modeling is discovering and representing the feedback processes, which determine the dynamics of a system. Feedback is important in a variety of systems (Bordetsky & Mark, 2000). All dynamics arise from the interaction of just two types of feedback loops, positive (or self-reinforcing) and negative (or self-correcting) loops. Positive loops tend to reinforce or amplify whatever is happening in the system: The more information technology is used in the organization, the more IT skills users develop, leading to even greater use of information technology in the organization, as illustrated in Figure 2.1.

The + signs at the arrowheads indicate that the effect is positively related to the cause: An increase in information technology user skills causes the use of information technology to rise above what it would have been.

An example of a negative feedback loop in information technology is illustrated in Figure 2.2. The idea in the model is that more investments in

Figure 2.1. A positive feedback loop in information technology

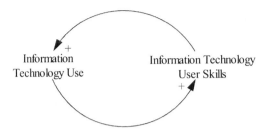

Figure 2.2. A negative feedback loop in information technology

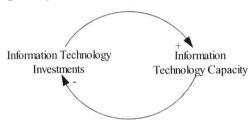

information technology lead to higher information technology capacity. Assuming that the use does not change, capacity utilization drops, leading to lower information technology investments.

The negative minus (-) polarity for the link from information technology capacity means that an increase in information technology capacity leads to reduction in information technology investments. When the two loops are connected, we might find a dynamic system as illustrated in Figure 2.3. Here we have two negative feedback loops and one positive feedback loop.

From a management perspective, Figure 2.3 can be interpreted in different ways. One simulation would be to focus on information technology capacity utilization. We might start with a high capacity utilization, leading both to higher investments and reduced use. After a while, capacity utilization drops as a consequence.

An example might be IT helpdesk. We can think of a staff of five persons working at the desk. Response times and service levels drop as a consequence of high capacity utilization. Another person is hired. At the same time, users stop contacting the help desk, leading to lower capacity utilization and the questioning of why this sixth person was hired.

Figure 2.3. Dynamic system in information technology

Another possible example based on Figure 2.3 is illustrated in Figure 2.4. As information technology capacity utilization increases, information technology investments increase, leading to a decline in capacity utilization. Since there are delays involved in decision-making, the firm might experience fluctuations and long-term decline in capacity utilization, as illustrated in Figure 2.4. While decision-makers probably don't like this development, they have themselves caused it by making information technology invest-

Figure 2.4. Fluctuations in information technology capacity utilization caused by event-oriented investment decision-making

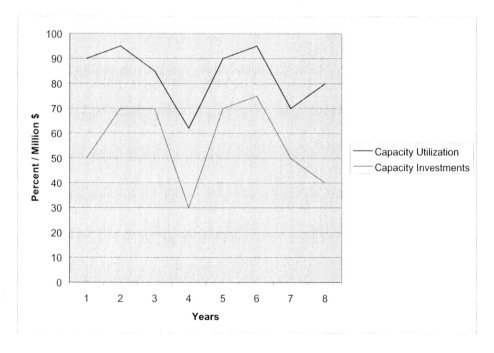

ment decisions based on events rather than an understanding of the feedback structure in Figure 2.3.

System Dynamics Modeling

System dynamics is a methodology for studying and managing complex systems, such as one finds in business and other social systems. It is used to address a variety of feedback systems. Feedback refers to the situation of X affecting Y and Y in turn affecting X, perhaps through a chain of causes and effects. The methodology identifies a problem, develops a dynamic hypothesis explaining the cause of the problem, builds a computer simulation model of the system, tests the model, devises and tests in the model alternative policies, and implements the best solution (Society, 2006).

The system dynamics methodology is an integrated multi-disciplinary modeling approach for identifying, conceptualizing, representing, and analyzing operational, tactical, and strategic business issues. The value of simulation models lies in its ability to help users draw conclusions about a real business situation or system by studying and analyzing the model. Simulation models are therefore tools for helping managers to imagine, experience, and manage the future, before it arrives (Powersim, 2006).

In this book, we limit our application of system dynamics modeling to causal loop diagrams and reference modes. This is sufficient for the purpose of this book, which is to illustrate the dynamics of information technology management. For those interested in building simulation models, we refer readers to the standard textbook by Sterman (2000). However, just to give an introduction, this section describes the steps in modeling.

In the modeling process, the causal loop diagram is transformed into a stock and flow map (Moxnes & Saysel, 2004). Stocks are accumulations. They characterize the state of the system and generate the information upon which decisions and actions are based. Stocks create delays by accumulating the difference between the inflow to a process and its outflow.

Stocks and flows are familiar to management. While information technology capacity is a stock, investments in information technology is a flow. By investing more information technology (flow), management will cause an increase in information technology capacity (stock). Stocks characterize the state of the system and provide the basis for actions.

After turning the causal loop diagram into a stock and flow map, a simulation model is formulated. Formulation of the simulation model consists of specifying structure and decision rules, estimating parameters, behavioral relationships, and initial conditions, and testing for consistency with the purpose and boundary. The testing consists of:

- **Comparison to reference mode:** Does the model reproduce the behavior adequately for management purpose?
- **Robustness under extreme conditions:** Does the model behave realistically when stressed by extreme conditions?
- **Sensitivity:** How does the model behave given uncertainty in parameters, initial conditions, model boundary, and aggregation?

When the model has successfully passed these tests, then it can be applied for policy design and evaluation. Policy design means answers to questions such as: What new decision rules, strategies, and structures might be tried in the real world? How can they be represented in the model? What if something else happens? What are the effects of various policies? How robust are the policy recommendations under different scenarios and given uncertainties? Do the policies interact? Are there synergies or compensatory responses?

Many software packages are available for system dynamics modeling. Vensim is used in this book. Vensim from Ventana (2006) is a visual modeling tool that allows the model developer to conceptualize, document, simulate, analyze, and optimize models of dynamic systems. Vensim provides a way of building simulation models from causal loop or stock and flow diagrams.

By connecting words with arrows, relationships among system variables are entered and recorded as causal connections. This information is used by an equation editor to help form a complete simulation model. The model can be analyzed throughout the building process, looking at causes and uses of a variable, and also at the loops involving the variable. When the model is built and tested, Vensim enables ways to explore the behavior of the model (Ventana, 2006).

An alternative software package is Powersim (2006). Powersim's approach to business planning involves the building of mathematical models (representations of the real situation or system) for computer simulation. The models are based on the system dynamics paradigm, which is the use of feedback theory to organize the system structure and the use of computer simulation to deduce the behavior of the business system.

System dynamics modeling has over the years been applied to a variety of business, regional, national, and global issues. One example is found in the *Journal of Computer Information Systems*, in which Chen (2004) presented a decision support system for tourism development. The model was developed to simulate visitor dynamics in response to different environmental changes and investment scenarios. The model is a system dynamics-based interactive decision support system. It is designed in the Powersim program.

Organizational Performance

Despite the importance to researchers, managers, and policy makers of how information technology contributes to organizational performance, there is uncertainty and debate about what we know and do not know. A review of the literature conducted by Melville, Kraemer, and Gurbaxani (2004) reveals that studies examining the association between IT and organizational performance are divergent in how they conceptualize key constructs and their interrelationships.

IT business value research examines the organizational performance impacts of information technology. Previous research has shown that information technology may indeed contribute to the improvement of organizational performance (e.g., Brynjolfsson & Hitt, 1996). The dimensions and extent of IT business value depend on a variety of factors, including the type of IT, management practices, and organizational structure, as well as the competitive and macro environment. Research also suggests that firms do not appropriate all of the value they generate from IT; value may be captured by trading partners or competed away by end customers in the form of lower prices and better quality.

Melville et al. (2004) developed a model of IT business value based on the resource-based theory of the firm that integrates the various strands of research into a single framework. The resource-based theory has been used to examine the efficiency and competitive advantage implications of specific firm resources such as entrepreneurship, culture, and organizational routines. It is also useful in the IT context, providing a robust framework for analyzing whether and how IT may be associated with competitive advantage.

Based on how Melville et al. (2004) mode'
a causal loop diagram as illustrated in F
value generation is the organization that
which might be called the focal firm. Bt
shaping the extent to which IT business '
In particular the competitive environme
diagram in Figure 2.5.

In Figure 2.5, the information technolog
cal IT resource and the human IT res(
can be further categorized into IT infra
and technology services across the or;
plications that utilize the infrastructure ....
analysis tools, and so forth. The technological IT resource thus includes both
hardware and software. The separation into infrastructure and business applications is consistent with how companies view their physical IT assets.
The human IT resource denotes both technical and managerial knowledge.
Examples of technical expertise include application development, integration
of multiple systems, and maintenance of existing systems. Managerial skills
include the ability to identify appropriate projects, marshal adequate resources,
and lead and motivate development teams to complete projects according to
specification and within time and budgetary constraints. Although technical
and managerial expertise are often intertwined, they are nonetheless distinct
concepts, and their conceptualization as such is necessary for precision in
describing IT investment impacts.

Although it is possible to apply IT for improved organizational performance
with few organizational changes, successful application of IT is often ac-
companied by significant organizational change, including policies and rules,

Figure 2.5. IT business value model

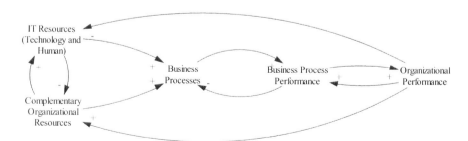

...cture, workplace practices, and organizational culture. ...between IT and other firm resources exist, we call the latter ...y organizational resources, as illustrated in Figure 2.5.

...rocesses in Figure 2.5 are activities underlying value-generating ...es (transforming inputs to outputs). Business process performance is ...perational efficiency of specific business processes, measures of which ...clude customer service, flexibility, information sharing, and inventory management. Organizational performance is the overall firm performance, including productivity, efficiency, profitability, market value, and competitive advantage (Melville et al., 2004).

Santhanam and Hartono (2003) applied the resource-based theory and tested empirically whether information technology capability influences firm performance. Their results indicate that firms with superior IT capability indeed exhibit superior current and sustained firm performance when compared to average industry performance, even after adjusting for effects of prior firm performance.

According to the resource-based theory, the benefits of superior IT capability must be sustainable over time. Sustained competitive advantage does not imply that the benefits will last forever, but indicates that it will not be competed away by the duplication efforts of other firms. The concept of IT capability was developed using the premise that while resources can be easily duplicated, a unique set of capabilities mobilized by a firm cannot be easily duplicated and will result in sustained competitive advantages. Information technology investments are often made with long-term goals, and there is a time lag in obtaining benefits. Therefore, the sustained effects of IT investments in terms of IT capability are important.

In their empirical study, Santhanam and Hartono (2003) found sustained effects of IT capability. The leader firms were identified as having superior IT capability. Similar results were obtained in another study by Ravichandran and Lertwongsatien (2005), who found that variation in firm performance was explained by the extent to which IT was used to support and enhance a firm's core competencies. Their results also support the proposition that an organization's ability to use IT to support its core competencies is dependent on IT functional capabilities, which, in turn, are dependent on the nature of human, technology, and relationship resources of the IT department.

Ravichandran and Lertwongsatien applied the resource-based theory and tested empirically the effect of information technology resources and capabilities on firm performance. They defined capabilities as socially complex routines that determine the efficiency with which firms transform inputs into outputs. IT capabilities are the routines within the IT department that enable it to deliver IT services to the organization.

While a variety of IT capabilities have been identified in the literature, Ravichandran and Lertwongsatien limit their focus to the capabilities in the core functional areas such as planning, systems development, IT support, and IT operations. Building on the notion that capabilities are determined by organizational routines, they adopted a process focus and defined IT capabilities in terms of the quality and sophistication of IT processes.

When measuring organizational performance, Ravichandran and Lertwongsatien distinguished between operating performance and market-based performance. Operating performance was measured using a four-item scale that assessed the extent to which the profitability, productivity, and financial performance exceeded those of their competitors in the past three years. Market-based performance was measured using a three-item scale that assessed the success of the firm in entering new markets and in bringing new products and services to the market during the past three years.

References

Bordetsky, A., & Mark, G. (2000). Memory-based feedback controls to support groupware coordination. *Information Systems Research, 11*(4), 366-385.

Brynjolfsson, E., & Hitt, L. (1996). Paradox lost? Firm-level evidence on the returns to information systems spending. *Management Science, 42*(4), 541-558.

Callejón, M., & Segarra, A. (1999). Business dynamics and efficiency in industry and regions: The case of Spain. *Small Business Economics, 13*, 253-271.

Chen, K. C. (2004). Decision support system for tourism development: System dynamics approach. *Journal of Computer Information Systems,* Fall, 104-112.

McCullagh, K. (2003). Situating technological change within social and business dynamics. *Design Management Journal,* Spring, 10-16.

Melville, N., Kraemer, K., & Gurbaxani, V. (2004). Information technology and organizational performance: An integrative model of IT business value. *MIS Quarterly, 28*(2), 283-322.

Moxnes, E., & Saysel, A. K. (2004). *Misperceptions of global climate change: Information policies.* University of Bergen, Norway: The System Dynamics Group, Department of Information Science.

OECD (2004). Business dynamics and policies. *OECD Economic Studies, 38,* 9-36.

Powersim Studio: User's Guide. (2006). Powersim Software. www.powersim.no

Ravichandran, T., & Lertwongsatien, C. (2005). Effect of information systems resources and capabilities on firm performance: A resource-based perspective. *Journal of Management Information Systems, 21*(4), 237-276.

Santhanam, R., & Hartono, E. (2003). Issues in linking information technology capability to firm performance. *MIS Quarterly, 27*(1), 125-153.

Shen, W., & Cannella, A. A. (2002). Power dynamics within top management and their impacts on CEO dismissal followed by inside succession. *Academy of Management Journal, 45*(6), 1195-1206.

Society (2006). What is System Dynamics. *System Dynamics Society.* www.albany.edu/cpr/sds/

Sterman, J. D. (2000). *Business dynamics: Systems thinking and modeling for a complex world.* Boston: McGraw-Hill.

Vensim: Ventana Simulation Environment. (2006). User's guide version 5. www.ventana.com.

Chapter III

Information Technology Governance

In many organizations, information technology has become crucial in the support, the sustainability, and the growth of the business. This pervasive use of technology has created a critical dependency on IT that calls for a specific focus on IT governance, which consists of the leadership and organizational structures and processes that ensure that the organization's IT sustains and extends the organization's strategy and objectives (Grembergen et al., 2004).

IT governance matters because it influences the benefits received from IT investments. Through a combination of practices (such as redesigning business processes and well-designed governance mechanisms) and appropriately matched IT investments, top-performing enterprises generate superior returns on their IT investments (Weill, 2004).

However, IT governance should be developed and managed according to the resource-based theory that is relevant for the value configuration and in a dynamic perspective. This means that IT governance is concerned with exploring and exploiting strategic IT resources in support of the organization's value configuration(s) over time.

IT governance can be defined as specifying decision rights and accountability framework to encourage desirable behavior in the use of IT (Weill & Ross, 2004). There are several examples of other definitions. First, IT governance is the structures and processes that ensure that IT supports the organization's mission. The purpose is to align IT with the enterprise, maximize the benefits of IT, use IT resources responsibly, and manage IT risks; Second, it is a structure of relationships and processes to direct and control the enterprise in order to achieve the enterprise's goals by adding value, while balancing risk vs. return over IT and its processes. Third, IT governance is the responsibility of the board of directors and executive management. It is an integral part of enterprise governance and consists of the leadership and organizational structures and processes that ensure that the organization's IT sustains and extends the organization's strategies and objectives. Fourth,IT governance is the system by which an organization's IT portfolio is directed and controlled. IT Governance describes (a) the distribution of decision-making rights and responsibilities among different stakeholders in the organization, and (b) the rules and procedures for making and monitoring decisions on strategic IT concerns (Peterson, 2004).

IT governance is further defined as the patterns of authority for key IT activities in business firms, including IT infrastructure, IT use, and project management and is conceptually different from IT management. IT management involves making and implementing approved technology decisions, while governance addresses the inputs and decision rights to drive desirable behaviors.

Weill and Ross (2004) use political archetypes (monarchy, feudal, federal, duopoly, anarchy) to describe the combinations of people who have either decision rights or input to IT decisions:

1. **Business monarchy:** In a business monarchy, senior business executives make IT decisions affecting the entire enterprise. It is a group of business executives or individual executives (CxOs), including committees of senior business executives (may include CIO). It excludes IT executives acting independently.

2. **IT monarchy:** In an IT monarchy, IT professionals make IT decisions. It is a group of IT executives or individual CIOs.

3. **Feudal:** The feudal model is based on the traditional idea that princes and princesses or their designated knights make their own decisions,

optimizing their local needs. It is business unit leaders, key process owners, or their delegates.

4. **Federal:** The federal decision-making model has a long tradition in government. Federal arrangements attempt to balance the responsibilities and accountability of multiple governing bodies, such as country or states. It is c-level executives and business groups (e.g., business units or processes). It may also include IT executives as additional participants. It is equivalent of the central and state governments working together.

5. **IT duopoly:** The IT duopoly is a two-party arrangement where decisions represent a bilateral agreement between IT executives and one other group (e.g., CxO or business unit or process leaders). The IT executives may be a central IT group or team of central and business unit IT organizations.

6. **Anarchy:** Within an anarchy, individuals or small groups make their own decisions based only on their local needs. Anarchies are the bane of the existence of many IT groups and are expensive to support and secure. It can be each individual user.

Peterson (2004) discusses decision makers and decision rights in terms of centralization vs. decentralization. Over the past decade, organizations have set out to achieve the best of both worlds by adopting a *federal* IT governance structure. In a federal IT governance model, IT infrastructure decisions are centralized, and IT application decisions are decentralized. The federal IT governance model thus represents a hybrid model of both centralization and decentralization.

The discussion of whether to centralize or decentralize IT governance is based on a rational perspective of the organization, in which choices are reduced to one of internal efficiency and effectiveness. This view assumes a system of goal consonance and agreement on the means for achieving goals, that is, rational and logical trade-off between (a) efficiency and standardization under centralization, vs. (b) effectiveness and flexibility under decentralization.

In general, it is assumed that centralization leads to greater specialization, consistency, and standardized controls, while decentralization provides local control, ownership, and greater responsiveness and flexibility to business needs. However, flexibility under decentralization may lead to variable standards, which ultimately result in lower flexibility, and specialization under centralization incurs risks due to bounded rationality and information overload (Peterson, 2004).

A federal approach toward IT governance challenges managers in local business units to surrender control over certain business-specific IT domains for the wellbeing of the enterprise, and to develop business-to-corporate and business-to-IT partnerships. The potential risk in contemporary business environments is that either centralization or decentralization fits the organization into a fixed structure. The challenge is therefore to balance the benefits of decentralized decision-making and business innovation, and the benefits of central control and IT standardization (Peterson, 2004).

Weill and Ross (2004) identified five decision categories for decision makers. These five decision categories are IT principles, IT architecture, IT infrastructure, IT applications, and IT investments. These categories will be presented in the framework of system dynamics in this chapter.

Dynamics of IT Principles

IT Principles are a related set of high-level statements about how IT is used in the business. Once articulated, IT principles become part of the enterprise's management lexicon and can be discussed, debated, supported, overturned, and evolved. The hallmark of an effective set of IT principles is a clear trail of evidence from the business to the IT management principles. For Mead-Westvaco, described by Weill and Ross (2004), architectural integrity (IT principle two) provides both standardized processes and technologies (business principle two) and cost control and operational efficiency (business principle four); rapid deployment of new applications (IT principle four) promotes alignment and responsiveness to negotiated business requirements (business principle five); a consistent, flexible infrastructure (IT principle three) should enable all five business principles. IT principles can also be used as a tool for educating executives about technology strategy and investment decisions.

Depending on quantitative parameters in the system dynamics model, the causal loop diagram in Figure 3.1 might cause the behavior over time as illustrated with the reference mode in Figure 3.2.

In Figure 3.1, a positive sign at the arrowhead means change in the same direction. When one variable goes up, then the other variable goes up. When one variable goes down, then the other variable goes down. A negative sign

Figure 3.1. Causal loop diagram for IT principles dynamics

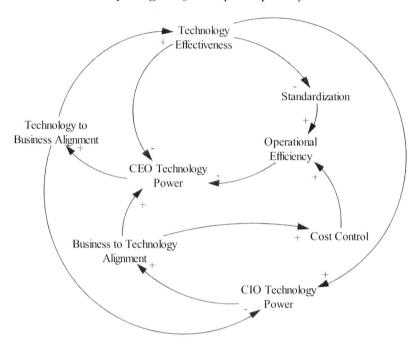

Figure 3.2. Reference mode for IT principles dynamics

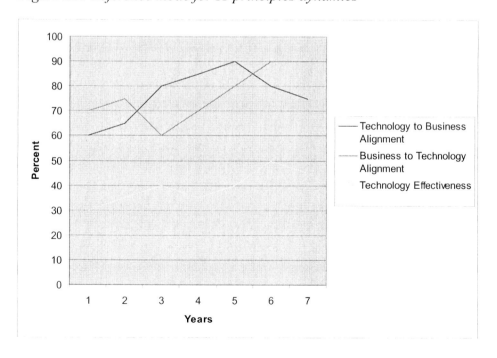

at the arrowhead means change in opposite direction. When one variable goes up, then the other variable goes down. When one variable goes down, then the other variable goes up.

Technology effectiveness is directly improved by technology to business alignment and indirectly improved by business to technology alignment. Technology to business alignment means that IT principles are primarily concerned with the alignment of information technology to business strategy. Business to technology alignment means that IT principles are primarily concerned with exploiting the potential of modern information technology in the business.

Dynamics of IT Infrastructures

IT infrastructure is the foundation of planned IT capability (both technical and human) available throughout the business as shared and reliable services and used by multiple applications. Foresight in establishing the right infrastructure at the right time enables rapid implementation of future electronically enabled business initiatives as well as consolidation and cost reduction of current business processes. Over-investing in infrastructure—or worse, implementing the wrong infrastructure—results in wasted resources, delays, and a system not compatible with business partners. Infrastructure base are the technology components, such as computers, printers, database software packages, operating systems, and scanners. The technology components are converted into useful shared services by a human IT infrastructure composed of knowledge, skills, standards, and experience (Weill & Ross, 2004).

IT infrastructure can further be defined as the base foundation of the IT portfolio (including both technical and human assets), shared throughout the firm in the form of reliable services. The IT infrastructure capability includes both the technical and managerial expertise required to provide reliable services. The IT infrastructure capability of a firm can be assessed using three measures (Broadbent et al., 1999): the extent of the firm's infrastructure services, the provision of boundary-crossing infrastructure services, and the firm's reach and range in the market place.

One of the interesting feedback loops in Figure 3.3 is the dynamic relationship between infrastructure visits and infrastructure capabilities. This posi-

Figure 3.3. Causal loop diagram for IT infrastructure dynamics

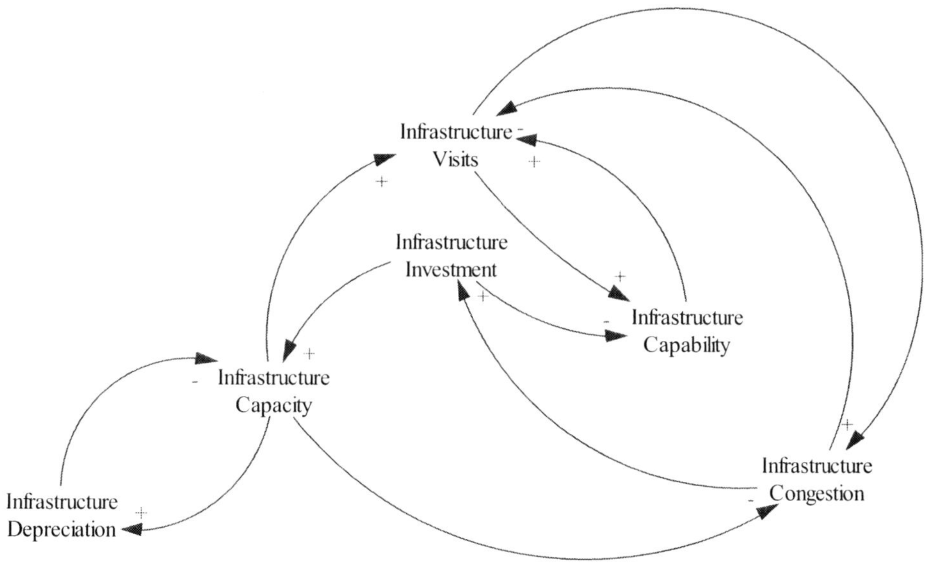

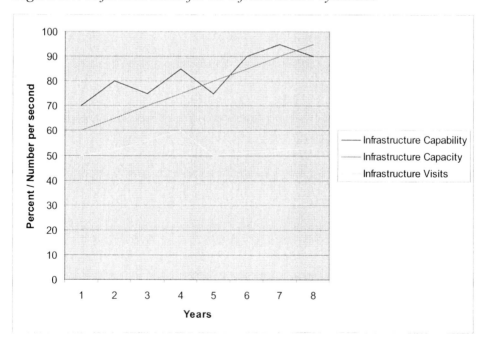

Figure 3.4. Reference mode for IT infrastructure dynamics

tive feedback loop says that more advanced infrastructure capability will attract more sophisticated infrastructure use, causing even more advanced infrastructure capability to emerge from infrastructure investments.

Depending on quantitative parameters in the system dynamics model, the causal loop diagram in Figure 3.3 might cause the behavior over time as illustrated with the reference mode in Figure 3.4. While both infrastructure capacity and capability grow over time, a major setback in infrastructure visits occurs in year five. This long-term setback is caused by the short-term setback in infrastructure capability.

Dynamics of IT Architectures

IT architecture is the organizing logic for data, applications, and infrastructure, captured in a set of policies, relationships, and technical choices to achieve

Figure 3.5. Causal loop diagram for IT architecture dynamics

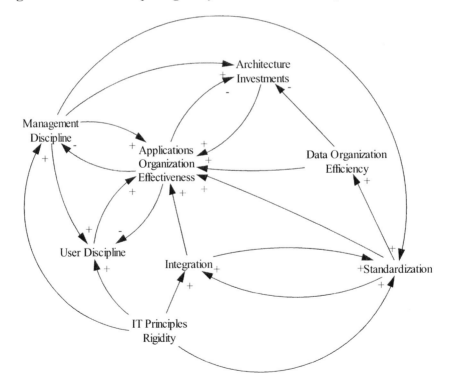

desired business and technical standardization and integration. By providing a road map for infrastructure and applications (and, consequently, investment decisions), architecture decisions are pivotal to effective IT management and use. By clarifying how IT supports business principles, IT principles state—implicitly or explicitly—the requirements for process standardization and integration. The key to process standardization is discipline—adherence to a single, consistent way of doing things. Process integration allows multiple business units to provide a single face to a customer or to move seamlessly from one function to another (Weill & Ross, 2004).

In the causal loop diagram in Figure 3.5, we have introduced a feedback loop between standardization and integration. Standardization enables integration, while integration stimulates standardization.

Depending on quantitative parameters in the system dynamics model, the causal loop diagram in Figure 3.5 might cause the behavior over time as illustrated with the reference mode in Figure 3.6. Deteriorating management discipline in terms of architecture leads to reduced standardization. However, at the same time, integration is improving when the rigidity of IT principles remains or is reinforced.

Figure 3.6. Reference mode for IT architecture dynamics

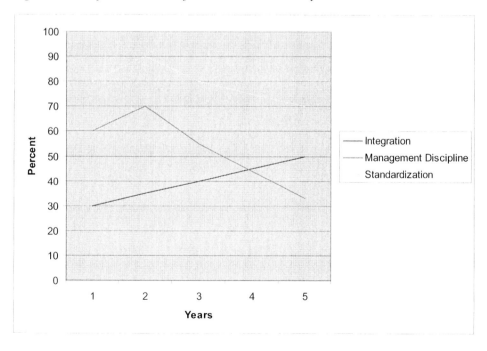

Dynamics of IT Applications

Business application needs often has two conflicting objectives—creativity and discipline. Creativity is about identifying new and more effective ways to deliver customer value using IT. Creativity involves identifying business applications that support strategic business objectives and facilitate business experiments. Discipline is about architectural integrity—ensuring that applications leverage and build out the enterprise architecture rather than undermine architectural principles. Discipline is also about focus—committing the necessary resources to achieve project and business goals.

New business applications often build on IT innovations. An information technology innovation can be defined as the creation and new organizational application of digital computer and communication technologies. IT innovations result from exponential improvements in computing speed and data storage functions that have over time led to radically enhanced functionality in processing, storage, transfer, and display of information (Lyytinen & Rose, 2003). The ability to innovate through IT applications is an important contributor to organizational success (Fichman, 2001).

Business application needs decisions require reconciling complex change and opposing organizational forces. Managers responsible for defining requirements must distinguish core process requirements from nonessentials and know when to live within architectural constraints. They must design experiments knowing that actual benefits could be different from anticipated benefits—or if there are no benefits, they must pull the plug. Most importantly, they must know how to design organizational change and then make it happen. Business application needs decisions require creative thinkers and disciplined project managers, and are probably the least mature of the five IT decisions (Weill & Ross, 2004).

Depending on quantitative parameters in the system dynamics model, the causal loop diagram in Figure 3.7 might cause the behavior over time as illustrated with the reference mode in Figure 3.8. As the number of application errors increase, no more applications are acquired, both leading to a decline in the business benefits from IT applications.

Chillarege (2002) suggested a marriage of business dynamics and software engineering. Although software engineering is a special branch within IT application, it is still worthwhile to read his thoughts on the topic of business dynamics. He argues that few technology disciplines have the emotion and belief wrapped around the issue of process that software engineering does.

Figure 3.7.Causal loop diagram for IT applications dynamics

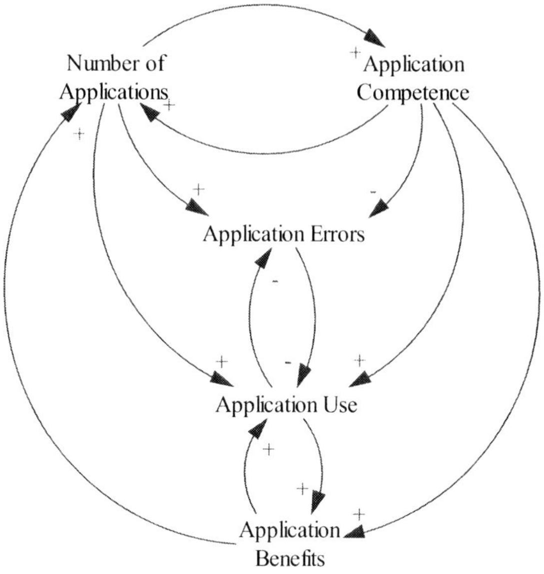

Figure 3.8. Reference mode for IT applications dynamics

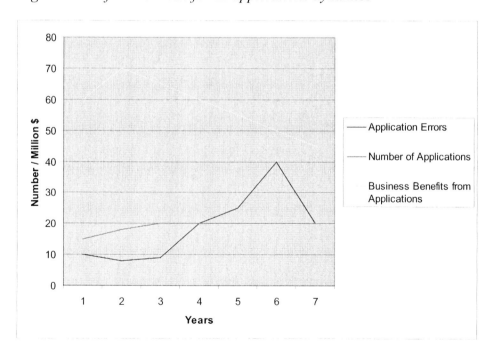

However, a software engineering process is only as good as its ability to create products that meet market needs.

If we fail to realize that business dynamics drive software development—with cost, time, and product quality as outcomes—we make bad judgments. Chillarege (2002) argues:

To better understand how software process and product intertwine, we must focus on both software development fundaments and market dynamics. We also need a realistic view of what is both humanly and technically possible. Evolution takes time, and implementing industry best practices won't raise productivity levels if organizational resources can't realistically support them. (p. 43)

What makes this article interesting is the way it links business dynamics to software engineering along the time dimension. The lifecycle of products consists of entry, growth, stability, and sunset. A good marriage between business dynamics and software engineering process arises from a good match between market values and process attributes. An information system should help deliver a product while accentuating market value.

Abdel-Hamid (1988) built a system dynamics model of software development. The model had variables for error generation, detection, and correction. One of the feedback loops in the model portrayed how project work is accomplished through the utilization of project resources (manpower, facilities, equipment). As work is accomplished on the project, it is reported through a project control system. Such reports cumulate and are processed to create the project's forecast completion time, that is, adding to the current date the indicated time remaining on the job. The feedback loop is completed (closed) as the difference, if any, between the scheduled completion date and the forecast completion date causes adjustments in the magnitude or allocation of the project's resources.

Dynamics of IT Investments

IT investment and prioritization is often the most visible and controversial of the five key IT decisions. Some projects are approved, others are bounced, and the rest enter the organizational equivalent of suspended animation with the dreaded request from the decision makers to "redo the business case" or "provide more information." Enterprises that get superior value from IT focus their investments on their strategic priorities, cognizant of the distinction between "must have" and "nice to have" IT capabilities. IT investment decisions address three dilemmas: how much to spend, where to spend it, and how to reconcile the needs of different constituencies. Probably the most important attribute of a successful IT investment process is ensuring that the enterprise's IT spending reflects strategic priorities. Investment processes must reconcile the demands of individual business units as well as demands to meet companywide needs. Many enterprises value the interdependence of their business units and support their efforts to invest in IT according to business unit strategy. Most enterprises also emphasize the importance of companywide efficiencies and even integration. Enterprises that attempt to persuade independent business units to fund shared infrastructure are likely to experience resistance. Instead, business leaders must articulate the companywide objectives of shared infrastructure and provide appropriate

Figure 3.9. Causal loop diagram for IT investments dynamics

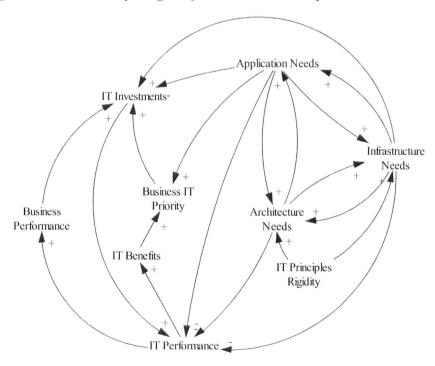

Figure 3.10. Reference mode for IT investments dynamics

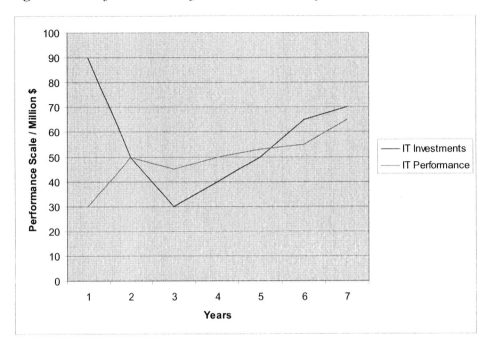

incentives for business unit leaders to sacrifice business unit needs in favor of companywide needs (Weill & Ross, 2004).

Again, depending on quantitative parameters in the system dynamics model, the causal loop diagram in Figure 3.9 might cause the behavior over time as illustrated with the reference mode in Figure 3.10. Reduction in IT investments might have several causes in the diagram, such as poor business performance or lack of application needs, lack of infrastructure needs, or business putting low priority on IT investments compared to other investments. At the same time, IT performance can improve, for example because the firm now has an information architecture that works well and because the information technology infrastructure works well.

IT Governance Capability

IT governance capability is the capability to integrate IS/IT effort with business purpose and activity. The ability to deal with interdependencies that arise between the business and IS function falls into this category. Being a management capability, it is typically developed between the IT manager or CIO and the general manager or CEO, but also between the CIO and the management of other business departments (Heijden, 2001).

Four behaviors reflect this capability. The first indicator refers to the quality of the executive relationship between the CIO and the other executives. High-performance CIOs build and develop quality relationships with their peer executives in the firm. Another behavior associated with this capability is the ability to arrive at shared objectives and visions. Shared objectives involve the alignment of business objectives and IT objectives. The alignment can be intellectual, social, or both. The intellectual dimension refers to whether IS and business executives understand each other's objectives and plans.

Fostering an appropriate culture in the IT department is a third behavior associated with IS/IT governance. There is often a cultural gap between IT departments and business departments. This gap is often fostered by "hard" elements (power and control structures), but also by the rituals, routines, stories, and myths and symbols that set the IT department apart from the other departments. Therefore, strong IS/IT governance capabilities are associated with cultural alignment between IT and business departments (Heijden, 2001).

The fourth and final behavior is that of incorporating best practices in management with this capability. Best practices, which is a broad term originating from the total quality management movement, is usually defined as the acquisition and implementation of (management) processes with superior performance on a continuous basis. Thus, the search for continuous improvement of processes is associated with strong IS/IT governance capability (Heijden, 2001).

A construct related to IT governance capability is IT governance maturity. Again, we can apply resource-based theory. Specifically, we can apply resource-advantage theory, which is a moderately socialized and embedded theory of competition that draws on and is applied by other disciplines including economics, management, public policy, and marketing. The resource-advantage theory would predict that an asset available to a firm, but not necessarily owned by the firm and still available to other firms, could provide competitive advantage since resource innovation is endogenous. For example, using the information technology infrastructure library (ITIL) and/or the control objectives for information and related technology (COBIT) in IT governance are examples of such assets (Gottschalk, 2006). If ITIL and CO-

BIT can be considered resources that provide advantages when implemented in the organization, then IT governance maturity might be conceptualized in terms of the extent of implementation.

References

Abdel-Hamid, T. K. (1988, September). The economics of software quality assurance: A simulation-based case study. *MIS Quarterly*, 395-411.

Broadbent, M., Weill, P., & St. Clair, D. (1999). The implications of information technology infrastructure for business process redesign. *MIS Quarterly, 23*(2), 159-182.

Chillarege, R. (2002). The marriage of business dynamics and software engineering. *IEEE Software,* November/December, 43-49.

Fichman, R. G. (2001). The role of aggregation in the measurement of IT-related organizational innovation. *MIS Quarterly, 25*(4), 427-455.

Gottschalk, P. (2006). *E-business strategy, sourcing and governance*. Hershey, PA: Idea Group Publishing.

Grembergen, W. V., Haes, S. D., & Guldentops, E. (2004). Structures, processes and relational mechanisms for IT governance. In: W. V. Grembergen (Ed.), *Strategies for information technology governance* (pp. 1-36). Hershey, PA: Idea Group Publishing.

Heijden, H. V. D. (2001). Measuring IT core capabilities for electronic commerce. *Journal of Information Technology, 16,* 13-22.

Lyytinen, K., & Roose, G. M. (2003). The disruptive nature of information technology innovations: The case of Internet computing in systems development organizations, *MIS Quarterly, 27*(4), 557-595.

Peterson, R. R. (2004). Integration strategies and tactics for information technology governance. In: W. V. Grembergen (Ed.), *Strategies for information technology governance* (pp. 37-80). Hershey, PA: Idea Group Publishing.

Weill, P. (2004). *Don't just lead, govern: How top-performing firms govern IT* (CISR WP No. 341). Cambridge, MA: Massachusetts Institute of Technology, Sloan School of Management.

Weill, P., & Ross, J. W. (2004). *IT governance*. Boston: Harvard Business School Press.

Chapter IV

Dynamics of E-Business Infrastructure

The contingent and dynamic approach to information technology management is illustrated in this chapter by the case of business models for electronic business. The need for information technology services in an organization depends on e-business models. Furthermore, e-business models depend on value configurations.

Thus, e-business is about much more than just the use of the Internet. According to the resource-based theory, e-business is about developing and applying internal and external resources for competitive advantage. It is about applying an e-business model that supports the current or desired value configuration of a value chain, value shop, and/or value network. And finally, it is about making progress over time, as both technology and market conditions evolve. This requires an understanding of system dynamics, where feedback loops between company actions and market reactions create or destroy infrastructure initiatives.

The term "commerce" is defined by some as describing transactions conducted between business partners. When this definition of commerce is used, some people find the term "electronic commerce" (EC) to be fairly narrow. Thus, many use the term "e-business." E-business refers to a broader definition of

EC, not just the buying and selling of goods and services, but also servicing customers, collaborating with business partners, and conducting electronic transactions within an organization (Turban, King, Lee, Warkentin, & Chung, 2002).

E-commerce is part of e-business, as illustrated in Figure 4.1. The difference can be demonstrated using a business example. The business example is concerned with handling of customer complaints. As long as customers do not complain, then e-commerce may be sufficient for electronic transactions with customers. The front end of the business is electronic, and this front end is the only contact customers have with the business.

However, if a customer complains, then other parts of the business may have to get involved, as illustrated in Figure 4.2. For example, if the customer has received a computer that is found deficient, the customer gets in touch with the vendor. The vendor has to decide whether the complaint is justified. If it is, then the vendor has to decide whether to fix the product, replace the product, or refund the money paid for the product.

This kind of decision-making will typically involve other departments in addition to marketing and sales departments. These other departments may be the technical department, the production department, and the finance department. While the marketing and sales departments have electronic communication with the customer using information systems, other departments may not be connected to the same information systems.

Figure 4.1. E-commerce is part of e-business

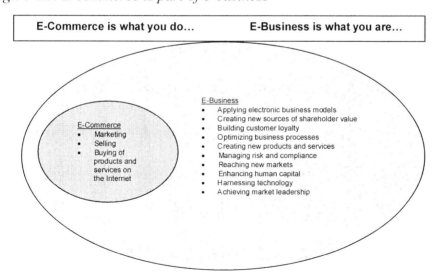

In this situation, the internal handling of a customer complaint in the business is not transparent to and accessible for the customer. The customer may experience time passing by without any information from the vendor. A complaining customer was angry already at the time of the complaint, and the anger and frustration rise as the customer receives no response. The customer is unable to obtain information from the vendor by electronic means, since the vendor is doing e-commerce, not e-business.

If the vendor were an e-business, then the business process of handling customer complaints would be an integrated information system to which the customer has access. Then it is possible for the customer to follow the complaint-handling process, and it is possible for departments other than marketing and sales to stay in direct contact with the complaining customer to resolve the issues. This business process is illustrated in Figure 4.2.

Weill and Vitale (2001) use the following working definition of e-business: marketing, buying, selling, delivering, servicing, and paying for products, services, and information across (nonproprietary) networks linking an enterprise and its prospects, customers, agents, suppliers, competitors, allies, and complementers. The essence of this definition is the conduct of business and business processes over computer networks based on nonproprietary standards. The Internet is the exemplar of a nonproprietary network used today for e-business. Given its low cost and universal access, the Internet

Figure 4.2. Customer complaint handling business process in company with e-commerce but no e-business

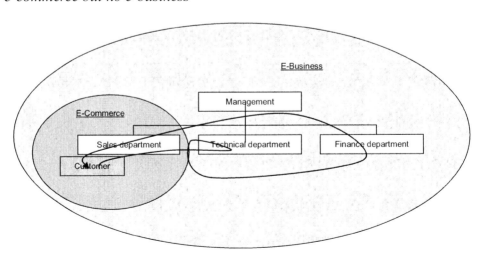

will be the major infrastructure for the foreseeable future. However, new access technologies already on the horizon (e.g., use of wireless application protocol from mobile telephones) will supplement the Internet.

E-business embodies the most pervasive, disruptive, and disconcerting form of change: It leaves no aspect of managing organizations untouched, it challenges long-accepted business models, and organization leaders have little to draw on from past experience to manage its effects. In particular, its capacity to transform business processes is no longer in dispute. The new technologies at the heart of e-business open up myriad possibilities not just to reconsider the reengineering of existing processes, but also to design, develop, and deploy fundamentally new ways of conceiving and executing business processes. Senior executives in every organization thus confront a central challenge: How should they endeavor to capture, analyze, and project the transformational impact of e-business on their organization's most critical or core processes? Later in this book we put forward that knowledge management provides one useful vehicle for doing so (Fahey, Srivastava, Sharon, & Smith, 2001).

In spite of its pervasiveness, visibility, and impact, e-business often remains a poorly understood phenomenon in many industries. E-business constitutes the ability of a firm to electronically connect, in multiple ways, many organizations, both internal and external, for many different purposes. It allows an organization to execute electronic transactions with any individual entity along the value creation—suppliers, logistics providers, wholesalers, distributors, service providers, and end customers. Increasingly, e-business allows an organization to establish real-time connections simultaneously among numerous entities for some specific purpose, such as optimizing the flow of physical items (raw materials, components, finished products) through the supply chain (Fahey et al., 2001).

E-business raises a number of critical business issues, each of which in turn generates distinct knowledge issues and challenges specific to the e-business transformation of processes. First, e-business is transforming the solutions available to customers in almost every industry, that is, the breadth of solutions and how the solutions are obtained and experienced. Consumers can now buy books, food, clothing, and a lot of other goods over the Internet in ways that allow distinct forms of customization. Industrial purchasers can now use the Internet to scour the offerings of many providers and procure components and supplies in combinations, prices, and delivery schedules that dramatically lower the costs of search, speed delivery, and reduce prices.

These new solutions open up possibilities for customer value creation and delivery that were simply unimaginable few years ago (Fahey et al., 2001).

Second, the creators and purveyors of the new customer value propositions represent new types of rivals. Traditional booksellers are confronted by Amazon.com; Merrill Lynch faces E*TRADE. These new entities recast the profile of rivals in many industries and, partly as a consequence, reshape the contours and boundaries of most traditional competitive spaces or industries (Fahey et al., 2001).

Third, in part due to the competitive context changes just noted, the nature and content of strategy, and by implication the dynamics of marketplace rivalry, are undergoing profound change. No longer can most firms rely on making modest, incremental changes to long-established strategy success formulas. Strategy in product domains as diverse as financial services, household furnishings, computers, automobiles, and industrial components increasingly revolves around inventing new product solutions, and/or new ways of interacting with customers in designing, developing, and delivering these solutions. In fact, organizations are adjusting their strategies according to the new notion of the customer in which customer intimacy, customer relationship management, one-to-one marketing, and the concept of the customer, as opposed to the product, as the new asset of the organization and real carrier of value, dominate. In short, e-business offers the platform for new forms of marketplace strategy models—a significant element of any firm's business model—that will change the competitive rules of the game (Fahey et al., 2001).

Fourth, e-business requires firms to refocus and reconfigure almost every type of tangible and intangible asset. It places an especially heavy premium on developing and leveraging intangible assets, including many different types of new skills, new forms of integrated and intensive relationships with external entities, new sets of perceptions held by customers, channels, and suppliers, and significant new knowledge (Fahey et al., 2001).

Fifth, e-business is dramatically reshaping every traditional business process: from developing new products and managing customer relationships, to acquiring human resources and procuring raw materials and components. By enabling major new tasks to be added to individual processes, e-business broadens their scope, content, and value-generating capability. For example, customer relationship management has been essentially reinvented through e-business's ability to access large bodies of heretofore unavailable data, manipulate and mine such data in radical new ways, and customize the outputs of such analysis to customer segments, and in many cases, to individual customers. And, by integrating traditionally largely separate processes, e-business in effect creates what might well be described as new business processes (Fahey et al., 2001).

Electronic Business Models

A business model can be defined as the method by which a firm builds and uses its resources to offer its customers better value than its competitors and to make money doing so. It details how a firm makes money now and how it plans to do so in the long run. The model is what enables a firm to have a sustainable competitive advantage, to perform better than its rivals in the long term. A business model can be conceptualized as a system that is made up of components, linkages between the components, and dynamics (Afuah & Tucci, 2003).

Weill and Vitale (2001) define an e-business model as a description of the roles and relationships among a firm's consumers, customers, allies, and suppliers that identifies the major flows of product, information, and money, and the major benefits to participants.

There are many different ways to describe and classify e-business models. Weill and Vitale (2001) propose that there are a finite number of atomic e-business models, each of which captures a different way to conduct e-business. Firms can combine atomic e-business models as building blocks to create tailored e-business models and initiatives, using their competencies as their guide. Weill and Vitale (2001) identified eight atomic e-business models, each of which describes the essence of conducting business electronically.

1. **Direct to customer:** The distinguishing characteristic of this model is that buyer and seller communicate directly, rather than through an intermediary. The seller may be a retailer, a wholesaler, or a manufacturer. The customer may be an individual or a business. Examples of the direct-to-customer model are Dell Computer Corporation and Gap, Inc.

    Infrastructure: The direct-to-customer model requires extensive electronic connection with the customer, including online payment systems.

Many direct-to-customer implementations include an extranet to allow customized Web pages for major business-to-business (B2B) customers. Operating a direct-to-customer e-business requires significant investment in the equivalent of the store, the Web site. Direct-to-customer businesses spend millions of dollars developing easy-to-navigate and easy-to-use Web sites with the goal of improving the B2B or business-to-customer (B2C) shopping experience online. Lands End has devised a feature by which women can build and store a three-dimensional model of themselves to "try on" clothes electronically.

In their field research, Weill and Vitale (2001) found that firms with e-business initiatives containing the direct-to-customer e-business model needed and were investing more heavily in three areas of infrastructure services: application infrastructure, communications, and IT management.

Direct-to-customer firms particularly needed payment transaction processing to process online customer payments, enterprise-wide resource planning (ERP) to process customer transactions, workflow infrastructure to optimize business process performance, communication network services linking all points in the enterprise to each other and the outside world (often using TCP/IP protocol), the installation and maintenance of workstations and local area networks supporting the large number of people required to operate a direct-to-customer model, and service-level agreements between the business and the IT group or outsourcer to ensure, monitor, and improve the systems necessary for the model.

Sources of revenue: The main source of revenue in the direct-to-customer model is usually direct sales to customers. Supplemental revenues come from advertising, the sale of customer information, and product placement fees.

Critical success factors: Critical success factors are the things a firm must do well to flourish. The following list shows the critical success factors for the direct-to-customer model: create and maintain customer awareness, in order to build a critical mass of users to cover the fixed cost of building an electronic presence; reduce customer acquisition costs; strive to own the customer relationship and understand individual customer needs; increase repeat purchases and average transaction size; provide fast and efficient transaction processing, fulfillment, and payment; ensure adequate security for the organization and its customers;

and provide interfaces that combine ease of use with richness of experience, integrating multiple channels.

2.   **Full-service provider:** A firm using the full-service provider model provides total coverage of customer needs in a particular domain, consolidated via a single point of contact. The domain could be any major area of customer needs requiring multiple products and services, for example, financial services, health care, or industrial chemicals. The full-service provider adds value by providing a full range of products, sourced both internally and externally, and consolidated them using the channel chosen by the customer. Examples of the full-service provider are the Prudential Advisor and GE Supply Company.

Infrastructure: Virtually all businesses aspire to getting one hundred percent of their customers' business, or at least to getting as much of that business as they can profitably handle. Yet the number of full-service providers remains small. Part of the reason for this is required infrastructure. The missing piece of infrastructure in many businesses is often a database containing information about the customer and the products that the customer owns. Without owning these data, a provider does not own the customer relationship, and therefore some of the customer's transactions are likely to take place directly with other providers. All of the important interactions with customers occurring across any channel or business unit must be recorded in the firm-wide customer database.

Weill and Vitale (2001) identified in their field research databases and data warehouses as some of the most important infrastructure services associated with the full-service provider model. Other important infrastructure services included the following: the ability to evaluate proposals for new information systems initiatives to coordinate IT investments across a multibusiness-unit firm with the goal of a single point of contact for the customer; centralized management of IT infrastructure capacity to integrate across multiple business units within the firm and third-party providers—the full-service provider model is not readily workable if each business unit optimizes its own IT needs; installation and maintenance of workstations and local area networks to operate the online business linking all the business units and third-party providers; electronic support for groups to coordinate the cross-functional teams required to implement this model; and the identification and testing of new technologies to find cost-effective ways to deliver this complex business model to the customer across multiple channels.

Sources of revenue: A full-service provider gains revenues from selling its own products and those of others, and possibly also from annual membership fees, management fees, transaction fees, commissions on third-party products, advertising or listing fees from third-party providers, and fees for selling aggregated data about customers.

Critical success factors: One important critical success factor is the brand, credibility, and trust necessary for a customer to look to the firm for its complete needs in an area. Another is owning the customer relationship in one domain and integrating and consolidating the offering of many third parties into a single channel or multiple channels. A third factor is owning more of the customer data in the relevant domain than any other player. A final factor is enforcement of policies to protect the interests of internal and external suppliers, as well as customers.

3. **Whole of enterprise:** The single point of contact for the e-business customer is the essence of the whole-of-enterprise atomic business model. Although many of this model's breakthrough innovations have occurred in public-sector organizations, the model is applicable in both the for-profit and the public sectors. An example of this model is the Australian state of Victoria with its Business Channel and Health Channel

Infrastructure: For the whole-of-enterprise model, infrastructure needs to link the different systems in the various business units and provide a firm-wide perspective for management. The field research by Weill and Vitale (2001) revealed that the following infrastructure services are the most important for implementing this model: centralized management of infrastructure capacity to facilitate integration and capture economies of scale; identification and testing of new technologies to find new ways to integrate the often different systems in many business units into a single point of customer contact; management of key data independent of applications and the creation of a centralized repository for firm-wide information; electronic means of summarizing data from different applications and platforms to manage the complexity arising from a single point of contact for multiple business units; development of an ERP service to process the transactions instigated by customers interacting with several different business units, often requiring consolidating or linking several ERPs in the firm; payment transaction processing, either on a firm-wide basis or by linking several systems across the business units; large-scale data-processing facilities to process transactions from multiple business units, often centralized to achieve economies of scale; and integrated mobile computing applications, which provide another channel to the customer.

Sources of revenue: In the for-profit sector, revenues are generated by provision of goods and services to the customer by the business units. There may also be the opportunity to charge an annual service or membership fee for this level of service. In the government sector, the motivation is usually twofold: improved service and reduced cost. Service to the community is improved through continuous, round-the-clock operation and faster service times. Government costs can potentially be reduced by sharing more infrastructure and eliminating the need to perform the same transaction in multiple agencies.

Critical success factors: The following list details the critical success factors for the whole-of-enterprise model: changing customer behavior to make use of the new model, as opposed to the customer continuing to interact directly with individual units; reducing costs in the individual business units as the direct demands on them fall and managing the transfer pricing issues that will inevitably arise; altering the perspective of the business units to take an enterprise-wide view, which includes broad product awareness, training, and cross-selling; in the integrated implementation, reengineering the business processes to link into life events at the front end and existing legacy processes and systems at the back end; and finding compelling and practical life events that customers can use as triggers to access the enterprise.

4. **Intermediaries** such as portals, agents, auctions, aggregators, and other intermediaries. E-business is often promoted as an ideal way for sellers and buyers to interact directly, shortening old-economy value chains by disintermediating some of their members. Yet some of the most popular sites on the Internet, both for consumers and for business users, are in fact intermediaries—sites that stand between the buyer and the seller. The services of intermediaries include search (to locate providers of products and services), specification (to identify important product attributes), price (to establish the price, including optional extras such as warranties), sale (to complete the sales transaction, including payment and settlement), fulfillment (to fulfill the purchase by delivering the product or service), surveillance (to conduct surveillance of the activities of buyers and sellers in order to report aggregate activity and prices and to inform and regulate the market), and enforcement (to enforce

proper conduct by buyers and sellers). Examples of intermediaries are electronic malls, shopping agents, specialty auctions, electronic markets, electronic auctions, and portals.

Infrastructure: Intermediaries generate value by concentrating information and bringing together buyers and sellers, operating entirely in space and thus relying on IT as the primary infrastructure. Weill and Vitale (2001) found in their field interviews that the most important infrastructure services for firms pursuing the intermediary atomic business model are the following: knowledge management, including knowledge databases and contact databases that enable the codification and sharing of knowledge in this highly information-intensive business; enforcing Internet and e-mail policies to ensure proper and consistent use of electronic channels to buyers, sellers, and intermediaries; workstation networks to support the products and services of this all-electronic business model; centralized management of e-business applications, ensuring consistency and integration across product offerings; information systems planning to identify the most effective uses of IT in the business; and information systems project management to ensure that business value is achieved from IT investments.

Sources of revenue: An intermediary may earn revenues from buyers, sellers, or both. Sellers may pay a listing fee, a transaction fee, a sales commission, or some combination of these. Similarly, buyers may pay a subscription fee, a success fee, or a sales commission.

Critical success factors: The chief requirement for survival as an intermediary is sufficient volume of usage to cover the fixed costs of establishing the business and the required infrastructure. Attracting and retaining a critical mass of customers is therefore the primary critical success factor. Another important critical success factor is building up infrastructure just quickly enough to meet demand as it increases.

5. **Shared infrastructure:** The firm provides infrastructure shared by its owners. Other suppliers, who are users of the shared infrastructure, but not owners, can also be included. Customers who access the shared infrastructure directly are given a choice of suppliers and value propositions. The owner and the non-owner suppliers are generally represented objectively. In some situations, goods or services flow directly from the shared infrastructure to the customer. In other situations, a message is sent by the shared infrastructure to the supplier, who then completes the transaction by providing the goods or services to the customer.

An example illustrating the features of the shared-infrastructure business model is the system from 2000 consisting of America's largest automakers, some of their dealers, and IBM, Motorola, and Intel. The initiative was named Covisint (collaboration vision integrity). General Motors, Ford, and DaimlerChrysler see stronger potential benefits from cooperating on supply-chain logistics than from competing.

Infrastructure: The shared-infrastructure business model requires competitors to cooperate by sharing IT infrastructure and information. This level of cooperation requires agreement on high-level IT architectures as well as operational standards for applications, data communications, and technology. Effective implementation of the shared-infrastructure model also requires enforcement of these standards, and most shared-infrastructure models have a joint committee to set and enforce standards. Another role of these committees is to implement the policies of the shared infrastructure about what information, if any, is shared and what information is confidential to partner firms. Weill and Vitale (2001) found in their field research that the most important infrastructure services required by firms implementing the shared-infrastructure atomic business model all concerned architectures and standards: specification and enforcement of high-level architectures for data, technology, applications, communications, and work that are agreed to by alliance partners; and specification and enforcement of detailed standards for the high-level architectures.

Sources of revenue: Revenues can be generated both from membership fees and from transaction fees. The alliance may be run on a nonprofit basis or on a profit-making basis. Not-for-profit shared infrastructures are typically open to all eligible organizations and distribute any excess revenues back to their members. The for-profit models are typically owned by a subset of the firms in a given segment, which split up any profits among themselves.

Critical success factors: Critical success factors for the shared-infrastructure model include the following: no dominant partner that gains more than any other partner; an unbiased channel and objective presentation of product and service information; critical mass of both alliance partners and customers; management of conflict among the ongoing e-business initiatives of the alliance partners; compilation and delivery of accurate and timely statements of the services and benefits provided to each member of the alliance; and interoperability of systems.

6. **Virtual community**: Virtual communities deserve our attention, and not only because they are the clearest, and perhaps the last, surviving embodiment of the original intent of the Internet. By using IT to leverage the fundamental human desire for communication with peers, virtual communities can create significant value for their owners as well as for their members. Once established, a virtual community is less susceptible to competition by imitation than any of the other atomic business models. In this business model, the firm of interest—the sponsor of the virtual community—sits in the center, positioned between members of the community and suppliers. Fundamental to the success of this model is that members are able, and in fact are encouraged, to communicate with one another directly. Communication between members may be via e-mail, bulletin boards, online chat, Web-based conferencing, or other computer-based media, and it is the distinguishing feature of this model. Examples of this model are Parent Soup, a virtual community for parents, and Motley Fool, a virtual community of investors.

    Infrastructure: Virtual communities depend on IT to exist. In particular, the creation and continual enhancement of an Internet site is essential if a virtual community is to survive. Many virtual-community sites include not just static content and links, but also tools of interest to potential members. Weill and Vitale (2001) found in their field research that the infrastructure services most important for the virtual-community business model are the following: training in the use of IT for members of the community; application service provision (ASP) to provide specialized systems virtual communities need such as bulletin boards, e-mail, and Internet service provider access; IT research and development, including infrastructure services for identifying and testing new technologies and for evaluating proposals for new information systems initiatives; information systems planning to identify and prioritize potential investments in IT in this completely online business; and installation and maintenance of workstations and local area networks to support the electronic world of the virtual community.

    Sources of revenue: A sponsoring firm can gain revenue from membership fees, direct sales of goods and services, advertising, click-throughs and sales commissions. A firm sponsoring a virtual community as an adjunct to its other activities may receive no direct revenue at all from the virtual community. Rather, the firm receives less tangible benefits, such as customer loyalty and increased knowledge about its customer base.

Critical success factors: The critical success factors for a virtual community include finding and retaining a critical mass of members; building and maintaining loyalty with an appropriate mix of content and features; maintaining privacy and security for member information; balancing commercial potential and members' interests; leveraging member profile information with advertisers and merchants; and engendering a feeling of trust in the community by its members.

7. **Value net integrator:** Traditionally, most firms operate simultaneously in two worlds, the physical and the virtual. In the physical world, goods and services are created in a series of value-adding activities connecting the supply side (suppliers, procurement, and logistics) with the demand side (customers, marketing, and shipping). In the virtual world, information about the members of the physical value chain are gathered, synthesized, and distributed along the virtual value chain. E-business provides the opportunity to separate the physical and virtual value chains. Value net integrators take advantage of that split and attempt to control the virtual value chain in their industries by gathering, synthesizing, and distributing information. Value net integrators add value by improving the effectiveness of the value chain by coordinating information. A pure value net integrator operates exclusively in the virtual value chain, owning a few physical assets. To achieve the gathering, synthesizing, and distributing of information, the value net integrator receives and sends information to all other players in the model. The value net integrator coordinates product flows from suppliers to allies and customers. The product flows from the suppliers to customers may be direct or via allies. In some cases, the value net integrator may sell information or other products to the customer. The value net integrator always strives to own the customer relationship with the other participants in the model, thus knowing more about its operations than any other player. Examples of value net integrators are Seven-Eleven Japan and Cisco Systems.

    Infrastructure: The value net integrator succeeds in its role by gathering, synthesizing, and distributing information. Thus, for a value net integrator, data and electronic connectivity with allies and other players are very important assets. Field research carried out by Weill and Vitale (2001) suggests that the most important infrastructure services required for a value net integrator include middleware, linking systems on different platforms across the many players in the value net; a centralized data warehouse that collects and summarizes key information for analysis from decentralized databases held by several players across the value net; specification and enforcement of high-level architectures and detailed standards for data, technology, applications, and communications to link together different technology platforms owned by different firms; call centers to provide advice and guidance for partners and allies in getting the most value from the information provided by the value net generator; and high-capacity communications network service to support the high volumes of information flowing across the value net.

Sources of revenue: In this model, revenues generally come from fees or margins on the physical goods that pass through the industry value net. By using information about consumers, the value net integrator is able to increase prices by meeting consumer demand. By using information about suppliers, the value net integrator reduces costs by cutting inventories and lead times.

Critical success factors: The critical success factors for the value net integrator atomic business model are as follows: reducing ownership of physical assets while retaining ownership of data; owning or having access to the complete industry virtual value chain; establishing a trusted brand recognized at all places in the value chain; operating in markets where information can add significant value, such as those that are complex, fragmented, regulated, multilayered, inefficient, and large with many sources of information; presenting the information to customers, allies, partners, and suppliers in clear and innovative ways that provide value; and helping other value chain participants capitalize on the information provided by the value net integrator.

8. **Content provider:** Like many terms associated with e-business, "content provider" has different meanings to different people. We define content provider as a firm that creates and provides content (information, products, or services) in digital form to customers via third parties. The physical-world analogy of a content provider is a journalist, recording artist, or stock analyst. Digital products such as software, electronic travel guides, and digital music and video are examples of content. A virtual-world example of a content provider is weather forecasters such as Storm Weather Center.

    Infrastructure: Content providers must excel at tailoring and manipulating their core content to meet the specific needs of customers. Content providers must categorize and store their content in well-indexed modules so it can be combined and customized to meet customer needs via a wide variety of channels. Customers and transactions tend to be relatively few, at least compared with the number of end consumers and their transactions. Often, complex and unique IT infrastructures are needed to support the particular needs of the specialized professionals employed by the content provider. Field research by Weill and Vitale (2001) identified the most important infrastructure services: multimedia storage farms or storage area network infrastructures to deal with large amounts of information; a strong focus on architecture, including setting and enforcing standards particularly for work; detailed data architectures to structure, specify, link manipulate, and manage the core intellectual property; workstation network infrastructures to enable the fundamentally online business of a content provider; and a common systems development environment to provide compatible and integrated systems, ensuring the systems can provide content across multiple channels to their customers.

Sources of revenue: The primary source of revenue for a content provider is fees from its third parties or allies. These fees may be based on a fixed price per month or year, or on the number of times the third party's own customers access the content. In some situations, the fees paid are lower for content branded by the provider, and higher for unbranded content, which then appears to the customer to have been generated by the third party itself.

Critical success factors: To succeed, a content provider must provide reliable, timely content in the right format and at the right price. The critical success factors for this model include the following: branding (the value of content is due in part to reputation), recognized as best in class (the business of content provision will be global and competitive), and network (establishing and maintaining a network of third parties through which content is distributed.

One way of comparing these e-business models is to analyze to what extent each model creates integration with customers and to what extent each model creates integration with partners. As illustrated in Figure 4.3, the direct to customer business model creates mainly integration with customers, while shared infrastructure creates mainly integration with partners.

Figure 4.3. E-business models integration with customers versus partners

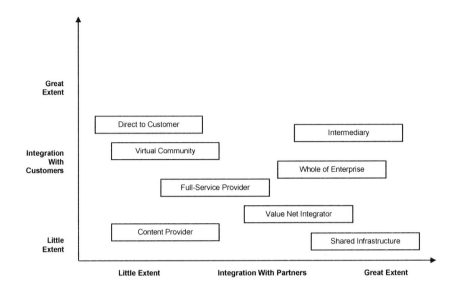

Determining Appropriate Models

Despite works by Weill and Vitale (2002) and others, how an e-business model must be defined and specified is largely an open issue. Business decision makers tend to use the notion in a highly informal way, and usually there is a big gap between the business view and that of IT developers.

The electronic business landscape is confusing for many new entrants, and many of them face the paradox that hesitation would run the risk of being left behind, but rushing in and making an incorrect choice regarding electronic business initiatives could have dire consequences for organizations. According to Hayes and Finnegan (2005), Internet-only or "dot-com" models have proven particularly vulnerable. For example, the dot-com implosion of spring 2000 led to a large number of high-profile collapses including boo, ClickMango, and eToys. "Clicks and mortar" strategies have also met with mixed success, as in the case of Wall Street Journal Interactive and Fyffes' World-of-Fruit.

The Internet age has produced many Internet business models. For example, Afuah and Tucci (2003) describe the following nine: brokerage model, advertising model, infomediary model, merchant model, manufacturing model, affiliate model, community model, subscription model, and utility model. An Internet business model—sometimes labeled b-web—is a business on the Internet that represents a distinct system of suppliers, distributors, commerce service providers, infrastructure providers, and customers that use the Internet for their primary business communication and transactions.

Another classification of Internet business models is presented by Laudon and Laudon (2005):

- **Virtual storefront:** Sells physical products directly to consumers or to individual businesses (Amazon.com, EPM.com)

- **Information broker:** Provides product, pricing, and availability information to individuals and businesses. Generates revenue from advertising or from directing buyers to sellers (Edmunds.com, Kbb.com, Insweb.com, IndustralMall.com)

- **Transaction broker:** Saves users money and time by processing online sales transactions, generating a fee each time a transaction occurs. Also provides information on rates and terms (etrade.com, Expedia.com)

- **Online marketplace:** Provides a digital environment where buyers and sellers can meet, search for products, display products, and establish prices for those products (eBay.com, Priceline.com, ChemConnect.com, Pantellos.com)

- **Content provider:** Creates revenue by providing digital content, such as digital news, music, photos, or video, over the Web (WSJ.com, CNN.com, TheStreet.com, Gettyimages.com, MP3.com)

- **Online service provider:** Provides online service for individuals and businesses. Generates revenue from subscription or transaction fees, from advertising, or from collecting marketing information from users (@Backup.com, Xdrive.com, Employease.com, Salesforce.com)

- **Virtual community:** Provides online meeting place where people with similar interests can communicate and find useful information (Motocross.com, iVillage.com, Sailnet.com)

- **Portal:** Provides initial point of entry to the Web along with specialized content and other services (Yahoo.com, MSN.com, StarMedia.com)

Hayes and Finnegan (2005) present several classifications of e-business models. One classification includes e-shops, e-malls, e-procurement, third-party marketplaces, e-auction, virtual community, collaboration platform, value chain service providers, value chain integration, information brokerage, and trust services. Another classification includes aggregation, agora/open market, alliance, and value chain. Another classification includes catalogue hubs, other hubs, yield managers, exchanges, forward aggregators, and reverse aggregators. A final classification consists of a long list including click-and-mortar merchant models, virtual merchants, catalogue merchants, virtual malls, metamediaries, distributors, manufacturer models, buy/sell fulfillment, market exchange, bounty brokers, auction brokers, reverse auction, vertical Web community, specialized portal, knowledge networks, open-source models, content services, trust services, and transaction brokers.

Electronic business poses significant challenges for organizations, as it affects both how organizations relate to external parties (customers, suppliers, partners, competitors, and markets) and how they operate internally in managing activities, processes, and systems. Porter (2001) argues that the companies that succeed with e-business will be those that use the Internet in conjunction with their traditional business models and activities.

Hayes and Finnegan (2005) argue that business models are possibly the most discussed yet least understood area of electronic business. They refer the point that consultants, executives, researchers, and journalists frequently use the phrase "business model" but have rarely given a precise definition of what they exactly meant, and that this has lead to the loss of credibility of the concept.

A business model can be understood as a blend of three streams: value, revenue, and logistics. The value stream is concerned with the value proposition for buyers, sellers, and market makers. The revenue stream identifies how the organizations will earn revenue, and the logistics stream involves detailing how supply chain issues will affect the organizations involved (Hayes & Finnegan, 2005).

A business model can also be understood as an architecture for product, service, and information flows, incorporating a description of the sources of revenue, the actors involved, their roles, and the benefits to them. An electronic business model is comprised of components, linkages, and dynamics. Components are factors such as customer scope, product (goods and services) scope, customer value, pricing, revenue sources, connected activities, implementation, capabilities of the firm, and sustainability. Linkages exist when one activity affects another in terms of cost-effectiveness, and trade-offs and optimization are sought to find the right blend to achieve competitive advantage. The dynamics represent how a firm reacts to or initiates change to attain a new competitive advantage, or to sustain an existing one, to have sustainable competitive advantage and to perform better than its rivals in the long term (Hayes & Finnegan, 2005).

While the atomic business models by Weill and Vitale (2002) were distinguished by dimensions such as infrastructure, sources of revenue, and critical success factors, we can think of other criteria to classify e-business models. For example, three major areas that impact the sustainability and growth of an e-business are revenue streams, value streams, and logistical streams. These three elements are interrelated, with changes to any one impacting the others. Furthermore, e-business models can be classified in terms of integration with customers versus integration with partners, as illustrated in Figure 4.3.

At the moment, there is no single, comprehensive, and cogent taxonomy of the Web business models. Businesses face questions as to which business model is appropriate for them. This is made more difficult when we consider that companies in the same industry often pursue different Internet business models. For example, companies in the automobile industry have industry consortia models such as shared infrastructure, while others have virtual community models.

As a result, determining and employing an appropriate Internet business model has become a major business issue. The problem is that there is no well-developed or complete framework to aid the decision of choosing a model.

In addition to outlining the components of a business model, some authors offer a set of business model representation tools. Weill and Vitale (2001) have developed a formalism to assist analyzing e-business initiatives, which they call e-business model schematic. The schematic is a pictorial representation, aiming to highlight a business model's important elements. This includes characteristics of the firm of interest, its suppliers and allies, the major flows of product, information, and money, and finally the revenues and other benefits each participant receives.

In determining an appropriate e-business model, several criteria can be used, such as:

- **Involved parties**, such as business-to-business, business-to-consumer, and/or consumer-to-consumer.

- **Revenue sources**, such as transaction fee, product price, and/or exposure fee.

- **Value configuration**, such as value chain, value shop, and/or value network.

- **Integration** with customers and/or partners.

- **Relationships**, such as one-to-many, many-to-many, and/or many-to-one.

- **Knowledge**, such as know-how, know-what, and know-why.

Unfortunately, e-business models still fall under open and weak theory domains. An open domain is one that cannot be realistically modeled. A weak theory domain is a domain in which relationships between important concepts are uncertain. General knowledge in such domains is theoretically uncertain, incomplete and subject to changes. Methods that rely on deductive proofs are not readily applicable. Concepts and statements in Internet business models are more or less plausible, stronger or weaker supported, rather than true or false.

Fortunately, new research on e-business models is emerging. For example, Hayes and Finnegan (2005) present different approaches to understanding e-business models. One approach is e-business model ontology, which can be defined as a rigorous definition of the e-business issues and their interdependencies in a company's business model. The e-business model ontology focuses on four aspects of the organization, product innovation, infrastructure management, customer relationship, and financials.

Dimensions of product innovation are target customer segment, value proposition, and capabilities. Dimensions of customer relationship are information strategy, feel and serve, and trust and loyalty. Dimensions of infrastructure management are resources, activity configuration, and partner network, while dimensions of financials are revenue model, cost structure, and profit/loss.

Architectures for business models can be identified through the deconstruction and reconstruction of the value configuration. Value configuration elements are identified as well as the possible ways that information can be integrated in the value configuration and between the respective value configurations of the parties that are interacting.

As we have seen, decision makers are faced with an enormous range of electronic business models from which to choose. The process of fully researching each of these models can prove daunting. Such research is a feature of what has been termed the intelligence phase of decision-making. This phase is important, as options excluded at this stage do not get considered at a later stage. Hayes and Finnegan (2005) developed a framework for use at the intelligence phase to exclude models that are incompatible with prevailing organizational and supply chain characteristics.

The framework assesses the following characteristics: economic control, supply chain integration, functional integration, innovation, and input sourcing:

- **Economic control** refers to the degree to which a market is hierarchical or self-organizing. This characteristic can be measured in terms of the extent of regulatory bodies, government policy, customers, asset specificity, switching costs, proprietary products, capital requirements, and access to necessary inputs for new entrants in this industry.

- **Supply chain integration** is considered to be a measure of the degree to which the business functions and processes of an organization are integrated with those of their supply chain partners. This characteristic can be measured in terms of shipping scheduling, transportation management, tax reporting, negotiating customer credit terms, negotiating supplier credit terms, determining freight charges and terms, resource planning, and inventory control.

- **Functional integration** refers to the degree to which multiple functions are integrated in a business model. In order to measure the degree to which functions within an organization are integrated, a scale that considers a detailed list of processes can be applied. Examples of process integrations are purchase order processing with servicing functions, shipping scheduling with manufacturing, transportation management with financial functions, tax reporting with financial functions, negotiating customer credit terms with distribution, and negotiating supplier credit terms with distribution.

- **Innovation** is the degree of innovation of an e-business model, which can be defined as the extent to which processes can be performed via the Internet that were not previously possible. Innovation can be divided into internal and external components based on the firm's ability (internal) to innovate or assimilate innovations within the innovative environment of the industrial sector (external).

- **Sourcing** refers to the way in which inputs are sourced by the organization, either systematically from a long-term supplier or through spot markets. The issue of sourcing raw materials is more straightforward, as manufacturing and operating inputs are either sourced systematically or on spot markets.

Hayes and Finnegan (2005) believe that their framework has the potential to help decision makers by providing a method of excluding from consideration those electronic business models that are unsuitable given prevailing organizational and environmental characteristics. Business models are excluded based on scale ratings for items measuring economic control, supply chain integration, functional integration, innovation, and sourcing. For each scale, the decision-maker needs to determine the number of attributes that are applicable to their organization.

Infrastructure Capabilities

As firms integrate e-business into their existing business, they migrate from traditional physical business models to combined physical and virtual models. This shift increases the role of the information technology infrastructure because information and online transaction processing become more important. However, the large number of infrastructure investment options can easily overwhelm senior management. To help, Weill and Vitale (2002) classified e-business initiatives by the building blocks they use (which are called atomic e-business models), and they examined the main IT infrastructure services that these models need. The business models require surprisingly different IT infrastructure services, so categorization should help executives prioritize their IT infrastructure investments based on their business goals. At the heart of this prioritization process is the firm's IT governance process, which should ensure that IT knows of upcoming IT infrastructure needs early in the strategizing process.

Weill and Vitale (2002) define a firm's information technology portfolio as its total investment in computing and communications technology. The IT portfolio thus includes hardware, software, telecommunications, electronically stored data, devices to collect and represent data, and the people who provide IT services.

IT Infrastructure

The foundation of an IT portfolio is the firm's information technology infrastructure. This internal IT infrastructure is composed of four elements: IT components (the technologist's view of the infrastructure building blocks), human IT infrastructure (the intelligence used to translate the IT components into services that users can draw upon), shared IT services (the user's view of the infrastructure), and shared and standard applications (fairly stable uses of the services) as illustrated in Figure 4.4.

- **IT components:** At the base of the internal infrastructure are the technical components, such as computers, printers, database software packages, operating systems, and scanners. These components are commodities and are readily available in the marketplace. Traditionally, IT infrastructures have been described in terms of these components. Unfortunately, while technologists understand the capabilities of these components, business people do not—components are not business language to them. Thus, technologists and business people have had difficulty discussing infrastructure needs and business models because they have not had a common language (Weill & Vitale, 2002).

- **Human IT infrastructure:** Describing IT components in business terms requires a translation. That translation is handled by people, and

Figure 4.4. The hierarchy of IT infrastructure

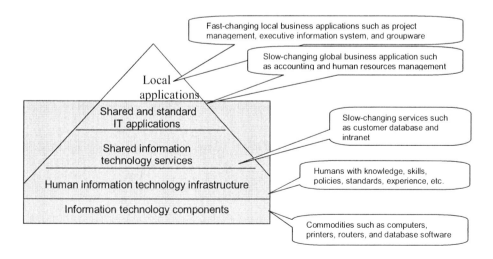

is performed in this layer, which builds on the IT components layer. The human IT infrastructure layer consists of knowledge, skills, standards, and experience. These tools are used to bind IT components into reliable services, which are services business people can understand (Weill & Vitale, 2002).

- **Shared IT services:** This layer views the infrastructure as a set of services that users can understand, draw upon, and share, to conduct their business. For example, to link with customers and partners, they can draw on channel management services. To manage data, they can draw on data management services. To handle security, they can draw on security and risk services. In all, Weill and Vitale (2002) identified nine service areas needed by IT-enabled business models, with 70 services in all. Therefore, describing IT infrastructure as a set of reliable services allows business people and technologists to discuss business models and their underlying infrastructure needs because the two parties speak the same language.

- **Shared and standard applications:** The top piece of the IT infrastructure consists of stable applications, such as human resource management, budgeting, and accounting. In the last five to seven years, there has been a significant trend by multi-business firms to standardize their common business processes and the associated IT applications. The driver for some firms was improving and reengineering their business processes; for others, it was implementation of large enterprise resource planning (ERP) systems. As a result, shared and standard applications have been added to the typical firm's IT infrastructure (Weill & Vitale, 2002).

Based on these layers, a firm's IT infrastructure capability is its integrated set of reliable IT infrastructure services available to support both existing applications and new initiatives.

The time required to implement a new e-business initiative depends in part on the firm's infrastructure capability. For example, in building a new Web-based housing loan system, a large bank needed to use the following information technology infrastructure services: mainframe and server processing, customer databases, both local area and national communications networks, and security procedures and systems. Having most of these infrastructure services already in place significantly reduced the time and cost to build the loan system (Weill & Vitale, 2002).

Infrastructure Services

Weill and Vitale (2002) identified nine service areas with 70 services needed by IT-enabled e-business models. The service areas were (number of services in parenthesis): applications infrastructure (13), communications (7), data management (6), IT management (9), security (4), architecture and standards (20), IT research and development (2), and IT education (2):

Applications infrastructure

1. Internet policies such as employee access

2. Enforce Internet policies

3. E-mail policies such as inappropriate and personal mail, harassment policies, filtering policies

4. Enforce e-mail policies

5. Centralized management of e-business applications such as common standards

6. Centralized management of infrastructure capacity such as server traffic

7. Integrated mobile computing applications such as access for internal users

8. ERP (enterprise resource planning) services

9. Middleware linking systems on different platforms

10. Wireless applications such as Web applications for wireless devices

11. Application services provision to business units

12. Workflow applications such as groupware

13. Payment transaction processing such as EFT (electronic funds transfer)

Communications

14. Communications network services

15. Broadband communication services

16. Intranet capabilities to support publishing, directories, and so forth.

17. Extranet capabilities to support information and applications

18. Workstation networks

19. EDI (electronic data interchange) linkages to customers and suppliers

20. Electronic support to groups

Data management

21. Manage key data independent of applications

22. A centralized data warehouse that summarizes key information from decentralized databases

23. Data management advice and consultancy

24. Electronic provision of management information

25. Storage farms or storage area networks

26. Knowledge management in terms of contract database, information databases, and communities of practice

IT management

27. Large-scale data processing facilities

28. Server farms including mail server, Web servers, and printer servers

29. Installation and maintenance of workstations and LANs (local area networks)

30. Information systems planning for strategy

31. Information systems project management

32. Negotiate with suppliers and outsourcers

33. Service-level agreements

34. Common systems development environment

35. Pilot e-business initiatives such as pilot Web shop fronts

Security

36. Security policies for use of information systems

37. Enforce security policies for information systems

38. Disaster planning for business applications

39. Firewall on secure gateway services

Architecture and standards

40. Specify architectures for data by setting high level guidelines for data use and integration

41. Specify architectures for technology by setting high-level guidelines for technology use and integration

42. Specify architectures for communications by setting high-level guidelines for communications use and integration

43. Specify architectures for applications by setting high-level guidelines for applications use and integration

44. Specify architectures for work by setting high-level guidelines for the way work will be conducted

45. Enforce architectures for data

46. Enforce architectures for technology

47. Enforce architectures for communications

48. Enforce architectures for applications

49. Enforce architectures for work

50. Specify architecture standards for data

51. Specify architecture standards for technology

52. Specify architecture standards for communications

53. Specify architecture standards for applications

54. Specify architecture standards for work

55. Enforce architecture standards for data

56. Enforce architecture standards for technology

57. Enforce architecture standards for communications

58. Enforce architecture standards for applications

59. Enforce architecture standards for work

Channel management

60. Electronic file transfer protocols

61. Kiosks

62. Web sites

63. Call centers

64. IVRs
65. Mobile phones
66. Mobile computing

IT research and development
67. Identify and test new technologies for business purposes
68. Evaluate proposals for new information systems initiatives

IT education
69. Training and use of IT
70. Management education for generating value from IT use

These 70 infrastructure services were identified by Weill and Vitale (2002) when they studied IT infrastructure services and e-business. They studied 50 e-business initiatives in 15 firms. Based on their study, they identified eight atomic business models, nine infrastructure areas with 70 infrastructure services. The nine infrastructure areas were defined as follows:

- **Applications infrastructure:** An application is a software program that resides on a computer for the purpose of translating electronic input into meaningful form. Applications management includes purchasing software, developing proprietary applications, modifying applications, providing installation and technical support, and other tasks related to ensuring that applications are meeting the needs of the organization.

- **Communications:** Technology that facilitates digital communication both within the organization and with the outside world is relevant here. It includes the management of hardware and software to facilitate communication via computer, telephone, facsimile, pagers, mobile phones, and other communication and messaging services. It includes the cabling and any other communication linkages required to create an effective communications network, in addition to the necessary hardware and applications to meet the needs of the organization.

- **Data management:** This refers to the way the organization structures and handles its information resources. Data may be sourced from internal or external databases. Data management includes data collection, database design, sorting and reporting information, creating links to external databases, assuring data compatibility, and other activities surrounding the effective management of electronic information.

- **IT management:** Information technology management includes many of the professional and strategic activities of the information technology group including negotiation, IS planning, project management, and other tasks. IS project management is defined as the coordination and control of all of the activities required to complete an information systems project.

- **Security:** To protect data, equipment, and processing time, organizations restrict access to certain data and protect data and applications from manipulation and contamination. Recovery refers to the need for a plan to maintain computer operations and information should a disaster occur.

- **Architecture and standards:** Information technology architecture is a set of policies and rules that govern the use of information technology and plot a migration path to the way business will be done in the future. In most firms it provides technical guidelines rather than rules for decision-making. Architecture has to cope with both business uncertainty and technological change, making it one of the most difficult tasks for a firm. A good architecture evolves over time and is documented and accessible to all managers in the firm. Each architecture decision needs a sound business base to encourage voluntary agreement and compliance across the business. A standard is a detailed definition of the technical choices to implement an architecture. Five elements of architectures and standards are important: data, technology, communications, applications, and work. It can be distinguished between specifying architecture or standards and enforcement.

- **Channel management:** New and emerging technologies allow direct connections or distribution channels to customers.

- **IT research and development:** The information systems market develops rapidly, particularly with the rise of new e-business technologies. It is thus necessary to continually test applications and hardware to assist with planning decisions. IT research and development includes identifying and testing new technologies for business purposes and evaluating proposals for new information systems initiatives.

- **IT education:** Training and education in the use of IT can be defined as formal classes, individual training, and technology-based self-training programs for users ensuring hands-on computer proficiency levels meeting corporate requirements. IS management education can be defined as education aimed at senior levels in the firm designed to generate value from IT use.

Our above presentation of Weill and Vitale's (2002) work on infrastructure services indicate the number and complexity of services that must constitute the IT infrastructure in an organization to enable electronic business. Successfully implementing e-business initiatives depends on having the necessary IT infrastructure in place. E-business initiatives can be decomposed into their underlying atomic e-business models, which can have quite different IT infrastructure requirements.

For example, the most critical IT infrastructure service for the first business model of content provider might be storage farms or storage area networks, which is a data management service, number 25 on the list. Here it can be argued that as a content provider, the quality, quantity, and availability of content by electronic means is the most critical service. For the next e-business model, direct-to-customer, getting paid in an efficient way might be the most critical factor for success, leading to the need for IT infrastructure service number 13, which is payment transaction processing.

Infrastructure Dynamics

To study the performance of electronic business and the evolution of infrastructure services to support e-business, a causal loop diagram is presented in Figure 4.5. Please notice that this diagram is one out of very many possible diagrams that can be drawn. The selection of variables in the diagram, as well as the cause-and-effect relationships, very much depend on the focus that is desired.

In the case of Figure 4.5, the focus is the evolution of e-business as determined by interactions between e-business model capability, e-business experience, and the priority management has for e-business versus other management issues.

A possible development over time is illustrated in Figure 4.6 based on the causal loops in Figure 4.5. Both e-business priority and e-business perfor-

Figure 4.5. Causal loop diagram for infrastructure dynamics in e-business

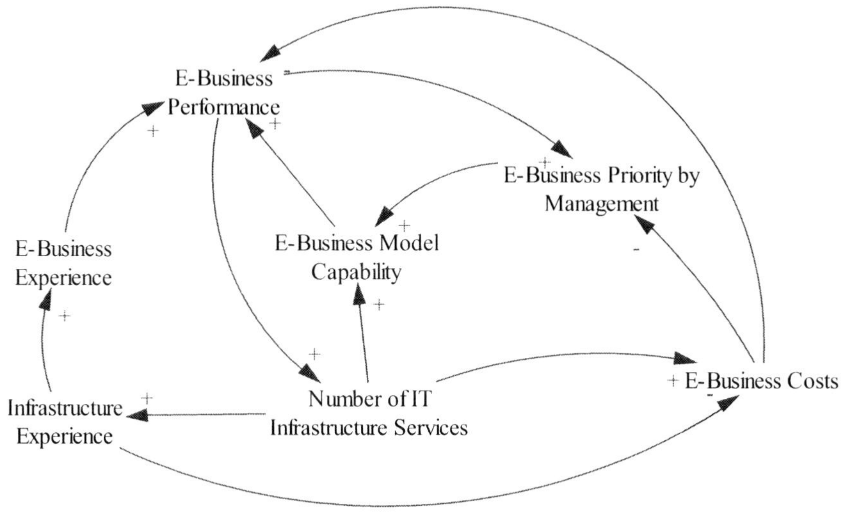

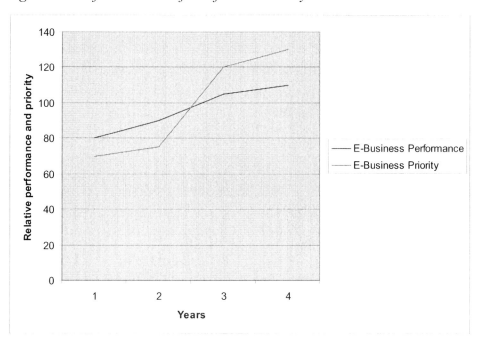

Figure 4.6. Reference mode for infrastructure dynamics in e-business

mance improve over time. The link between the two is found in Figure 4.5, where e-business performance influences e-business priority by management in a positive way.

E-business priority is a relative concept, whereby a priority below 100 means that most other issues have a higher priority. E-business performance is here also a relative concept, where performance below 100 means that other parts of the business are more profitable than the corporate e-business.

Strategic Agility

Companies need to build IT infrastructure for strategic agility. Strategic agility is defined by the set of business initiatives an enterprise can readily implement. Many elements contribute to agility, including customer base, brand, core competence, infrastructure, and employees' ability to change. Organizing and coordinating these elements into an integrated group of resources results in an enterprise capability, which, if superior to that of competitors, becomes a distinctive competence. Research conducted by Weill, Subramani, and Broadbent (2002) demonstrated a significant correlation between strategic agility and IT infrastructure capability. This suggests that if managers can describe their desired strategic agility, they then can identify the IT infrastructure service clusters that need to be above the industry average, and thus can create a distinctive competence.

Strategic agility is the ability of a firm to continually sense and explore customer and marketplace enrichment opportunities and respond with the appropriate configurations of capabilities and capacities to exploit these opportunities with speed, surprise, and competitive success. According to Sambamurthy and Zmud (2004), enriching customers, leveraging capabilities and capacities, nurturing interorganizational cooperation, and mastering change and uncertainty are the four building blocks of strategic agility.

Enriching customers can include the following activities:

- **Solution-centricity:** Deliver total solutions for current and anticipated customer needs. Solutions are customizable bundles of products and services.

- **Customer-centricity:** Heighten customer convenience, including space, time, speed, and personalized convenience.

- **Accelerate solution and product innovation to continually refresh customer offerings:** Portfolio of incremental, architectural, and radical innovation projects.

- **Co-opt customers in the innovation process:** Customers are sources of ideas for product and solution offerings. Customers are co-creators of innovative ideas.

Leveraging capabilities and capacities is the next building block. First, an ecosystem of capabilities has to be built. The ecosystem might consist of customer relationship management, selling-chain management, supply-demand synchronization, manufacturing management, financial engineering, brand management, human capital management, and information technology management. Next, world-class excellence has to be nurtured. This implies focus on a balanced set of metrics, such as adaptiveness, responsiveness, speed, cost, effectiveness, and quality. This also implies applying continuous improvement methods for capability enhancement and investing in and developing enabling information infrastructures and services platforms.

Nurturing inter-organizational cooperation is concerned with value net concept, value net posture, and value net integration. In the context of strategic agility, value nets are configurations of sourcing and partnership structures for building the extended enterprise. This definition is different from our main definition of value network as a value configuration in this book. In the context of strategic agility, value nets are architected to leverage other firms' capabilities and assets that complement core capabilities and assets within a firm. Value net posture is concerned with the governance of the value net, which can be either prescriptive or collaborative. Value net integration requires focus on the value net and expertise replication or expertise integration. In addition, the following actions are important in nurturing interorganizational cooperation:

- Identify and certify potential partners with regard to desired competencies (assets, capabilities) and their financial solvency
- Develop and continually assess working relationships with partners

- Develop abilities to work with partners through a variety of contractual mechanisms
- Develop competencies to quickly establish (and remove) the technology, process, and managerial interfaces needed when initiating business arrangements with new partners

Mastering change and uncertainty is the fourth and final building block of strategic agility. It requires strategic foresight, strategic insight, and organizational learning. The following actions are important in mastering change and uncertainty:

- Sense, anticipate and exploit trends, opportunities, and threats
- Quickly and seamlessly marshal the combinations of capabilities necessary in shaping innovative moves
- Quickly reconfigure capabilities necessary in shaping innovative moves
- Execute and learn from strategic experiments and from strategic actions

The evidence from leading enterprises indicates that implementing different types of electronic business initiatives based on atomic e-business models requires different high-capability IT infrastructures. Strategic agility requires time, money, leadership, and focus—an understanding of which distinct patterns of high-capability infrastructures are needed where. Investing in IT infrastructure is like buying an option. If used successfully, infrastructure enables faster time to market; if not, it will prove an unnecessary cost. To ensure that investments in IT infrastructure support the organization's strategic goals and business initiatives, Weill et al. (2002) consider it critical for the enterprise's most senior executives to understand which specific IT infrastructure capabilities are needed for which kinds of initiatives. That way, they can have some assurance that the investments they make today will serve the strategies of tomorrow.

One approach to improving strategic agility is utility computing. Utility computing proposes to allow clients to buy computing capacity as they do electricity—just by plugging in. For clients the cost is variable and based on the actual capacity they demand, rather than a fixed cost for a capacity they only use during peak periods. They can get the capacity they need whenever they need it, without expending resources and effort to regularly monitor and upgrade capacity (Ross & Westerman, 2004)

The vision of utility computing goes beyond traditional outsourcing of IT services. It includes all potential combinations of sourcing options, as we shall see in part two of this book. Vendors are promising to offer applications and business processes, including computing, applications, and expert staff, in an on-demand format, just as many firms now buy call center and payroll processes (Ross & Westerman, 2004).

Utility computing relies on several important technical capabilities to deliver these promised services. First, grid computing enables a network of processors to provide shared processing capacity by seamlessly accessing unused capacity elsewhere. Second, autonomic computing technology enables a network to be self-healing, and thus provides higher reliability across a system than is currently available. Third, Web services provide technical standards that facilitate integration across systems. In combining these three capabilities in a one-to-many business model, vendors expect to offer on-demand computing capacity and a wide range of plug-and-play technology and process components (Ross & Westerman, 2004).

Another approach to improving strategic agility is organizational architecture work. Organizations often relegate the job of aligning business needs and technology support to IT or operations, but with the strategic uncertainties of e-business, Sauer and Willcocks (2002) find that a separate coordinating role of organizational architect may be the only solution.

The shifting competitive landscape is creating a larger gap between strategists and technologists. Executives are busy creating and refining visions and have little time to focus on technology. Technologists are busy keeping the platform current and have little time to understand the business in depth. Without a mechanism to force communication, each group retreats into its specialty.

Among companies that were successfully aligning business and technology in e-business, Sauer and Willcocks (2002) identified a series of bridging activities that amounted to the creation of what they call an organizational architect. An organizational architect is someone who is neither all strategist nor all technologist, who guides the translation of a strategic vision to a flexible, integrated platform. Organizational architects sustain a dialogue between visionaries and technologists as they define and design the right combination of structures, processes, capabilities, and technologies. This combination has a greater chance of improving strategic agility by being responsive to shifting organizational goals.

Sauer and Willcocks (2002) surveyed chief executive officers and chief information officers at 97 companies in the United States, Europe, and Australia that had moved or were moving to e-business. Most were responding to an increasingly volatile business environment by shrinking their development and planning cycles. Half of the companies did not extend their plans beyond one year, and half of those with infrastructure plans updated them quarterly.

Lacking some mechanism to bridge the interests of strategists and technologists, information technology cannot prepare for change, and senior business executives end up guiding and funding short-term technology initiatives. Organizational architects work with both strategists and technologists to identify and grow the organizational and technical capabilities needed to see a vision through to its supporting platform. The architect sees the vision through three main translation phases (Sauer & Willcocks, 2002):

- **Phase 1. From vision to organization:** The organizational architect sets design parameters for the organizational structures, processes, and capabilities that make the vision possible.

- **Phase 2. From organization to technology requirements:** The architect now works to map the organizational needs to platform characteristics.

- **Phase 3. From technology requirements to actual platform:** The architect is now ready to get a fix on reality by talking with technology experts about what they can actually do.

An organizational architect is a significant investment for a business, so it will be important to underwrite the position even though it is essentially a staff function with no immediately visible commercial benefits. Sauer and Willcocks (2002) argue that persistence will be required particularly in difficult economic times.

Sambamurthy and Zmud (2004) define the evolution toward strategic agility in terms of four generations. The first generation is total quality management, while the second is lean management and mass customization. Then follows organizational adaptiveness before strategic agility emerges. Each generation of corporate transformation has emphasized specific types of capabilities and performance enhancement. Path-dependent progression through each of these waves is essential as the learning that occurs within each wave produces necessary changes in orientation and capacity.

Total quality management has efficiency as its competitive base, while lean management and mass customization have customer centricity and product variety as its base. Organizational adaptiveness is characterized by flexibility and partnerships, while strategic agility has entrepreneurial sense making and improvisation as its competitive base. Furthermore, strategic agility has the design objective of innovation and disruption and the decision architecture of external-internal collaboration.

The evolution toward agility in terms of information architecture started with data and metrics rationalization (total quality management), moved on to process rationalization and data integration (lean management and mass customization), then to metaprocess rationalization and metadata integration (organizational adaptiveness), and finally to information visibility and information probing (strategic agility).

According to Sambamurthy and Zmud (2004), information technologies can enable agility in several ways. First, the strategic role of IT can shift to fluid decision, authority, and collaboration structures. Second, the IT architecture can shift to modular form. Next, key technologies will be Web services, objects, intelligent agents, and distributed collaboration technologies. Fourth, key IT partnerships will include partners' market experts. Finally, IT investment focus will no longer be cost reduction, productivity improvement, time-to-market, or product life cycle refreshment. Rather, IT investment will focus on real options, market prototyping, time-to-solution, and relationship capital.

Of critical importance is IT investment in IT infrastructure. Strategic agility requires a distinct pattern of high-capability infrastructures. Getting the right balance is difficult. Under-investing reduces strategic agility and slows time to market. Also, infrastructure investments must be made before investments in business applications because doing both at the same time results in infrastructure fragmentation. But if the infrastructure is not used or is the wrong kind, a company is over-investing and wasting resources (Weill et al., 2002).

Sambamurthy and Zmud (2004) provide the following managerial guidelines for strategic agility:

- Adaptiveness enables competitive success in the digital economy
- Strategic agility enables competitive leadership

- Adaptiveness requires the co-integration of customer- and solution-centricity, capabilities built around information, process, and information technology infrastructures, and value net architectures

- Additionally, strategic agility requires the mastery of change and uncertainty through entrepreneurial orientation and sensing capabilities

- Strategic agility is nurtured at multiple levels: competitive agility, innovation agility, and functional agility

- The evolution toward strategic agility occurs through the learning gained by prior investments in total quality management, lean management, and value net integration

- Information technology management facilitates strategic agility as a digital options generator by representing a platform for process innovation, for value net integration, and for innovation and strategic experimentation

- Attention must be focused on significant transformations of the IT function, such as IT architecture, IT investment, IT partnerships, and organizing logic

Strategic agility is an emerging concept that needs research concerning both organizational and technology issues. Organizational issues include competency development and organizational architecture as demonstrated by the need for organizational architects. Technology issues include distributed intelligence, interfacing intelligent agents and humans, knowledge-discovery technologies and processes, rapid start-up and integration initiatives, metadata and process architectures, and end-to-end value chain information visibility (Sambamurthy & Zmud, 2004).

One approach to organizational actions for strategic agility is organization capital readiness. Kaplan and Norton (2004) define organization capital as the ability of the organization to mobilize and sustain the process of change required to execute strategy. Organization capital provides the capability for integration so that individual intangible human and information capital assets, as well as tangible physical and financial assets, are not only aligned to the strategy, but are all integrated and working together to achieve the organization's strategic objectives. An enterprise with high organization capital has a shared understanding of vision, mission, values, and strategy, is strongly led, has created a performance culture around the strategy, and shares knowledge across the organization.

If managers can describe their desired strategic agility, they then can identify the IT infrastructure services that need to be above the industry average, and thus can create a distinctive competence. Although none of the enterprises Weill et al. (2002) evaluated had all 70 infrastructure services presented earlier, those with the highest degree of strategic agility had more services in each of the 10 clusters, broader implementations of each service and more demanding service-level agreements.

Important drivers of strategic agility are strategy, sourcing, and governance. Strategy describes paths to the desired future, sourcing describes access to resources for the desired future, while governance describes management mechanisms to lead into the desired future.

References

Afuah, A., & Tucci, C. L. (2003). *Internet business models and strategies* (2nd ed.). New York: McGraw-Hill.

Fahey, L., Srivastava, R., Sharon, J. S., & Smith, D. E. (2001). Linking e-business and operating processes: The role of knowledge management. *IBM Systems Journal, 40*(4), 889-907.

Hayes, J., & Finnegan, P. (2005). Assessing the potential of e-business models: Towards a framework for assisting decision-makers. *European Journal of Operational Research, 160,* 365-379.

Kaplan, R. S., & Norton, D. P. (2004). *Strategy maps.* Boston: Harvard Business School Press.

Porter, M. E. (2001). Strategy and the Internet. *Harvard Business Review,* March, 63-78.

Ross, J. W., & Westerman, G. (2004). Preparing for utility computing: The role of IT architecture and relationship management. *IBM Systems Journal, 43*(1), 5-19.

Sambamurty, V., & Zmud, R. (2004, March). *Steps toward strategic agility: Guiding corporate transformations.* Paper presented at Michigan State University and University of Oklahoma.

Sauer, C., & Willcocks, L. P. (2002). The evolution of the organizational architect. *MIT Sloan Management Review,* Spring, 41-49.

Turban, E., King, D., Lee, J., Warkentin, M., & Chung, H. M. (2002). *Electronic commerce: A managerial perspective.* Sidney, Australia: Pearson Education, Prentice Hall.

Weill, P., Subramani, M., & Broadbent, M. (2002). Building IT infrastructure for strategic agility. *MIT Sloan Management Review,* Fall, 57-65.

Weill, P., & Vitale, M. R. (2001). *Place to space: Migrating to e-business models.* Boston: Harvard Business School Press.

Weill, P., & Vitale, M. R. (2002). What IT infrastructure capabilities are needed to implement e-business models? *MIS Quarterly Executive, 1*(1), 17-34.

Chapter V

Dynamics of
Knowledge
Management
Systems

Knowledge management systems refer to a class of information systems applied to manage organizational knowledge. These systems are IT applications to support and enhance the organizational processes of knowledge creation, storage and retrieval, transfer, and application (Alavi & Leidner, 2001).

According to the resource-based theory, the difference between successful and unsuccessful companies is their respective abilities to mobilize and utilize their resources. In the knowledge economy, the most important resource is knowledge. Strategic knowledge resources are characterized by being valuable, rare, inimitable, nontransferable, nonsubstitutable, combinable, and applicable.

Knowledge resources are applied within the value configuration(s) of the organization. In the value chain, knowledge is applied in areas such as logistics and production. In the value shop, knowledge is applied in areas such as problem diagnosis and problem solving. In the value network, knowledge is applied in areas such as subscriber recruiting and service extensions.

Knowledge resources are applied in actions at the individual, group, and organization levels. Such actions create reactions, which the individual, group, or organization has to respond to. In these interactions dynamics occur, and such business dynamics are modeled using system dynamics in this book.

The knowledge management technology stage model presented in this chapter is a multistage model proposed for organizational evolution over time. Stages of knowledge management technology is a relative concept concerned with IT's ability to process information for knowledge work. The knowledge management technology stage model consists of four stages (Gottschalk, 2005).

Characteristics of Knowledge

Knowledge is an important organizational resource. Unlike other, inert organizational resources, the application of existing knowledge has the potential to generate new knowledge. Not only can knowledge be replenished in use, it can also be combined and recombined to generate new knowledge. Once created, knowledge can be articulated, shared, stored, and recontextualized to yield options for the future. For all of these reasons, knowledge has the potential to be applied across time and space to yield increasing returns (Garud & Kumaraswamy, 2005).

The strategic management of organizational knowledge is a key factor that can help organizations sustain competitive advantage in volatile environments. Organizations are turning to knowledge management initiatives and technologies to leverage their knowledge resources. Knowledge management can be defined as a systemic and organizationally specified process for acquiring, organizing, and communicating knowledge of employees so that other employees may make use of it to be more effective and productive in their work (Kankanhalli, Tan, & Wei, 2005).

Knowledge management is also important in interorganizational relationships. Interorganizational relationships have been recognized to provide two distinct potential benefits: short-term operational efficiency and longer-term new knowledge creation. For example, the need for continual value innovation is driving supply chains to evolve from a purely transactional focus to leveraging interorganizational partnerships for sharing information and, ultimately, market knowledge creation. Supply chain partners are engaging in interlinked processes that enable rich (broad-ranging, high-quality, and privileged) information sharing, and building information technology infrastructures that allow them to process information obtained from their partners to create new knowledge (Malhotra, Gosain, & El Sawy, 2005).

Knowledge is a renewable, reusable, and accumulating resource of value to the organization when applied in the production of products and services. Knowledge cannot as such be stored in computers; it can only be stored in the human brain. Knowledge is what a knower knows; there is no knowledge without someone knowing it.

The need for a knower in knowledge existence raises the question as to how knowledge can exist outside the heads of individuals. Although knowledge cannot originate outside the heads of individuals, it can be argued that knowledge can be represented in and often embedded in organizational processes, routines, and networks, and sometimes in document repositories. However, knowledge is seldom complete outside of an individual.

In this book, knowledge is defined as information combined with experience, context, interpretation, reflection, intuition, and creativity. Information becomes knowledge once it is processed in the mind of an individual. This knowledge then becomes information again once it is articulated or communicated to others in the form of text, computer output, spoken or written words, or other forms. Six characteristics of knowledge can distinguish it from information: Knowledge is a human act, knowledge is the residue of thinking, knowledge is created in the present moment, knowledge belongs to communities, knowledge circulates through communities in many ways, and new knowledge is created at the boundaries of old. This definition and these characteristics of knowledge are based on current research (e.g., Poston & Speier, 2005; Ryu, Kim, Chaudhury, & Rao, 2005; Sambamurthy & Subramani, 2005; Tanriverdi, 2005; Wasko & Faraj, 2005).

Today, any discussion of knowledge quickly leads to the issue of how knowledge is defined. A pragmatic definition defines the topic as the most valuable form of content in a continuum starting at data, encompassing information, and ending at knowledge. Typically, data is classified, summarized, transferred, or corrected in order to add value and become information within a certain context. This conversion is relatively mechanical and has long been facilitated by storage, processing, and communication technologies. These technologies add place, time, and form utility to the data. In doing so, the information serves to inform or reduce uncertainty within the problem domain. Therefore, information is united with the context, that is, it only has utility within the context (Grover & Davenport, 2001).

Knowledge has the highest value, the most human contribution, the greatest relevance to decisions and actions, and the greatest dependence on a specific situation or context. It is also the most difficult of content types to manage, because it originates and is applied in the minds of human beings. People who are knowledgeable not only have information, but also have the ability to integrate and frame the information within the context of their experience, expertise, and judgment. In doing so, they can create new information that expands the state of possibilities, and in turn allows for further interaction with experience, expertise, and judgment. Therefore, in an organizational context, all new knowledge stems from people. Some knowledge is incorporated in organizational artifacts like processes, structures, and technology. However, institutionalized knowledge often inhibits competition in a dynamic context, unless adaptability of people and processes (higher order learning) is built into the institutional mechanisms themselves.

Our concern with distinctions between information and knowledge is based on real differences as well as technology implications. Real differences between information and knowledge do exist, although for most practical purposes these differences are of no interest at all. Information technology implications are concerned with the argument that computers can only manipulate electronic information, not electronic knowledge. Business systems are loaded with information, but without knowledge.

Davenport and Prusak (1998) define knowledge as a fluid mix of framed experience, values, contextual information, and expert insights that provides a framework for evaluating and incorporating new experiences and information. It originates and is applied in the minds of knowers. In organizations, it often becomes embedded not only in documents or repositories but also in organizational routines, processes, practices, and norms. Distinctions are often made among data, information, knowledge, and wisdom:

- **Data** are letters and numbers without meaning. Data are independent, isolated measurements, characters, numerical characters, and symbols.

- **Information** is data that are included in a context that makes sense. For example, "40 degrees" can have different meanings depending on the context. There can be a medical, geographical, or technical context. If a person has a fever of 40 degrees Celsius, that is quite serious. If a city is located 40 degrees north, we know that it is far south of Norway. If an angle is 40 degrees, we know what it looks like. Information is data that make sense, because it can be understood correctly. People turn data into information by organizing it into some unit of analysis, such as dollars, dates, or customers. Information is data endowed with relevance and purpose.

- **Knowledge** is information combined with experience, context, interpretation, and reflection. Knowledge is a renewable resource that can be used over and over, and that accumulates in an organization through use and combination with employees' experience. Humans have knowledge; knowledge cannot exist outside the heads of individuals in the company. Information becomes knowledge when it enters the human brain. This knowledge transforms into information again when it is articulated and communicated to others. Information is an explicit representation of knowledge; it is in itself no knowledge. Knowledge can both be truths and lies, perspectives and concepts, judgments and expectations. Knowledge is used to receive information by analyzing, understanding, and evaluating; by combining, prioritizing, and decision making; and by planning, implementing, and controlling.

- **Wisdom** is knowledge combined with learning, insights, and judgmental abilities. Wisdom is more difficult to explain than knowledge, since the levels of context become even more personal, and thus the higher-level nature of wisdom renders it more obscure than knowledge. While knowledge is mainly sufficiently generalized solutions, wisdom is best thought of as sufficiently generalized approaches and values that can be applied in numerous and varied situations. Wisdom cannot be created like data and information, and it cannot be shared with others like knowledge. Because the context is so personal, it becomes almost exclusive to our own minds and incompatible with the minds of others without extensive transaction. This transaction requires not only a base of knowledge and opportunities for experiences that help create wisdom, but also the processes of introspection, retrospection, interpretation, and contemplation. We can value wisdom in others, but we can only create it ourselves.

These are the definitions applied in this book. Grover and Davenport (2001) call these definitions pragmatic, as a continuum is used starting from data, encompassing information, and ending at knowledge in this book. The most valuable form of content in the continuum is knowledge. Knowledge has the highest value, the most human contribution, the greatest relevance to decisions and actions, and the greatest dependence on a specific situation or context. It is also the most difficult of content types to manage, because it originates and is applied in the minds of human beings.

It has been argued that expert systems using artificial intelligence are able to do knowledge work. The chess-playing computer called Deep Blue by IBM is frequently cited as an example. Deep Blue can compete with the best human players because chess, though complex, is a closed system of unchanging and codifiable rules. The size of the board never varies, the rules are unambiguous, the moves of the pieces are clearly defined, and there is absolute agreement about what it means to win or lose (Davenport & Prusak, 1998). Deep Blue is no knowledge worker; the computer does only perform a series of computations at extremely high speed.

While knowledge workers develop knowledge, organizations learn. Therefore, the learning organization has become a term frequently used. The learning organization is similar to knowledge development. While knowledge development is taking place at the individual level, organizational learning is taking place at the firm level. Organizational learning occurs when the firm is able to exploit individual competence in new and innovative ways. Organizational learning also occurs when the collective memory—including local language, common history, and routines—expands. Organizational learning causes growth in the intellectual capital. Learning is a continuous, never-ending process of knowledge creation. A learning organization is a place where people are constantly driven to discover what has caused the current situation and how they can change the present. To maintain competitive advantage, an organization's investment decisions related to knowledge creation are likely to be strategic in nature (Chen & Edgington, 2005).

Alavi and Leidner (2001) make the case that the hierarchy of data-information-knowledge can be of a different nature. Specifically, they claim that knowledge can be the basis for information, rather than information the basis for knowledge. Knowledge must exist before information can be formulated and before data can be measured to form information. As such, raw data do not exist—the thought or knowledge processes that led to its identification and collection have already influenced even the most elementary piece of data. It is argued that knowledge exists that, when articulated, verbalized, and structured, becomes information that, when assigned a fixed representation and standard interpretation, becomes data:

Critical to this argument is the fact that knowledge does not exist outside an agent (a knower): It is indelibly shaped by one's needs as well as one's initial stock of knowledge. Knowledge is thus the result of cognitive processing triggered by the inflow of new stimuli. Consistent with this view, we posit that information is converted to knowledge once it is processed in the mind of individuals and the knowledge becomes information once it is articulated and presented in the form of text, graphics, words, or other symbolic forms. A significant implication of this view of knowledge is that for individuals to arrive at the same understanding of data or information, they must share a certain knowledge base. Another important implication of this definition of knowledge is that systems designed to support knowledge in organizations may not appear radically different from other forms of information systems, but will be geared toward enabling users to assign meaning to information and to capture some of their knowledge in information and/or data. (Alavi & Leidner 2001, p. 109)

Knowledge Value Level

It is not difficult to agree with this reasoning. In fact, our hierarchy from data via information to knowledge is not so much a road or direction, as it is a way of suggesting resource value levels. Knowledge is a more valuable resource to the organization than information, and information is a more valuable resource than data. This is illustrated in Figure 5.1. The figure illustrates that it is less the knowledge existing at any given time per se than the organization's ability to effectively apply the existing knowledge to develop new knowledge and to take action that forms the basis for achieving long-term competitive advantage from knowledge-based assets.

According to Grover and Davenport (2001), knowledge processes lie somewhere between information and the organization's source of revenue, its products and services. This process can be generically represented in three subprocesses: knowledge generation, knowledge codification, and knowledge transfer/realization. Knowledge generation includes all processes involved in the acquisition and development of knowledge. Knowledge codification involves the conversion of knowledge into accessible and applicable formats. Knowledge transfer includes the movement of knowledge from its point of generation or codified form to the point of use.

Figure 5.1. Value levels of resources in the organization

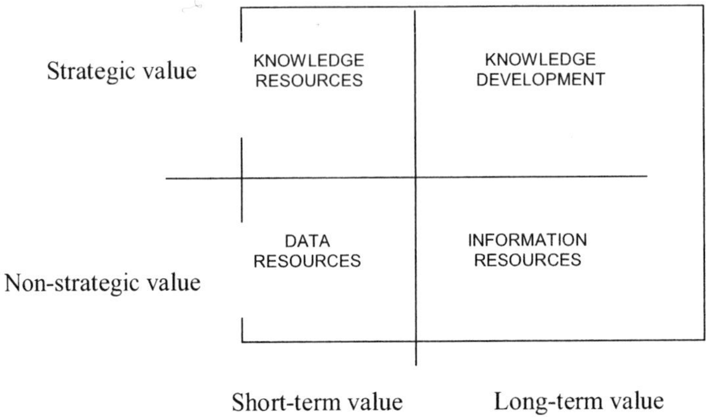

Strategic value	KNOWLEDGE RESOURCES	KNOWLEDGE DEVELOPMENT
Non-strategic value	DATA RESOURCES	INFORMATION RESOURCES
	Short-term value	Long-term value

One of the reasons that knowledge is such a difficult concept is because this process is recursive, expanding, and often discontinuous. According to Grover and Davenport (2001), many cycles of generation, codification, and transfer are concurrently occurring in businesses. These cycles feed on each other. Knowledge interacts with information to increase the state space of possibilities and provide new information, which can then facilitate generations of new knowledge. The knowledge process acts on information to create new information that allows for greater possibilities to fulfill old or possibly new organizational needs. This process is often discontinuous, where new needs and their fulfillment mechanism could be created.

In our resource-based perspective of knowledge, data is raw numbers and facts, information is processed data, and knowledge is information combined with human thoughts. Knowledge is the result of cognitive processing triggered by the influx of new stimuli. Information is converted to knowledge once it is processed in the mind of individuals, and the knowledge becomes information once it is articulated and presented to others. A significant implication of this view of knowledge is that for individuals to arrive at the same understanding of information, they must share the same knowledge framework.

In Figure 5.1, we can imagine that data are assigned meaning and become information, that information are understood and interpreted by individuals and become knowledge, and that knowledge is applied and develops into new knowledge. We can also imagine the opposite route. Knowledge develops in the minds of individuals. This knowledge development causes an increase in knowledge resources. When the new knowledge is articulated, verbalized, and structured, it becomes information and causes an increase in information resources. When information is assigned a fixed representation and standard interpretation, it becomes data and causes an increase in data resources.

There are alternatives to our perspective of knowledge as a resource in the organization. Alavi and Leidner (2001) list the following alternatives: Knowledge is state of mind, knowledge is an object to be stored, knowledge is a process of applying expertise, knowledge is a condition of access to information, and knowledge is the potential to influence action.

This book applies the resource-based theory of the organization, where the knowledge-based perspective identifies the primary role of the organization as integrating the specialist knowledge resident in individuals into goods and services. The task of management is to establish the coordination necessary for this knowledge integration. The knowledge-based perspective serves as a platform for a view of the organization as a dynamic system of knowledge production and application.

Identification of Knowledge Needs

To classify knowledge as a resource, there has to be a need for that knowledge. Hence, identification of knowledge needs in an organization is important. Three supplementary methods exist to identify needs for knowledge as illustrated in Figure 5.2:

- **Problem decision analysis:** This method aims at identifying and specifying problems that knowledge workers have, solutions they can find, decisions they have to make, and what knowledge they need to solve problems and make decisions. For a lawyer, the problem can be an insurance claim by a client, the decision can be how to approach the insurance company, and the knowledge need can be outcomes of similar cases handled by the law firm.

- **Critical success factors:** This method aims at identifying and specifying what factors cause success. Success can be at firm level, individual level, or individual case level. For a lawyer, critical success factors

Figure 5.2. Methods to identify knowledge needs

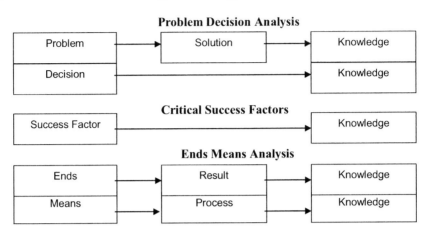

at the individual case level can be quality of legal advice and service level of advice delivery. Critical knowledge in this case includes legal knowledge as well as procedural knowledge.

- **Ends means analysis:** This method aims at identifying and specifying external demands and expectations to goods and services from the firm. For a lawyer, the client expectation might be that she or he wins the case. The end is winning the case. Knowledge needs associated with winning a case includes legal, procedural, and analytical knowledge of successful cases in the past. The means for winning a case might be access to resources of various kinds, such as client documents and client funds. Knowledge needs associated with means include historical records and analysis of legal client practice.

Knowledge Categories

Many researchers have tried to define categories and dimensions of knowledge. A common distinction is made between explicit and tacit knowledge. Explicit knowledge can be expressed in words and numbers and shared in the form of data, scientific formulae, specifications, manuals, and the like. This kind of knowledge can be readily transmitted between individuals both formally and systematically. Tacit knowledge is on the other hand highly personal and hard to formalize, making it difficult to communicate or share with others. Subjective insights, intuitions, and hunches fall into this category of knowledge. Tacit knowledge is deeply rooted in an individual's actions and experience as well as in the ideals, values, or emotions he or she embraces. Tacit knowledge is embedded in the human brain and cannot be expressed easily, while explicit knowledge can be easily codified. Both types of knowledge are important, but Western firms have focused largely on managing explicit knowledge (Grover & Davenport, 2001).

Tacitness may be considered as a variable, with the degree of tacitness being a function of the extent to which the knowledge is or can be codified and abstracted. Knowledge may dynamically shift between tacit and explicit over time, although some knowledge always will remain tacit. Nonaka, Toyama, and Konno (2000) have suggested that knowledge creation is a spiraling process of interactions between explicit and tacit knowledge. This spiraling process consists of socialization, externalization, combination, and internalization, as we will see later in this chapter.

The concept of tacit knowledge corresponds closely to the concept of knowledge with a low level of codification. Codification is the degree to which knowledge is fully documented or expressed in writing at the time of transfer between two persons. The complexity of knowledge increases with lower levels of codification. A similar distinction which scholars frequently make is between practical, experience-based knowledge and the theoretical knowledge derived from reflection and abstraction from that experience.

A distinction is sometimes made between codification and personalization. This distinction is related to the tacit versus explicit concept. It involves an organization's approach to knowledge transfer. Companies using codification approaches rely primarily on repositories of explicit knowledge. Personalization approaches imply that the primary mode of knowledge transfer is direct interaction among people. Both are necessary in most organizations, but an increased focus on one approach or the other at any given time within a specific organization may be appropriate (Grover & Davenport, 2001).

Explicit knowledge is sometimes called articulable knowledge (Hitt, Bierman, Shumizu, & Kochhar, 2001). Articulable knowledge can be codified and thus can be written and easily transferred. Tacit knowledge is not articulable and therefore cannot be easily transferred. Tacit knowledge is often embedded in uncodified routines and in a firm's social context. More specifically, it is partially embedded in individual skills and partially embedded in collaborative working relationships within the firm. Tacit knowledge is integral to professional skills. As a result, tacit knowledge is often unique, difficult to imitate, and uncertain. It has a higher probability of creating strategic value than articulable knowledge.

Distinctions can be made among core, advanced, and innovative knowledge. These knowledge categories indicate different levels of knowledge sophistication. Core knowledge is that minimum scope and level of knowledge required for daily operations, while advanced knowledge enables a firm to be competitively viable, and innovative knowledge is the knowledge that enables the firm to lead its industry and competitors.

- **Core knowledge** is the basic knowledge required to stay in business. This is the type of knowledge that can create efficiency barriers for entry of new companies, as new competitors are not up to speed in basic business processes. Since core knowledge is present at all existing competitors, the firm must have this knowledge even though it will provide the firm with no advantage that distinguishes it from its competitors. Core knowledge is that minimum scope and level of knowledge required just to play the game. Having that level of knowledge and capability will not assure the long-term competitive viability of the firm, but does present a basic industry knowledge barrier to entry. Core knowledge tends to be commonly held by members of an industry and therefore provides little advantage other than over nonmembers (Zack, 1999).

  In a law firm, examples of core knowledge include knowledge of the law, knowledge of the courts, knowledge of clients, and knowledge of procedures. For a student inbusiness school, core knowledge includes knowledge of what subjects to study this term and where the lectures take place.

  According to Tiwana (2002), core knowledge is the basic level of knowledge required just to play the game. This is the type of knowledge that creates a barrier for entry of new companies. Since this level of knowledge is expected of all competitors, you must have it even though it will provide your company with no advantage that distinguishes it from its competitors. Let's take two examples, one from the consumer electronics (hard product) business and one from Internet programming (soft product). To enter the modem manufacturing market, a new company must have extensive knowledge of these aspects: a suitable circuit design, all electronic parts that go into a modem, fabricating surface mount (SMD) chip boards, how to write operating system drivers for modems, and familiarity with computer telephony standards. Similarly, a company developing Web sites for, say, florists, needs server hosting capabilities, Internet programming skills, graphic design skills, clearly identified target markets, and necessary software. In either case, just about any competitor in those businesses is assumed to have this knowledge in order to compete in their respective markets; such essential knowledge therefore provides no advantage over other market players.

- **Advanced knowledge** is what makes the firm competitively visible and active. Such knowledge allows the firm to differentiate its products and services from that of a competitor through the application of superior knowledge in certain areas. Such knowledge allows the firm to compete head-on with its competitors in the same market and for the same set of customers. Advanced knowledge enables a firm to be competitively viable. The firm may have generally the same level, scope, or quality of knowledge as its competitors though the specific knowledge content will often vary among competitors, enabling knowledge differentiation. Firms may choose to compete on knowledge head-on in the same strategic position, hoping to know more than a competitor. They instead may choose to compete for that position by differentiating their knowledge (Zack, 1999).

In a law firm, examples of advanced knowledge include knowledge of law applications, knowledge of important court rulings, and knowledge of successful procedural case handling. For a student in business school, advanced knowledge includes knowledge of important articles and books, which are compulsory literature in subjects this term.

According to Tiwana (2002), advanced knowledge is what makes your company competitively viable. Such knowledge allows your company to differentiate its product from that of a competitor, arguably through the application of superior knowledge in certain areas. Such knowledge allows your company to compete head-on with its competitors in the same market and for the same set of customers. In the case of a company trying to compete in modem manufacturing markets, superior or user-friendly software or an additional capability in modems (such as warning online users of incoming telephone calls) represents such knowledge. In case of a Web site development firm, such knowledge might be about international flower markets and collaborative relationships in Dutch flower auctions that the company can use to improve Web sites delivered to its customers.

- **Innovative knowledge** allows a firm to lead its entire industry to an extent that clearly differentiates it from competition. Such knowledge allows a firm to change the rules of the game by introducing new business practices. Such knowledge enables a firm to expand its market share by winning new customers and by increasing service levels to existing customers. Innovative knowledge is that knowledge that enables a firm to lead its industry and competitors and to significantly differentiate itself from its competitors. Innovative knowledge often enables a firm to change the rules of the game itself (Zack, 1999).

In a law firm, examples of innovative knowledge include knowledge of standardizing repetitive legal cases, knowledge of successful settlements and knowledge of modern information technology to track and store vast amounts of information from various sources. For a student in business school, innovative knowledge includes knowledge of important topics within subjects, links between subjects, typical exam questions, and knowledge of business cases where theory can be applied.

According to Tiwana (2002), innovative knowledge allows a company to lead its entire industry to an extent that clearly differentiates it from competition. Innovative knowledge allows a company to change the rules of the game. Patented technology is an applicable example of changing the rules. Innovative knowledge cannot always be protected by patents, as the lawsuit between Microsoft and Apple in the 1980s should serve to remind us. Apple sued Microsoft for copying the look and feel of its graphical user interface (GUI). The Supreme Court ruled that things like look and feel cannot be patented; they can only be copyrighted. Microsoft won the case, since it copied the look and feel but used entirely different code to create it in the first place.

Many more categories and dimensions of knowledge have been suggested by researchers. The problem with most of these classifications is that they do not seem to satisfy three important criteria for classification. The first requirement is that a classification should always be complete, there should be no category missing. The second requirement is that each category should be different from all other categories, that is, there should be no overlap between categories. The final requirement is that each category should be at the same level, and there should be no category including another category. Consider the following categories suggested by researchers: formal knowledge, instrumental knowledge, informal knowledge, tacit knowledge, metaknowledge, and context-independent knowledge. These categories seem to violate some of the classification rules. For example, there seems to be an overlap between informal knowledge and tacit knowledge. Maybe Long and Fahey's (2000) classification into human knowledge, social knowledge, and structured knowledge satisfy our requirements:

- **Human knowledge:** This constitutes the know-what, know-how, and know-why of individuals. Human knowledge is manifested in individual skills (e.g., how to interview law firm clients) or expertise (e.g., why this case is similar to a previous case). Individual knowledge usually combines explicit and tacit knowledge. This type of knowledge may be located in the body, such as knowing how to touch-type on a PC or how to ride a bicycle. This type of knowledge may be cognitive, that is, largely conceptual and abstract.

- **Social knowledge:** This kind of knowledge exists only in relationships between individuals or within groups. For example, high-performing teams of tax lawyers share certain collective knowledge that is more than the sum of the individual knowledge of the team's members. Social or collective knowledge is mainly tacit knowledge, shared by team members, and develops only as a result of team members working together. Its presence is reflected by an ability to collaborate effectively.

- **Structured knowledge:** This is embedded in an organization's systems, processes, tools, routines, and practices. Knowledge in this form is explicit and often rule-based. A key distinction between structured knowledge and the first two types of knowledge is that structured knowledge is assumed to exist independently of individual knowers. It is, instead, an organizational resource. However, to be complete, this knowledge has to be in the heads of individuals.

Two dimensions have been introduced to classify knowledge. The first dimension is concerned with whether an individual knows. The second dimension is concerned with whether an individual knows whether he or she knows. This is illustrated in Figure 5.3. I can either have the knowledge (I do no) or not have the knowledge (I don't know). I can either be aware of it (I know it) or not be aware of it (I don't know it).

Some researchers have argued that the real tacit knowledge is found in the right upper quadrant. In this dimension, I do know, but I don't know that

Figure 5.3. Dimensions of individual knowledge

	I know it	I don't know it
I do know	I know that I know	I don't know that I know
I don't know	I know that I don't know	I don't know that I don't know

I know. Tacit knowledge in this sense is also called hidden knowledge or non-accessible knowledge. In this book, we do not use this extremely limited definition of tacit knowledge. We define tacit knowledge as personal and difficult, but not impossible, to communicate.

Classification of knowledge into categories and dimensions may depend on industry. For example, there are likely to be different knowledge categories in a bank and in a law firm. At the same time, there will be certain generic knowledge categories, such as market intelligence and technology understanding, in most companies independently of industry. When classifying knowledge in a firm, it is important to do the analysis without the organization chart. If you classify knowledge into technology knowledge, production knowledge, marketing knowledge, and financial knowledge, it may be because the firm according to the organization chart consists of a development department, production department, marketing department, and financial department. It might be more useful to introduce new knowledge categories such as product knowledge, which includes knowledge of development, production, marketing, and finance. By identifying cross-sectional knowledge categories and dimensions, solutions for improved knowledge flows in the organization will emerge.

A law firm is a good example. A law firm is organized according to legal disciplines. Some lawyers work in the tax department, while others work in the department for mergers and acquisitions. The types of knowledge involved in the practice of law can be categorized as administrative, declarative, procedural, and analytical knowledge (Edwards & Mahling, 1997):

- **Administrative knowledge** includes all the nuts and bolts information about firm operations, such as hourly billing rates for lawyers, client names and matters, staff payroll data, and client invoice data.

- **Declarative knowledge** is knowledge of the law, the legal principles contained in statutes, court opinions, and other sources of primary legal authority; law students spend most of their law school time acquiring this kind of knowledge.

- **Procedural knowledge** involves knowledge of the mechanisms of complying with the law's requirements in a particular situation: how documents are used to transfer an asset from Company A to Company B, or how forms must be filed where to create a new corporation. Declarative knowledge is sometimes labeled know-that and know-what, while procedural knowledge is labeled know-how.

- **Analytical knowledge** pertains to the conclusions reached about the course of action a particular client should follow in a particular situation. Analytical knowledge results, in essence, from analyzing declarative knowledge (i.e., substantive law principles) as it applies to a particular fact setting.

Classification of knowledge into categories and dimensions has important limitations. For example, the classification into explicit and tacit knowledge may create static views of knowledge. However, knowledge development and sharing are dynamic processes, and these dynamic processes cause tacit knowledge to become explicit, and explicit knowledge to become tacit over time. Tacit and explicit knowledge depend on each other, and they influence each other. In this perspective, Alavi and Leidner (2001) argue that whether tacit or explicit knowledge is the more valuable may indeed miss the point. The two knowledge categories are not dichotomous states of knowledge, but mutually dependent and reinforcing qualities of knowledge: Tacit knowledge forms the background necessary for assigning the structure to develop and interpret explicit knowledge.

According to Alavi and Leidner (2001), the linkage of tacit and explicit knowledge suggests that only individuals with a requisite level of shared knowledge are able to exchange knowledge. They suggest the existence of a shared knowledge space that is required in order for individual A to understand individual B's knowledge. The knowledge space is the underlying overlap in knowledge base of A and B. This overlap is typically tacit knowledge. It may be argued that the greater the shared knowledge space, the less the context needed for individuals to share knowledge within the group and, hence, the higher the value of explicit knowledge. For example, in a law firm, lawyers in the maritime law department may have a large knowledge space so that even a very limited piece of explicit knowledge can be of great value to the lawyers. Alavi and Leidner (2001) discuss knowledge space in the following way:

Whether tacit or explicit knowledge is the more valuable may indeed miss the point. The two are not dichotomous states of knowledge, but mutually dependent and reinforcing qualities of knowledge: Tacit knowledge forms the background necessary for assigning the structure to develop and interpret explicit knowledge. The inextricable linkage of tacit and explicit knowledge suggests that only individuals with a requisite level of shared knowledge can truly exchange knowledge: If tacit knowledge is necessary to the understanding of explicit knowledge, then in order for Individual B to understand Individual A's knowledge, there must be some overlap in their underlying knowledge bases (a shared knowledge space). However, it is precisely in applying technology to increase 'weak ties' in organizations, and thereby increase the breadth of knowledge sharing, that IT holds promise. Yet, absent a shared knowledge space, the real impact of IT on knowledge exchange is questionable. This is a paradox that IT researchers have somewhat eschewed, and that organizational researchers have used to question the application of IT to knowledge management. To add to the paradox, the very essence of the knowledge management challenge is to amalgamate knowledge across groups for which IT can play a major role. What is most at issue is the amount of contextual information necessary for one person or group's knowledge to be readily understood by another.

It may be argued that the greater the shared knowledge space, the less the context needed for individuals to share knowledge within the group and, hence, the higher the value of explicit knowledge and the greater the value of IT applied to knowledge management. On the other hand, the smaller the existing shared knowledge space in a group, the greater the need for contextual information, the less relevant will be explicit knowledge, and hence the less applicable will be IT to knowledge management. (p.112)

Some researchers are interested in the total knowledge within a company, while others are interested in individual knowledge. Dixon (2000) was interested in the knowledge that knowledge workers develop together in the organization. Employees gain this knowledge from doing the organization's tasks. This knowledge is called common knowledge to differentiate it from book knowledge or lists of regulations or databases of customer information. Some examples of common knowledge are what medical doctors in a hospital have learned about how to carry out certain kinds of surgery, what an organization has learned about how to introduce a new drug into the diabetes market, how to reduce costs on consulting projects, and how to control the amount of analysis in maritime law cases. These examples all include the how-to rather than the know-what of school learning. Moreover, it is know-how that is unique to a specific company. In the law firm example, procedural knowledge was classified as know-how.

Knowledge Management Systems

As we trace the evolution of computing technologies in business, we can observe their changing level of organizational impact. The first level of impact was at the point work got done and transactions (e.g., orders, deposits, reservations) took place. The inflexible, centralized mainframe allowed for little more than massive number crunching, commonly known as electronic *data* processing. Organizations became data heavy at the bottom and data management systems were used to keep the data in check. Later, the management *information* systems were used to aggregate data into useful information reports, often prescheduled, for the control level of the organization—people who were making sure that organizational resources like personnel, money, and physical goods were being deployed efficiently. As information technology (IT) and information systems (IS) started to facilitate data and information overflow, and corporate attention became a scarce resource, the concept of *knowledge* emerged as a particularly high-value form of information (Grover & Davenport, 2001).

Information technology can play an important role in successful knowledge management initiatives. However, the concept of coding and transmitting knowledge in organizations is not new: Training and employee development programs, organizational policies, routines, procedures, reports, and manuals have served this function for many years. What is new and exciting in the knowledge management area is the potential for using modern information technology (e.g., the Internet, intranets, extranets, browsers, data warehouses, data filters, software agents, expert systems) to support knowledge creation, sharing, and exchange in an organization and between organizations. Modern information technology can collect, systematize, structure, store, combine, distribute, and present information of value to knowledge workers (Nahapiet & Ghoshal, 1998).

According to Davenport and Prusak (1998), more and more companies have instituted knowledge repositories, supporting such diverse types of knowledge as best practices, lessons learned, product development knowledge, customer knowledge, human resource management knowledge, and methods-based knowledge. Groupware and intranet-based technologies have become standard knowledge infrastructures. A new set of professional job titles—the knowledge manager, the chief knowledge officer (CKO), the knowledge coordinator, and the knowledge-network facilitator—affirms the widespread legitimacy that knowledge management has earned in the corporate world.

The low cost of computers and networks has created a potential infrastructure for knowledge sharing and opened up important knowledge management opportunities. The computational power as such has little relevance to knowledge work, but the communication and storage capabilities of networked computers make it an important enabler of effective knowledge work. Through e-mail, groupware, the Internet, and intranets, computers and networks can point to people with knowledge and connect people who need to share knowledge independent of time and place.

For example, electronic networks of practice are computer-mediated discussion forums focused on problems of practice that enable individuals to exchange advice and ideas with others based on common interests. Electronic networks make it possible to share information quickly, globally, and with large numbers of individuals. Electronic networks that focus on knowledge exchange frequently emerge in fields where the pace of technological change requires access to knowledge unavailable within any single organization (Wasko & Faraj, 2005).

In the knowledge-based view of the firm, knowledge is the foundation of a firm's competitive advantage and, ultimately, the primary driver of a firm's value. Inherently, however, knowledge resides within individuals and, more specifically, in the employees who create, recognize, archive, access, and apply knowledge in carrying out their tasks. Consequently, the movement of knowledge across individual and organizational boundaries, into and from repositories, and into organizational routines and practices is ultimately dependent on employees' knowledge sharing behaviors (Bock, Zmud, & Kim, 2005).

According to Grover and Davenport (2001), most knowledge management projects in organizations involve the use of information technology. Such projects fall into relatively few categories and types, each of which has a key objective. Although it is possible, and even desirable, to combine multiple objectives in a single project, this was not normally observed in a study of 31 knowledge management projects in 1997 (Davenport & Prusak, 1998). Since that time, it is possible that projects have matured and have taken on more ambitious collections of objectives.

Regardless of definition of knowledge as the highest value of content in a continuum starting at data, encompassing information, and ending at knowledge, knowledge managers often take a highly inclusive approach to the content with which they deal. In practice, what companies actually manage under the banner of knowledge management is a mix of knowledge, information, and unrefined data—in short, whatever anyone finds that is useful and easy to store in an electronic repository. In the case of data and information, however, there are often attempts to add more value and create knowledge. This transformation might involve the addition of insight, experience, context, interpretation, or the myriad of other activities in which human brains specialize (Grover & Davenport, 2001).

Identifying, nurturing, and harvesting knowledge is a principal concern in the information society and the knowledge age. Effective use of knowledge-facilitating tools and techniques is critical, and a number of computational tools have been developed. While numerous techniques are available, it remains difficult to analyze or compare the specific tools. In part, this is because knowledge management is a young discipline. The arena is evolving rapidly as more people enter the fray and encounter new problems (Housel & Bell, 2001).

In addition, new technologies support applications that were impossible before. Moreover, the multidisciplinary character of knowledge management combines several disciplines, including business and management, computer science, cybernetics, and philosophy. Each of these fields may lay claim to the study of knowledge management, and the field is frequently defined so broadly that anything can be incorporated. Finally, it is difficult to make sense of the many tools available. It is not difficult to perform a search to produce a list of more than one hundred software providers. Each of the software packages employs unique visions and aims to capture its share of the market (Housel & Bell, 2001).

Ward and Peppard (2002) find that there are two dominant and contrasting views of IS/IT in knowledge management: the engineering perspective and the social process perspective. The engineering perspective views knowledge management as a technology process. Many organizations have taken this approach in managing knowledge, believing that it is concerned with managing pieces of intellectual capital. Driving this view is the idea that knowledge can be codified and stored—in essence, that knowledge is explicit knowledge and therefore is little more than information.

The alternative view is that knowledge is a social process. As such, it asserts that knowledge resides in people's heads and that it is tacit. As such, it cannot be easily codified and is only revealed through its application. As tacit knowledge cannot be directly transferred from person to person, its acquisition occurs only through practice. Consequently, its transfer between people is slow, costly, and uncertain. Technology, within this perspective, can only support the context of knowledge work. It has been argued that IT-based systems used to support knowledge management can only be of benefit if used to support the development and communication of human meaning. One reason for the failure of IT in some knowledge management initiatives is that the designers of the knowledge management systems fail to understand the situation and work practices of the users and the complex human processes involved in work.

While technology can be used with knowledge management initiatives, Ward and Peppard (2002) argue that it should never be the first step. Knowledge management is to them primarily a human and process issue. Once these two aspects have been addressed, the created processes are usually very amenable to being supported and enhanced by the use of technology.

What, then, is knowledge management technology? According to Davenport and Prusak (1998), the concept of knowledge management technology is not only broad but also a bit slippery to define. Some infrastructure technology that we don't ordinarily think of in this category can be useful in facilitating knowledge management. Examples are videoconferencing and the telephone. Both of these technologies don't capture or distribute structured knowledge, but they are quite effective at enabling people to transfer tacit knowledge.

Our focus here, however, is on technology that captures, stores, and distributes structured knowledge for use by people. The goal of these technologies is to take knowledge that exists in human heads and partly in paper documents, and make it widely available throughout an organization. Similarly, Alavi and Leidner (2001) argue that information systems designed to support knowledge in organizations may not appear radically different from other forms of IT support, but will be geared toward enabling users to assign meaning to information and to capture some of their knowledge in information. Therefore, the concept of knowledge management technology in this book is less concerned with any degree of technology sophistication and more concerned with the usefulness in performing knowledge work in organizations and between organizations.

Moffett and McAdam (2003) illustrate the variety of knowledge management technology tools by distinguishing between collaborative tools, content management, and business intelligence. Collaborative tools include groupware technology, meeting support systems, knowledge directories, and intranets/extranets. Content management includes the Internet, agents and filters, electronic publishing systems, document management systems, and office automation systems. Business intelligence includes data warehousing, decision support systems, knowledge-based systems and workflow systems.

In addition to technologies, we also present techniques in this book. The term technique is defined as a set of precisely described procedures for achieving a standard task (Kettinger, Teng, & Guha, 1997).

Knowledge Technology Stages

Stages of growth models have been used widely in both organizational research and information technology management research. According to King and Teo (1997), these models describe a wide variety of phenomena—the organizational life cycle, product life cycle, biological growth, and so forth. These models assume that predictable patterns (conceptualized in terms of stages) exist in the growth of organizations, the sales levels of products, and the growth of living organisms. These stages are sequential in nature, occur as a hierarchical progression that is not easily reversed, and involve a broad range of organizational activities and structures.

Benchmark variables are often used to indicate characteristics in each stage of growth. A one-dimensional continuum is established for each benchmark variable. The measurement of benchmark variables can be carried out using

Guttman scales (Frankfort-Nachmias & Nachmias, 2002). Guttman scaling is a cumulative scaling technique based on ordering theory that suggests a linear relationship between the elements of a domain and the items on a test.

In the following main part of this chapter, a four-stage model for the evolution of information technology support for knowledge management is proposed and empirically tested. The purpose of the model is both to understand the current situation in an organization in terms of a specific stage and to develop strategies for moving to a higher stage in the future. We are concerned with the following question: Do organizations move through various stages of growth in their application of knowledge management technology over time, and is each theoretical stage regarded as an actual stage in an organization?

Stages of Growth Models

Various multistage models have been proposed for organizational evolution over time. These models differ in the number of stages. For example, Nolan (1979) introduced a model with six stages for IT maturity in organizations, which later was expanded to nine stages. Earl (2000) suggested a stages of growth model for evolving the e-business, consisting of the following six stages: external communication, internal communication, e-commerce, e-business, e-enterprise, and transformation. Each of these models identifies certain characteristics that typify firms in different stages of growth. Among these multistage models, models with four stages seem to have been proposed and tested most frequently (King & Teo, 1997).

In the area of knowledge management, Housel and Bell (2001) described a knowledge management maturity model. The knowledge management maturity (KMM) model is used to assess the relative maturity of a company's knowledge management efforts. The KMM model defines the following five levels:

1. **Level one** is the default stage in which there is low commitment to managing anything other than essential, necessary survival-level tasks. At level one formal training is the main mechanism for learning, and all learning is taken to be reactive. Moreover, level-one organizations fragment knowledge into isolated pockets that are not explicitly documented.

2. **Level two** organizations share only routine and procedural knowledge. Need-to-know is characteristic, and knowledge awareness rises with the realization that knowledge is an important organizational resource that must be managed explicitly. Databases and routine tasks exist but are not centrally compiled or managed.

3. **Level three** organizations are aware of the need for managing knowledge. Content fit for use in all functions begins to be organized into a knowledge life cycle, and enterprise knowledge-propagation systems are in place. However, general awareness and maintenance are limited.

4. **Level four** is characterized by enterprise knowledge sharing systems. These systems respond proactively to the environment and the quality, currency, utility, and usage of these systems is improved. Knowledge processes are scaled up across the organization, and organization knowledge boundaries become blurred. Benefits of knowledge sharing and reuse can be explicitly quantified, and training moves into an ad hoc basis as the technology infrastructure for knowledge sharing is increasingly integrated and seamless.

5. At **level five**, knowledge sharing is institutionalized and organizational boundaries are minimized. Human know-how and content expertise are integrated into a seamless package, and knowledge can be most effectively leveraged. Level-five organizations have the ability to accelerate the knowledge life cycle to achieve business advantage. (Housel & Bell, 2001, p. 136)

According to Kazanjian and Drazin (1989), the concept of stages of growth is widely employed. A number of multistage models have been proposed which assume that predictable patterns exist in the growth of organizations, and that these patterns unfold as discrete time periods best thought of as stages. These models have different distinguishing characteristics. Stages can be driven by the search for new growth opportunities or as a response to internal crises. Some models suggest that firms progress through stages, while others argue that there may be multiple paths through the stages.

Kazanjian (1988) applied dominant problems to stages of growth. Dominant problems imply that there is a pattern of primary concerns that firms face for each theorized stage. In the area of IT maturity, dominant problems can shift from lack of skills to lack of resources to lack of strategy associated with different stages of growth.

Kazanjian and Drazin (1989) argue that either implicitly or explicitly, stage of growth models share a common underlying logic. Organizations undergo transformations in their design characteristics, which enable them to face the new tasks or problems that growth elicits. The problems, tasks, or environments may differ from model to model, but almost all suggest that stages emerge in a well-defined sequence, so that the solution of one set of problems or tasks leads to the emergence of a new set of problems or tasks that the organization must address. Growth in areas such as IT maturity can be viewed as a series of evolutions and revolutions precipitated by internal crises related to leadership, control, and coordination. The striking characteristic of this view is that the resolution of each crisis sows the seeds for the next crisis. Another view is to consider stages of growth as responses to the firm's search for new growth opportunities once prior strategies have been exhausted.

Stages of growth models may be studied through organizational innovation processes. Technological innovation is considered the primary driver of improvements in many businesses today. Information technology represents a complex organizational technology, that is, technology that, when first introduced, imposes a substantial burden on would-be adopters in terms of the competence needed to use it effectively (Levina & Vaast, 2005). According to Fichman and Kemerer (1997), such technology typically has an abstract and demanding scientific base—it tends to be fragile in the sense that it does not always operate as expected, it is difficult to test in a meaningful way, and it is unpackaged in the sense that adopters cannot treat the technology as a black box.

Embodying such characteristics, organizational learning and innovation diffusion theory can be applied to explain stages of growth models. Organizational learning is sometimes placed at the center of innovation diffusion theory through a focus on institutional mechanisms that lower the burden of organizational learning related to IT adoption. Organizations may be viewed, at any given moment, as possessing some bundle of competence related to their current operational and managerial processes. In order to successfully assimilate a new process technology, an organization must somehow reach a state where its bundle of competence encompasses those needed to use the new technology (Fichman & Kemerer, 1997).

Innovations through stages of growth can be understood in terms of technology acceptance over time. Technology acceptance has been studied for several decades in information systems research. Technology acceptance models explain perceived usefulness and usage intentions in terms of social influence and cognitive instrumental processes. For example, Venkatesh and Davis (2000) found that social influence processes (subjective norm, voluntariness, and image) and cognitive instrumental processes (job relevance, output quality, result demonstrability, and perceived ease of use) significantly influenced user acceptance. Similarly, Venkatesh (2000) identified determinants of perceived ease of use, a key driver of technology acceptance, adoption, and usage behavior.

Stages of growth models have been criticized for a lack of empirical validity. Benbasat, Dexter, Drury, and Goldstein (1984) found that most of the benchmark variables for stages used by Nolan (1979) were not confirmed in empirical studies. Based on empirical evidence, Benbasat et al. wrote the following critique of Nolan's stage hypothesis:

The stage hypothesis on the assimilation of computing technology provides one of the most popular models for describing and managing the growth of administrative information systems. Despite little formal evidence of its reliability or robustness, it has achieved a high level of acceptance among practitioners. We describe and summarize the findings of seven empirical studies conducted during the past six years that tested various hypotheses derived from this model. The accumulation of evidence from these studies casts considerable doubt on the validity of the stage hypothesis as an explanatory structure for the growth of computing in organizations.

For example, Nolan (1979) proposed that steering committees should be constituted in later stages of maturity. However, an empirical study showed that of 114 firms, 64 of which had steering committees, the correlation between IT maturity and steering committees was not significant. In practice, organizations adopt steering committees throughout the development cycle rather than in the later stages.

Another example is charge-back methods. In a survey, approximately half of the firms used charge-back systems and the other half did not. In the Nolan (1979) structure, as firms mature through later stages, they should have adopted charge-back systems. Yet, in the empirical analysis, there were no significant correlations between maturity indicators and charge-back system usage, according to Benbasat et al. (1984). Benchmark variables such as steering committees and charge-back systems have to be carefully selected and tested before they are applied in survey research.

The concept of stages of growth has created a number of skeptics. Some argue that the concept of an organization progressing unidirectionally through a series of predictable stages is overly simplistic. For example, organizations may evolve through periods of convergence and divergence related more to shifts in information technology than to issues of growth for specific IT. According to Kazanjian and Drazin (1989), it can be argued that firms do not necessarily demonstrate any inexorable momentum to progress through a linear sequence of stages, but rather that observed configurations of problems, strategies, structures, and processes will determine firms' progress.

Kazanjian and Drazin (1989) addressed the need for further databased research to empirically examine whether organizations in a growth environment shift according to a hypothesized stage of growth model, or whether they follow a more random pattern of change associated with shifts in configurations that do not follow such a progression. Based on a sample of 71 firms they found support for the stage hypothesis.

To meet the criticism of lacking empirical validity, this research presentation describes the careful development, selection, and testing of a variety of instrument parts to empirically validate a knowledge management technology stage model.

Guttman Scaling for Cumulative Growth

Benchmark variables in stages of growth models indicate the theoretical characteristics in each stage of growth. The problem with this approach is that not all indicators of a stage may be present in an organization, making it difficult to place the organization in any specific stage.

Guttman scaling is also known as **cumulative scaling** or **scalogram analysis.** Guttman scaling is based on ordering theory that suggests a linear relationship between the elements of a domain and the items on a test. The purpose of Guttman scaling is to establish a one-dimensional continuum for a concept to measure. We would like a set of items or statements so that a respondent who agrees with any specific question in the list will also agree with all previous questions. This is the ideal for a stage model—or for any progression. By this we mean that it is useful when one progresses from one state to another, so that upon reaching the higher stage one has retained all the features of the earlier stage (Trochim, 2002).

For example, a cumulative model for knowledge transfer could consist of six stages: awareness, familiarity, attempt to use, utilization, results, and impact. Byers and Byers (1998) developed a Guttman scale for knowledge levels consisting of stages by order of learning difficulty. Trochim (2002) developed the following cumulative six-stage scale for attitudes towards immigration:

1. I believe that this country should allow more immigrants in.
2. I would be comfortable with new immigrants moving into my community.
3. It would be fine with me if new immigrants moved onto my block.
4. I would be comfortable if a new immigrant moved next door to me.
5. I would be comfortable if my child dated a new immigrant.
6. I would permit a child of mine to marry an immigrant.

Guttman (1950) used scalogram analysis successfully during the war in investigating morale and other problems in the United States Army. In scalogram analysis, items are ordered such that, ideally, organizations that answer a given question favorably all have higher ranks than organizations that answer the same question unfavorably. According to Guttman (1950), the ranking of organizations provides a general approach to the problem of scaling:

We shall call a set of items of common content a scale if an organization with a higher rank than another organization is just as high or higher on every item than the other organization. (p. 62)

Kline (1998) discusses three problems with Guttman scales, which may he claims may render them of little scientific value:

1. ***The underlying measurement model:*** *The first concerns the fact that items correlate perfectly with the total scale score or the attribute being measured. This is unlikely of any variable in the real world. In general terms, it means the measurement model does not fit what is being measured. This is not dissimilar to the difficulty that in psychological measurement it is simply assumed that the attribute is quantitative.*

2. ***Unidimensionality of the scale:*** *It has been argued that all valid measuring instruments must be unidimensional. Now the construction of a Guttman scale does not ensure unidimensionality. It would be perfectly possible to take items from different scales, each item of a considerably different level of difficulty, and these would form a Guttman scale. This is because the scaling characteristics of Guttman scales are dependent only on difficulty levels. Thus Guttman scales may not be unidimensional. The only practical way round the problem is to factor the items first, but then it may prove difficult to make a Guttman scale with so restricted an item pool.*

3. ***Ordinal measurement:*** *The construction of Guttman scales may only permit ordinal measurement. This severely restricts the kinds of statistical analyses, which can be used with Guttman scales.* (p. 75)

These problems also occurred in the conducted empirical tests of the knowledge management technology stage model in Norway and Australia, as is evident in the book by Gottschalk (2005).

The KMT Stage Model

Stages of knowledge management technology (KMT) is a relative concept concerned with IT's ability to process information for knowledge work. At later stages, IT is more useful to knowledge work than IT at earlier stages. The relative concept implies that IT is more directly involved in knowledge work at higher stages, and that IT is able to support more advanced knowledge work at higher stages.

The KMT stage model consists of four stages. The first stage is general IT support for knowledge workers. This includes word processing, spreadsheets, and e-mail. The second stage is information about knowledge sources. An information system stores information about who–knows-what within the firm and outside the firm. The system does not store what they actually know. A typical example is the company intranet. The third stage is information representing knowledge. The system stores what knowledge workers know in terms of information. A typical example is a database. The fourth and final stage is information processing. An information system uses information to evaluate situations. A typical example here is an expert system.

Figure 5.4. The knowledge management technology stage model

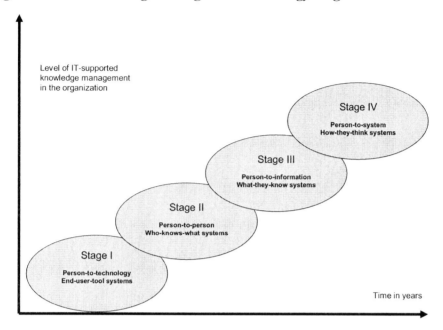

The contingent approach to firm performance implies that stage one may be right for one firm, while stage four may be right for another firm. Some firms will evolve over time from stage one to higher stages as indicated in Figure 5.4. The time axis ranging from 1990 to 2020 in Figure 5.4 suggests that it takes time for an individual firm and a whole industry to move through all stages. As an example applied later in this chapter, the law firm industry is moving slowly in its use of information technology.

Stages of IT support in knowledge management are useful for identifying the current situation as well as planning for future applications in the firm. Each stage is described in the following:

I.   **Tools for end users** are made available to knowledge workers. In the simplest stage, this means a capable networked PC on every desk or in every briefcase, with standardized personal productivity tools (word processing, presentation software) so that documents can be exchanged easily throughout a company. More complex and functional desktop infrastructures can also be the basis for the same types of knowledge support. Stage one is recognized by widespread dissemination and use of end-user tools among knowledge workers in the company. For example, lawyers in a law firm will in this stage use word processing, spreadsheets, legal databases, presentation software, and scheduling programs.

Stage one can be labeled *end-user-tools* or *people-to-technology,* as information technology provides knowledge workers with tools that improve personal efficiency.

II. **Information about who-knows-what** is made available to all people in the firm and to selected outside partners. Search engines should enable work with a thesaurus, since the terminology in which expertise is sought may not always match the terms the expert uses to classify that expertise.

According to Alavi and Leidner (2001), the creation of corporate directories, also referred to as the mapping of internal expertise, is a common application of knowledge management technology. Because much knowledge in an organization remains uncodified, mapping the internal expertise is a potentially useful application of technology to enable easy identification of knowledgeable persons.

Here we find the cartographic school of knowledge management (Earl, 2001), which is concerned with mapping organizational knowledge. It aims to record and disclose who in the organization knows what by building knowledge directories. Often called yellow pages, the principal idea is to make sure knowledgeable people in the organization are accessible to others for advice, consultation, or knowledge exchange. Knowledge-oriented directories are not so much repositories of knowledge-based information as gateways to knowledge, and the knowledge is as likely to be tacit as explicit.

Information about who-knows-what is sometimes called metadata, representing knowledge about where the knowledge resides. Providing taxonomies or organizational knowledge maps enables individuals to rapidly locate the individual who has the needed knowledge, more rapidly than would be possible without such IT-based support.

One starting approach in stage two is to store curriculum vitae (CV) for each knowledge worker in the firm. Areas of expertise, projects completed, and clients helped may over time expand the CV. For example, a lawyer in a law firm works on cases for clients using different information sources that can be registered on yellow pages in terms of an intranet.

At stage two, firms apply the personalization strategy in knowledge management. According to Hansen, Nohria, and Tierney (1999), the personalization strategy implies that knowledge is tied to the person who developed it and is shared mainly through direct person-to-person contact. This strategy focuses on dialogue between individuals: Knowledge is transferred mainly in personal e-mail, meetings, and one-on-one conversations.

The creation of a knowledge network is an important part of stage two. Unless specialists can communicate easily with each other across platform types, expertise will deteriorate. People have to be brought together both virtually and face-to-face to exchange and build their collective knowledge in each of the specialty areas. The knowledge management effort is focused on bringing the experts together so that important knowledge can be shared and amplified, rather than on mapping expertise or benchmarking which occurs in stage three.

Electronic networks of practice are computer-mediated discussion forums focused on problems of practice that enable individuals to exchange advice and ideas with others based on common interests. Electronic networks have been found to support organizational knowledge flows between geographically dispersed coworkers and distributed research and development efforts. These networks also assist cooperative open-source software development and open congregation on the Internet for individuals interested in a specific practice. Electronic networks make it possible to share information quickly, globally, and with large numbers of individuals (Wasko & Faraj, 2005).

The knowledge network is built on modern communication technology. Advances in portable computers such as palm pilots and laptops, in conjunction with wireless network technologies, have engendered mobile computing. In a mobile computing environment, users carrying portable computers are permitted to access the shared computing resources on the network through wireless channels regardless of their physical locations.

According to Earl (2001), knowledge directories represent more of a belief in personalized knowledge of individuals than the codified knowledge of knowledge bases and may demonstrate organizational preferences for human, not technology-mediated, communication and exchange. The knowledge philosophy of firms that settle in stage two can be seen as one of people connectivity. Consequently, the principal contribution from IT is to connect people via intranets and to help them locate knowledge sources and providers using directories accessed by the intranet. Extranets and the Internet may connect knowledge workers to external knowledge sources and providers.

Communication competence is important at stage two. Communication competence is the ability to demonstrate skills in the appropriate communication behavior to effectively achieve one's goals. Communication between individuals requires both the decoding and encoding of messages (Ko, Kirsch, & King, 2005). Lin, Geng, and Whinston (2005) found that knowledge transfer depends on the completeness or incompleteness of the sender's and the receiver' information sets.

The dramatic reduction in electronic communication costs and ease of computer-to-computer linkages has resulted in opportunities to create new channel structures, fueling interest in interorganizational systems. Interorganizational systems are planned and managed ventures to develop and use IT-based information exchange systems to support collaboration and strategic alliances between otherwise independent actors. These systems allow for the exchange of information between partners for the purpose of coordination, communication, and cooperation (Malhotra et al., 2005).

Stage two can be labeled who-knows-what or people-to-people as knowledge workers use information technology to find other knowledge workers.

III. **Information from knowledge workers** is stored and made available to everyone in the firm and to designated external partners. Data mining techniques can be applied here to find relevant information and combine information in data warehouses. On a broader basis, search engines are Web browsers and server software that operate with a thesaurus, since the terminology in which expertise is sought may not always match the terms used by the expert to classify that expertise.

One starting approach in stage three is to store project reports, notes, recommendations, and letters from each knowledge worker in the firm. Over time, this material will grow fast, making it necessary for a librarian or a chief knowledge officer (CKO) to organize it. In a law firm, all client cases will be classified and stored in databases using software such as Lotus Notes.

An essential contribution that IT can make is the provision of shared databases across tasks, levels, entities, and geographies to all knowledge workers throughout a process (Earl, 2001). For example, Infosys Technologies—a U.S. $1 billion company with over 23,000 employees and globally distributed operations—created a central knowledge portal called KShop. The content of KShop was organized into different content types, for instance, case studies, reusable artifacts, and downloadable software. Every knowledge asset under a content type was associated with one or more nodes (representing areas of discourse) in a knowledge hierarchy or taxonomy (Garud & Kumaraswamy, 2005).

According to Alavi and Leidner (2001), one survey found that 74% of respondents believed that their organization's best knowledge was inaccessible and 68% thought that mistakes were reproduced several times. Such a perception of failure to apply existing knowledge is an incentive for mapping, codifying, and storing information derived from internal expertise.

However, sifting though the myriad of content available through knowledge management systems can be challenging, and knowledge workers may be overwhelmed when trying to find the content most relevant for completing a new task. To address this problem, system designers often include rating schemes and credibility indicators to improve users' search and evaluation of knowledge management system content (Poston & Speier, 2005).

According to Alavi and Leidner (2001), one of the most common applications is internal benchmarking with the aim of transferring internal best practices. To be successful, best practices have to be coded, stored, and shared among knowledge workers.

In addition to (i) best practices knowledge within a quality or business process management function, other common applications include (ii) knowledge for sales purposes involving products, markets, and customers, (iii) lessons learned in projects or product development efforts, (iv) knowledge around implementation of information systems, (v) competitive intelligence for strategy and planning functions, and (vi) learning histories or records of experience with a new corporate direction or approach (Grover & Davenport, 2001).

In stage three, access both to knowledge (expertise, experience, and learning) and to information (intelligence, feedback, and data analyses) is provided by systems and intranets to operatives, staff, and executives. The supply and distribution of knowledge and information are not restricted. Whereas we might say in stage one, "give knowledge workers the tools to do the job," we now add, "give knowledge workers the knowledge and information to do the job." According to Earl (2001), this is another way of saying that the philosophy is enhancing the firm's capabilities with knowledge flows.

Although most knowledge repositories serve a single function, Grover and Davenport (2001) found that it is increasingly common for companies to construct an internal portal so that employees can access multiple repositories and sources from one screen. It is also possible and increasingly popular for repositories to contain information as well as pointers to experts within the organization on key knowledge topics. Often called knowledge yellow pages, these systems facilitate contact and knowledge transfer between knowledgeable people and those who seek their knowledge. Stored, codified knowledge is combined with lists of individuals who contributed the knowledge and could provide more detail or background on it.

An enterprise information portal is viewed as a knowledge community. Enterprise information portals are of multiple forms, ranging from Internet-based data management tools that bring visibility to previously dormant data so that their users can compare, analyze, and share enterprise information to a knowledge portal, which enables its users to obtain specialized knowledge that is related to their specific tasks (Ryu et al., 2005).

Individuals' knowledge does not transform easily into organizational knowledge even with the implementation of knowledge repositories. According to Bock et al. (2005), individuals tend to hoard knowledge for various reasons. Empirical studies have shown that the greater the anticipated reciprocal relationships are, the more favorable the attitude toward knowledge sharing will be.

Electronic knowledge repositories are electronic stores of content acquired about all subjects for which the organization has decided to maintain knowledge. Such repositories can comprise multiple knowledge bases as well as the mechanisms for acquisition, control, and publication of the knowledge. The process of knowledge sharing through electronic knowledge repositories involves people contributing knowledge to populate repositories (e.g., customer and supplier knowledge, industry best practices, and product expertise) and people seeking knowledge from repositories for use (Kankanhalli et al., 2005).

In stage three, firms apply the codification strategy in knowledge management. According to Hansen et al. (1999), the codification strategy centers on information technology: Knowledge is carefully codified and stored in knowledge databases and can be accessed and used by anyone. With a codification strategy, knowledge is extracted from the person who developed it, is made independent of the person, and stored in the form of interview guides, work schedules, benchmark data, and so forth. It is then searched and retrieved and used by many employees.

According to Grover and Davenport (2001), firms increasingly view attempts to transform raw data into usable knowledge as part of their knowledge management initiatives. These approaches typically involve isolating data in a separate warehouse for easier access and the use of statistical analysis or data mining and visualization tools. Since their goal is to create data-derived knowledge, they are increasingly addressed as part of knowledge management in stage three.

Stage three can be labeled *what-they-know* or *people-to-docs,* as information technology provides knowledge workers with access to information that is typically stored in documents. Examples of documents are contracts and agreements, reports, manuals and handbooks, business forms, letters, memos, articles, drawings, blueprints, photographs, e-mail and voice mail messages, video clips, script and visuals from presentations, policy statements, computer printouts, and transcripts from meetings.

Sprague (1995) argues that concepts and ideas contained in documents are far more valuable and important to organizations than facts traditionally organized into data records. A document can be described as a unit of recorded information structured for human consumption. It is recorded and stored, so a speech or conversation for which no transcript is prepared is not a document. A document is a snapshot of some set of information that can incorporate many complex information types, exist in multiple places across a network, depend on other documents for information, change as subordinate documents are updated, and be accessed and modified by many people simultaneously.

IV. **Information systems solving knowledge problems** are made available to knowledge workers and solution seekers. Artificial intelligence is applied in these systems. For example, neural networks are statistically oriented tools that excel at using data to classify cases into one category or another. Another example is expert systems that can enable the knowledge of one or a few experts to be used by a much broader group of workers requiring the knowledge.

According to Alavi and Leidner (2001), an insurance company was faced with the commoditization of its market and declining profits. The company found that applying the best decision-making expertise via a new underwriting process, supported by a knowledge management system based on best practices, enabled it to move into profitable niche markets and, hence, to increase income.

According to Grover and Davenport (2001), artificial intelligence is applied in rule-based systems, and more commonly, case-based systems are used to capture and provide access to resolutions of customer service problems, legal knowledge, new product development knowledge, and many other types of knowledge.

Biodiversity is a data-intense science, drawing as it does on data from a large number of disciplines in order to build up a coherent picture of the extent and trajectory of life on earth. Bowker (2000) argues that as sets of heterogeneous databases are made to converge, there is a layering of values into the emergent infrastructure. This layering process is relatively irreversible, and it operates simultaneously at a very concrete level (fields in a database) and at a very abstract one (the coding of the relationship between the disciplines and the production of a general ontology).

Knowledge is explicated and formalized during the knowledge codification phase that took place in stage three. Codification of tacit knowledge is facilitated by mechanisms that formalize and embed it in documents, software, and systems. However, the higher the tacit elements of the knowledge, the more difficult it is to codify. Codification of complex knowledge frequently relies on information technology. Expert systems, decision support systems, document management systems, search engines, and relational database tools represent some of the technological solutions developed to support this phase of knowledge management. Consequently, advanced codification of knowledge emerges in stage four, rather than in stage three, because expert systems and other artificial intelligence systems have to be applied to be successful.

Stage four can be labeled how-they-think or people-to-systems where the system is intended to help solve a knowledge problem. The label how-they-think does not mean that the systems as such think. Rather, it means that the thinking of people has been implemented in the systems.

Stage one is a technology-centric stage, while stage two is a people-oriented stage, stage three is a technology-driven stage, while stage four is a process-centric stage. A people-oriented perspective draws from the work of Nonaka et al. (2000). Essential to this perspective of knowledge sharing and knowledge creation is that people create knowledge and that new knowledge or the increasing of the extant knowledge base occurs as a result of human cognitive activities and the effecting of specific knowledge transformations (Wasko and Faraj, 2005). A technology-driven perspective to knowledge management at stage three is often centered on the computerized technique of data mining and the many mathematical and statistical methods available to transform data into information and then meaningful knowledge (e.g., Poston & Speier, 2005). A process-centric approach tries to combine the essentials of both the people-centric and the technology-centric and technology-driven perspectives in the earlier stages. It emphasizes the dynamic and ongoing nature of the process, where artificial intelligence might help people understand how to proceed in their tasks. Process-centered knowledge generation is concerned with extraction of critical and germane knowledge in a decision-making perspective (Bendoly, 2003).

When companies want to use knowledge in real-time, mission-critical applications, they have to structure the information base for rapid, precise access. A Web search yielding hundreds of documents will not suffice when a customer is waiting on the phone for an answer. Representing and structuring knowledge is a requirement that has long been addressed by artificial intelligence researchers in the form of expert systems and other applications. Now their technologies are being applied within the context of knowledge management. Rule-based systems and case-based systems are used to capture and provide access to customer service problem resolution, legal knowledge, new product development knowledge, and many other types of knowledge. Although it can be difficult and labor-intensive to author a structured knowledge base, the effort can pay off in terms of faster responses to customers, lower cost per knowledge transaction, and lessened requirements for experienced, expert personnel (Grover & Davenport, 2001).

Expert systems are in stage four in the proposed model. Stewart (1997) argues for stage two, stating that knowledge grows so fast that any attempt to codify it all is ridiculous; but the identities of in-house experts change slowly.

Corporate yellow pages should be easy to construct, but it's remarkable how few companies have actually done this. A simple system that connects inquirers to experts saves time, reduces error and guesswork, and prevents the reinvention of countless wheels.

What may be stored in stage three, according to Stewart (1997), are lessons learned and competitor intelligence. A key way to improve knowledge management is to bank lessons learned—in effect, prepare checklists of what went right and wrong, together with guidelines for others undertaking similar projects. In the area of competitor intelligence, companies need to organize knowledge about their suppliers, customers, and competitors.

Information technology can be applied at four different levels to support knowledge management in an organization, according to the proposed stages of growth. At the first level, end user tools are made available to knowledge workers. At the second level, information on who knows what is made available electronically. At the third level, some information representing

Figure 5.5. Examples of IS/IT in different knowledge management stages

STAGES TASKS	I END USER TOOLS people-to-technology	II WHO KNOWS WHAT people-to-people	III WHAT THEY KNOW people-to-docs	IV WHAT THEY THINK people-to-systems
Distribute knowledge	Word Processing Desktop Publishing Web Publishing Electronic Calendars Presentations	Word Processing Desktop Publishing Web Publishing Electronic Calendars Presentations	Word Processing Desktop Publishing Web Publishing Electronic Calendars Presentations	Word Processing Desktop Publishing Web Publishing Electronic Calendars Presentations
Share knowledge		Groupware Intranets Networks E-mail	Groupware Intranets Networks E-mail	Groupware Intranets Networks E-mail
Capture knowledge			Databases Data Warehouses	Databases Data Warehouses
Apply knowledge				Expert systems Neural networks Intelligent agents

knowledge is stored and made available electronically. At the fourth level, information systems capable of simulating human thinking are applied in the organization. These four levels are illustrated in Figure 5.5, where they are combined with knowledge management tasks. The entries in the figure only serve as examples of current systems.

One reason for stage three emerging after stage two is the personalization strategy versus the codification strategy. The individual barriers are significantly lower with the personalization strategy, because the individual professional maintains the control through the whole knowledge management cycle. According to Disterer (2001), the individual is recognized as an expert and is cared for.

Knowledge management strategies focusing on personalization could be called communication strategies, because the main objective is to foster personal communication between people. Core IT systems with this strategy are yellow pages (directories of experts, who-knows-what systems, people-finder databases) that show inquirers who they should talk to regarding a given topic or problem. The main disadvantages of personalization strategies are a lack of standards and the high dependence on communication skills and the will of the professionals. Such disadvantages make firms want to advance to stage three. In stage three, independence in time among knowledge suppliers and knowledge users is achieved (Disterer, 2002).

When we look for available computer software for the different stages, we find a variety of offers from software vendors. At stage one, we find Microsoft software such as Word, Outlook, Excel, and Powerpoint. At stage two, we find knowledge software such as Knowledger from Knowledge Associates. The Knowledger 4.0 helps companies collect and categorize internal and external information. It allows individuals to capture information together with its context into a knowledge repository.

At stage three, we find Novo Knowledge Base Enterprise, Confluence the Enterprise Wiki, and Enterprise Edition X1 Technologies. While Novo's KnowledgeBase provides Web support and documentation solutions, Atlassian's JIRA is tracking and managing the issues and bugs that emerge during a project.

Finally, at stage four, we find DecisionScript by Vanguard Software Corporation and CORVID Knowledge Automation Expert System Software by Xsys. Vanguard provides decision-support system software ranging from desktop tools for managing decision-making to server-based systems that help the entire organization work better. Vanguard's desktop software, DecisionPro, is designed for managers, consultants, and analysts who make business decisions based on uncertain estimates and imperfect information. Exsys argues that its software and services enable businesses, government, and organizations to distribute a company's most valuable asset—expert knowledge—to the people who need it, through powerful interactive Web-enabled systems.

Gottschalk (2005) developed benchmark variables for the stages of growth model. Benchmark variables indicate the theoretical characteristics in each stage of growth. Examples of benchmark variables include trigger of IT, management participation, critical success factor, and performance indicator.

Technology Stage Dynamics

The stages of growth model for knowledge management technology is mainly a sequential and accumulative model. However, in practice the model can also be applied in a cyclical mode. For example, when a firm reaches 2020 in Figure 5.4, the firm might return to stage three to improve information sources and information access at stage three that will improve the performance of systems applied at stage four. Therefore, in a short-term perspective the stages model is sequential, while in a long-term perspective it consists of several cycles.

The knowledge management technology stage model was tested empirically in Norway and Australia. Surveys of law firms were conducted in both countries (Gottschalk, 2005).

The largest law firms in Norway were obtained from the Web site www. paragrafen.no. This Web site lists all law firms in Norway that have a home page on the Internet. The largest law firms were selected by identifying all law firms that had at least five lawyers in the firm. This procedure resulted in a total of 102 law firms. It was possible to obtain email addresses for managing directors and chief executive officers in 95 of these law firms by contacting the firms. Most law firms in Norway are small. While knowledge management technology for sharing information is dependent on a minimum number of lawyers to make sense, only law firms with a minimum of five lawyers were selected for this survey.

Questionnaires were prepared and sent to the CEO in each firm. The questionnaire was developed in QuestBack, an online tool for electronic research. The service is built around three modules: QuestDesigner to create and publish surveys, QuestReporter for analysis of incoming responses, and QuestManager to administer ongoing QuestBack initiatives. QuestBack has a reminder function, which was used for two follow-ups at one and two weeks after the date of the initial mailings. Five firms declined participation, citing that the questionnaire was too long. Nineteen firms returned useable responses, providing a response rate of 20%.

Characteristics of respondents are listed in Figure 5.6. Although most respondents indicated the job title of lawyer, their current position was managing partner or chief executive officer. The average responding law firm had a total of 43 lawyers, which by Norwegian standards are large law firms. Fourteen of these lawyers were partners in the firm. The IT budget constituted 2.3% of the income budget, while IT staff was 1.7% of total staff in the average firm.

Figure 5.7 shows the number of responding firms currently operating in each stage of growth. This is based on the part of the survey instrument describing extensively the four stages of growth. Generally, the results show that what-they-know occurs most often, followed by who-knows-what and end-user-tools. Only one firm reported stage four of how-they-think.

Figure 5.6. Characteristics of law firm respondents

Characteristic	Response
Job title of most respondents	Lawyer
Years with the firm on average	6 years
Persons in the firm	65 persons
Lawyers in the firm	43 lawyers
Partners in the firm	14 partners
Income budget	10 Mill. US $
IT budget	0,2 Mill. US $
Persons in IT function in the firm	1.1 persons

Figure 5.7. Distribution of stages of growth

Stage of Growth	Number	Percent
End-user-tools (people-to-technology)	3	16
Who-knows-what (people-to-people)	4	21
What-they-know (people-to-docs)	11	58
How-they-think (people-to-systems)	1	5
Total	19	100

Figure 5.8. Paths of evolution

Paths of Evolution	Number	Percent
I End-user-tools to **II** who-knows-what to **III** what-they-know	4	50.0
I End-user-tools to **III** what-they-know	1	12.5
II Who-knows-what **III** what-they-know	1	12.5
I End-user-tools to **III** what-they-know to **II** who-knows-what	1	12.5
III what-they-know to **II** who-knows-what to **I** end-user-tools	1	12.5
Total	8	100.0

Figure 5.8 shows the various paths of evolution reported by the respondent firms. Unfortunately, only 8 out of 19 respondents filled in this part of the questionnaire. As expected, the path of evolution generally proceeds from end-user-tools to who-knows-what to what-they-know. This was the case for three respondents. However, the remaining five respondents show varying patterns of reciprocal behavior as illustrated in Figure 5.9.

In our perspective of applying system dynamics to information technology, the paths of evolution in Figure 5.9 demonstrate the dynamics in applying knowledge management technology. Figure 5.10 makes an attempt at explaining the paths in a causal loop diagram.

In Figure 5.10, the more person-to-tools systems in the firm, the more the firm can focus on person-to-person systems in the future. Similarly, the more person-to-person systems in the firm, the more the firm can focus on person-to-information systems, and finally on person-to-application systems. Those causal relationships move from left to right in the diagram.

Moving from right to left we see the need for improving the basis. For example, all stages two to four require more person-to-tools systems to develop

Figure 5.9. Paths of evolution

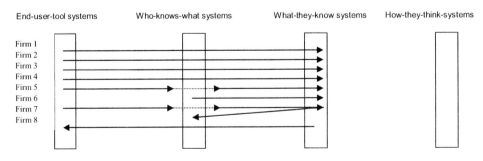

Figure 5.10. Causal loop diagram for stages of growth dynamics

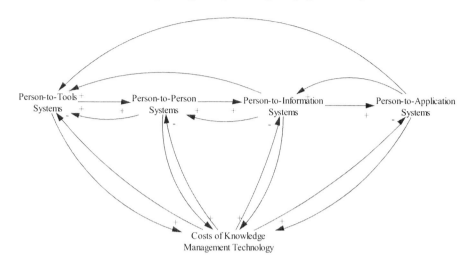

further. For example, to expand person-to-person systems, each person might need access to more tools. Another example is the information basis for stage four systems, which are accumulated at stage three.

In the survey in Norway, stages of growth were measured in terms of tools and systems. Each stage was measured through a multiple item scale consisting of five items. Reliability for each scale is listed in Figure 5.11. The second scale on who-knows-what systems had an unacceptable reliability even when items were deleted.

Scores in Figure 5.11 are illustrated in Figure 5.12. The visual picture supports stages of growth in terms of less systems use at higher stages. When

Figure 5.11. Average response to systems use at each stage (1 little extent, 6 great extent)

Multiple item scale	Norway Score	Australia Score	Norway Alpha	Australia Alpha
End-user-tool systems	4,7	4,3	.69	.79
Who-knows-what systems	3,7	2,9	-	-
What-they-know systems	3,0	3,2	.77	.80
How-they-think systems	1,4	1,5	.89	.85

Figure 5.12. Average response to systems use at each stage (1 little extent, 6 great extent)

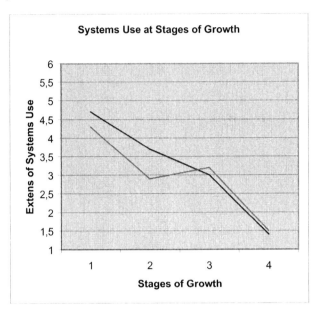

this picture is combined with an earlier figure on paths of evolution, stronger support is present for the stages of growth model for knowledge management technology in law firms. While the earlier figure on paths of evolution supports the sequence suggested by the model, Figure 5.12 supports declining use suggested by the model.

References

Alavi, M., & Leidner, D. E. (2001). Knowledge management and knowledge management systems: Conceptual foundations and research issues. *MIS Quarterly, 25*(1), 107-136.

Benbasat, I., Dexter, A. S., Drury, D. H., & Goldstein, R. C. (1984). A critique of the stage hypothesis: Theory and empirical evidence. *Communications of the ACM, 27*(5), 476-485.

Bendoly, E. (2003). Theory and support for process frameworks of knowledge discovery and data mining from ERP systems. *Information & Management, 40,* 639-647.

Bock, G. W., Zmud, R. W., & Kim, Y. G. (2005). Behavioral intention formation in knowledge sharing: Examining the roles of extrinsic motivators, social-psychological forces, and organizational climate. *MIS Quarterly, 29*(1), 87-111.

Bowker, G. C. (2000). Biodiversity datadiversity. *Social Studies of Science, 30*(5), 643-683.

Byers, C., & Byers, W. A. (1998, June). *Sliding scale: A technique to optimize the assessment of knowledge level through ordering theory.* Paper presented at the Annual Conference of the International Personnel Management Association Assessment Council, Chicago. Retrieved from http://www.ipmaac.org/conf98/byers.pdf

Chen, A. N. K., & Edgington, T. M. (2005). Assessing value in organizational knowledge creation: Considerations for knowledge workers. *MIS Quarterly, 29*(2), 279-309.

Davenport, T. H., & Prusak, L. (1998). *Working knowledge.* Boston: Harvard Business School Press.

Disterer, G. (2001). *Individual and social barriers to knowledge transfer.* Proceedings of the 34th Hawaii International Conference on Systems Sciences, IEEE, USA.

Disterer, G. (2002). *Veränderungen der Rechtsberufe durch neue Technologien. Beispiel: Wissensmanagement bei Anwälten.* Arbeidspapier 68/2002, Fachbereich Wirtschaft, Fachhochschule Hannover, Germany.

Dixon, N. M. (2000). *Common knowledge.* Boston: Harvard Business School Press.

Earl, M. J. (2000). Evolving the e-business, *Business Strategy Review, 11*(2), 33-38.

Earl, M. J. (2001). Knowledge management strategies: Toward a taxonomy. *Journal of Management Information Systems, 18*(1), 215-233.

Edwards, D. L., & Mahling, D. E. (1997). Toward knowledge management systems in the legal domain. *Proceedings of the International ACM SIGGROUP Conference on Supporting Group Work Group '97,* The Association of Computing Machinery ACM, (pp. 158-166).

Fichman, R. G., & Kemerer, C. F. (1997). The assimilation of software process innovations: An organizational learning perspective. *Management Science, 43*(10),1345-1363.

Frankfort-Nachmias, C., & Nachmias, D. (2002). *Research methods in the social sciences* (5th ed.). UK: Arnold.

Garud, R., & Kumaraswamy, A. (2005). Vicious and virtuous circles in the management of knowledge: The case of Infosys Technologies. *MIS Quarterly, 29*(1), 9-33.

Gottschalk, P. (2005). *Strategic knowledge management technology.* Hershey, PA: Idea Group Publishing.

Grover, V., & Davenport, T. H. (2001). General perspectives on knowledge management: Fostering a research agenda. *Journal of Management Information Systems, 18*(1), 5-21.

Guttman, L. (1950). The basis for scalogram analysis. In S. A. Stouffer, L. Guttman, E. A. Suchman, P. F. Lazardsfeld, S. A. Star, & J. A. Clausen (Eds.), *Measurement and prediction*: *Studies in social psychology in World War II* (Vol. 4, pp. 60-90). Princeton, NJ: Princeton University Press.

Hansen, M. T., Nohria, N., & Tierney, T. (1999). What's your strategy for managing knowledge? *Harvard Business Review,* March-April, 106-116.

Hitt, M. A., Bierman, L., Shumizu, K., & Kochhar, R. (2001). Direct and moderating effects of human capital on strategy and performance in professional service firms: A resourced-based perspective. *Academy of Management Journal, 44*(1), 13-28.

Housel, T., & Bell, A. H. (2001). *Measuring and managing knowledge.* New York: McGraw-Hill Irwin.

Kankanhalli, A., Tan, B. C. Y., & Wei, K. K. (2005). Contributing knowledge to electronic knowledge repositories: An empirical investigation. *MIS Quarterly, 29*(1), 113-143.

Kazanjian, R. K. (1988). Relation of dominant problems to stages of growth in technology-based new ventures. *Academy of Management Journal, 31*(2), 257-279.

Kazanjian, R. K. & Drazin, R. (1989). An empirical test of a stage of growth progression model. *Management Science, 35*(12), 1489-1503.

Kettinger, W. J., Teng, J. T. C., & Guha, S. (1997). Business process change: A study of methodologies, techniques, and tools. *MIS Quarterly,* March, 55-79,

King, W. R., & Teo, T. S. H. (1997). Integration between business planning and information systems planning: Validating a stage hypothesis. *Decision Sciences, 28*(2), 279-307.

Kline, P. (1998). *The new psychometrics: Science, psychology and measurement.* UK: Routledge

Ko, D. G., Kirsch, L. J., & King, W. R. (2005). Antecedents of knowledge transfer from consultants to clients in enterprise system implementations. *MIS Quarterly, 29*(1), 59-85.

Levina, N., & Vaast, E. (2005). The emergence of boundary spanning competence in practice: Implications for implementation and use of information systems. *MIS Quarterly, 29*(2), 335-363.

Lin, L., Geng, X., & Whinston, A. B. (2005). A sender-receiver framework for knowledge transfer. *MIS Quarterly, 29*(2), 197-219.

Long, D. W. & Fahey, L. (2000). Diagnosing cultural barriers to knowledge management. *Academy of Management Executive, 14*(4), 113-127.

Malhotra, A., Gosain, S., & El Sawy, O. A. (2005). Absorptive capacity configurations in supply chains: Gearing for partner-enabled market knowledge creation. *MIS Quarterly, 29*(1), 145-187.

Moffett, S., & McAdam, R. (2003). Contributing and enabling technologies for knowledge management. *International Journal of Information Technology and Management, 2*(1/2), 31-49.

Nahapiet, J., & Ghoshal, S. (1998). Social capital, intellectual capital, and the organizational advantage. *Academy of Management Review, 23*(2), 242-266.

Nolan, R. L. (1979). Managing the crises in data processing. *Harvard Business Review,* March-April, 115-126.

Nonaka, I., Toyama, R., & Konno, N. (2000). SECI, Ba and leadership: A unified model of dynamic knowledge creation. *Long Range Planning, 33*(1), 5-34

Poston, R. S., & Speier, C. (2005). Effective use of knowledge management systems: A process model of content ratings and credibility indicators. *MIS Quarterly, 29*(2), 221-244.

Ryu, C., Kim, Y. J., Chaudhury, A., & Rao, H. R. (2005). Knowledge acquisition via three learning processes in enterprise information portals: Learning-by-investment, learning-by-doing, and learning-from-others. *MIS Quarterly, 29*(2), 245-278.

Sambamurthy, V., & Subramani, M. (2005). Special issue on information technologies and knowledge management. *MIS Quarterly, 29*(1), 1-7; and *29*(2), 193-195.

Sprague, R. H. (1995, March). Electronic document management: Challenges and opportunities for information systems managers. *MIS Quarterly*, 29-49.

Stewart, T. A. (1997). *Intellectual capital: The new wealth of organizations.* UK: Nicholas Brealy Publishing.

Tanriverdi, H. (2005). Information technology relatedness, knowledge management capability, and performance of multibusiness firms. *MIS Quarterly, 29*(2), 311-334.

Tiwana, A. (2002). The knowledge management toolkit: Practical techniques for building a knowledge management system (2nd ed.). Upper Saddle River, NJ: Prentice Hall.

Trochim (2002). *Guttman scaling.* <http://trochim.human.cornell.edu/kb/scalgutt.htm>

Venkatesh, V. (2000). Determinants of perceived ease of use: Integrating control, intrinsic motivation, and emotion into the technology acceptance model. *Information Systems Research, 11*(4), 342-365.

Venkatesh, V., & Davis, F. D. (2000). A theoretical extension of the technology acceptance model: Four longitudinal field studies. *Management Science, 46*(2), 186-204.

Ward, J., & Peppard, J. (2002). *Strategic planning for information systems.* UK: Wiley.

Wasko, M. M., & Faraj, S. (2005). Why should I share? Examining social capital and knowledge contribution in electronic networks of practice. *MIS Quarterly, 29*(1), 35-57.

Zack, M. H. (1999). Developing a knowledge strategy. *California Management Review, 41*(3), 125-145.

Chapter VI

Dynamics of Outsourcing Relationships

Given the potential headaches of managing IT, it is tempting to hand the job over to someone else. Indeed, outsourcing once appeared to be a simple solution to management frustrations, and senior management teams at many companies negotiated contracts with large service providers to run their entire IT functions (Gottschalk & Solli-Sæther, 2006). At a minimum, these providers were often able to provide IT capabilities for a lower cost and with fewer hassles than the companies had been able to themselves. But many of these outsourcing arrangements resulted in dissatisfaction, particularly as a company's business needs changed.

Service providers, with their standard offerings and detailed contracts, provided IT capabilities that were not flexible enough to meet changing requirements, and they often seemed slow to respond to problems. Furthermore, a relationship with a supplier often required substantial investments of money and time, which entrenched that supplier in the company's strategic planning and business processes. The company then became particularly vulnerable if the supplier failed to meet its contractual obligations (Ross & Weill, 2002).

In our dynamic perspective of knowledge resources, outsourcing relationships are not just about transactions between a vendor and a supplier. The resource-based theory argues that the firm's ability to mobilize and utilize both internal and externally available resources determines its ability to succeed in the market place. If the firm is short of important resources such as IT resources, an outsourcing arrangement might help overcome the problem as the vendor makes IT resources available to the firm for a price.

The quality of an outsourcing relationship will vary over time. For example, when the client's behavior in the relationship changes, then a reaction from the vendor should be expected. The vendor's reaction will have to be responded to by the client. In this manner, the relationship might dynamically improve or deteriorate over time. We apply system dynamics to understand such developments over time.

Often, the vendor will have a different value configuration than the client. The vendor being a solutions provider makes it a value shop, while the client might be a value chain, value shop, or value network. Understanding how different value configurations interact will improve the relationship. For example, if the client is a value chain, then information systems operated by the vendor have the main purpose of making production more efficient and effective at the client site. If the client is also a value shop, the information systems operated by the vendor have the main purpose of adding value to the problem solution work done by the client for its customers.

Agency Theory

Agency theory has broadened the risk-sharing literature to include the agency problem that occurs when cooperating parties have different goals and division of labor. The cooperating parties are engaged in an agency relationship defined as a contract under which one or more persons (the principal/s) engage another person (agent) to perform some service on their behalf which involves delegating some decision-making authority to the agent (Jensen & Meckling, 1976). Agency theory describes the relationship between the two parties using the metaphor of a contract. In an IT outsourcing relationship this is a client-vendor relationship and an outsourcing contract.

According to Eisenhardt (1985), agency theory is concerned with resolving two problems that can occur in agency relationships. The first is the agency problem that arises when the desires or goals of the principal and agent conflict and it is difficult or expensive for the principal to verify what the agent is actually doing. The second is the problem of risk sharing that arises when the principal and agent have different risk preferences. These problems are well known in IT outsourcing. An example might be that the client organization wants to reduce its IT costs, while the vendor organization wants to maximize profits. The agency problem arises when the two parties do not share productivity gains. The risk-sharing problem might be the result of different attitudes toward the use of new technologies. Because the unit of analysis is the contract governing the relationship between the two parties, the focus of the theory is on determining the most efficient contract governing the principal-agent relationship given assumptions about people (e.g., self-interest, bounded rationality, risk aversion), organizations (e.g., goal conflict of members), and information (e.g., information is a commodity which can be purchased). Thus the question becomes: Is a behavior-oriented contract more efficient than an outcome-oriented contract? Outsourcing contracts are to a great extent tied up to service-level agreements, where the outcome of the service is the focal point.

The agency theory is applicable when describing client-vendor relationships in IT outsourcing arrangements. Typically, the client organization (principal) transfers property rights to the vendor organization (agent). In the context of IT, assets transferred might be infrastructure, systems and documentation, and employees. For a certain amount of money, the vendor organization provides services to the client organization. This implies a change in legal relationships, and IT services are carried out using a more formal transaction process. The status of personal relationships also changes, from that of a manager and a subordinate, to that of a client-manager and a vendor. According to agency theory, control mechanisms also change, from that of behavioral control, to that of outcome-based control. If both parties to the relationship are trying to maximize their utility, there is good reason to believe that the vendor organization will not always act in the best interests of the client. Monitoring and bonding activities in reducing agency costs include auditing, formal control systems, budget restrictions, and the establishment of incentive compensation systems which serve to more closely identify the manager's interests with those of the outside equity holder.

The original impetus for the development of agency theory was large corporations' separation of control from ownership. Thus, its focus was never on organizational boundaries, as with transaction cost theory. Agency theory's primary interest is not the decision to source via the hierarchy or via the market. Although all contractual arrangements contain important elements of agency, agency theory is essentially concerned with the delegation of work by the principal to the agent via a contract, whether or not they are both within the same organization. However, agency and transaction cost theories share several concepts, such as opportunism, uncertainty, and bounded rationality, and there is a rough correspondence between transaction cost economics' hierarchies and markets and agency theory's behavior-based contracts and outcome-based contracts.

According to Hancox and Hackney (2000), the choice of contract type depends on the agency costs, which include the principal's effort in assessing the agent's performance and the agent's efforts in assuring the principal of his commitment. Agency theory holds that human beings act through self-interest and therefore, as contracting parties, they may have divergent goals. An important aspect of the theory is that both principal and agent wish to avoid risk when dealing with each other. The principal may prefer to place risk with the agent via an outcome-based contract, whereas the agent may prefer to avoid risk by having a behavior-based contract.

Outcome-based contracts are claimed to reduce agent opportunism because the rewards of both agent and principal depend on the same actions. Behavior-based contracts need the principal to have sufficient information to identify two possible dangers: First, whether there is adverse selection (the agent does not possess the skills he claims), and second, whether there is a moral hazard—the agent is shirking. Overall risk may be reduced by sourcing via the hierarchy, but agency costs also exist in hierarchies. Problems between agents and principals are greater in complex organizations with many managerial layers. Given that many public sector bodies are large and complicated both in the range of their activities and the structures adopted to manage and account for those activities, it may be that agency costs are inclined to be higher in the public sector. Nonmarket organizations may be especially susceptible to influence costs, where employees pursue their own agenda. This might imply that within a public sector organization, if the employees of one department were motivated by self-interest, then workers in other departments would be inconvenienced and resent the action, unless, perhaps, they themselves were pursuing a similar or compatible agenda.

The technological and business complexity of IT means that there may be major problems for the principal in choosing a suitable agent and in monitoring the agent's work. Only the agent knows how hard he is working, and that can be especially important in multilateral contracting where one agent acts for several principals. This is often the case in IT outsourcing because of the market dominance of one large firm. Given the difficulties of behavior-based contracts suggested by agency theory, it is reasonable to assume that the overwhelming majority of clients would insist on outcome-based contracts when acquiring IT products and services. Such a strategy can only succeed if the client can confidently specify current and future requirements. But accurate predictions by the client may not always be in the vendor's interests, since vendor account managers often are rewarded according to contract profitability, which is principally achieved through charging the client extra for anything, which is not in the contract.

Hancox and Hackney (2000) interviewed IT managers to find support for the agency theory in IT outsourcing. In their interviews, it was difficult to find examples of some of the ideas from agency theory, although a minority of the organizations had been disappointed with aspects of vendor performance and behavior.

Partnership and Alliance Theory

Partnership appears to be a less rigorously defined analytical framework than the theories of core competencies, transaction cost economics, and theories that are typically applied to explain outsourcing (Gottschalk & Solli-Sæther, 2006). Indeed, the very word "partnership" has a more everyday ring to it and is associated with the readily understood characteristics, which may be found in a relationship between two or more parties in a particular context. Partnership's treatment in the information systems literature seems largely nontheoretical, perhaps reflecting a wide diversity of practical arrangements and the absence of a single commonly recognized theory. Although the sharing of risk and reward is sometimes mentioned in the information systems literature, often the emphasis is on intangibles such as trust, comfort, understanding, flexibility, cooperation, shared values, goals, and problem solving, good interpersonal relations, and regular communication. The influential Kodak-IBM outsourcing deal had much to do with a sense of honor and a chemistry between the parties, and changed the common perception of IT outsourcing from an arm's length relationship to one of strategic partnership (Hancox & Hackney, 2000).

Partnership, often referred to as an alliance, has frequently been noted as a major feature of IT outsourcing. Partnership can reduce the risk of inadequate contractual provision, which may be comforting for clients about to outsource a complex and high-cost activity such as IT. However, in the relationship between vendor and client, the latter may be overly dependent on the former, and goals are not necessarily shared. A client may be more comfortable if he knows the vendor already. In partner selection, cultural compatibility is vital and shared values and objectives inform all stages of the partnership development process. This may make a successful relationship especially difficult if the putative partners are from fundamentally different domains and bring fundamentally different perspectives, as might well be argued is the case in a private sector/public sector arrangement. The difficulty may be compounded where, as in the UK government's compulsory competitive tendering policy, the outsourcing can be involuntary.

Hancox and Hackney (2000) found that few organizations claim to be in a strategic partnership with their IT suppliers. The contract is more likely to favor the vendor because he has greater experience in negotiation. Clients with loose contracts were more likely to regard outsourcing as a failure; yet most respondents in a study used the vendor's standard contract as a basis for outsourcing agreement and most did not use external technical or legal advice. It was found that 80% of clients wished that they had more tightly defined contracts. Partly the client's view of IT influences its relationship with the vendor, such that firms regarding IT as a core competence capability are more likely to look upon outsourcing as an alliance. Clients who view IT as a core are also more likely to be satisfied with the outsourcing arrangements because they negotiate from a more knowledgeable position.

Hancox and Hackney (2000) interviewed IT managers to find support for the partnership theory in IT outsourcing. Despite assurances found in vendors' marketing literature, most clients were skeptical about partnership. If partnership did exist, it was usually as a collection of some of the intangibles mentioned earlier, rather than as a formalized arrangement. Partnership was more likely to be claimed in the area of systems development, where vendors needed to have a greater understanding of the organization, than in outsourcing of operations and IT infrastructure support. There seemed to be no correlation between those organizations regarding IT as strategic and those regarding relationships with vendors as partnerships.

Das and Teng (2002) studied how alliance conditions change over the different stages of alliance development to understand the development processes of strategic alliances such as an IT outsourcing relationship. They defined the following stages in the alliance development process:

- **Formation stage:** Partner firms approach each other and negotiate the alliance. Partner firms then carry out the agreement and set up the alliance by committing various types of resources. The alliance is initiated and put into operation. Alliances will be formed only under certain conditions. These conditions include a relatively high level of collective strengths, a low level of inter partner conflicts, and a high level of interdependencies.

- **Operation stage:** Not only is the formation stage directly influenced by alliance conditions, the transition from the formation stage to the operation stage is also dictated by the same alliance conditions variables. During the operation stage, partner firms collaborate and implement all agreements of the alliance. The alliance will likely grow rapidly in size during this stage, somewhat akin to the growth stage of organizational life cycles. Other than the growth route, an alliance may also be reformed and/or terminated at this stage.

- **Outcome stage:** During this stage, alliance performance becomes tangible, and can thus be evaluated with some certainty. There are four possible outcomes for an alliance at this stage: stabilization, reformation, decline, and termination. A combination of outcomes is also possible, such as a termination after reformation. Alliance reformation and alliance termination do not necessarily signal alliance failure. Reformation and termination may be the best option under certain circumstances, such as the achievement of preset alliance objectives. Alliance condition variables continue to play a decisive role in the outcome stage. The particular alliance outcome will depend on the condition of the alliance.

Das and Teng (2003) discussed partner analysis and alliance performance. An important stream of research in the alliance literature is about partner selection. It emphasizes the desirability of a match between the partners, mainly in terms of their resource profiles. The approach is consistent with the resource-based theory of the firm, which suggests that competitors are defined by their resources profiles. They found a lack of agreement concerning alliance performance. This lack of agreement reflects an underlying conceptual puzzle: What does effective alliance performance mean? There are two distinct loci of alliance performance in the literature: the alliance itself and the partners forming the alliance. On the one hand, when alliances are viewed as separate entities, alliance performance is the success of these separate entities, in terms of, say, profitability or growth rate. On the other hand, because partner firms use alliances to achieve certain strategic objectives, alliance performance ought to be measured in terms of the aggregated results for the partner firms.

Alliances are broadly defined as collaborative efforts between two or more firms in which the firms pool their resources in an effort to achieve mutually compatible goals that they could not easily achieve alone. Resources here are defined as any tangible or intangible entity available for use by a firm to compete in its marketplace. When interfirm business relationships are collaborative, rather than adversarial, in nature, a variety of types of these relationships may be classified as alliances, for example outsourcing. According to Lambe, Spekman, and Hunt (2002), the popularity of alliances is growing. Alliances account for anywhere from 6 to 25%of the market value of the typical company. Yet alliance success remains elusive. Studies find that as many as 70%of alliances are not successful. Thus, an important question for researchers and practicing managers is, what makes alliances succeed? They argue that alliance competence contributes to alliance success, both directly and through acquisition and creation of resources. Using survey data gathered from 145 alliances, empirical tests provide support for the posited explanation of alliance success.

Alliance competence has three facets, which Lambe et al. (2002) labeled alliance experience, alliance manager development capability, and partner identification propensity. Furthermore, consistent with competence-based theory and resource-advantage theory conceptualizations of a competence (a higher-order resource that is a distinct combination of lower-order resources), the researchers proposed that these three facets are the three lower-order resources that collectively comprise the higher-order resource of an alliance competence. That is, more of each of these three lower-order resources will contribute to increasing a firm's competence in finding, developing, and managing alliances:

- **Alliance experience** is a resource that can be leveraged across an organization because it contributes to knowledge about how to manage and use alliances.
- **Alliance manager development capability** enables firms to plan and navigate the mechanisms of an alliance so that roles and responsibilities are clearly articulated and agreed upon. In addition, these managers have the ability to review continually the fit of the alliance to the changing environment to make modifications as necessary.

- **Partner identification propensity** enables firms to systematically and proactively scan for and identify partners that have the complementary resources that are needed to develop a relationship portfolio or mix that complements existing competencies and enables them to occupy positions of competitive advantage.

Lambe et al. (2002) posited that two specific types of resources affect alliance success: idiosyncratic and complementary resources. In terms of resource-advantage theory, complementary resources may be thought of as lower-order resources that are brought to the alliance and idiosyncratic resources as the higher-order resources that are developed by the alliance through the process of combining the complementary resources of the partner firms. Idiosyncratic resources are resources that are developed during the life of the alliance, are unique to the alliance, and facilitate the combining of the distinct lower-order resources contributed by the partner firms. Idiosyncratic resources may be tangible, such as computers and cables, or intangible, such as developing a methodology or a process together. Similarly, some researchers refer to idiosyncratic investments or assets.

Relational Exchange Theory

Contracts are often extremely imperfect tools for controlling opportunism. While relational contracts may mitigate some opportunistic behavior, significant residual opportunism may remain. It is possible that transactors using relational contracts may incur significant ex-post bargaining costs as they periodically negotiate contract adjustments (Artz & Brush, 2000). Relational exchange theory is based on relational norms. According to this theory, the key to determining how efficiently contract governance is carried out lies in the relational norms between the transactors. For example, the degree to which transactors engage in joint planning or their extent of interfirm information sharing are process elements that determine the costs associated with periodically renegotiating contracts. Those transactors who have established behavioral norms that can simplify and smooth the renegotiation process can reasonably expect to incur lower ex post bargaining costs than those who have not.

Artz and Brush (2000) examined supplier relationships that were governed by relational contracts, and they found support for the relational exchange theory. By altering the behavioral orientation of the alliance, relational norms lowered exchange costs. In their measurement of relational norm, Artz and Brush (2000) included collaboration, continuity expectations, and communication strategies. Collaboration refers to the willingness of the client and vendor to work together to create a positive exchange relationship and improve alliance performance. Collaborative actions can act to enhance the client-vendor relationship as a whole and curtail opportunistic behaviors. For example, joint planning and forecasting can allow both the customer and the supplier to participate in determining the roles and responsibilities of each and foster mutually beneficial expectations. Continuity expectations refer to the extent to which the customer and the supplier expect the relationship to continue for the foreseeable future. Expectations of a long-term supply relationship can encourage cooperation by providing the opportunity for one alliance partner to retaliate if the other behaved opportunistically. Specifically, opportunistic behavior by one party in one period can be matched by opportunistic behavior by the other partner in the next. Similarly, cooperation can be met with cooperation. "Communication strategies" refers to the type of communications the customer and vendor use in their bargaining sessions to try to influence the negotiations. Such strategies can be grouped into either coercive or noncoercive communications. Partners using coercive communications attempt to achieve their desired goals by applying direct pressure with adverse consequences of noncompliance stressed. Examples of coercive communications include using threats or legalistic pleas, in which one party argues that compliance is required by the formal contract terms. When one firm attempts to coerce another in order to gain a more favorable negotiation outcome, that firm is likely to be viewed by its alliance partner as exploitative rather than accommodative, and retaliatory behavior often results. In contrast, noncoercive strategies attempt to persuade rather than demand. Noncoercive communications center on beliefs about business issues and involve little direct pressure. Examples include simple requests or recommendations, in which one party stresses the benefits the other party will receive by complying.

Kern and Blois (2002) considered the role of norms within networks by describing how BP Exploration outsourced its information technology function, a major business activity. This outsourcing venture led to the formation of a consortium of vendors. However, this attempt was found to have failed. They suggested that central to the failure of the consortium, as an outsourcing arrangement was the issue of norms. Norms create expectations of behavior and imply a certain action and are shared by the actors. It is believed that society shares a number of common norms that make it necessary for contracts to contain certain features but not necessary to include statements about others. Yet norms vary a great deal between and within societies, as is illustrated by international contracts in which a foreigner's requirements as to what should go into a contract will often surprise us but what we would not consider necessary to include may surprise them.

Businesses recognize the impossibility of a contract meeting every eventuality, so there is a need for adaptability within a contract and the completion of a contract is frequently dependent upon workers being able to take up a lot of the uncertainty. Both the normal economic models of a market transaction and the legal model of a contract tend to obscure the degree to which large numbers of contracts are agreements to deliver an indefinite good or service for an indefinite price. Without such willingness to be adaptable many business relationships would grind rapidly and regularly to a halt. Norms are in a sense the lubricants that keep relationships from being stymied by their contractual terms.

In the case of BP Exploration, three problems arose. First, the consortium's members, though competitors, were expected to work closely with each other as the senior partner on some sites and as the junior partner on others. Yet neither BP Exploration nor any member of the consortium recognized in advance that the norms that they usually applied in their relationships with their clients would not be applicable to this situation. Consequently, their staff was working with norms that were at best not appropriate to the new situation and at worst made for difficulties. For example, a company's norms do not normally encourage the acceptance of flexibility, information exchange, and solidarity in contacts with competitors, all of which are needed if sound relationships are to be developed between organizations. Second, BP Exploration's line managers conducted their relationships with the consortium members as if they were buying a commodity service. Yet a major reason for outsourcing was BP Exploration's desire to obtain a state-of-the-art IT service. Its behavior toward the consortium was therefore based on norms that were inappropriate relative to its stated objectives. The third problem was that one of the vendors was not familiar with European modes of operations and had a horrendous job trying to adapt to a non-U.S. culture.

Norms are formed in different ways. Some norms' roots can be related to cultural backgrounds, but the roots of others are more difficult to identify.

However, how norms develop when new industries or, as in the case of BP, new forms of organization evolve is far from apparent. In relationships such as the one described in this case, which develop in a new environment, the relative power of the parties involved is presumably a major factor. Thus, where one organization is very dominant in a new market it seems probable that their values and approaches to business will be very influential. Within business relationships the nature of exchanges that occur between the personnel involved can vary a great deal. Sometimes the relationships at a senior level are more relaxed than those at a junior level. Yet the opposite can be true with junior staff making the relationship work on a day-to-day level in spite of adversarial behavior among the directors. Many classifications of norms have been proposed, but no one is regarded as dominant. It has been proposed that relational norms are a higher-order construct consisting of three dimensions (Kern & Blois, 2002):

- **Flexibility**, which defines a bilateral expectation of the willingness to make adaptations as circumstances change.

- **Information exchange**, which defines a bilateral expectation that parties will proactively provide information useful to the partner.

- **Solidarity**, which defines a bilateral expectation that a high value is placed on the relationship. It prescribes behaviors directed specifically toward relationship maintenance.

Many factors led to BP Exploration being a less than successful experiment in outsourcing. However, a major contribution was a failure to recognize the need for establishing norms of behavior that were appropriate to the consortium form of organization (Kern & Blois, 2002).

Norms are expectations about behavior that are at least partially shared by a group of decision makers. Norms are important in relational exchange because they provide the governance rules of the game. These rules depend on the game, which from an exchange perspective has been described as either discrete or relational. Discrete exchange norms contain expectations about an individualistic or competitive interaction between exchange partners. The individual parties are expected to remain autonomous and pursue strategies aimed at the attainment of their individual goals. In contrast, relational exchange norms are based on the expectation of mutuality of interest, essentially prescribing stewardship behavior, and are designed to enhance the well-being of the relationship as a whole. In the evolutionary model of relational exchange, relational norm development takes place during an extended period of time through many interactions between the partners. For example, tacit relational norms emerge as partners interact during the exploration stage of relational development (Lambe, Spekman, & Hunt, 2000).

Relational exchange is an interactive process where commitments are made, outcomes are observed, and further investments are made, if outcomes meet or exceed expectations. Based on previous interactions as well as expectations about the future, a mutual orientation develops resulting in a common language and mutual knowledge. The exchange is embedded in a normative structure that determines the functioning of the system. Patterns of behavior are taken for granted. The actors share common expectations about expected and accepted behavior, and collective interests are incorporated into the preferences and belief structures of the actors (Rokkan & Haugland, 2002). Discrete and relational exchange can be regarded as polar cases. Pure discrete exchange is consistent with the underlying assumptions of neoclassical economic theory. Relational exchange, on the other hand, accounts for the social and historical context in which exchange takes place. The fundamental norms of discrete exchange are discreteness and presentation, which means that any transaction is separated from all else between the participants at the same time and before and after, and that all future obligations and actions are brought into the present. Relational exchange, on the other hand, is based on norms such as role integrity, conflict resolution, and preservation of the relationship.

Rokkan and Haugland (2002) studied the effect of power on relational exchange. Power is related to whether the relationship is symmetrical or unbalanced. A key characteristic of long-term relationships is mutual power relations. Actor A's power in the relationship with actor B is the inverse of B's dependence upon A. Dependence or interdependence thus affects and constrains the behavior of the actors, but it may also create opportunities. This factor is important in relation to relational exchange, as it is closely linked to the question of equity or fair dealing. They hypothesized that dependence asymmetry would have a negative effect on relational exchange, but they did not find empirical support in their survey for this hypothesis.

Partnership Quality Determinants

Increasing attention is paid to building successful partnerships in information technology outsourcing. Lee and Kim (1999) have studied the effect of partnership quality on IS outsourcing success. They define partnership as an interorganizational relationship to achieve the participants' shared goals. Partnership is not a new concept in the management area. Marketing and interorganizational systems research has explored relationships between customer and vendor, buyer and seller, manufacturer and distributor, or auditor and client, and so on. A number of different views emerged concerning interorganizational relationships.

Research has classified the relationship between organizations into two types: transactional style and partnership style. A transactional style relationship develops through the formal contract in which rules of the game are well-specified and the failure to deliver on commitments by either party should be resolved through litigation or penalty clauses in the contract. In contrast, the requirements of a partnership style relationship include risk and benefit sharing, the need to view the relationship as a series of exchanges without a definite endpoint, and the need to establish a range of mechanisms to monitor and execute its operations.

In traditional IS management, the role of a service provider was limited in terms of the size of the contract and the type of service. Maintenance of hardware or program subcontracting has traditionally been the typical IS service provider. However, the type of relationship in outsourcing is changing from such buyer-seller relationships to the more strategic partnership relationship. Therefore, a necessary condition to move away from self-interest is a belief that the exchange relationship is a win-win situation for organizations to gain competitive advantages.

Relevant theories to analyze the interorganizational relationship include the resource-dependency theory, transaction-cost theory, and agent-cost theory from the economic viewpoint, and social exchange theory and power-political theory from the social viewpoint. Economic theories aim at explaining the characteristics of governance or contract. They treat each sourcing decision as an independent event regardless of prior relationships that affect the ongoing sourcing decision. This treatment may be inappropriate where organizations repeatedly enter transactions with each other. Explaining the relationship between organizations from a purely economic point of view is unjustifiable because interorganizational relationships form from the social learning experiences based on specific sequential interactions (Lee & Kim, 1999).

Social theorists assume that processes evolve over time as participants mutually and sequentially demonstrate their trustworthiness, whereas in the economic perspective, the organization's exchange activities are enforceable. Social theorists understand a relationship as a dynamic process through specific sequential interactions in which two participants carry out activities toward one another. However, a good relationship does not always bring about the participants' desired results. According to social theories, two mechanisms, trust and power, can explain the relationship between organizations. Trust, a feature of relationship quality, has been conceptualized as the firm's belief that the other company will perform actions that will result in a positive outcome for the firm, and will not take unexpected actions that would result in negative outcomes for the firm. Power is determined by the relative dependence between two actors in an exchange relationship, and the concept of power is only meaningful when compared with another organization. While social exchange theory uses the concept of trust to explain interactions between participants, power-political theory relies on the power derived from offering valuable resources that few other sources can provide (Lee & Kim, 1999).

Partnership is an effective way to improve economies of scale and scope provided by the traditional modes of organization. However, partnership does not guarantee a desired outcome. Therefore, careful attention needs to be paid to the partnership problems that may lead to an unstable and conflicting relationship. Partnership quality is an important concept in this respect. Quality is treated as having two dimensions: fitness of use (does the product or service does what it is supposed to do? Does it possess the features that meet the customer's needs?), and reliability (to what extent is the product free from deficiencies?) If we apply the first dimension to partnership, partnership quality may be expressed as how well the outcome of a partnership matches the participants' expectations (Lee & Kim, 1999).

From this outset, partnership quality can be viewed as an antecedent of the outsourcing success. High partnership quality may be a necessary condition for outsourcing success, but not a sufficient condition. For instance, if the main objective of the outsourcing was cost reduction but the outsourcing vendor failed to meet the objective, such an outsourcing project would be a failure regardless of the partnership quality between the service receiver and provider. Thus, Lee and Kim (1999) distinguish the concept of partnership quality from that of outsourcing success, and empirically tested whether outsourcing is successful when high-quality partnership exists. They identified the following five factors that make up partnership quality: trust (degree of confidence and willingness between partners), business understanding (degree of understanding of behaviors, goals, and policies between partners), benefit/risk share (degree of articulation and agreement on benefit and risk between partners), conflict (degree of incompatibility of activities, resource share, and goals between partners), and commitment (degree of the pledge of relationship continuity between partners).

Partnership quality is affected by organizational, human, and environmental factors. However, most literature does not explicitly distinguish the components of partnership quality from the factors that affect it. Lee and Kim (1999) introduced the factors from previous literature as potential determinants of partnership quality and presented the hypotheses related to each factor. They expected to find a positive relationship between each of the hypothesized determinants of partnership quality and trust, business understanding, benefit/ risk share, and commitment among the components of partnership quality, and a negative relationship between each of the hypothesized determinants of partnership quality and conflict.

Figure 6.1 illustrates their findings. Participation was found to be significantly related to partnership quality. From a social perspective, participation is prescribed as a remedy when there is conflict, frustration, and vacillation in the group. Active participation of the partnership members plays a major part in enhancing the sustainability of their partnerships over time. When one partner's actions influence the ability of the other to compete effectively, the need for participation in specifying roles, responsibilities, and expectations increases. Accordingly, the higher the degree of participation, the higher the quality of partnership. Communication quality was found to be significantly related to partnership quality. According to the social exchange literature, effective communication between partners is essential in order to achieve the intended objectives. Intensive communication should lead to better-informed parties, which in turn should make each party more confident in the relationship and more willing to keep it alive. Communication quality is treated as an antecedent of trust in the research literature. Accordingly, higher communication quality is believed to enhance the quality of partnership. Information sharing is the third significant determinant in Figure 6.1. Information sharing is the extent to which critical or proprietary information is communicated to one's partner. Partnerships can create a competitive advantage through the strategic sharing of organizations' key information. Closer relationships

Figure 6.1. Partnership quality affected by determinants and effecting outsourcing success

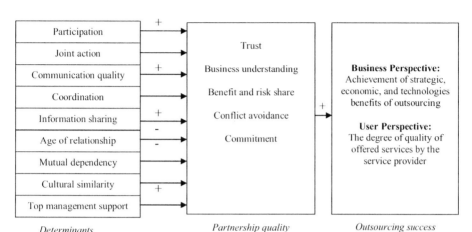

result from more frequent and relevant information exchanges among high-performance partners. Participants are expected to sustain more effective relationships over time by sharing information and by being knowledgeable about each other's organization.

Age of relationship had a significant negative effect on the partnership quality. Among the components of partnership quality, conflict and commitment were significantly associated with age of relationship. However, contrary to many expectations, age of relationship had a positive effect on conflict and a negative effect on commitment. Interestingly, mutual dependency was also negatively associated with partnership quality. This means that the degree of partnership quality was lower when mutual dependency was higher. Although mutual dependency had a significant effect on business understanding, benefit and risk share, and conflict, these results were contrary to the researchers' expectation. The relationship between top management support and partnership quality was significant. Top management support also was significantly associated with trust and business understanding, while it was not related to benefit and risk share, conflict, or commitment.

In Figure 8.6, there is a causal relationship between partnership quality and outsourcing success. Successful partnership enables participants to achieve organizational objectives and to build a competitive advantage that each organization could not easily attain by itself. To gain these advantages of partnership, participants should try to enhance their partnership quality to reflect the extent of intimacy between partners. Therefore, a higher quality of partnership is likely to lead to a successful outsourcing relationship.

Outsourcing success can be viewed as the level of fitness between the customer's requirements and the outsourcing outcomes. Lee and Kim (1999) measured outsourcing success in terms of both business and user perspectives in the following way: They expected to find a positive relationship between outsourcing success and components of partnership quality such as trust, business understanding, benefit/risk share, and commitment, and a negative relationship between outsourcing success and conflict. In a business perspective, outsourcing is motivated by the promise of strategic, economic, and technological benefits. The success of outsourcing, then, should be assessed in terms of attainment of these benefits. Strategic benefits refer to the ability of a firm to focus on its core business by outsourcing routine information technology activities. Economic benefits refer to the ability of a firm to use expertise and economies of scale in human and technological resources of the service provider and to manage its cost structure through unambiguous contractual arrangements. Technological benefits refer to the ability of a firm to gain access to leading edge IT and to avoid the risk of technological obsolescence that results from dynamic changes in IT. From a user perspective, outsourcing success may also be the level of quality of offered services. A decision to outsource on the basis of saving costs without analysis of the quality of service frequently leads to higher costs and lower user satisfaction. Therefore, it is imperative to conduct a proper analysis of the service quality before building a relationship with a service provider for a successful outsourcing project.

In their statistical analysis, Lee and Kim (1999) found that the quality of outsourcing partnership had a strong positive relationship with both business satisfaction and user satisfaction, as well as with overall outsourcing success. Trust showed a strong positive relationship with business satisfaction, while it had no effect on user satisfaction. This indicates that trust is a critical predictor of outsourcing success in terms of the business perspective, as opposed to the user perspective. Unlike the result with trust, business understanding was not a good predictor of business satisfaction, while it significantly influenced user satisfaction. This means that the outsourcing outcome matched the users' requirements as understanding of its partner's business increased. Benefit and risk share showed a strong positive relationship with both business satisfaction and user satisfaction, as well as with overall outsourcing success.

Although conflict was a predictor of business satisfaction, it had no effect on the overall outsourcing success and user satisfaction. Lee and Kim's (1999) finding for the conflict variable indicated that outsourcing success was not affected by the degree of conflict between the service receiver and provider. Their study also indicated that commitment was significantly associated with outsourcing success in terms of both the business and the user perspective. In summary, all partnership quality variables except conflict were significantly related to outsourcing success.

Partnership Quality Dynamics

As has become quite well known by reading this book so far, the findings in Figure 6.1 have obvious limitations. Rather than focusing on determinants that have a one-on-one relationship with partnership quality, there are interactions, as illustrated in Figure 6.2. Figure 6.2 illustrates some of the cause and effect relationships and feedback loops when partnership quality is studied as a function of time.

Figure 6.2. Causal loop diagram for outsourcing partnership quality dynamics

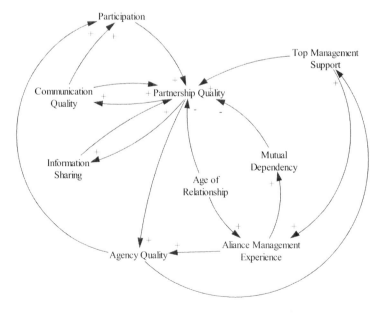

Figure 6.3. Reference mode for outsourcing partnership quality

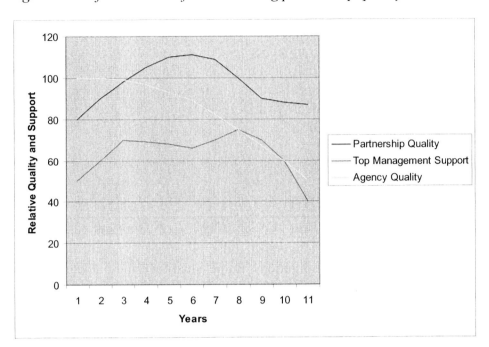

The causal loop diagram in Figure 6.2 might produce different simulation results depending on parameters for quantitative relationships. One possible outcome is illustrated in Figure 6.3. We see partnership quality initially rising in the first years of the outsourcing relationship. In year 6, the relationship reaches its top quality, before it starts to deteriorate. Top management support for the outsourcing arrangement remains for 2s more years, but this variable as well starts to deteriorate in year 8. Because of such developments, the vendor starts to practice opportunistic behavior, causing a fast deterioration in agency quality.

References

Artz, K. W., & Brush, T. H. (2000). Asset specificity, uncertainty and relational norms: An examination of coordination costs in collaborative strategic alliances. *Journal of Economic Behavior & Organization, 41,* 337-362.

Das, T. K., & Teng, B.-S. (2002). The dynamics of alliance conditions in the alliance development process. *Journal of Management Studies, 39*(5), 725-746.

Das, T. K., & Teng, B.-S. (2003). Partner analysis and alliance performance. *Scandinavian Journal of Management, 19,* 279-308.

Eisenhardt, K. M. (1985). Control: Organizational and economic approaches. *Management Science, 31*(2), 134-149.

Gottschalk, P., & Solli-Sæther, H. (2006). *Managing successful IT outsourcing relationships.* Hershey, PA: Idea Group Publishing.

Hancox, M., & Hackney, R. (2000). IT outsourcing: Frameworks for conceptualizing practice and perception. *Information Systems Journal, 10*(3), 217-237.

Jensen, M. C., & Meckling, W. H. (1976). Theory of the firm: Managerial behavior, agency costs and ownership structures. *Journal of Financial Economics, 3*(4), 305-360.

Kern, T., & Blois, K. (2002). Norm development in outsourcing relationship. *Journal of Information Technology, 17,* 32-42.

Lambe, C. J., Spekman, R. E., & Hunt, S. D. (2000). Interimistic relational exchange: Conceptualization and propositional development. *Journal of the Academy of Marketing Science, 28*(2), 212-225.

Lambe, C. J., Spekman, R. E., & Hunt, S. D. (2002). Alliance competence, resources, and alliance success: Conceptualization, measurement, and initial test. *Journal of the Academy of Marketing Science, 30*(2), 141-158.

Lee, J.-N., & Kim, Y.-G. (1999). Effect of partnership quality on IS outsourcing success: Conceptual framework and empirical validation. *Journal of Management Information Systems, 15*(4), 29-61.

Rokkan, A. I., & Haugland, S. A. (2002). Developing relational exchange: Effectiveness and power. *European Journal of Marketing, 36*(1), 211-230.

Ross, J. W., & Weill, P. (2002, November). Six IT decisions your IT people shouldn't make. *Harvard Business Review*, 84-91.

Chapter VII

Corporate Strategic Management

Over the last several decades, strategy researchers have devoted attention to the question of how corporate elites (i.e., corporate executives and directors) affect corporate strategy. The CEO as a person in position shapes the scope of the firm, while the CIO as a person in another position shapes the scope of IT in the firm. Jensen and Zajac (2004) proposed and tested the notion that while differences in individual characteristics of corporate elites may imply different preferences for particular corporate strategies such as diversification and acquisitions, these basic preferences, when situated in different agency contexts (e.g., CIO, CEO) generate very different strategic outcomes.

This kind of strategy dynamics caused by the relationship between the CIO and the organization will be discussed in the next chapter. First, we will discuss business dynamics caused by information technology strategy in this chapter.

Strategy can simply be defined as principles, a broad-based formula, to be applied in order to achieve a purpose. These principles are general guidelines guiding the daily work to reach business goals. Strategy is the pattern of resource allocation decisions made throughout the organization. These encapsulate both desired goals and beliefs about what are acceptable and, most critically, unacceptable means for achieving them.

While the business strategy is the broadest pattern of resource allocation decisions, more specific decisions are related to information systems and information technology. Information Systems must be seen both in a business and an IT context. Information Systems is in the middle because IS supports the business while using IT. This will be discussed later in this book in terms of IT governance as strategic alignment.

Why is strategic IS/IT planning undertaken within business organizations? Hann and Weber (1996) see IS/IT planning as a set of activities directed toward achieving the following objectives:

1. Recognizing organizational opportunities and problems where IS/IT might be applied successfully

2. Identifying the resources needed to allow IS/IT to be applied successfully to these opportunities and problems

3. Developing strategies and procedures to allow IS/IT to be applied successfully to these opportunities and problems

4. Establishing a basis for monitoring and bonding IT managers so their actions are more likely to be congruent with the goals of their superiors

5. Resolving how the gains and losses from unforeseen circumstances will be distributed among senior management and the IT manager

6. Determining the level of decision rights to be delegated to the IT manager

Empirical studies of IS/IT planning practices in organizations indicate that wide variations exist. Hann and Weber (1996) found that organizations differ in terms of how much IS/IT planning they do, the planning methodologies they use, the personnel involved in planning, the strength of the linkage between IS/IT plans and corporate plans, the focus of IS/IT plans (e.g., strategic systems versus resource needs), and the way in which IS/IT plans are implemented.

It has been argued that the Internet renders strategic planning obsolete. In reality, it is more important than ever for companies to do strategic planning:

Many have argued that the Internet renders strategy obsolete. In reality, the opposite is true. Because the Internet tends to weaken industry profitability without providing proprietary operational advantages, it is more important than ever for companies to distinguish themselves through strategy. The winners will be those that view the Internet as a complement to, not a cannibal of, traditional ways of competing. (Porter 2001, p. 63)

The Y model provides a coherent step-by-step procedure for development of an IS/IT strategy, as will be explained a little later in this book.

Strategic Planning

Often, strategy development is equated with strategic planning procedures. They represent the design approach to managing strategy. Such procedures may take the form of highly systematized, step-by-step, chronological procedures involving many different parts of the organization. For example, the annual strategic planning cycle in a company may follow a procedure like this:

1. **May:** Broad strategic direction.
2. **June:** Review of current strategy.
3. **August:** Goals for business units.
4. **September:** Strategies for business units.
5. **October:** Board meeting to agree strategic plan.
6. **November:** Board meeting to agree operational plan and budget.

Some of the key concepts in strategic planning are future thinking, controlling the future, decision making, integrated decision –making, and a formalized procedure to produce an articulated result in the form of an integrated process of decisions. Strategic planning is the process of deciding on the projects that the organization will undertake and the approximate amount of resources that will be allocated to each program over the next several years.

"Planning" represents the extent to which decision-makers look into the future and use formal planning methodologies. Planning is something we do in advance of taking action; it is anticipatory decision making. We make decisions before action is required. The focus of planning revolves around objectives, which are the heart of a strategic plan. According to Mintzberg (1994), planning has the following characteristics:

- **Planning is future thinking:** It is taking the future into account. Planning denotes thinking about the future. Planning is action laid out in advance.

- **Planning is controlling the future:** It is not just thinking about it but achieving it, enacting it. Planning is the design of a desired future and of effective ways of bringing it about. It is to create controlled change in the environment.

- **Planning is decision making:** Planning is the conscious determination of courses of action designed to accomplish purposes. Planning entails those activities that are concerned specifically with determining in advance what actions and/or human and physical resources are required to reach a goal. It includes identifying alternatives, analyzing each one, and selecting the best ones.

- **Planning is integrated decision making:** It means fitting together ongoing activities into a meaningful whole. Planning implies getting somewhat more organized, and making a feasible commitment around which already available courses of action get organized. This definition may seem close to the preceding one. But because it is concerned not so much with the making of decisions as with the conscious attempt to integrate different ones, it is fundamentally different and begins to identify a position for planning.

- **Planning is a formalized procedure to produce an articulated result, in the form of an integrated system of decisions:** What captures the notion of planning above all—what most clearly distinguishes its literature and differentiates its practice from other processes—is its emphasis on formalization, the systemization of the phenomenon to which planning is meant to apply. Planning is a set of concepts, procedures, and tests. Formalization here means three things: (a) to decompose, (b) to articulate, and (c) to rationalize the process by which decisions are made and integrated in organizations.

Given that this is planning, the question becomes, why do it? Mintzberg (1994) provides the following answers:

- Organizations must plan to coordinate their activities.

- Organizations must plan to ensure that the future is taken into account.

- Organizations must plan to be rational in terms of formalized planning.

- Organizations must plan to control.

"Strategy" is both a plan for the future and a pattern from the past; it is the match an organization makes between its internal resources and skills (sometimes collectively called competencies) and the opportunities and risks created by its external environments. Strategy is the long-term direction of an organization. Strategy is a course of action for achieving an organization's purpose. Strategy is the direction and scope of an organization over the long term, which achieves advantage for the organization through its configuration of resources within a changing environment and fulfills stakeholder expectations (Johnson & Scholes, 2002).

Strategy as a plan is a direction, a guide, or course of action into the future, a path to get from here to there. Strategy as a pattern is a consistency in behavior over time. Strategy as a position is the determination of particular products in particular markets. Strategy as perspective is an organization's way of doing things (Mintzberg, 1994).

Strategic planning does not attempt to make future decisions, as decisions can be made only in the present. Planning requires that choices be made among possible events in the future, but decisions made in their light can be made only in the present. Once made, these decisions may have long-term, irrevocable consequences. Strategic planning has many benefits for an organization:

- It can provide a structured means of *analysis and thinking* about complex strategic problems, at its best requiring managers to *question and challenge* the received wisdom they take for granted.

- It can encourage a *longer-term view* of strategy than might otherwise occur. Planning horizons vary, of course. In a fast-moving consumer goods company, 3- to 5-year plans may be appropriate. In companies which have to take very long-term views on capital investment, such as those in the oil industry, planning horizons can be as long as 14 years (in Exxon) or 20 years (in Shell).

- It can be used as a means of *control* by regularly reviewing performance and progress against agreed-upon objectives or previously agreed-upon strategic direction.

- It can be a useful means of *coordination*, for example by bringing together the various business unit strategies within an overall corporate strategy, or ensuring that resources within a business are coordinated to put strategy into effect.

- Strategic planning may also help to *communicate* an intended strategy.

- It can be used as a way of involving people in strategy development, therefore perhaps helping to create *ownership* of the strategy.

- *Planning systems may provide a sense of security and logic for the organization and, in particular, management, who believe they should be proactively determining the future strategy and exercising control over the destiny of the organization.* (Johnson & Scholes, 2002, p. 61)

In the strategic planning perspective on strategy formation, strategies are intentionally designed, much as an engineer designs a bridge. Building a bridge requires a long formulation phase, including extensive analysis of the situation, the drawing up of a number of rough designs, evaluation of these alternatives, choice of a preferred design, and further detailing in the form of a blueprint. Only after the design phase has been completed do the construction companies take over and build according to plan. Characteristic of such a planning approach to producing bridges and strategies is that the entire process can be disassembled into a number of distinct steps that need to be carried out in a sequential and orderly way. Only by going through these steps in a conscious and structured manner will the best results be obtained (Wit & Meyer, 2004).

The whole purpose of strategizing is to give organizations direction, instead of letting them drift. Organizations cannot act rationally without intentions —if you do not know where you are going, any behavior is fine. By first setting a goal and then choosing a strategy to get there, organizations can get organized. A structure can be chosen, tasks can be assigned, responsibilities can be divided, budgets can be allotted and targets can be set. Not unimportantly, a control system can be created to measure results in comparison to the plan, so that corrective action can be taken (Wit & Meyer, 2004).

Another advantage of the planning approach to strategy formation is that it allows for the formalization and differentiation of strategy tasks. Because of its highly structured and sequential nature, strategic planning lends itself well to formalization. The steps of the strategic planning approach can be captured in planning procedures to enhance and organize the strategy formation process. In such planning procedures, not all elements of strategy formation need to be carried out by one and the same person, but can be divided among a number of people. The most important division of labor is often between those formulating the plans and those implementing them (Wit & Meyer, 2004).

In many large companies the managers proposing the plans are also the ones implementing them, but deciding on the plans is passed up to a higher level. Often, other tasks are spun off as well, or shared with others, such as diagnosis (strategy department or external consultants), implementation (staff departments), and evaluation (corporate planner and controller). Such task differentiation and specialization can lead to better use of management talent, much as the division of labor has improved the field of production. At the same, having a formalized procedure allows for sufficient coordination and mutual adjustment, to ensure that all specialized elements are integrated back into a consistent organization-wide strategy (Wit & Meyer, 2004).

An important advantage of strategic planning is that it encourages long-term thinking and commitment. Strategic planning directs attention to the future. Managers making strategic plans have to take a more long-term view and are stimulated to prepare for, or even create, the future. Instead of just focusing on small steps, planning challenges managers to define a desirable future and to work toward it. Instead of wavering and opportunism, strategic planning commits the organization to a course of action and allows for investments to be made at the present that may only pay off in the long run (Wit & Meyer, 2004).

Corporate strategy is concerned with the strategic decisions at the corporate level of organizationswhich decisions may affect many business units. Managers at this level are acting on behalf of shareholders, or other stakeholders, to provide services and, quite possibly, strategic guidance to business units which they themselves seek to generate value by interacting with customers. In these circumstances a key question is to what extent and how might the corporate level add value to what the businesses do, or at the least how it might avoid destroying value (Johnson & Scholes, 2002).

A multibusiness company structure may consist of a number of business units grouped within divisions and a corporate center or head office providing, perhaps, legal services, financial services, and the staff of the chief executive. There are different views as to what is meant by corporate strategy and what represents corporate at distinct from business-level strategy. Johnson and Scholes (2002) argue that anything above the business unit level represents corporate activity.

The levels of management above business units are often referred to as the corporate parent. So, for example, the divisions within a corporation, which look after several businesses, act in a corporate parenting role. The corporate parenting role can be as:

- **The portfolio manager:** A corporate parent acting as an agent on behalf of financial markets and shareholders with a view to enhancing the value attained from the various businesses in a more efficient or effective way than financial markets could. Their role is to identify and acquire undervalued assets or businesses and improve them.

- **The restructurer:** A corporate parent identifying restructuring opportunities in businesses and having the skills to intervene to transform performance in those businesses. They may well hold a diverse range of businesses within their portfolio. However, they do have a limited role at business-unit level, which is to identify ways in which businesses can be turned around or fitness improved and to manage the restructuring period.

Figure 7.1. Corporate strategy above other levels

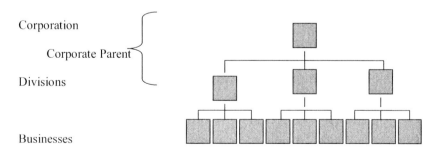

- **The synergy manager:** Synergy is often seen as the main reason for the existence of the corporate parent. Potentially, synergy can occur in situations where two or more activities or processes complement each other, to the extent that their combined effect is greater than the sum of the parts. In terms of corporate strategy, the logic is that value can be enhanced across business units. This can be done in a number of ways—activities might be shared, and there may exist common skills or competencies across businesses.

- **The parental developer:** A corporate parent seeks to employ its own competencies as a parent to add value to its businesses. Here, the issue is not so much about how it can help create or develop benefits across business units or transference between business units, as in the case of managing synergy. Rather, parental developers have to enhance the potential of business units. (Johnson & Scholes, 2002)

In our strategic planning perspective, corporate strategy will depend on the main role of the corporate parent. The portfolio manager is not directly intervening in the strategies of business units. Rather, they are setting financial targets, making central evaluations about the well-being and future prospects of such businesses and investing or divesting accordingly. The restructurer is directly intervening in business units, as it is likely that the business restructuring opportunities that will be sought will be those that match the skills of the corporate center. The synergy manager will initiate activities and develop resources that are shared across business units. Managers in the businesses have to be prepared to cooperate in such transference and sharing (Johnson & Scholes, 2002).

Finally, the parental developer has to enhance the potential of business units in various ways. Suppose, for example, it has a great deal of experience in globalizing domestically based businesses, or a valuable brand that may enhance the performance of image of a business, or perhaps specialist skills in financial management, brand marketing, or research and development. If such parenting competencies exist, corporate managers then need to identify a parenting opportunity—a business or businesses which are not fulfilling their potential and where improvement could be made by the application of the competencies of the parent (Johnson & Scholes, 2002).

Strategic management includes understanding the strategic position of an organization, strategic choices for the future, and turning strategy into action.

Understanding the strategic position is concerned with impact on strategy of the external environment, internal resources and competences, and the expectations and influence of stakeholders. Strategic choices involve understanding the underlying bases for future strategy at both the corporate and business unit levels and the options for developing strategy in terms of both the directions in which strategy might move and the methods of development. Translating strategy into action is concerned with ensuring that strategies are working in practice. A strategy is not just a good idea, a statement, or a plan. It is only meaningful when it is actually being carried out (Johnson & Scholes, 2002).

Generally, there are some characteristics of strategic decisions that are usually associated with the word "strategy":

- Strategy is likely to be concerned with long-term direction of an organization.
- Strategic decisions are normally about trying to achieve some advantage for the organization over competition.
- Strategic decisions are likely to be concerned with the scope of an organization's activities.
- Strategy can be seen as the matching of the resources and activities of an organization to the environment in which it operates.
- Strategy can also be seen as building on or expanding an organization's resources and competencies to create opportunities or to capitalize on them.
- Strategies may require major resource changes for an organization.
- Strategic decisions are likely to affect operational decisions.
- The strategy of an organization is affected not only by environmental forces and resource availability, but also by the values and expectations of those who have power in and around the organization. (Johnson & Scholes, 2002)

The notion of strategic fit is developing strategy by identifying opportunities in the business environment and adapting resources and competences so as to take advantage of these. The correct positioning of the organization is important, for example in terms of the extent to which it meets clearly identified market needs. Strategic position is concerned with the impact on strategy of the external environment, internal resources, and competencies, and the expectations and influence of stakeholders (Johnson & Scholes, 2002).

Strategy development is here equated with strategic planning procedures. They represent the design approach to managing strategy, which views strategy development as the deliberate positioning of the organization through a rational, analytic, structured, and directive process. "Strategy as design" is an important strategy lens. Alternative and supplementing lenses are "strategy as experience" and "strategy as ideas." "Strategy as experience" suggests that strategies develop in an adaptive fashion and change gradually. Strategy is here understood in terms of continuity—once an organization has adopted a particular strategy, it tends to develop from and within that strategy, rather than fundamentally changing direction. "Strategy as ideas" sees strategy as the emergence of order and innovation from the variety and diversity that exists in and around an organization. New ideas, and therefore innovation, may come from anywhere in an organization or from stimuli in the world around it (Johnson & Scholes, 2002).

In addition to strategic planning, strategy development and strategy formation are also concerned with concepts such as strategic leadership, organizational politics, strategic incrementalism, the learning organization, imposed strategy, and multiple processes of strategy development. A strategic leader is an individual upon whom strategy development and change are seen to be dependent. Managers often suggest that the strategy being followed by the organization is really the outcome of organizational politics in terms of the bargaining and power politics that go on between important executives. Managers may have a view of where they want the organization to be in years to come and try to move toward this position incrementally, where strategic incrementalism can be though of as the deliberate development of strategy by learning through doing over time. The concept of the "learning organization" and strategy as a learning process implies continual regeneration of strategy from the variety of knowledge, experience, and skills of individuals with a culture, which encourages mutual questioning and challenge around a shared purpose or vision. Forces or agencies external to the organization may cause imposed strategy that the organization has to follow. Different lenses and different strategy development processes may cause multiple processes of strategy development, since there is no right way in which strategies are developed (Johnson & Scholes, 2002).

At the beginning of this subchapter on strategic planning, strategy was defined as a course of action for achieving an organization's purpose. Where managers have a clear understanding of their organization's purpose, this can provide strong guidance during processes of strategic thinking, strategy formation, and strategic change. The organizational purpose can function as a fundamental principle against which strategic options can be evaluated. "Organizational purpose" can be defined as the reason for which an organization exists. The broader set of fundamental principles giving direction to strategic decision making, of which organizational purpose is the central element, is referred to as the corporate mission. The corporate mission may have elements such as organizational beliefs, organizational values, and business definition (Wit & Meyer, 2004).

Some authors distinguish between deliberate strategy and emergent strategy as two alternative processes of strategy formulation. According to Christensen and Raynor (2003), deliberate strategy, such as strategic planning, is the appropriate tool for organizing action if three conditions are met. First, the strategy must encompass and address correctly all of the important details required to succeed, and those responsible for implementation must understand each important detail in management's deliberate strategy. Second, if the organization is to take collective action, the strategy needs to make as much sense to all employees as they view the world from their own context as it does to top management, so that they will all act appropriately and consistently. Finally, the collective intentions must be realized with little unanticipated influence from outside political, technological, and market forces.

"Emergent strategy" bubbles up from within the organization, and is the cumulative effect of day-to-day prioritization and investment decisions made by middle managers, engineers, salespeople, and financial staff. These tend to be tactical, day-to-day operating decisions that are made by people who are not in a visionary, futuristic, or strategic state of mind (Christensen & Raynor, 2003).

Some authors distinguish between intended strategy and realized strategy. Intended strategy is an expression of desired strategic direction deliberately formulated and planned by managers. Realized strategy is the strategy actually being followed by an organization in practice. Strategic drift occurs when an organization's strategy gradually moves away from relevance to the forces at work in its environment. (Johnson & Scholes, 2002).

As we will see throughout this book, strategic planning procedures apply methods for analysis, choice, and implementation. A general method is available in terms of strategy maps as defined by Kaplan and Norton (2004), which represent interesting perspectives on strategy development and strategy formation. Strategy maps are used to describe how the organization creates value, and they were developed for the balanced scorecard. The strategy map is based on several principles:

- **Strategy balances contradictory forces:** Investing in intangible assets for long-term revenue growth usually conflicts with cutting costs for short-term financial performance.

- **Strategy is based on a differentiated customer value proposition:** Satisfying customers is the source of sustainable value creation.

- **Value is created through internal business processes:** The financial and customer perspectives in strategy maps and balanced scorecards describe the outcomes, that is, what the organization hopes to achieve.

- **Strategy consists of simultaneous, complementary themes:** Operations management, customer management, innovation, regulations, and societal expectations deliver benefits at different points in time.

- **Strategic alignment determines the value of intangible assets:** Human capital, information capital, and organization capital are intangible assets.

Understanding the strategic position of an organization and considering the strategic choices open to it are of little value unless the strategies managers wish to follow can be turned into organizational action. Strategies cannot take effect until they take shape in action. Such action takes form in the day-to-day processes and relationships that exist in organizations, and these need to be managed desirably in line with the intended strategy (Johnson & Scholes, 2002).

Translating strategies into action is no simple task. First, it is important to organize for success by introducing appropriate structure, processes, relationships, and boundaries. Second, it is important to enable success by managing people, managing information, managing finance, managing technology, and integrating resources. Finally, strategic change has to be managed by diagnosing the change situation, applying relevant styles and roles, and implementing levers for managing strategic change, such as organizational routines and symbolic processes (Johnson & Scholes, 2002).

The design school of strategic planning is built on the belief that strategy formation is a process of conception—the use of a few basic ideas to design strategy. Of these, the most essential is that of congruence, or fit, between external and organizational factors. A number of premises underlie the design school (Mintzberg, 1994):

1.   Strategy formation should be a controlled, conscious process of thought.

2.   Responsibility for the process must rest with the chief executive officer; that person is *the* strategist.

3.   The model of strategy formation must be kept simple and informal.

4.   Strategies should be unique: The best ones result from a process of creative design.

5.   Strategies must come out of the design process fully developed.

6.   The strategies should be made explicit and, if possible, articulated, which means they have to be kept simple.

7.   Finally, once these unique, full-blown, explicit, and simple strategies are fully formulated, they must then be implemented.

Strategic Planning and Firm Performance

Numerous researchers and executives advocate strategic planning. They argue that an explicit planning process rather than haphazard guesswork results in the collection and interpretation of data critical to creating and maintaining organization-environment alignment. They argue that planning generally produces better alignment and financial results than does trial-and-error learning (Miller & Cardinal, 1994).

Despite the intuitive appeal of these arguments, several researchers have countered that explicit strategic planning is dysfunctional, or at best irrelevant. One of the most widely circulated criticisms is that planning yields too much rigidity. Proponents of the rigidity hypothesis maintain than a plan channels attention and behavior to an unacceptable degree, driving out important in-novations that are not part of the plan. Given that the future parameters of even relatively stable industries are difficult to predict, these theoreticians consider any reduction in creative thinking and action dysfunctional (Miller & Cardinal, 1994).

Miller and Cardinal (1994) developed a model that might explain the inconsistent planning-performance findings reported in previous research. Results from the model suggest that strategic planning positively influences firm performance. Researchers who have concluded that planning does not generally benefit performance appear to have been incorrect.

Measurement of Competitive Strategy

The measurement of competitive strategy is an important issue in strategic management. Porter (1985) first defined three generic competitive strategies: cost leadership, differentiation, and focus. Attempts to measure these strategies seek to capture differences in the extent to which firms emphasize various competitive dimensions. Competitive strategy is traditionally measured at the business level. Yet businesses often consist of product portfolios in which a different competitive strategy is used for each product. Thus, business-level measures may not be good indicators of product-level competitive strategy. Further, business-level analyses have found combined cost-leadership and differentiation strategies. But if competitive strategies are formulated at the product level, it is unclear whether combined strategies exist at that level.

Nayyar (1993) examined these issues. He found that business-level measures are not good indicators of product-level competitive strategies. I also found no evidence supporting the existence of combined competitive strategies at the product level. He found that cost-leadership and differentiation are mutually exclusive at the product level. They do not appear to be two dimensions of any strategy. Previously used business-level measures tend to identify combined competitive strategies, a result that may reflect the existence of product portfolios rather than combined competitive strategies.

These findings suggest a need for a reexamination of the concept of competitive strategies. It appears that firms use competitive strategies for products and then construct product portfolios to obtain overall cost, differentiation, and preemption advantages. Within any industry, different firms may construct different product portfolios.

In his measurement of competitive strategy, Nayyar (1993) used the following competitive dimensions associated with a cost-leadership strategy: operating efficiency, cost control, pricing below competitors, managing raw materials cost and availability, trade sales promotion, manufacturing process improvements and innovation, and product cost reduction. The following competitive dimensions were associated with a differentiation strategy: new product development, extensive customer service, building and maintaining brand equity, marketing innovation, influence over distribution channels, targeting high-priced segment/s, advertising, building and maintaining the firm's reputation, providing product/s with many features, and premium product quality. The following competitive dimensions were associated with a focus strategy: serving special market segment/s and manufacturing and selling customized products.

Instead of measuring competitive strategy in terms of alternative strategies, Julien and Ramangalahy (2003) measured competitive strategy in terms of intensity. The more competitive a strategy is, the more intense is the competitive strategy. The intensity was measured in terms of marketing differentiation, segmentation differentiation, innovation differentiation, and products service. Marketing differentiation is based on competitive pricing, brand development, control over distribution, advertising, and innovation in terms of marketing techniques. Segmentation differentiation relies on the ability to offer specialized products to specific customer groups. Innovation differentiation is based on the ability to offer new and technologically superior products. Product service is based on the quality of the products and services provided by customers.

Competitive strategy must drive other strategies in the firm, such as knowledge strategy. Executives must be able to articulate why customers buy a company's products or services rather than those of its competitors. What value do customers expect from the company? How does knowledge that resides in the company add value for customers? Assuming the competitive strategy is clear, managers will want to consider three further questions that can help them choose a primary knowledge management strategy (Hansen, Nohria, & Tierny, 1999):

- **Do you offer standardized or customized products?** Companies that follow a standardized product strategy sell products that do not vary much, if at all. A knowledge management strategy based on reuse fits companies that are creating standardized products.

- **Do you have a mature or innovative product?** A business strategy based on mature products typically benefits most from a reuse of existing knowledge.

- **Do your people rely on explicit or tacit knowledge to solve problems?**
  Explicit knowledge is knowledge that can be codified, such as simple
  software code and market data.

Strategic planning in a turbulent environment is challenging. The challenge of
making strategy when the future is unknowable encourages reconsideration
of both the process of strategy formulation and the nature of organizational
strategy. Attempts to reconcile systematic strategic planning with turbulent, un-
predictable business environments included the following (Grant, 2003):

- **Scenario planning:** Multiple scenario planning seeks not to predict
  the future but to envisage alternative views of the future in the form
  of distinct configurations of key environmental variables. Abandoning
  single-point forecasts in favor of alternative futures implies forsaking
  single-point plans in favor of strategy alternatives, emphasizing strategic
  flexibility that creates option values.

- **Strategic intent and the role of vision:** If uncertainty precludes planning in any detailed sense, then strategy is primarily concerned with
  establishing broad parameters for the development of the enterprise
  with regard to domain selection and domain navigation. Uncertainty
  requires that strategy is concerned less with specific actions and more
  with establishing clarity of direction within which short-term flexibility
  can be reconciled with overall coordination of strategic decisions.

- **Strategic innovation:** If established companies are to prosper and
  survive, new external environments require new strategies. Strategic
  planning may be a source of institutional inertia rather than innovation.
  Yet systematic approaches to strategy can be encouraging to managers to explore alternatives beyond the scope of their prior experiences.
  Strategic inertia may be more to do with the planners than of planning
  per se.

- **Complexity and self-organization:** Often faced with a constantly
  changing fitness landscape, an organization's maximizing survival
  implies constant exploration, parallel exploration efforts by different
  organizational members, and the combination of incremental steps. A
  key feature of strategic processes is the presence of semi structures that
  create plans, standards, and responsibilities for certain activities while
  allowing freedom elsewhere. One application of the semi structure

concept to strategy formulation concerns the use of simple rules that permit adaptation while establishing bounds that can prevent companies from falling off the edge of chaos.

Hopkins and Hopkins (1997) investigated relationships among managerial, environmental, and organizational factors, strategic planning intensity, and financial performance in U.S. banks. The results suggested that the intensity with which banks engage in the strategic planning process has a direct, positive effect on banks' financial performance, and mediates the effects of managerial and organizational factors on banks' performance. Results also indicated a reciprocal relationship between strategic planning intensity and performance. That is, strategic planning intensity causes better performance and, in turn, better performance causes greater strategic planning intensity.

Strategic planning takes many different forms in different organizations. However, Boyd and Reuning-Elliotts' (1998) study of strategic planning provide strong support for the measurement properties of the strategic planning construct. In particular, the study results indicate that strategic planning is a construct that can be reliably measured through seven indicators: mission statement, trend analysis, competitor analysis, long-term goals, annual goals, short-term action plans, and ongoing evaluation. This evidence is important because previous researchers neither tested often for dimensionality of the planning construct, nor did most studies report tests of the reliability of their measures.

A small, entrepreneurial startup may operate without any explicit strategy. The firm's strategy is likely to exist only in the head of the founder, and apart from being articulated through verbal communication with employees, suppliers, and other interested parties, may have been made explicit only when a business plan was required by outside investors. Most corporations with an established management structure tend to have some form of strategic planning process, though in small, single-business companies the strategy process may be highly informal, with no regular cycle, and may result in little documentation. Most larger companies, especially those with multiple businesses, have more systematic strategic planning processes, the outcome of which is a documented plan that integrates the business plans of the individual divisions (Grant, 2003).

Whether formal or informal, systematic or ad hoc, documented or not, the strategy formulation process is an important vehicle for achieving coordination within a company. The strategy process occupies multiple roles within the firm. It is in part a coordination device encouraging consistency between the decisions being made at different levels and in different parts of the organization. And it is in part a mechanism for driving performance by establishing consensus around ambitious long-term targets and by inspiring organizational members through creating vision and a sense of mission. In these roles, the strategy process can be important in achieving both coordination and cooperation (Grant, 2003).

The system through which strategy is formulated varies considerably from company to company. Even after the entrepreneurial startup has grown into a large company, strategy making may remain the preserve of the chief executive. Medium-sized, single-business companies typically have simple strategic planning processes where functional managers provide key inputs such as financial projections and market analysis, but the key elements of strategy—goals, new business developments, capital investment, and key competitive initiatives—are decided by the chief executive (Grant, 2003).

The more systematized strategic planning processes typical of large companies with separate divisions or business units traditionally follow an annual cycle. Strategic plans tend to be for three to five years and combine top-down initiatives (indications of performance expectations and identification of key strategic initiatives) and bottom-up business plans (proposed strategies and financial forecasts for individual divisions and business units). After discussion between the corporate level and the individual businesses, the business plans are amended and agreed and integrated into an overall corporate plan that is presented to and agreed by the board of directors (Grant, 2003).

The resulting strategic plan typically comprises the following elements (Grant, 2003):

- A statement of the goals the company seeks to achieve over the planning period with regard to both financial targets and strategic goals.

- A set of assumptions or forecasts about key developments in the external environment to which the company must respond.

- A qualitative statement of how the shape of the business will be changing in relation to geographical and segment emphasis, and the basis on which the company will be establishing and extending its competitive advantage.

- Specific action steps with regard to decisions and projects, supported by a set of mileposts stating what is to be achieved by specific dates.

- A set of financial projections, including a capital expenditure budget and outline operating budgets.

Although directed toward making decisions that are documented in written strategic plans, the important elements of strategic planning form the strategy process: the dialog through which knowledge is shared and ideas communicated, the establishment of consensus, and the commitment to action and results (Grant, 2003).

The Y Model for Strategy Work

In all kinds of strategy work, there are three steps. The first is concerned with analysis. The second step is concerned with choice (selection and decision), and the final step is concerned with implementation.

We now introduce a model for strategy work. This is illustrated in Figure 7.2. The model consists of seven stages covering analysis, choice, and implementation. The stages are as follows (Gottschalk, 2005):

1. **Describe current situation:** The current IS/IT situation in the business can be described using several methods. The benefits method identifies benefits from use of IS/IT in the business. Distinctions are made between rationalization benefits, control benefits, organizational benefits, and market benefits. Other methods include the three-era model, management activities, and stages of growth.

2. **Describe desired situation:** The desired business situation can be described using several methods. Examples of methods are value configuration, competitive strategy, management strategy, business process redesign, knowledge management, the Internet and electronic business, and information technology benefits (Gottschalk, 2005).

3. **Analyze and prioritize needs for change:** After descriptions of the current situation and the desired situation, needs for change can be identified. The gap between desired and current situation is called needs for change. Analysis is to provide details on needs, what change is needed, and how changes can take place. *What*-analysis will create an understanding of vision and goals, knowledge strategy, market strategy,

and corporate problems and opportunities. *How*-analysis will create an understanding of technology trends and applications. These analyses should result in proposals for new IS/IT in the organization.

4. **Seek alternative actions:** When needs for change have been identified and proposals for filling gaps have been developed, alternative actions for improving the current situation can be developed. New IS/IT can be developed, acquired, and implemented in alternative ways. For example, an information system can be developed in-house by company staff, it can be purchased as a standard application from a vendor, or it can be leased from an application systems provider (ASP).

5. **Select actions and make an action plan:** When needs for change and alternative actions have been identified, several choices have to be made and documented in an action plan. Important issues here include development process, user involvement, time frame, and financial budget for IS/IT projects.

6. **Implement plan and describe results:** This is the stage of action. Technical equipment such as servers, PCs, printers, and cables are installed. Operating systems are installed. Application packages, software programs, programming tools, end user tools, and database systems are installed. Development projects are organized. Management and user training takes place. Document results over time.

7. **Evaluate results:** Implementation results are compared with needs for change. It is determined to what extent gaps between desired and current situation have been closed. This is the beginning of the IS/IT strategy revision process, where a new process through the Y model takes place. Typically, a new IS/IT strategy process should take place every other year in business organizations.

While stages 1 to 3 cover *analysis*, 4 and 5 cover *choice*, and 6 and 7 cover *implementation*. In some strategy models, stage 2 is listed as the first stage. It is here recommended to do stage 1 before stage 2. It is easier to describe the ideal situation when you know the current situation. If you start out with stage 2, it often feels difficult and abstract to describe what you would like to achieve. Having done stage 1 first makes the work more relevant. Stage 3 is a so-called gap analysis, looking at the difference between the desired and actual situation. This stage also includes prioritizing. Stage 4 is a creative

Figure 7.2. The Y model for IS/IT strategy work

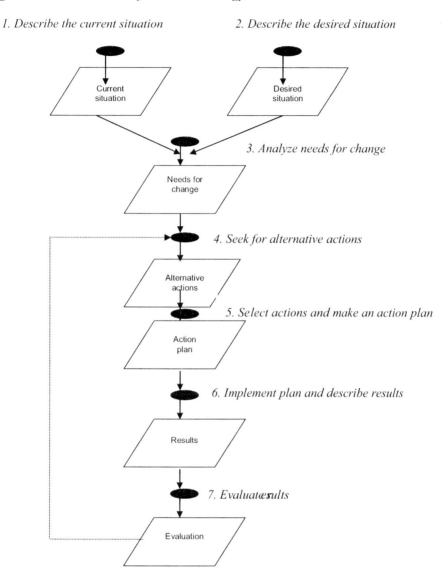

session as it calls for ideas and proposals for alternative actions. Stages 5 and 6 are typical planning stages. The final stage 7 is important because we can learn from performing an evaluation.

Resource-Based Strategy

Strategic management models traditionally have defined the firm's strategy in terms of its product/market positioning—the products it makes and the markets its serves. The resource-based approach suggests, however, that firms should position themselves strategically based on their unique, valuable, and inimitable resources and capabilities rather than the products and services derived from those capabilities. Resources and capabilities can be thought of as a platform from which the firm derives various products for various markets. Leveraging resources and capabilities across many markets and products, rather than targeting specific products for specific markets, becomes the strategic driver. While products and markets may come and go, resources and capabilities are more enduring. Therefore, a resource-based strategy provides a more long-term view than the traditional approach, and a more robust view in uncertain and dynamic competitive environments. Competitive advantage based on resources and capabilities therefore is potentially more suitable than that based solely on product and market positioning (Zack, 1999).

According to Hitt, Bierman, Shumizu, and Kochhar (2001), scholars argue that resources form the basis of firm strategies and are critical in the implementation of those strategies as well. Therefore, firm resources and strategy seem to interact to produce positive returns. Firms employ both tangible resources (such as buildings and financial resources) and intangible resources (like human capital and brand equity) in the development and implementation of strategy. Outside of natural resource monopolies, intangible resources are more likely to produce a competitive advantage because they are often rare and socially complex, thereby making them difficult to imitate.

Following Barney (2001), resource-based theory includes a very simple view about how resources are connected to the strategies a firm pursues. It is almost as though once a firm becomes aware of the valuable, rare, costly to imitate, and nonsubstitutable resources it controls, the actions the firm should take to exploit these resources will be self-evident. That may be true some of the time. For example, if a firm possesses valuable, rare, costly to imitate, and nonsubstitutable economies of scale, learning curve economies, access to low-cost factors of production, and technological resources, it seems clear that the firm should pursue a cost leadership strategy. However, it will often be the case that the link between resources and the strategy of a firm is not being so obvious. Resource-based strategy has to determine when, where and how resources may be useful. Such strategy is not obvious, since a firm's resources may be consistent with several different strategies, all with the ability to create the same level of competitive advantage. In this situation, how should a firm decide which of these several different strategies it should pursue? According to Barney (2001), this and other questions presented by Priem and Butler (2001) concerning the resource-based theory of the firm indicate that the theory is still a theory in many respects, and that more conceptual and empirical research has to be conducted to make the theory more useful to business executives who develop resource-based strategies for their firms.

Resource-based strategy is concerned with the mobilization of resources. Since perceived resources merely represent potential sources of value-creation, they need to be mobilized to create value. Conversely, for a specific resource to have value it has to increase or otherwise facilitate value-creation. The activity whereby tangible and intangible resources are recognized, combined, and turned into activities with the aim of creating value is the process here called resource mobilization. The term "resource mobilization" is appropriate, as it incorporates the activity-creation based on both individual and organizational resources, as well as tangibles and intangibles. According to Haanaes (1997), alternative terms such as resource allocation, resource leveraging, or resource deployment are appropriate when describing the value-creation based on tangible resources, but less so for intangibles. For example, a competence cannot be allocated, as the person controlling it has full discretion over it. Moreover, the competence can be used in different ways. An engineer can choose to work for a different organization and to work with varying enthusiasm. Also, the same engineer can choose not to utilize his or her competence at all. The term resource mobilization is thus meant to cover the value-creation based on all types of resources, and it recognizes that all activity creation has a human aspect.

In strategic management and organization theory, the importance for the firm of reducing uncertainty and its dependence on key resources that it cannot fully control has received much attention. If a large part of the resource accumulation takes place in terms of increased competencies that key professionals could easily use for the benefit of other employers, the firm needs to set priorities in terms of linking these individually controlled resources to the firm. Løwendahl (2000) suggests three alternative strategies. The simplest strategy, which may be acceptable to some firms, involves minimizing the dependence on individual professionals and their personal competence. In this sense, the firm chooses to avoid the dependence on individual tangibles. A second strategy is that of linking the professionals more tightly to the firm and reducing the probability of losing them. The third alternative strategy involves increasing the organizationally controlled competence resources without reducing the individually controlled resources. Such a strategy leads to a reduction in the relative impact of individual professionals on total performance, without reducing the absolute value of their contributions. Firms that have been able to develop a high degree of organizationally controlled resources, including relational resources that are linked to the firm rather than to individual employees, are likely to be less concerned about the exit and entry of individual professionals and more concerned about the development and maintenance of their organizational resource base.

According to Maister (1993), there is a natural but regrettable tendency for professional firms, in their strategy development process, to focus on new things: What new markets does the firm want to enter? What new clients does the firm want to target? What new services does the firm want to offer? This focus on new services and new markets is too often a cop-out. A new specialty (or a new office location) may or may not make sense for the firm, but it rarely does much (if anything) to affect the profitability or competitiveness of the vast majority of the firm's existing practices. On the other hand, an improvement in competitiveness in the firm's core businesses will have a much higher return on investment since the firm can capitalize on it by applying it to a larger volume of business. Enhancing the competitiveness of the existing practice will require changes in the behavior of employees. It implies new methods of operating, new skill development, and new accountabilities. Possible strategies for being more valuable to clients can be found in answers to the following questions (Maister, 1993):

- Can we develop an innovative approach to *hiring* so that we can be more valuable to clients by achieving a higher caliber of staff than the competition?

- Can we *train* our people better than the competition in a variety of technical and counseling skills so that they will be more valuable on the marketplace than their counterparts at other firms?

- Can we develop innovative *methodologies* for handling our matters (or engagements, transactions, or projects) so that our delivery of services becomes more thorough and efficient?

- Can we develop systematic ways of helping, encouraging, and ensuring that our people are skilled at client *counseling* in addition to being top suppliers?

- Can we become better than our competition at accumulating, disseminating, and building our firm-wide expertise and experience, so that each professional becomes more valuable in the marketplace by being *empowered* with a greater breadth and depth of experience?

- Can we organize and *specialize* our people in innovative ways, so that they become particularly skilled and valuable to the market because of their focus on a particular market segment's needs?

- Can we become more valuable to our clients by being more systematic and diligent about *listening* to the market—collecting, analyzing, and absorbing the details of their business—than our competition?

- Can we become more valuable to our clients by investing in research and *development* on issues of particular interest to them?

In resource-based strategy, there has to be consistency between resources and business. The logic behind this requirement is that the resources should create a competitive advantage in the business in which the firm competes. To meet this requirement, corporate resources can be evaluated against key success factors in each business. When doing so, it is important to keep in mind that in order to justify retaining a business, or entering a business, the resources should convey a substantial advantage. Merely having pedestrian resources that could be applied in an industry is seldom sufficient to justify entry or maintain presence in an attractive industry. Moreover, managers must remember that, regardless of the advantage a particular corporate resource appears to yield, the firm must also compete on all the other resources that are required to produce and deliver the product or service in each business. One great resource does not ensure a successful competitive position, particularly if a firm is disadvantaged on other resource dimensions (Collis & Montgomery, 1997).

Activity-Based Strategy

The goal of strategy formulation in the resource-based theory is to identify and increase those resources that allow a firm to gain and sustain superior rents. Firms owning strategic resources are predicted to earn superior rents, while firms possessing no or few strategic resources are thought to earn industry average rents or below average rents. The goal of strategy formulation in the activity-based theory is to identify and explore drivers that allow a firm to gain and sustain superior rents. Drivers are a central concept in the activity-based theory. To be considered drivers, firm-level factors must meet three criteria: They are structural factors at the level of activities, they are more or less controllable by management, and they impact the cost and/or differentiation position of the firm. The definition of drivers is primarily based on what drivers do. Drivers are abstract, relative, and relational properties of activities. For example, scale of an activity is a driver, as the size of the activity relative to competitors may represent a competitive advantage.

The analytical focus of the resource-based theory is potentially narrower than that of the activity-based theory. While the activity-based theory takes the firm's entire activity set as its unit of analysis, the resource-based theory focuses on individual resources or bundles of resources. Having a narrower focus means that the resource-based theory may not take into account the negative impact of resources, how a resource's value may change as the environment changes, or the role of non-core resources in achieving competitive advantage.

The activity-based and resource-based theories are similar as they both attempt to explain how firms attain superior positions through factors that increase firm differentiation or lower firm cost. While drivers and resources share a common goal of achieving and sustaining superior positions, the manner by which they are seen to reach a profitable position is different. With the resource-based theory it is the possession or control of strategic resources that allow a firm to gain a profitable position. On the other hand, drivers within the activity-based theory are not unique to the firm. They are generic, structural factors, which are available to all firms in the industry in the sense that they are conceptualized as properties of the firm's activities. A firm gains a profitable position by configuring its activities using drivers. It is this position that a firm may own, but only if it is difficult for rivals to copy the firm's configuration.

The sustainability of superior positions created by configuring drivers or owning resources is based on barriers to imitation. The sustainability of competitive advantage as per the activity-based theory is through barriers to imitation at the activity level. If the firm has a competitive advantage, as long as competitors are unable to copy the way activities are performed and configured through the drivers, the firm should be able to achieve above-average earnings over an extended period. The sustainability of superior profitability in the resource-based theory is through barriers to imitation of resources and immobility of resources. If resources are easily copied or substituted then the sustainability of the position is suspect.

Sheehan (2002) concludes his discussion by finding similarities between the resource-based theory and the activity-based theory. Resources in the resource-based theory are similar to drivers in the activity-based theory, as both are based on earning efficiency rents. Furthermore, capabilities in the resource-based theory are similar to activities in the activity-based theory, as both imply action.

Strategic Alignment

Alignment between business strategy and IT strategy is widely believed to improve business performance (Sabherwal & Chan, 2001). Therefore, strategic alignment is both a top management concern and also an important characteristic of the attributes of effective CIOs.

While the business strategy is the broadest pattern of resource allocation decisions, more specific decisions are related to IS and IT. Information systems must be seen both in a business and an IT context, and IS is in the middle because IS supports the business while using IT.

Business strategy is concerned with achieving the mission, vision, and objectives of a company, while IS strategy is concerned with use of IS/IT applications and IT strategy is concerned with the technical infrastructure. A company typically has several IS/IT applications. The connection between them is also of great interest, as interdependencies should prevent applications from being separate islands. Furthermore, the arrows in the illustration in Figure 7.3 are of importance. Arrows from business strategy to IS strategy and from IS to IT strategy represent the alignment perspective; they illustrate the *what* before the *how*. Arrows from IT to IS strategy, and from IS to business strategy represent the extension from *what* to *how* to *what*. This is the impact perspective, representing the potential impacts of modern information technology on future business options.

Necessary elements of a business strategy include mission, vision, objectives, market strategy, knowledge strategy, and our general approach to the use of information, information systems, and information technology.

"Mission" describes the reason for firm existence. For example, the reason for law firm existence is clients' need for legal advice. The mission addresses

Figure 7.3. Relationships between strategies at three levels

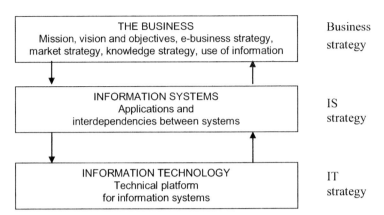

the organization's basic question of "What business are we in?" This single, essential, question should include no quantification, but must unambiguously state the purpose of the organization and should just as carefully define what the organization does not do. The mission is an unambiguous statement of what the organization does and its long-term, overall purpose. Its primary role is to set a direction for everyone to follow. It may be short, succinct, and inspirational, or contain broad philosophical statements that tie an organization to certain activities and to economic, social, ethical, or political ends. Values are also frequently stated alongside the mission. Three differing examples of missions are: To help people move from one place to another; to provide medical treatment to sick people; and to enable electronic communication between people.

"Vision" describes what the firm wants to achieve. For example, a law firm wants to become the leading law firm in Norway. The vision represents the view that senior managers have for the future of the organization— it is what they want it to become. This view gives a way to judge the appropriateness of all potential activities that the organization might engage in. The vision gives a picture, frequently covering many aspects that everyone can identify with, of what the business will be in the future, and how it will operate. It exists to bring objectives to life, and to give the whole organization a destination that it can visualize, so that every stakeholder has a shared picture of the future aim.

"Objectives" describe where the business is heading. For example, the law firm can choose to merge with another law firm to become the leading law firm in Norway. Objectives are the set of major achievements that will accomplish the vision. These are usually small in number, but embody the most important aspects of the vision, such as financial returns, customer service, manufacturing excellence, staff morale, and social and environmental obligations.

"Market strategy" describes market segments and products. For example, the law firm can focus on corporate clients in the area of tax law.

Necessary elements of an IS strategy include future IS/IT applications, future competence of human resources (IS/IT professionals), future IS/IT organizational structure, and control of the IS/IT function. An important application area is KMS. The future applications are planned according to priorities, how they are to be developed or acquired (made or bought), how they meet user requirements, and how security is achieved. The future competence is planned by types of resources needed, motivation and skills needed (managers, users, IS/IT professionals), salaries, and other benefits. The future IS/IT organization defines tasks, roles, management, and possibly outsourcing.

Necessary elements of an IT strategy include selection of IT hardware, basic software, and networks, as well as how these components should interact as a technological platform, and how required security level is maintained. The IT platform consists of hardware, systems software, networks and communications, standards, and support from selected vendors.

An IS/IT strategy is a combined strategy including business context, the IS in a narrow sense, and the technological platform. Necessary elements of an IS/IT strategy include business direction and strategy (mission, vision, objectives, knowledge strategy), applications (knowledge management systems), people (future competence of human resources), organization (future organization and control of IT function), and IT platform (future technical infrastructure). Hence, IS/IT is quite a broad term. The term is broad to take care of all connections and interdependencies in a strategy, as changes in one element will have effect on all other elements, as illustrated in Figure 7.4.

The same thinking is represented in a famous model called Leavitt's Diamond (Gottschalk, 2005). Everything is connected, and changes in one element affect all the others, as illustrated in Figure 7.5. Tasks are performed using systems, structure is important for support functions, and people represent the competence. The Diamond can only create change in a desired strategic business direction if all interdependencies between elements are taken care of over time.

Figure 7.4. IS/IT strategy elements and interdependencies

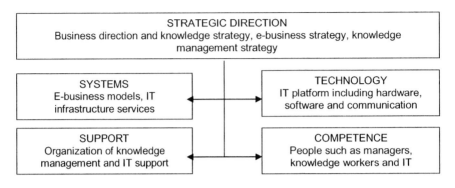

Figure 7.5. Leavitt's Diamond of elements and interrelationships

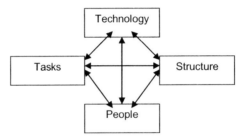

Most large companies in the United States and Europe have long struggled with the need for tighter relationships between IT and business management. This perennial management problem is echoed once again in a study of how French CEOs and CIOs view the performance of information systems within their organizations. Insights from the study suggest that CEOs are growing keener to find a solution, and that both CIOs and the leaders of business units may soon be held more accountable for business ownership of IT (Monnoyer, 2003).

In the survey, CEOs say that IT is not meeting their (admittedly high) performance expectations, particularly in providing systems and tools to support managerial decision-making and in gaining the scale advantages of deploying common systems and processes across business units. The CEOs attribute the gap between expected and actual performance mainly to the insufficient involvement of business units in IT projects, to the weak oversight and management of these projects, and to IT's inadequate understanding of their business requirements (Monnoyer, 2003).

Strategic Management Dynamics

So far, we have looked at the traditional and common way of strategy making and strategy planning. In the author's opinion there is nothing wrong with it. The only concern is the lack of understanding of how this kind of strategic planning causes organizational performance over time. Few executives realize that they themselves are part of business dynamics through their decision-making behavior. Such insight can be generated and presented when using system dynamics.

A possible system dynamics causal loop diagram is found in Figure 7.6. More needs for strategic change (analysis phase) lead to more strategic change decisions (choice phase). Increased strategic change decisions cause more strategic actions for change (implementation phase). For implementation to be successful, strategic resources have to be mobilized.

Figure 7.6. Causal loop diagram for business performance from strategic decision making

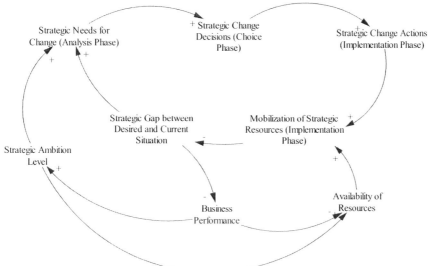

Figure 7.7. Reference mode for business performance from strategic decision making

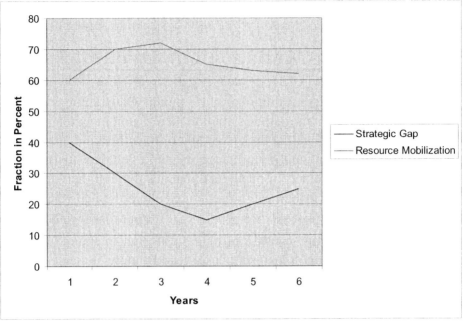

Depending on parameters and quantitative relationships in the causal diagram in Figure 7.6, the firm may experience a development as illustrated in Figure 7.7. One of the reasons for a final rise in strategic gap is the negative relationship between business performance and availability of resources. The argument for this polarity is the typical management behavior of reducing resource use as the firm approaches a business goal.

References

Barney, J. B. (2001). Is the resourced-based "view" a useful perspective for strategic management research? Yes. *Academy of Management Review, 26*(1), 41-56.

Boyd, B. K., & Reuning-Elliott, E. (1998). A measurement model of strategic planning. *Strategic Management Journal, 19,* 181-192.

Christensen, C. M., & Raynor, M. E. (2003). *The innovator's solution.* Boston: Harvard Business School Press.

Collis, D. J., & Montgomery, C. A. (1997). *Corporate strategy; Resources and the scope of the firm.* Chicago: McGraw-Hill.

Gottschalk, P. (2005). *Strategic knowledge management technology.* Hershey, PA: Idea Group Publishing.

Grant, R. M. (2003). Strategic planning in a turbulent environment: Evidence from the oil majors. *Strategic Management Journal, 24,* 491-517.

Haanes, K. B. (1997). *Managing resource mobilization: Case studies of Dynal, Fiat Auto Poland and Alcatel Telecom Norway.* Unpublished doctorial dissertation, Copenhagen Business School, Copenhagen, Denmark.

Hann, J., & Weber, R. (1996). Information systems planning: A model and empirical tests. *Management Science, 42*(7), 1043-1064.

Hansen, M. T., Nohria, N., & Tierny, T. (1999, March-April). What's your strategy for managing knowledge? *Harvard Business Review*, 106-116.

Hitt, M. A., Bierman, L., Shumizu, K., & Kochhar, R. (2001). Direct and moderating effects of human capital on strategy and performance in professional service firms: A resource-based perspective. *Academy of Management Journal, 44*(1), 13-28.

Hopkins, W. E., & Hopkins, S. A. (1997). Strategic planning: Financial performance relationships in banks: A causal examination. *Strategic Management Journal, 18*(8), 635-652.

Jensen, M., & Zajac, E. J. (2004). Corporate elites and corporate strategy: How demographic preferences and structural position shape the scope of the firm. *Strategic Management Journal, 25,* 507-524.

Johnson, G., & Scholes, K. (2002). *Exploring corporate strategy.* Harlow, Essex, UK: Pearson Education, Prentice Hall.

Julien, P. A., & Ramangalahy, C. (2003). Competitive strategy and performance of exporting SMEs: An empirical investigation of the impact of their export enformation search and competencies. *Entrepreneurship Theory and Practice,* Spring, 227-245.

Kaplan, R. S., & Norton, D. P. (2004). *Strategy maps.* Boston: Harvard Business School Press.

Løwendahl, B. R. (2000). *Strategic management of professional service firms* (2nd ed.). Copenhagen, Denmark: Copenhagen Business School Press.

Maister, D. H. (1993). *Managing the professional service firm*. New York: Free Press.

Miller, C. C., & Cardinal, L. B. (1994). Strategic planning and firm performance: A synthesis of more than two decades of research. *Academy of Management Journal, 37*(6), 1649-1665.

Mintzberg, H. (1994). Rounding out the manager's job. *Sloan Management Review, 36*(1), 11-26.

Monnoyer, E. (2003). What CEOs really think about IT. *McKinsey Quarterly, 3,* 80-82.

Nayyar, P. R. (1993). On the measurement of competitive strategy: Evidence from a large multiproduct U.S. firm. *Academy of Management Journal, 36*(6), 1652-1669.

Porter, M. E. (1985). *Competitive strategy*. New York: The Free Press.

Porter, M. E. (2001, March). Strategy and the Internet. *Harvard Business Review*, 63-78.

Priem, R. L., & Butler, J. E. (2001). Is the resourced-based "view" a useful perspective for strategic management research? *Academy of Management Review, 26*(1), 22-40.

Sabherwal, R., & Chan, Y. E. (2001). Alignment between business and IS strategies: A study of prospectors, analyzers, and defenders. *Information Systems Research, 12*(1), 11-33.

Wit, B. D., & Meyer, R. (2004). *Strategy: Process, content, context* (3rd ed.). London: Thomson Learning.

Zack, M. H. (1999). Developing a knowledge strategy. *California Management Review, 41*(3), 125-145.

Chapter VIII

Dynamics of
CIO Performance

The CIO can be defined as the highest-ranking IT executive who typically exhibits managerial roles requiring effective communication with top management, a broad corporate perspective in managing information resources, influence on organizational strategy, and responsibility for IT planning to cope with a firm's competitive environment. This definition is in line with research, which applied the following criteria when selecting CIOs for empirical observation: (1) highest-ranking information technology executive; (2) reports no more than two levels from the CEO, that is, either reports to the CEO or reports to one of the CEOs direct reports; (3) areas of responsibility include information systems, computer operations, telecommunications and networks, office automation, end-user computing, help desks, computer software, and applications; and (4) responsibility for strategic IS/IT planning.

According to Gartner (2005), only a few CEOs view CIOs as boardroom peers. Most CEOs view their CIOs as effective operational leaders. Yet only a few view them as full business leaders. There is an opportunity for CIOs to build their relationship with their CEO and other stakeholders, to increase their influence, and to enhance the contribution of information systems and information technology.

When applying to a resource-based theory of the firm, two perspectives emerge. First, the CIO represents a resource for the organization. Next, the CIO manages IT resources in the organization. Having a CIO who represents a strategic resource and develops IT resources into strategic resources will help the firm succeed.

When applying value configurations, more perspectives emerge. If the firm is a value chain, the CIO will be concerned with information systems in areas such as logistics and supply chains. If the firm is a value shop, the CIO will concentrate on knowledge management systems. If the firm is a value network, the CIO will work mainly on IT infrastructure and architecture that makes a difference to firm performance.

The Chief Information Officer

The CIO position emerged in the 1970s as a result of increased importance of IT. In the early 1980s, the CIO was often portrayed as the corporate savior who was to align the worlds of business and technology. The CIOs were described as the new breed of information managers who were businessmen first, managers second, and technologists third (Grover, Jeong, Kettinger, & Lee, 1993). It was even postulated that in the 1990s, as information became a firm's critical resource, the CIO would become the logical choice for the chief executive officer (CEO) position.

As a manager of people, the CIO faces the usual human resource roles of recruiting, staff training, and retention, and the financial roles of budget determination, forecasting, and authorization. As the provider of technological services to user departments, there remains a significant amount of work in publicity, promotion, and internal relations with user management. As a manager of an often-virtual information organization, the CIO has to coordinate sources of information services spread throughout and beyond the boundaries of the firm. The CIO is thus concerned with a wider group of issues than are most managers.

While information systems executives share several similarities with the general manager, notable differences are apparent. The CIO is not only concerned with a wider group of issues than most managers, but as the chief information systems strategist also has a set of responsibilities that must constantly evolve with the corporate information needs and with information technology itself. It has been suggested that the IT director's ability to add value is the biggest single factor in determining whether the organization views information technology as an asset or a liability.

According to Earl and Feeny (1994), CIOs have the difficult job of running a function that uses a lot of resources but that offers little measurable evidence of its value:

Chief information officers have the difficult job of running a function that uses a lot of resources but that offers little measurable evidence of its value. To make the information systems department an asset to their companies—and to keep their jobs—CIOs should think of their work as adding value in certain key areas. (p. 11)

Creation of the CIO role was driven in part by two organizational needs. First, accountability is increased when a single executive is responsible for the organization's processing needs. Second, creation of the CIO position facilitates the closing of the gap between organizational and IT strategies, which has long been cited as a primary business concern.

Alignment of business and IT objectives is not only a matter of achieving competitive advantage, but is essential for the firm's very survival. Though the importance of IT in creating competitive advantage has been widely noted, achieving these gains has proven elusive. Sustained competitive advantage requires not only the development of a single system, but the ability to consistently deploy IT faster, more cheaply, and more strategically than one's competitors. IT departments play a critical role in realizing the potential of IT. The performance of IT functions, in turn, often centers on the quality of leadership, that is, the CIO.

As early as 1984, some surveys suggested that one third of U.S. corporations had a CIO function, if not in title. While exact percentages differ, ranging from 40% to 70%, Grover et al. (1993) found that the number of senior-level information systems executive positions created over the past 10 years had grown tremendously. The earliest scientifically conducted research on the CIO position examined 43 of 50 top-ranked Fortune 500 service organizations in the US, and noted that 23 (58%) of these organizations had the CIO position. In 1990, the 200 largest Fortune 500 industrial and service organizations were examined, and it was found that 77% of the industrials had a CIO position, as compared with 64% of the service organizations. It is very likely that these numbers have increased in recent years.

Few studies have examined the reasons behind the creation of the CIO position in firms. Creation of the position effectively increases accountability by making a single executive responsible for corporate information processing needs. In a sample of Fortune 500 firms, that is, appearing on the list for 4 consecutive years, 287 firms with CIOs were compared in 1995 to firms without CIOs on a number of variables hypothesized to predict creation of the position. It was observed that a number of characteristics of the corporate board, including the number of outside directors and equity ownership of the directors, predicted the existence of the CIO position. A firm's information intensity was also found to be positively related to the creation of the CIO position. Furthermore, the CIO position was more likely to exist when the CEO appreciated the strategic value and importance of IT.

The CIO title itself has become a source of confusion. The term CIO has been somewhat loosely defined and is often used interchangeably with various titles such as IT director, vice president of IS, director of information resources, director of information services, and director of MIS, to describe a senior executive responsible for establishing policy and controlling information resources. Sometimes, the CIO label denotes a function rather than a title. Studies relating to the CIO have focused on the evolution of the position and the similarities between the CIO and other senior-level executives.

The CIO label itself has been met with resistance, and some firms have replaced the title with alternative labels such as knowledge manager, chief knowledge officer (CKO), or chief technology officer (CTO). It has been found that the CKO has to discover and develop the CEO's implicit vision of how knowledge management would make a difference, and how IT can support this difference.

There are differences between the tasks of a CTO, CIO, and CKO. While the CTO is focused on technology, the CIO focuses on information, and the CKO focuses on knowledge. When companies replace a CIO with a CKO, it should not only be a change of title. Rather, it should be a change of focus. Alternatively, as we shall see later in this book, the CIO might expand his or her powerbase by including the roles of the CTO and the CKO in the position of the CIO.

Applegate, McFarlan, and McKenney (1996) indicate that the CIO is becoming a member of the top management team and participates in organizational strategy development. Similarly, it has been stated that CIOs see themselves as corporate officers and general business managers. This suggests that CIOs must be politically savvy and that their high profile places them in contention for top line management jobs. The results of these studies indicate that today's CIO is more a managerially oriented executive than a technical manager. Some provide a profile of the ideal CIO as an open communicator with a business perspective, capable of leading and motivating staff, and as an innovative corporate team player. Karimi, Somers, and Gupta (2001) found that successful CIOs characterized themselves in the following way:

- I see myself as a corporate officer.
- In my organization I am seen by others as a corporate officer.
- I am a general business manager, not an IT specialist.
- I am a candidate for top line management positions.
- I have a high-profile image in the organization.
- I have political as well as rational perspectives of my firm.
- I spend most of my time outside the IT department focusing on the strategic and organizational aspects of IT.

Among the most significant roles that CIOs will likely fulfill in the digital era is that of business strategist, according to Sambamurthy, Straub, and Watson (2001). As a business strategist, the CIO must understand and visualize the economic, competitive, and industry forces impacting the business and the factors that sustain competitive advantage. Further, the CIO must be capable of plotting strategy with executive peers, including the CEO, chief operating officer (COO), and other senior business executives:

Business strategist is likely to be among the most significant roles that CIOs will fulfill in the digital era. As a business strategist, the CIO must understand and visualize the economic, competitive, and industry forces impacting the business and the factors that sustain competitive advantage. Further, the CIO must be capable of plotting strategy with executive peers, including the chief executive officer (CEO), chief operating officer (COO), and other senior business executives. Not only are CIOs drawn into the mainstream of business strategy, but also their compensation is being linked with the effectiveness of competitive Internet actions in many firms. With an understanding of current and emergent information technologies and an ability to foresee breakthrough strategic opportunities as well as disruptive threats, CIOs must play a lead role in educating their business peers about how IT can raise the competitive agility of the firm. Obviously, to be effective business strategists, the CIOs must be members of an executive leadership team and part of the dominant coalition that manages the firm. (Sambamurthy et al., 2001, p. 285)

With an understanding of current and emergent information technologies and an ability to foresee breakthrough strategic opportunities as well as disruptive threats, CIOs must play a lead role in educating their business peers about how IT can raise the competitive agility of the firm. To be effective business strategists, the CIOs must be members of an executive leadership team and part of the dominant coalition that manages the firm.

Reporting Levels

Although it was originally expected that the CIO would have high levels of influence within the firm, as the definition of job responsibilities would suggest, recent surveys indicate that this may not be the case. They may not actually possess strategic influence with top management, and they may lack operational and tactical influence with users. Some specific problems include higher-than-average corporate dismissal rates compared with other top executives, diminished power with belt tightening and budget cuts, high expectations of new strategic systems that CIOs may not be able to deliver, lack of secure power bases due to the fact that CIOs are viewed as outsiders by top management, and the fact that few CIOs take part in strategic planning, and many do not report to the CEO.

Over time, the number of CIOs reporting to CEOs seems to increase. In 1992, only 27% of surveyed CIOs in the US reported to CEOs, while this number had increased to 43% 5 years later, as listed in Figure 8.1. In 2005, Gartner (2005) found that 40% of the surveyed CIOs reported to the CEO, 18% to the CFO, 21% to the COO, and 21% to other executives.

In Norway, the numbers in Figure 8.1 seem to indicate a stable level above 40%, or maybe an insignificant decline in the fraction of CIOs reporting to the CEO. An interesting development is indirect reports moving from CFOs to other top executives.

Figure 8.1. CIO reporting in the US and Norway over time

Chief Information Officer (CIO) reporting to:	USA 1992	USA 1997	USA 2000	USA 2005	Norway 1997	Norway 1999	Norway 2000
Chief Executive Officer (CEO)	27 %	43 %	33 %	40 %	48 %	44 %	41 %
Chief Financial Officer (CFO)	44 %	32 %	20 %	18 %	21 %	23 %	16 %
Other top executive in the company	29 %	25 %	47 %	42 %	31 %	33 %	43 %

In a survey in the United States in 2000 cited by Schubert (2004), 33% of the CIOs reported to the CEO, while 20% reported to the CFO, and 47% reported to another top executive in the company, as listed in Figure 8.1. It is interesting to note that among those CIOs not reporting to the CEO in 2000 in the US, most of them reported to the chief operating officer (COO).

In most countries surveyed by Gartner (2005), CIOs tended to report to an executive other than the CEO. Not so in Japan and South Korea, where more than two thirds of IT executives had the CEO for a boss. Regardless of whom they reported to, CIOs in the US, Canada, South Korea, and Singapore said they spent the most time interacting with other business executives.

In a Gartner (2005) CIO 100 survey in the US, 40% of the respondents held the title of CIO, 7% were both CIO and executive vice president (EVP), 16% were both CIO and senior vice president (SVP), 22% were chief technology officers (CTO), and 15% had other titles such as director.

The CIO's pivotal responsibility of aligning business and technology direction presents a number of problems. Moreover, rapid changes in business and information environments have resulted in corresponding changes at the IT function helm. This role has become increasingly complex, causing many firms to look outside the organization for the right qualifications. Characteristics such as professional background, educational background, and current length of tenure have been examined in previous research. CIO problems seem to indicate that, when compared with other senior executives, CIOs do not have the authority or ability to achieve the kind of changes that were promised when the position was initially proposed. A second and possibly related explanation is that CIOs are experiencing managerial role conflicts that prevent them from meeting those expectations as originally envisioned in the CIO position.

The Chief Executive Officer

The CEO is the only executive at level one in the hierarchy of an organization (Carpenter & Wade, 2002). All other executives in the organization are at lower levels. At level two, we find the most senior executives. Level three includes the next tier of executives. In our perspective of promoting the CIO to be the next CEO, we first have to understand the role of the CEO. Therefore, the first chapter of this book is dedicated to the topic of CEO successions (Zhang & Rajagopalan, 2004).

Being a CEO involves handling exceptional circumstances and developing a high level of tacit knowledge and expertise; these characteristics and experiences contribute to the accumulation of firm-specific human capital. The time a CEO spends in the position represents a significant investment in firm-specific human capital for both the individual and the firm. The firm is investing its resources to compensate the CEO, and the CEO is investing his or her productive time. Both make these investments with the expectation of future return, so age is a major factor determining the level of firm-specific human capital investment (Buchholtz, Ribbens, & Houle, 2003).

Being a CEO means bearing full responsibility for a company's success or failure, but being unable to control most of what will determine it. It means having more authority than anyone else in the organization, but being unable to wield it without unhappy consequences. Porter, Lorsch, and Nohria (2004) make this sound like a very tough job. They argue that this comes as a surprise to CEOs who are new to the job.

Some of the surprises for new CEOs arise from time and knowledge limitations—there is so much to do in complex new areas, with imperfect information and never enough time. Other problems stem from unexpected and unfamiliar new roles and altered professional relationships. Still others crop up because of the paradox that the more power you have, the harder it is to use. While several of the challenges may appear familiar, Porter et al. (2004) discovered that nothing in a leader's background, even running a large business within his company, fully prepares him to be CEO.

CEOs have long been recognized as the principal architects of corporate strategy and major catalysts of organizational change, and the extent to which CEOs can effect change in corporate strategy is thought to be determined largely by the power they possess and how they decide to wield it (Bigley & Wiersema, 2002).

Bigley and Wiersema (2002) argue that CEOs' cognitive orientations should influence how they wield their power to affect corporate strategy. On the one hand, predictions about a CEO's use of power require an understanding of the CEO's cognitive orientation toward his or her firm's strategy, because power is simply the ability to bring about a preferred or intended effect. On the other hand, hypothesized associations between a CEO's cognitive orientation and corporate strategy presuppose that the CEO has sufficient power to bring about the preferred or intended effects.

The strategic beliefs of CEOs are likely to be instantiated to a significant degree in their firms' current strategies. When top executives' advice seeking confirms and/or restores their confidence in the correctness of their strategic beliefs, they will be less likely to change firm strategy. McDonald and Westphal (2003) theorize that relatively poor firm performance can prompt CEOs to seek more advice from executives of other firms who are their friends or similar to them, and less advice from acquaintances or dissimilar peers, and suggest how and why this pattern of advice seeking could reduce firms' propensity to change corporate strategy in response to poor performance.

McDonald and Westphal (2003) tested their hypotheses with a large sample. The results confirm their hypotheses and show that executives' social network ties can influence firms' responses to economic adversity, in particular by inhibiting strategic change in response to relatively poor firm performance. Additional findings indicate that CEOs' advice-seeking in response to low performance may ultimately have negative consequences for subsequent performance, suggesting how CEOs' social network ties could play an indirect role in organizational decline and downward spirals in firm performance.

In *MIT Sloan Management Review*, Johnson (2002) phrased the question, Do CEOs matter? To answer this question, he cites two critical dimensions that influence the magnitude of a CEO's impact on a company. First is resource availability, which is dependent upon an organization's level of debt (higher debt means less cash available to direct toward investments or acquisitions) and level of slack (that is, the number of extra people or amount of assets that the CEO can easily redeploy to take advantage of an opportunity). Second is opportunity availability, which is determined by independence, concentration, and growth. Those CEOs at the helms of companies with low debt levels and high slack levels—and thus high resource availability—will exert more powerful impact on their organizations, and CEO impact increases as opportunities become scarcer.

The CEO-CIO Relationship

Building strong social networks and coalitions within a firm is an essential task for those who aspire to be the CEO. When they are promoted to a firm's CEO position, inside successors not only have the approval of outside directors, but also have support within the top management group (Shen & Cannella, 2002a). For a CIO who aspires to become the next CEO, he or she needs to manage relationships, develop coalitions, and understand power dynamics in top management.

The quality of the CEO-CIO relationship influences the CIO's effectiveness and success as a business leader and the value gained from information technology. Many CEOs are demanding and not always clear about their expectations. That can create a situation in which their views are radically different from the CIO's perceptions, a situation fraught with risk for both. Both CEOs and CIOs often see the relationship between business and information differently. While CIOs tend to view their role and contribution optimistically, CEOs, by contrast, are more critical (Gartner, 2005).

The difference between how the CEO views the CEO-CIO relationship and how the CIO views this relationship creates the potential for a dangerous disconnect, limiting the value generated by information technology and the power of the executive team. Understanding the CEO's expectations and view of the CIO helps create the right relationship based on personal style and enterprise need.

In the survey conducted by Gartner (2005), CIOs believed they are trusted and respected business leaders, and to a great extent they are right. But few CEOs share the same unqualified view. This is partly because CEOs have a broad span of control, with IT just one of many priorities. It is also because of CIOs' technology and operations focus, which does not always allow them to show traditional business leadership styles and behaviors.

In the survey by Gartner (2005), responding CEOs found that healthy relationships with other executives (CXOs) are very important for the CIO. Furthermore, the CIO must ensure that IT objectives are aligned with the CEO's objectives and overall business strategy. Survey results indicate that CIOs and CEOs are in agreement on the most important skills for the CIO's success. They stress strategic thinking and planning, and understanding business processes and operations.

CEOs hire CIOs to fit with enterprise needs and the changing context, and CIOs must understand the type of relationship they are in and the actions required to reach the right relationship type. Four relationship types describe how CIOs relate to CEOs: at-risk, transactional, partnering, and trusted-ally. These relationships are not set in stone. Sudden events—a change of CEO or a strategic IT initiative—can change the balance. And if both CEO and CIO are open to the possibility, they can change the relationship.

The first step for the CIO is to understand where his or her relationship is now, through self-assessment and dialog with the CEO. Then the CIO uses that information to decide the next step, and then move one step at a time, cementing credibility and the enterprise's appetite for change at each level.

According to Gartner (2005), CIO success stems from a four-step cycle: leading, shaping demand, setting expectations, and delivering. The CIO is recommended to build an action plan based on this cycle, tailored to personal relationship type. The plan might have tangible, time-bounded goals. Embedded in the plan might be six powerful and proven practices: Get coaching and mentoring, make time for relationship building, take on non-IT responsibilities, build the strength of deputies, educate personally, and educate shareholders. This will increase the chances of achieving the right CEO-CIO relationship.

Gartner (2005) has the following note to CEOs:

The age of the operational CIO is almost over

Your relationship with your CIO matters. The CIO can be a powerful and positive member of your executive team. A recent study by Burson and Marsteller shows that 5%of Fortune Global 500 companies have CIO skills on their board. And these companies' stocks have outperformed the industry index by 6.4% per year since the CIO-skilled member was elected.

You set the tone of the relationship with your CIO. Successful CEOs are getting more from IT by building their CIO relationship. Getting CIO input into enterprise strategy has proved much more powerful than getting the CIO to execute a fixed strategy.

This trend is increasing, not decreasing, as enterprises become more reliant on IT to implement efficient processes and to drive sources of competitive advantage.

For an enterprise to be effective in using IT to drive innovation and growth, a good working relationship between the CEO and CIO is crucial. But there is still a lot of misunderstanding and suspicion among CEOs of CIOs and IT. To succeed, CIOs need to understand the CEO's perspective on them, and on IT's role in the enterprise.

Business Dynamics for Executive Performance

Based on the discussion so far, we are able to draw a variety of different causal loop diagrams to explain relationships and feedback loops for CIO and CEO performance. One example is illustrated in Figure 8.2.

CIO performance and CEO performance can be measured on a scale where 100 is the normal or expected performance. Performance above 100 is better than normal, while performance below 100 is worse than normal. In the simulation in Figure 8.3, the performance of the CEO stays above 100, while the behavior of the CIO fluctuates above and below the normal level of performance.

Figure 8.2. Causal loop diagram explaining executive performance

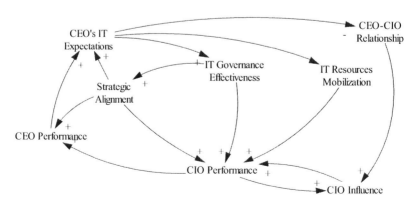

Figure 8.3. Reference mode simulating executive performance

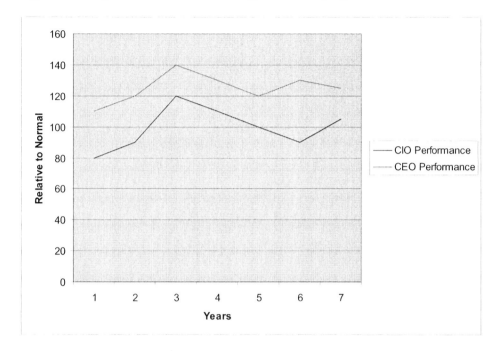

Changing Role of CIO to CEO

Both the CIO and the CEO are practicing leadership. One of the defining characteristics of leadership is the ability to develop and implement appropriate responses to a variety of problem situations. Leaders must solve an array of problems including resource allocation, interdepartmental coordination, interpersonal conflict, and subordinate morale, to name a few. In order to effectively solve such problems, leaders must draw on a body of knowledge gained from formal education, advice from other leaders, and personal experience (Hedlund, Forsythe, Horvath, Williams, Snook, & Sternberg, 2003).

Sternberg (2003) presented a model of leadership in organizations. According to this model, the three key components of leadership are wisdom, intelligence, and creativity, synthesized. The basic idea is that one needs these three components working together (synthesized) in order to be a highly effective leader.

Sternberg argues that one is not born a leader. Rather, wisdom, intelligence, and creativity are, to some extent, forms of developing expertise. One interacts with the environment in ways that utilize, to varying degrees, one's innate potentials. The environment strongly influences the extent to which leaders are able to utilize and develop whatever genetic potentials they have. Many people with substantial innate potential fail to take advantage of it, whereas others with lesser potential do take advantage of it.

Practical intelligence is the ability to solve everyday problems by utilizing knowledge gained from experience in order to purposefully adapt to, shape, and select environments. It thus involves changing oneself to suit the environment (adaptation), changing the environment to suit oneself (shaping), or finding a new environment within which to work (selection). Creativity refers to skill in generating ideas and products that are relatively novel, high in quality, and appropriate to the task at hand. Creativity is important in leadership because it is the component whereby one generates the ideas that others will follow. Wisdom consists of reasoning ability, sagacity, learning from ideas and environment, judgment, expeditious use of information, and perspicacity (Sternberg, 2003).

Demand Side CEO Requirements

From the demand side, there is a need for a new CEO. The question we raise is whether or not the CIO is a candidate for the job. Promoting the CIO to the post of CEO represents an inside succession. It can either be a relay or nonrelay succession. If the CIO is selected and crowned as an heir apparent it is a relay succession. An incumbent CEO works with the CIO as an heir apparent and passes the baton of leadership to the heir (Zhang & Rajagopalan, 2004).

To become an heir apparent, the CIO must be identified as a high-potential candidate. As the candidate enters the development pipeline, managers must constantly align education and on-the-job experience with the emerging landscape. And they must rigorously assess the candidates' performance at each development stage (Charan, 2005).

There is a need for a new CEO—is the CIO a candidate? Zhang and Rajagopalan (2004) did shed some interesting light on this question in their studies of inside or outside successions.

If a headhunting firm is involved, the chances of external recruitment might increase, thereby reducing the chances for the internal CIO to be promoted.

If the performance of the firm is poor, the chances of external recruitment increase, thereby reducing the chances for internal CIO to be promoted.

According to Charan (2005), it is important to be identified as one of those very rare people who might one day be CEO.

The demand side for a new CEO is dependent on firm performance, generally, and initiation of strategic changes in response to poor firm performance, specifically. In case of poor firm performance, corporate boards might have to initiate strategic changes. Part of the change will often be the departure of the current CEO. However, pluralistic ignorance on corporate boards sometimes prevents CEO succession. Pluralistic ignorance is typically defined at the group level as the extent to which group members (plural) underestimate the degree to which others share their concerns (Westphal & Bednar, 2005).

In another study, Westphal and Khanna (2003) considered the social process by which the corporate elite may have resisted pressure from stakeholders to adopt changes in corporate governance that limit managerial autonomy. Such resistance can influence both the likelihood of CEO succession and the potential selection of a CEO successor. For example, directors who are positive to CEO succession can experience social distancing and can be deterred from participating subsequently in governance changes that threaten the interests of fellow top managers.

Succession of the CEO can be solved by duality, where one executive holds two positions. For example, if the president is promoted to CEO, he or she may still remain in the president position. In this case, there is no real vacancy, and there is no demand for a new president. Similarly, when a CEO is promoted to chair of the board, the person might remain in the CEO position, and there will be no demand for a new CEO (Davidson, Nemic, & Worrell, 2001).

Supply Side CIO Qualifications

Taking a supply-side perspective, Zhang and Rajagopalan (2003) drew upon three theoretical perspectives—the executive human capital, agency theory, and power perspectives. First, the executive human capital argument indicates that the requirements of the CEO job are substantially different from those of other organizational positions (such as the CIO position). This is a position with considerable responsibility for overall firm performance, and hence only a small group of executives with experience at the highest levels of a firm are likely to possess the relevant managerial skills and expertise and to be considered serious candidates for this position. To improve his or her chances for promotion to CEO, the CIO must develop relevant executive human capital by involvement in tasks related to overall firm performance.

Second, the power perspective suggests that in order to qualify for consideration, an internal candidate needs an established power base, especially in relation to the incumbent CEO and the board of directors. Holding a formal job title like CIO may or may not evidence such a power base. To improve his or her chances for promotion to CEO, the CIO must develop a relevant and strong power base. Finally, from an agency theory perspective, a candidate is more likely to be considered seriously for the CEO position if the board of his or her firm has relevant information on the candidate's skills and competencies. Interactions with the board help to reduce the "adverse selection" problem that arises from information asymmetry between a board and a potential successor. One potential arena for such interactions is the presentation and discussion of IT strategy (see Chapter 10) with the board.

If the CIO is a qualified person, will he or she become the next CEO? In this book, we have seen some of the contingent answers to this question:

- Yes, if he or she can handle the power game
- Yes, if he or she has important decision rights concerning strategic resource allocations
- Yes, depending on stage of growth in terms of IT maturity
- Yes, depending on value configuration of the organization
- Yes, depending on reporting level two, three, or four
- Yes, depending on level of involvement in governance structures

In a survey by Earl (2000), some CIOs had experience being a CEO. The traditional responsibilities of the CIO job require technological competence plus the management know-how required to lead specialists and integrate the function with the rest of the business. Most CIOs in Earl's (2000) survey acquired these capabilities by having considerable experience in the IT function. The new responsibilities also involve business acumen and leadership skills. Those CIOs who had experience being a CEO of a business or head of a business unit considered that to be excellent training ground for developing these capabilities. In particular, they said it helped them judge where IT should lead or lag in business thinking. CEO experience from a subsidiary or another organization is likely to be considered strength when the CIO is a candidate for the CEO position in the current organization.

If the CIO has the chance of being a follower successor or contender successor, research by Shen and Cannella (2002b) is of interest. They studied effects of alternative successions on firm performance. They predicted a positive association between contender successor and postsuccession firm performance. The statistical coefficient for contender succession was positive, but not significant. Thus, the hypothesis was not supported. However, the coefficient for outsider successor and postsuccession operational performance was negative and significant. Based on this research, it seems that a CIO who would like to become the next CEO might choose the contender strategy if firm performance is bad, the departing CEO's position is weak, and the departing CEO's tenure is short.

Another study by Cannella and Shen (2003) is also of interest to CIOs aspiring to the CEO position. If the CIO is an heir apparent, two contrasting outcomes emerge: promotion to CEO or firm exit. Cannella and Shen (2003) propose that the distribution of power among an incumbent CEO, outside directors, and an heir apparent influences these outcomes. Results suggest that outside director and CEO powers are important influences on heir promotion and exit and that heirs who arise from within a firm are less likely to exit.

If the CIO is an heir apparent, his or her heir apparent power should be developed. As a competent and ambitious individual, the CIO is looking forward to run his or her own show as the CEO. Promotion to CEO is top priority for the CIO. As the second-in-command, an heir apparent also has her or his own sources of power, although the heir apparent is usually weaker in comparison to incumbent CEOs and outside directors. Further, some of the factors that are associated with CEO power are not correspondingly useful in gauging heir apparent power. For example, stock ownership, long a key measure of CEO power, is far less relevant for an heir apparent. Further, position tenure, certainly an important measure of CEO power, does not have a corresponding association with heir apparent power. An heir's tenure is designed to be relatively short. When it stretches longer than 5 or 6 years, the likelihood of the final promotion diminishes.

Canella and Shen's (2003) study examined two characteristics of heirs apparent—insider status and director status—as indicators of power. For example, an heir apparent who has many years of service at a firm may have already built his or her coalition and power base. Heir apparent power may have significant implications in a relay succession because, as research on executive turnover has shown, when firm performance is low, less powerful executives are more likely to be dismissed. Insider heirs and heirs who serve on their firms' boards may not only be able to reduce their risk of dismissal, but may also even use their power to challenge incumbents and promote their own ascensions to the CEO positions.

In addition, company tenure indicates the extent to which a person has invested time and effort in a firm, developing firm-specific knowledge and skills, and therefore the perception of a better chance of promotion. This perception makes heirs apparent with longer company tenures more reluctant to leave their employing firms for outside opportunities. Finally, heir apparent director status itself signals high commitment on the part of the incumbent CEO and outside directors to the heir. When a firm is highly committed to the heir apparent, it will grant more power (such as seat on the board) to that person. Therefore, it can be expected that an heir apparent who is promoted from within a firm and an heir who serves on its board of directors is more likely to be promoted to CEO and less likely to leave the firm, regardless of its performance (Cannella & Shen, 2003).

Changing Leadership Roles

Six out of ten leadership roles defined by Mintzberg (1994) were explored for the CIO earlier in this book. Four leadership roles were not considered relevant for the CIO by Grover et al. (1993). The six relevant roles were personnel leader, liaison, monitor, spokesman, entrepreneur, and resource allocator. The four irrelevant roles were figurehead, disseminator, disturbance handler, and negotiator. When the CIO moves from CIO to CEO, those four-neglected leadership roles become important.

The CEO as figurehead performs duties of ceremonial nature. In this role, the CEO is a symbolic head of the organization. The figurehead role belongs to the interpersonal roles together with liaison and personnel leader.

The CEO as disseminator transmits information to other organizational members and to external stakeholders. The chief executive expects to be questioned on detailed issues by various groups: union leaders, press, customers, politicians, and members of staff. The disseminator role belongs to the informational roles together with monitor and spokesman.

The CEO as disturbance handler and negotiator both belong to the decision roles, together with entrepreneur and resource allocator. However, chief executives might be constrained in their decision-making ability, as discussed in the first chapter. Chief executives have to negotiate with individuals. Mintzberg (1994) used 'negotiation' to refer to sessions in which chief executives met outsiders in attempts to reach agreements between their two organizations.

Then Comes CIO Succession

If a CIO becomes the next CEO, then the organization needs a new CIO. Perhaps this book suggests an acid test for selecting the new CIO. Does he or she have the potential to become CEO? If we could develop and appoint such executives, not only would we have CIOs fit for today's challenges, we would be lining up future CEOs (Earl, 2000).

Ordonez (2005) wrote about the art of being a CIO and his own role as CIO:

It takes a certain kind of individual to be a good CIO. You have to love the challenge of a rollercoaster industry. You have to learn constantly, not just about technology, but also about the world you operate in. And, you must learn from your peers. Our CEO is a good example of this, his dedication and passion for the job inspires me and keeps me on my toes. (p. 9)

References

Applegate, L. M., McFarlan, F. W., & McKenney, J. L. (1996). *Corporate information systems management* (4th ed.). USA: Irwin.

Bigley, G. A., & Wiersema, M. F. (2002). New CEOs and corporate strategic refocusing: How experience as heir apparent influences the use of power. *Administrative Science Quarterly, 47,* 707-727.

Buchholtz, A. K., Ribbens, B. A., & Houle, I. T. (2003). The role of human capital in postacquisition CEO departure. *Academy of Management Journal, 46*(4), 506-514.

Cannella, A. A., & Shen, W. (2003). So close and yet so far: Promotion versus exit for CEO heirs apparent. *Academy of Management Journal, 44*(2), 252-270.

Carpenter, M. A., & Wade, J. B. (2002). Microlevel opportunity structures as determinants of non-CEO executive pay. *Academy of Management Journal, 45*(6), 1085-1103.

Charan, R. (2005, February). Ending the CEO succession crisis. *Harvard Business Review*, 72-81.

Davidson, W. N., Nemic, C., & Worrell, D. L. (2001). Succession planning vs. agency theory: A test of Harris and Helfat's interpretation of plurality announcement market returns. *Strategic Management Journal, 22,* 179-184.

Earl, M. (2000). Are CIOs obsolete? *Harvard Business Review,* March-April, 60.

Earl, M. J., & Feeny, D. F. (1994). Is your CIO adding value? *Sloan Management Review, 35*(3), 11-20.

Gartner (2005). The changing role of the CIO. The State of the CIO Around the World. CIO 100 2005: The Bold 100. State of the CIO 2004: The CEO View. *Gartner Group Insight*, www.gartner.com

Grover, V., Jeong, S. R., Kettinger, W. J., and Lee, C. C. (1993). The chief information officer: A study of managerial roles. *Journal of Management Information Systems, 10*(2), 107-130.

Hedlund, J., Forsythe, G. B., Horvath, J. A., Williams, W. M., Snook, S., & Sternberg, R. J. (2003). Identifying and assessing tacit knowledge: Understanding the practical intelligence of military leaders. *The Leadership Quality, 14,* 117-140.

Johnson, L. K. (2002). Do CEOs matter? *MIT Sloan Management Review,* Winter, 8-9.

Karimi, J., Somers, T. M., & Gupta, Y. P. (2001). Impact of information technology management practices on customer service. *Journal of Management Information Systems, 17*(4), 125-158.

McDonald, M. L., & Westphal, J. D. (2003). Getting by with the advice of their friends: CEOs' advice networks and firms' strategic responses to poor performance. *Administrative Science Quarterly, 48,* 1-32.

Mintzberg, H. (1994). Rounding out the manager's job. *Sloan Management Review, 36*(1), 11-26.

Ordonez, A. (2005). When technology is your business, your business strategy, & your point of difference. In *CIO Leadership Strategies*. Aspatore Books.

Porter, M. E., Lorsch, J. W., & Nohria, N. (2004). Seven surprises for new CEOs. *Harvard Business Review,* October, 62-72.

Sambamurthy, V., Straub, D. W., & Watson, R. T. (2001). Managing IT in the digital era. In G. W. Dickson & G. DeSanctis (Eds.), *Information technology and the future enterprise: New models for managers* (pp. 282-305). :Prentice Hall.

Schubert, K. D. (2004). *CIO survival guide: The roles and responsibilities of the chief information officer.* Hoboken, NJ: John Wiley & Sons.

Shen, W., & Cannella, A. A. (2002a). Power dynamics within top management and their impacts on CEO dismissal followed by inside succession. *Academy of Management Journal, 45*(6), 1195-1206.

Shen, W., & Cannella, A. A. (2002b). Revisiting the performance consequences of CEO succession: The impacts of successor type, postsuccession senior executive turnover, and departing CEO tenure. *Academy of Management Journal, 45*(4), 717-733.

Sternberg, R. J. (2003). WICS: A model of leadership in organizations. *Academy of Management Learning and Education, 2*(4), 386-401.

Westphal, J. D., & Bednar, M. K. (2005). Pluralistic ignorance in corporate boards and firms' strategic persistence in response to low firm performance. *Administrative Science Quarterly, 50,* 262-298.

Westphal, J. D., & Khanna, P. (2003). Keeping directors in line: Social distancing as a control mechanism in the corporate elite. *Administrative Science Quarterly, 48,* 361-398.

Zhang, Y., & Rajagopalan, N. (2003). Explaining new CEO origin: Firm versus industry antecedents. *Academy of Management Journal, 46*(3), 327-338.

Zhang, Y., & Rajagopalan, N. (2004). When the known devil is better than an unknown god: An empirical study of the antecedents and consequences of relay CEO successions. *Academy of Management Journal, 47*(4), 483-500.

Chapter IX

Knowledge Business Examples

In this chapter, we move from information technology performance to the performance of value configurations based on information technology. Value configurations are value chains, value shops, and value networks, as exemplified throughout this book. In this chapter, only value shops are exemplified, as the knowledge economy creates more and more value shops and fewer and fewer value chains. First, law firms are used as an example, where the law firm performance is linked to knowledge management systems over time. Next, police investigation units are used as an example, where the extent of investigation success is linked to knowledge management systems over time.

Dynamics of Law Firm Performance

Earlier in this book, law firms were briefly used as an example to illustrate the iterative dimension of the stages of growth model for knowledge management technology. Here, law firms are used to illustrate the interactions between information technology and business dynamics in law firm business.

A law firm can be understood as a social community specializing in the speed and efficiency in the creation and transfer of legal knowledge (Nahapiet & Ghoshal, 1998). Many law firms represent large corporate enterprises, organizations, or entrepreneurs with a need for continuous and specialized legal services that can only be supplied by a team of lawyers. The client is a customer of the firm, rather than a particular lawyer. According to Galanter and Palay (1991), relationships with clients tend to be enduring:

Firms represent large corporate enterprises, organizations, or entrepreneurs with a need for continuous (or recurrent) and specialized legal services that could be supplied only by a team of lawyers. The client "'belongs to" the firm, not to a particular lawyer. Relations with clients tend to be enduring. Such repeat clients are able to reap benefits from the continuity and economies of scale and scope enjoyed by the firm. (p. 5)

Lawyers as Knowledge Workers

Lawyers can be defined as knowledge workers. They are professionals who have gained knowledge through formal education (explicit) and through learning on the job (tacit). Often, there is some variation in the quality of their education and learning. The value of professionals' education tends to hold throughout their careers. For example, lawyers in Norway are asked whether they got the good grade of 'laud', even thirty years after graduation. Professionals' prestige (which is based partly on the institutions from which they obtained their education) is a valuable organizational resource because of the elite social networks that provide access to valuable external resources for the firm (Hitt, Bierman, Shumizu, & Kochhar, 2001).

After completing their advanced educational requirements, most professionals enter their careers as associates in law. In this role, they continue to learn and thus gain significant tacit knowledge through "learning by doing." Therefore, they largely bring explicit knowledge derived from formal education into their firms and build tacit knowledge through experience.

Most professional service firms use a partnership form of organization. In such a framework, those who are highly effective in using and applying knowledge are eventually rewarded with partner status, and thus own stakes in a firm. On their road to partnership, these professionals acquire considerable knowledge, much of which is tacit. Thus, by the time professionals achieve partnership, they have built human capital in the form of individual skills (Hitt et al., 2001).

Because law is precedent-driven, its practitioners are heavily invested in knowing how things have been done before. Jones (2000) found that many attorneys, therefore, are already oriented toward the basic premises of knowledge management, though they have been practicing it on a more individualized basis and without the help of technology and virtual collaboration. As such, a knowledge management initiative could find the areas where lawyers are already sharing information and then introduce modern technology to support this information sharing to make it more effective.

Lawyers work in law firms, and law firms belong to the legal industry. According to Becker, Herman, Samuelson, & Webb (2001), the legal industry will change rapidly because of three important trends. First, global companies increasingly seek out law firms that can provide consistent support at all business locations and integrated cross-border assistance for significant mergers and acquisitions, as well as capital-market transactions. Second, client loyalty is decreasing as companies increasingly base purchases of legal services on a more objective assessment of their value, defined as benefits net of price. Finally, new competitors have entered the market, such as accounting firms and Internet-based legal services firms.

In this book, the term "lawyer" is used most of the time. Other terms, such as "attorney" and "solicitor," are sometimes used as synonyms in this book. In reality, these words can have different meanings, together with terms such as "barrister," "counselor," and "advocate." In Norwegian, a distinction is made between a lawyer (jurist) and a solicitor (advokat). There is no need to make such distinctions in this book.

Lawyers are knowledge workers. To understand the organizational form of lawyers as knowledge workers employed in companies such as law firms, there is a need to recognize the dual dependent relationship between knowledge workers and the organization. On the one hand, for the purpose of channeling the motivation and effort of employees to serve the interests of the firm, management will seek to exploit knowledge workers' need to rely on the organization for resources (for example, advanced computer software and hardware which are available at a high cost) to accomplish their work tasks. On the other hand, management depends on knowledge workers for their esoteric and advanced knowledge and their ability to synthesize theoretical and contextual knowledge. Management, therefore, needs to meet these employees' aspirations and expectations. As for knowledge workers, they need to depend on the organization as the locale to develop contextual knowledge and to create new knowledge. However, their ability to apply theoretical knowledge in other contexts, that is, in other organizations, means that to a certain extent, they are also able to pursue a limited form of marketization. This enables them to reap market-level rewards for their expertise (May, Korczynski, & Frenkel, 2002).

Knowledge Categories

To get started on this job, legal industry knowledge has to be understood. Edwards and Mahling (1997) have suggested that law firms have four categories of knowledge: administrative, declarative, procedural, and analytical knowledge, as defined earlier in this book. These knowledge categories are all important to the law firm. While any law firm needs to maintain efficient administrative records, there does not appear to be any significant possibility for gaining strategic advantage in the firm's core competency of providing sound legal advice to its clients by using these records. The detailed administrative knowledge they contain is essential to the operation of the law firm, but does not contribute to the substantive content. Declarative, procedural, and analytical knowledge offer greater possibilities for creating strategic value for the firm.

Edwards and Mahling (1997) present a case drawn from the case collection of one of the authors to illustrate the differences in strategic value among procedural, declarative, and analytical knowledge. In the early 1990s one of the authors, at the time engaged in the practice of law, represented a corporate client as seller in several sales of corporate businesses and real estate. At the time, buyers of businesses and real estate had become concerned about their possible liability for pollution existing on property when they purchased it. The U.S. federal laws governing the legal responsibility of landowners for environmental contamination on their property had been adopted a few years earlier and their full impact on sale of businesses was just beginning to be understood.

The relevant declarative knowledge was an understanding of several related state and federal laws and agency regulations governing liability for environmental contamination. The relevant procedural knowledge in part was to know how to transfer the environmental licenses and permits used by a given business to a new owner and how to transfer the real estate as an asset. The relevant analytical knowledge was to understand what risks the buyer of a contaminated property faced (legal and financial) and what contractual protections the seller could reasonably give to the buyer.

Law firms are interesting in themselves from both a knowledge and a management perspective. From a management perspective, law firm partners own a typical law firm. Among themselves, the partners appoint a board and a managing partner. In addition they hire a chief executive officer (CEO) to run all support functions in the firm, such as financial management (CFO), knowledge management (CKO), and information technology management (CIO).

Jones (2000) found that top-down directives are complicated in the legal industry. In large law firms in the US and UK, the power can be spread among as many as 150 partners, most of whom have different specialty areas, different work and management styles, and vastly different groups under their control. Earning a consensus is not an easy proposition—especially when the funding for new initiatives such as knowledge management initiatives is coming directly out of the partners' yearly income. At the same time, partners are the ones who have the most to gain if their firm is able to manage knowledge effectively to keep lucrative clients on board and draw new ones through new services.

The human capital embodied in the partners is a professional service firm's most important resource. Their experience, particularly as partners, builds valuable industry-specific and firm-specific knowledge, which is often tacit. Such knowledge is the least imitable form of knowledge. An important responsibility of partners is obtaining and maintaining clients. Partners build relationships with current and potential clients and, over time, develop social capital through their client networks. Therefore, the experience a professional gains as a partner contributes to competitive advantage (Hitt et al., 2001).

Partners with education from the best institutions and with the most experience as partners in particular legal areas represent substantial human capital to the firm. As partners, they continue to acquire knowledge, largely tacit and firm-specific, and to build social capital. This human capital should produce the highest-quality services to clients and thereby contribute significantly to firm performance. The job of partner differs from that of associate, and new skills must be developed. Partners must build the skills needed to develop and maintain effective relationships with clients. Importantly, partners in law firms serve as project and team leaders on specific cases and thus must develop managerial skills.

Partners own the most human capital in a firm and have the largest stakes using the firm's resources to the greatest advantage. One of the responsibilities of partners is to help develop the knowledge of other employees of the firm, particularly its associates. Associates at law firms need to learn internal routines, the situation of important clients, and nuances in the application of law (Hitt et al., 2001).

Information technology support for knowledge management in law firms has to consider the very special knowledge situation in each law firm. Edwards and Mahling (1997) argue that knowledge is dispersed among many different members of the firm, and others outside the firm may contribute to knowledge. Law firm knowledge has a wide variety of sources both inside and outside the firm. Much administrative knowledge is generated by the members of the firm as billing records for their services. The firm's administrative staff creates other administrative information. Attorneys are the major source of analytical, declarative, and procedural knowledge. Legal assistants have some declarative knowledge based on their experience. Declarative knowledge can also be found in publicly available sources intended for research purposes, primarily books, online subscription research sources, and CD-ROM resources. The quantity of publicly available research material for any given topic depends significantly on the size of the market for the information. The more specialized the legal area, the smaller the potential market for material and the less that is usually widely available. Experienced legal assistants are usually an invaluable source of procedural knowledge, since much procedural work is delegated to them. Legal assistants are common in countries such as the US and UK, but they are seldom found in law firms in countries such as Norway and Sweden.

Experienced legal secretaries may have a significant amount of procedural knowledge for transactions they handle often. Law firms in Norway employ many secretaries. It is common to find more than one secretary for every three lawyers in a law firm.

The role of others outside the law firm in generating analytical and procedural knowledge needs to be noted. While much of the useful procedural and analytical knowledge resides in firm employees, it is likely that there are sources outside the firm as well. One belief frequently expressed in the knowledge management literature is the view that learning is social: People learn in groups. These groups are known in the literature as communities of practice.

Communities of practice have been defined as groups of people who are informally bound to one another by exposure to a common class of problem. It is quite likely that the communities of practice for the lawyers in the firm include other members of professional associations such as bar associations. These groups usually have a number of committees devoted to practice areas, such as environmental law. In Norway, Den Norske Advokatforening (Norwegian Lawyers Association) has such committees.

Generally, the idea of communities of practice developed in the organizational learning movement. The idea posits that knowledge flows best through networks of people who may not be in the same part of the organization, or in the same organization, but have the same work interests. Some firms have attempted to formalize these communities, even though theorists argue that they should emerge in self-organizing fashion without any relationship to formal organizational structures (Grover & Davenport, 2001).

A few more technologically advanced lawyers may use the Internet or such subscription services as Counsel Connect in the US on the World Wide Web as a sounding board for analytical and procedural issues in a community of legal practice. These external sources can provide knowledge in the form of informal conversations, written newsletters and updates, briefs filed in relevant litigation, and other forms.

An obvious problem in law firms is that knowledge is not consistently documented, and documented knowledge is not always explicit. Much administrative information is captured in electronic form as part of the firm's billing records. Other administrative data resides in the firm's payroll and benefits records and file and records management systems. Much of the firm's declarative knowledge resides in the memories of the firm's attorneys and in their work product. As noted above, the firm has access to publicly available declarative knowledge in the form of published reference works, and declarative knowledge is typically the best-documented type of knowledge.

Much procedural knowledge is documented throughout the firm's files in the form of completed records of transactions, which provide guidance about what legal documents were necessary to complete a certain type of transaction. The knowledge of procedure reflected in these documents is often implicit rather than explicit. Explicit procedural knowledge is contained in a collection of written practice guides for popular areas like real estate transactions. These guides include standard checklists of items necessary to complete a particular transaction for the kinds of transactions that occur frequently.

Analytical knowledge resides primarily in attorneys' heads. Analytical knowledge is occasionally documented in client files through the notes of an attorney's thought processes. More often it is reflected in the completed contract documents or other transaction documents by the inclusion of specific clauses dealing with a particular topic. The analytical knowledge reflected in completed documents is very often not explicit, in the sense that it is often not clear from the face of the document what analytical issues are dealt with in the document.

Another law firm problem is that knowledge is often shared on an informal basis. Certain methods of sharing knowledge, at least within the firm, have traditionally been part of large law firm culture. One of the most important ways of sharing knowledge has been through the process of partners training associates to perform tasks. In larger firms, the practice of hiring young, bright law school graduates who were trained, supervised, and rewarded by a partner has been followed throughout most of this century. The method focuses on transmitting knowledge from more experienced attorneys to less experienced attorneys, as distinguished from transmitting it to other partners in the firm or to legal assistants and other support staff.

This attorney training customarily has relied on informal methods of transmitting knowledge, such as rotating young attorneys through a series of practice groups within the firm. Much of this informal training takes place via collaborative work on documents such as contracts and pleadings. Some of it occurs through informal consultation between a senior attorney and a junior attorney about the best way to handle a specific task. These consultations may be carried out by face-to-face discussions, e-mail, or telephone conversations. No attempt is usually made to capture the substance of the training through these informal methods, even where a form of communication, such as e-mail, may often be used that could produce documentation. It is important to note that this training often takes place under intense time pressure. Further, in an hourly billing system there is often little or no financial incentive to produce documentation, which cannot be billed directly to a client.

In addition to problems of knowledge dispersion, inconsistent documentation, and informal knowledge sharing, Edwards and Mahling (1997) argue that if knowledge has been documented, it is contained in a mixture of paper and electronic formats and located in dispersed physical locations. Administrative information typically exists in a combination of print and electronic formats. A large firm would customarily maintain computerized databases for key matters such as tracking lawyers' hourly billings, for its client contact data, and for staff assignments to projects but would usually generate paper invoices to clients. The data physically resides in the firm's computer network and in paper files.

Declarative, procedural, and analytical knowledge is often documented in attorney work product such as briefs, memoranda, and actual legal documents such as contracts, wills, and instruments of transfer. Work product documents typically are created in electronic form but are customarily stored in print-format client files. The electronic format materials are stored in standalone personal computers or on the network. Paper materials are located throughout the firm's offices.

Where knowledge has been documented in a law firm, often only a few simple tools exist to facilitate the retrieval of knowledge by topic. Attorney work files are usually indexed by client name and matter name but their contents are seldom indexed for subject matter in more than the most general way. An attorney creating a particular item of work product may place it in a firm's standard database maintained in electronic format. Other lawyers can then use these standard documents as examples or models. In a typical installation the standard forms library is stored on the network and is physically available to those who have network access. The standard forms library allows access to individual documents by name but subject matter classification is often limited to what can be included in a descriptive DOS format file name. Retrieving material from the forms library thus usually requires tedious sequential search and review of the contents of the library.

Access to the procedural and analytical knowledge embodied in client files is difficult at best for those not familiar with the files. The client files are often not indexed by subject matter, making it difficult to locate procedural or analytical knowledge on a particular topic if the contents of the file are not already familiar. Document management systems do support network-wide searches for documents in electronic form by selected attributes such as document author name or keywords appearing in the document. In the absence of a consistent system of classifying the document's contents by subject or topic, however, keyword searches by topic produce incomplete retrieval of all relevant documents.

Even if knowledge is documented by work product such as a memorandum to file, access to the implicit procedural and analytical knowledge embodied in the firm's files is often difficult at best. Client files that are indexed according to a subject-based system may offer some help in searching for analytical knowledge. A large transaction, however, may include dozens of analytical issues and it is unlikely that all of them would be indexed. Procedural knowledge is unlikely to be indexed at all. This means that the user must often rely on the ability to search by keywords for relevant fact patterns to retrieve relevant procedural or analytical knowledge.

Some knowledge in a law firm raises issues of security and confidentiality. There are few confidentiality concerns with declarative knowledge. This type of knowledge is meant to be public and readily accessible to all. Analytical and procedural knowledge within the firm can, however, raise issues of security and client confidentiality. Attorneys in the firm have professional ethical obligations to their clients to maintain the confidentiality of information furnished by the client. While these ethical obligations are customarily interpreted to permit sharing the information among the firm's members and staff, appropriate precautions still must be taken to avoid disclosures outside the firm.

Implications for Systems Design

Edwards and Mahling (1997) find that their observations have implications for system design. They believe that their observations about the characteristics of knowledge within large law firms have implications for the design of knowledge management tools for these firms. There is not a one-to-one correspondence between their observations and the implications for design, as some observations have a number of ramifications for the design tools. The following discussion of the implications for system specifications is important. A number of specification issues concern the roles of different end users of a knowledge management system in a large law firm. Gatekeepers, knowledge librarians, and other specialists should be named:

- A gatekeeper capable of evaluating materials for inclusion must be named.

- To assure accuracy, knowledge should be edited before being made accessible.

- To assure currency, the knowledge should be reviewed periodically after it has been placed in the knowledge base.

Another set of specifications deals with the strategy and trail of knowledge items, thus putting isolated knowledge pieces into organizational context:

- To maximize the strategic value created by a knowledge base, it must focus on the type of knowledge that has been identified as having the best potential strategic value. A selection process must be established for inclusion in the knowledge base. There should be agreement about the types of knowledge that are to be captured in the knowledge base as having strategic value to the firm.

- Users must have access to the name of the source of the knowledge. It must be easy to identify the creator of a particular item of knowledge.

- It must be easy to learn the history of a particular item in the knowledge base: The date it was added, the date of any revisions, the frequency with which it has been used.

- The tools must be able to extract the useful knowledge while preserving the confidentiality of client information. Some portions of the knowledge base must support restricted access.

The collaborative aspects of knowledge are related to specifications that border on the areas of organizational memory and collective intelligence:

- Because many firm members can create knowledge, all firm members should be able to share knowledge. All knowledge management tools should be in an electronic form and available on a network accessible by all firm members. Portions of the tools should be accessible by external users with appropriate security mechanisms.

- The system must facilitate the informal sharing of knowledge. Users should be able to identify creators of knowledge on a particular topic. The system should facilitate contact with the creator of knowledge by e-mail, telephone, or online conference. Users should also be able to transmit items readily by e-mail or other electronic communications.

- To encourage users to document their knowledge, it should be easy to add material to the knowledge base. As much as possible, the system should capture information without requiring much additional effort from the creator.

Knowledge acquisition and the solicitation of knowledge are crucial factors on the input side. Technical and organizational factors are concerned:

- User tools should be suitable for use by users with a wide variety of both substantive legal knowledge and technological sophistication.
- There should be incentives to document knowledge. When items are added to the system, the source must be identifiable. It should be possible to measure the use of an item once it is placed in the system.

An electronic format of structured and unstructured knowledge objects is a rather basic specification for knowledge management tools. Closely connected to this aspect is the retrieval and presentation of knowledge:

- The tools must be able to capture and manipulate knowledge in a variety of formats, both electronic (word processing, e-mail, and electronic database search results) and paper.
- Users should be able to retrieve knowledge in a format that can readily be exported to a word processor for inclusion in work product.
- The tools must permit at least rudimentary subject matter indexing. Users must be able to search, sort and retrieve knowledge in the system by subject.
- The system must facilitate the retrieval of implicit procedural and analytical knowledge. Users must be able to conduct keyword searches for relevant fact attributes that are not indexed. The use of other tools, such as intelligent agents and collaborative filtering programs, which could facilitate the retrieval of implicit knowledge, should be explored.

IT support for knowledge management is only at the beginning. But some law firms are making progress, and these firms may be ready for the next technology wave. According to Jones (2000), for the firms that have already embraced knowledge management, the next wave will likely include a stronger focus on client-facing extranets and the development of expert systems. Extranets are essential for ensuring lasting relationships with clients, not only because they increase a client's access to their counsel, but because the firm gets linked so tightly with the client that the client will remain with the firm. Expert systems are showing huge potential efficiency returns and hold promise for much of the transactional work-tax matters, real estate closings, and financial closings that make up the bulk of legal services. Capturing the knowledge upon which the systems are based is a more complicated process than setting up collaborative systems among practice groups.

Edwards and Mahling (1997) summarize the situation for IT support for knowledge management in law firms by stating that they believe a significant opportunity exists in large law firms for the successful use of knowledge management tools. These firms are currently performing some knowledge management tasks with tools that offer only rudimentary knowledge management capability and are not fully integrated with the firms' existing technology. None of the current available tools satisfies all of the user requirements they have identified. The tools that are currently available do not adequately support the informal knowledge sharing that is a key element of knowledge management in these firms. Tools must be configured to support and encourage informal collaboration and a stronger information-sharing culture. In these organizations, where performance is measured by the number of billable hours, knowledge management tools must minimize the amount of effort required of the user. They must become as invisible as possible.

Many authors are concerned with firm culture as a determining factor for knowledge management. O'Connor (2000) suggests that compensation, individuality, billing, and tradition are some of the most important barriers to knowledge management initiatives in today's firm:

- **Compensation:** Compensation models are one of the toughest hurdles. Although some firms have lock-step compensation models, where attorneys are not as adversely impacted for spending time on knowledge sharing activities, most don't. Even those that do typically place a premium on billable hours, and lawyers who do not hit billable targets feel the sting. The practical impact: It's a challenge to convince lawyers to contribute content into knowledge management systems.

- **Individuality:** Lawyers are lone wolves, and moving to team collaboration can be a tough transition. Law is intensely competitive, from getting in to the right school, to making the school's law review, to clerking for the right justice, to getting a job at the right firm. Competitiveness is ingrained in the legal psyche. Most lawyers remain intensely competitive, even in their own firms. How do you reconcile this mindset with demands to share knowledge with your coworkers? Lawyers must transition from believing that by transferring knowledge they somehow become less important, to believing the old adage that "All boats rise with the tide."

- **Billing:** Most firms still bill principally on a time and materials basis. Although clients are demanding fixed-price bids and not-to-exceed estimates, and competition ("'beauty contests") is thriving, many firms have not fully embraced new billing models. Old-school lawyers believe efficiency results in lower revenues. In their view, why spend lots of money to get more efficient, when it adversely impacts the business?

- **Tradition:** Attorneys are often skeptical about new ways of doing things. Tradition reigns, and it can be difficult to accept radically different approaches.

So, how can a firm address these challenges? O'Connor (2000) suggests that first and foremost, management must be committed to the knowledge management program and provide tangible support:

- Executive managers must understand why the firm is investing in KM, commit the necessary funds, and throw their weight behind the team doing the work. Ideally, firm leaders should prepare a one-minute-speech so that they can quickly and easily articulate the firm's KM strategy. Furthermore, second-tier management must be involved, that is, practice and department heads are also informed, and they must be active supporters. Discuss KM plans at partnership meetings and retreats; spread the message about why it is important.

- The first step is to conduct a knowledge audit. This involves spending time with the right people in the practice areas, and identifying how knowledge is created and transferred, with an eye for areas for improvement. Focus on the practice, and spend time with lawyers in the practice areas. Understand what they do and ascertain how we can improve the practice. Consider a broad-based knowledge management team, comprised of attorneys and staff, representative of the firm's practice areas and locations. For example, Shearman & Sterling, a law firm in the US, has created a Knowledge Advisory Board composed of just such a collection of lawyers and staff. They meet regularly to direct the strategy and overall plan for the firm's knowledge management initiative, with a real focus on best practices.

- The next step is to develop a plan to address the needs that have been distilled from this effort. It should focus on how the firm can capture and reuse important knowledge assets. Content is king. If we don't have a method and process for easily capturing and accessing helpful information, then we will not be successful.

- One of the key elements of the plan must be how we will create processes that facilitate knowledge sharing. They must be unobtrusive or they will not be followed, the content will provide marginal value, and the utility and benefits of the system will suffer. This may be the most important consideration of all. Sherman & Sterling created a role of knowledge coordinator in each practice group. These people not only help to determine what processes make sense, but they are also directly responsible for ensuring that their respective practice areas participate.

- Try a little marketing and shameless self-promotion. How we pitch KM in the firm may be a great determinant of its success. When considering KM, it all sounds too dramatic and complicated for lawyers to really embrace. Bonnie Speer-McGrath, of Speer Software Training, suggests that the same tactics used to sell new technology innovations to lawyers as part of the training process can also be used to get lawyers excited about KM. Finding ways to tangibly demonstrate how lawyers perform tasks today, coupled with how they could accomplish the same tasks faster and with better results is key. Given the structural impediments to implementing KM in law firms, firms must embrace a broad strategy for introducing it to their firms. Promotion and education can take many forms, from formal briefings, to hands-on training, to the use of success stories, where specific examples of the effective use of such tools and processes are highlighted. Lawyers want to know, "What's in it for me?"

- Focus on the needs of firm lawyers. Create a team to lead the effort that includes them. Spend time with them, ascertain needs, and focus efforts on building processes that will facilitate the incorporation of new content. If we've done a good job of understanding their needs and in providing useful content for them, then we can be sure that "If you build it, they will come."

Knowledge Management Matrix

To identify knowledge management applications, we can combine knowledge levels with knowledge categories. Core knowledge, advanced knowledge and innovative knowledge is combined with administrative knowledge, declara-

Figure 9.1. Knowledge management matrix

Levels Categories	Core Knowledge	Advanced Knowledge	Innovative Knowledge
Administrative Knowledge			
Declarative Knowledge			
Procedural Knowledge			
Analytical Knowledge			

Figure 9.2. Knowledge management matrix for the current IS/IT situation

Levels Categories	Core Knowledge	Advanced Knowledge	Innovative Knowledge
Administrative Knowledge	Accounting system Hours billing Clients database E-mail Word processing Spreadsheet Salary system	Competence database Client firm information Internet	
Declarative Knowledge	Library system Electronic law-book Electronic legal sources	Law database	
Procedural Knowledge	Case collection Document standards Procedural standards Document examples	Internal databases Intranet Public databases	
Analytical Knowledge	Law interpretations	Groupware	

Figure 9.3. Knowledge management matrix for desired IS/IT situation

Levels Categories	Core Knowledge	Advanced Knowledge	Innovative Knowledge
Administrative Knowledge	Accounting system Hours billing Clients database E-mail Word processing Spreadsheet Salary system *Electronic diary* *Electronic reception* *Office automation* *Message system*	Competence database Client firm information Internet *Videophone* *Video conference* *Quality system* *Financial services* *Intranet* *Net agent* *Electronic meetings*	*Client statistics* *Lawyer statistics* *Recruiting system* *Scanning* *Quality assurance* *Benchmarking* *Customer* *relationships* *Net-based services* *Electronic diary* *Mobile office* *Executive* *information*
Declarative Knowledge	Library system Electronic law- book Electronic legal sources *Document* *management* *Legal databases* *Commercial* *databases*	Law database *Electronic library* *Electronic law-book* *Extranet* *International legal* *sources*	*Law change base* *Precedence base* *Conference system* *Intelligent agents* *Artificial* *intelligence* *Portals* *Work flow systems*
Procedural Knowledge	Case collection Document standards Procedural standards Document examples *Planning system* *Standards archive* *Publishing system*	Internal databases Intranet Public databases *Experience* *database* *Image processing* *Document* *generation* *International law* *base* *Public web access*	*Video registration* *Case system* *Online services*
Analytical Knowledge	Law interpretations *Voice recognition* *Case* *interpretations*	Groupware *Intelligent agents* *Client monitoring* *Extranet* *Discussion groups* *Video conference*	*Expert register* *Expert system* *Research reports* *Subject database* *Data warehouse*

tive knowledge, procedural knowledge, and analytical knowledge in Figure 9.1. We have created a knowledge management matrix with twelve cells for IS/IT applications.

The knowledge management matrix can first be used to identify the current IS/IT that supports knowledge management in the firm, as illustrated in Figure 9.2.

Now the knowledge management matrix can be applied to identify future IS/IT, as illustrated in Figure 9.3. The systems do not only serve as examples, they illustrate that it is possible to find systems than can support all combinations of knowledge categories and knowledge levels.

Software and systems suitable for knowledge management in a law firm can now be identified using the knowledge management matrix. In Figure 9.4, examples of software to support systems in Figure 9.3 are listed.

Let us look at one example in Figure 9.4. Knowledger is listed as potential software in the innovative-analytical knowledge location. This is an ambitious location of a software product that has yet to demonstrate its real capabilities in knowledge firms. According to the vendor Knowledge Associates, Knowledger 3.0 is complete knowledge management software that can be integrated with other systems in the firm. Knowledger is Web-based and supports the firm by categorizing internal and external information, as well as linking incoming information to existing information.

Let us look at one more application in the most demanding location of innovative-analytical knowledge. There we find something called Summation. Summation is a system for document handling for use in large court cases. In the large court case of Balder in Norway, law firm Thommessen Krefting Greve Lund (TKGL) used Summation in 2001. The Balder case was a dispute between Exxon and Smedvig about the rebuilding of an offshore vessel costing 3 billion Norwegian crones. TKGL had more than 2,500 binders when the court case started in the city of Stavanger. All these documents were scanned into a database for use by Summation. When lawyers from TKGL present material in court, they submit it from their laptops. When new information emerges in court, then it is registered in Summation. When TKGL lawyers are to trace technical and financial developments for Balder, they make a search in the Summation database.

Another law firm is also using Summation. The law firm Bugge Arentz-Hansen Rasmussen (BA-HR) has the task of finding money after the late ship-owner Jahre. The money is expected to be in banks in countries where there are no

Figure 9.4. Knowledge management matrix for software supporting desired IS/IT situation

Levels / Categories	Core Knowledge	Advanced Knowledge	Innovative Knowledge
Administrative Knowledge	Microsoft Word Microsoft Excel Microsoft Outlook SuperOffice Timex Concorde XAL DBMS SuperOffice Microsoft Office Oracle Agresso Powermarkt Uni økonomi Datalex Justice Data Systems GroupWise Alta Law Office ESI Law	Microsoft Access Lotus Approach Corel Paradox Infotorg IFS Rubicon Concorde K-link Akelius dokument Windows NT Explorer CheckPoint Firewall RealMedia Advisor klient Completo Advokat Visma Business Advokat	Intranet Internet Extranet WAP PDA/Palm KnowledgeShare IFS Business performance Mikromarc 2 statistic IFS Front Office Psion Nomade Netscape Netcaster
Declarative Knowledge	NorLex CarNov RightOn Lovdata NORSOK	Lovdata Celex BibJure Shyster Finder Prjus BookWhere	Hieros Gamos Eudor Abacus Law Lawgic Netmeeting Lov chat LegalSeeker KG Agent Lotus K-station Domino Workflow
Procedural Knowledge	Jasper Karnov Mikas Aladdin ePaper Action Request System DocuShare CyberWorks Training Learning Space	Lotus Domino Domino.Doc DOCS Open HotDocs Adobe photoshop EUR-Lex ODIN eCabinet	Justice Autonomy LegalSeeker Expert Legal Systems Hieros Gamos Real Media Amicus Attorney

Figure 9.4. continued

Levels *Categories*	Core Knowledge	Advanced Knowledge	Innovative Knowledge
Analytical Knowledge	PDA/Palm Lotus LearningSpace Lotus Quickplace Lotus Sametime IBM Content Manager IBM Enterprise Portal Voice Express Collaborative Virtual Work Search Sugar Vchip	Lotus Notes iNotes Lotus K-Station Jasper Novell GroupWise Microsoft Exchange Netscape Communicator JSF Litigator's Notebook Empolis K42 Legal Files	Summation Knowledger Lotus Raven Shyster XpertRule Miner Expert Choice Dragon Dictate

taxes. The hunt for Jahre funds has been going on for almost a decade, and BA-HR has developed a large Summation database enabling BA-HR lawyers to present important information in the court in the city of Drammen.

According to Susskind (2000), six kinds of expert systems can play an important role in law firms in the future:

- **Diagnostic systems:** Those systems that offer specific solutions to problems presented to them. From the facts of any particular case, as elicited by such a system, it will analyze the details and draw conclusions, usually after some kind of interactive consultation. These systems are analogous to the medical diagnostic systems that make diagnoses on the basis of symptoms presented to them. An example of a diagnostic system in law would be a taxation system that could pinpoint the extent to which and why a person is liable to pay tax, doing so on the basis of a mass of details provided to it.

- **Planning systems:** In a sense, planning systems reason in reverse. For these systems are instructed as to a desired solution or outcome and their purpose is to identify scenarios, involving both factual and legal premises, which justify the preferred conclusion. In tax law, a planning system could recommend how best a taxpayer should arrange his affairs so as to minimize his exposure to liability. The knowledge held within planning systems can be very similar to that held within diagnostic systems; what is quite different is the way that that knowledge is applied.

- **Procedural guides:** Many complex tasks facing legal professionals require extensive expertise and knowledge that is in fact procedural in nature. Expert systems as procedural guides take their users through such complex and extended procedures, ensuring that all matters are attended to and done within any prescribed time periods. An example of such a system would be one that managed the flow of a complex tax evasion case, providing detailed guidance and support from inception through to final disposal.

- **The intelligent checklist:** This category of system has most often been used to assist in auditing or reviewing compliance with legal regulations. Compliance reviews must be undertaken with relentless attention to detail and extensive reference to large bodies of regulations. Intelligent checklists provide a technique for performing such reviews. They formalize the process. In taxation, an intelligent checklist approach could be used to assist in the review of a company's compliance with corporation tax.

- **Document modeling systems:** These systems—also referred to as document assembly systems—store templates set up by legal experts. These templates contain fixed portions of text together with precise indications as to the conditions under which given extracts should be used. In operation, such a system will elicit from its user all the details relevant to a proposed document. This is done by the user answering questions, responding to prompts, and providing information. On the basis of the user's input, the system will automatically generate a customized and polished document on the basis of its knowledge of how its text should be used.

- **Arguments generation systems:** It is envisaged that these systems are able to generate sets of competing legal arguments, in situations where legal resources do not provide definitive guidance. Rather than seeking to provide legal solutions (as diagnostic systems strive to do), argument generation systems will present sound lines of reasoning, backed both by legal authority and by propositions of principle and policy. These lines of reasoning will lead to a range of legal conclusions. Such systems would help users identify promising lines of reasoning in support of

Figure 9.5. Causal loop diagram for law firm performance

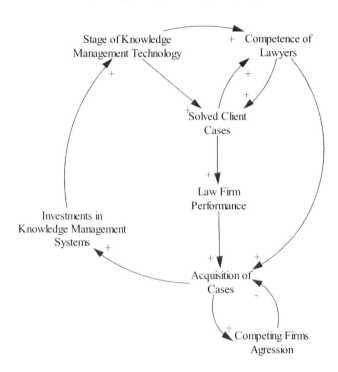

desired outcomes while, at the same time, advancing other arguments which may need to be refuted. (p. 163)

Returning to our main topic of business dynamics in information technology, Figure 9.5 illustrates the case of law firms. An important positive feedback loop in the diagram is the increased acquisition of cases based on improved law firm performance, leading to more investments in knowledge management systems and to a higher stage in knowledge management technology, causing further improvement in law firm performance.

A possible development over time for the law firm is illustrated in Figure 9.6 based on Figure 9.5. In this example, law firm performance and stage of knowledge management technology enter into a positive spiral over time.

Figure 9.6. Reference mode for law firm performance

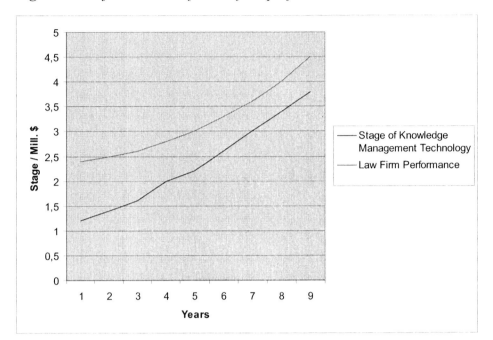

Dynamics of Police Investigation Performance

Police investigations are a complex undertaking that have both reactive and proactive dimensions to them. The knowledge required to effectively carry out an investigation is built upon "three pillars," a term employed by the Singapore Police Force, which are forensics, intelligence, and interviews (Dean, 2005).

A well-grounded forensic understanding of a crime scene is the foundation of any investigation. Intelligence gathering is a crucial activity for an investigation, particularly so for proactive investigations into organized crime and/or terrorist-related operations. With regard to interviews, the ability to derive relevant information from people through effective interviewing is seen by police as an essential activity in any investigation. Hence, as Chen et al. (2002) point out, police investigation units represent a knowledge-intensive and time-critical environment. The primary mission of any police force in the world is to protect life and property, preserve law and order, and prevent and detect crime (Luen & Al-Hawamdeh, 2001).

Value Shop

We treat police investigation as value shop activities. As can be seen in Figure 9.7, these five activities are interlocking, and while they follow a logical sequence, much like the management of any project the difference from a knowledge management perspective is the way in which knowledge is used as a resource to create value for the organization. Hence, the logic the five interlocking value shop activities in this example is of a police organization and how it engages in its core business of conducting reactive and proactive investigations.

Also noted on Figure 9.7 is how in practice these five sequential activities tend to overlap and link back to earlier activities, especially in relation to activity five (control and evaluation) in police organizations, when the need for control and command structures are a daily necessity because of the legal obligations that police authority entails. Hence, the diagram on Figure 9.7 is meant to illustrate the reiterative and cyclical nature of these five primary activities for managing the knowledge collected during and applied to a specific police investigation in a 'value shop' manner.

Briefly, these five activities in relation to a police investigation unit can be outlined as:

1. Problem-finding and acquisition involves working with parties to determine the exact nature of the crime. It involves deciding on the overall approach to police work for the case.

2. Problem solving is the actual generation of ideas and action plans for the investigation.

3. Choice represents the decision of choosing between alternatives. While the least important primary activity of the value shop in terms of time and effort, it is also the most important in terms of customer value. In this case, trying to ensure as far as is possible that is the action decided on is the best option to follow to get an effective investigative result.

4. Execution, as the name implies, represents communication, organizing, investigating, and implementing decisions.

Figure 9.7. Police investigation units as value shops

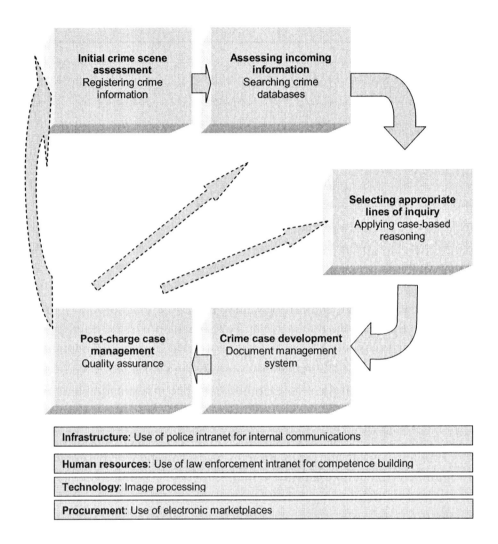

5.   Control and evaluation activities involve monitoring and measurement of how well the solution solved the original problem or met the original need. As noted above, this is where the command & control chain of authority comes into play for police organizations.

The public sector is turning to knowledge management, having recognized that it too faces competition in funding and from alternative services. Increasingly, customers of the public sector are demanding higher service quality, particularly in the area of e-government. Services, particularly e-services, are expected to be available all the time with immediate response, simplified and with one-stop processing. According to Luen and Al-Hawamdeh (2001), knowledge management is thus a natural solution to improve operations and enhance customer service. Large organizations around the world are implementing knowledge management.

The activities and work carried out by police forces are primarily in the areas of crime prevention, incident management, investigation, and community policing. Crime prevention implies the detection and hence prevention of crime. These activities can be carried out through both reactive and proactive means. Reactive measures such as roadblocks, spot-checks, and showing police presence are routinely carried out by police officers as part of their investigation duties. Proactive measures include public education to help prevent crime. Police forces routinely use mass media as a means to convey crime prevention advice relating to current crime trends. In Singapore, police officers also reach out to the community via grassroots and community agencies to educate the public on the latest crime trends and threats. Police officers performing both reactive and proactive measures effectively will need to know the latest legal and policy directions regarding these functions, as well the latest information on crime trends and the corresponding knowledge about the detection and prevention of crime.

Luen and Al-Hawamdeh (2001) find that the amount of information that police officers come into contact with in the course of their work is astounding. This and the vast knowledge that police officers need in order to perform their normal duties suggest the need for police officers to be proficient knowledge workers, being able to access, assimilate, and use knowledge effectively to discharge their duties.

Presently, such information and knowledge are captured within police organizations in various forms, ranging from computer records to documented institutional orders to the personal experiences of its officers. The crux of the issue is then how to surface such knowledge and bring it to bear on the problems faced by police officers in a timely and effective manner.

Knowledge Management

This is where knowledge management principles and practices can help. With the increased adoption of information technology within police organizations, and the increasing overall quality and IT competence of police officers, police organizations are well positioned to leverage knowledge management principles and practices. This, complemented by the enhanced skills, equipment, and empowerment given to the officers, will enable them to perform their duties at an optimal level.

In discussing the scope of knowledge management in police work, Luen and Al-Hawamdeh (2001) take into consideration the two definitions of knowledge within the context of knowledge management. These two definitions of knowledge—explicit and tacit knowledge—give rise to different implementation approaches, which are complementary rather than exclusive. Both of these implementation approaches are necessary if the organization is to reap full benefits of knowledge management.

Explicit knowledge is used as guidance for police actions and decision making. Explicit knowledge is captured in the form of documents (e.g., doctrines, police general orders, standard operating procedures) that have been verified and ascertained to be of value to police officers. Examples of these documents include procedures of arrest, handling a fire scene, and illegal parking.

The second type of knowledge is implicit or tacit knowledge. This includes the competence, experience, and skill of police officers. Tacit knowledge is usually dynamic and fast-changing, as compared with documented knowledge.

Documented or explicit knowledge is normally kept as routine records in official police documents. Examples of such documented information include crime threats, crime trends and statistics, criminal records, and situational information pertaining to the incident or crisis at hand.

Regarding tacit knowledge, the scope of knowledge management in police work is primarily in the areas of creating and sharing knowledge and information. The two main issues to be addressed here are the willingness of police officers to create and share knowledge and the ability of police officers to create and share knowledge.

According to Luen and Al-Hawamdeh (2001), the more difficult issue to tackle is = the willingness of police officers to create and share knowledge. There is a need for culture characterized by openness, collaboration, and sharing among police officers. This will require police officers to recognize the importance of collaboration and sharing knowledge with others.

The responsibility to surface knowledge lies with everyone in the police force, as knowledge is generated in all phases of work. In analyzing the content of the knowledge surfaced, it is necessary to check the subject matter of the knowledge as to what issues it addresses in relation to existing policies and procedures and whether such knowledge adds value for police officers. In assessing the complexity of the knowledge surfaced, it is necessary to check whether the knowledge is mostly explicit or tacit in nature. Explicit knowledge can be documented in writing with little loss in interpretation and understanding, while tacit knowledge tends to be difficult to document comprehensively due to its scope and nature (Luen & Al-Hawamdeh, 2001).

In police investigations, experienced officers not only check for a more complex and integrated set of traits, but they emphasize stable, generalized clues and actually look for fewer clues than recruits, according to Fielding (1984). Experienced officers have a more established idea of the important clues, which are then linked to lower-order clues. It has also been found that, compared to appearance, behavior is much more likely to be the basis of a classification of suspiciousness.

Analysis of police competence must acknowledge that police work aggravates several factors known to limit accurate judgment—for example, sources of information vary in credibility, and the police are particularly reliant on negative information (Fielding, 1984).

An interesting example of knowledge acquisition in police investigations is interrogation. Interrogation is concerned with the questioning of a person or persons suspected of a crime by police. Interrogation is to ask questions of a person, especially closely, thoroughly, and formally. In most criminal justice systems there is a frequent reliance on confession evidence, and in some cases it may be the only evidence.

To understand interrogation in terms of investigative interviewing, Crawshaw, Devlin, and Williamson (1998) find it necessary to place the interviewing of victims, witnesses, or suspects in the context of the investigation. In some cases the investigator may find that the victim is dead, there are no witnesses to the offence, the witnesses are too afraid to give evidence or information, or there may be no forensic evidence. In such cases the investigator has to rely on obtaining a confession from a suspect, and this is acceptable in those jurisdictions where a person may be found guilty by a court on the basis of an uncorroborated confession.

Since most interviews take place in private, where the suspect is alone with the interviewers and there is no independent record of what happened, there is a temptation for law enforcement officials to resort to physical and psychological abuse of the detainee in many countries. Sometimes the reasons for this can be understood, but such action is never justifiable (Crawshaw et al., 1998).

In most investigations it is normally the case that there are victims and witnesses from whom information can be obtained. Rather than relying too much on confession evidence, steps can be taken to identify witnesses who may be able to provide such relevant information. Sometimes enquiries for this purpose have to be made a considerable time after the event, and a number of methods have been found to be successful in tracing witnesses. For example, "house to house enquiries,"the methodological visiting of all premises in the vicinity of a crime in order to establish whether occupants are able to provide relevant information;appeals for witnesses through the news media; the distribution of leaflets giving details of a crime and appealing for information; dramatized reconstructions of a crime on television programs (Crawshaw et al., 1998).

Forensic science can contribute greatly to investigations. In some countries techniques may be basic but nevertheless sound—for example the physical (as opposed to technological) comparison of fingerprints found at the scene of a crime with those in a collection of previously convicted criminals. Other forensic science techniques, such as DNA profiling, are sophisticated and expensive, and previously only available in well-resourced police agencies. Regardless of the degree of sophistication of techniques or facilities available, it is essential that police officials should be aware of them and maximize their use so that they may be able to conduct an investigation that does not rely solely on confession evidence.

A fundamental flaw is created in many investigations when the investigator secures a confession from a suspect at an early stage, and then attempts to establish a case against the suspect by selectively building up supporting evidence around the confession. The key word here is "selectively," for it means that the investigator is prepared to ignore, and even conceal, evidence that does not support the case against the accused. This can be fatal to the proper conclusion of any investigation, but especially so if the suspect has falsely confessed to a crime which he or she has not committed. If a person is convicted of a crime on the basis of evidence produced by such an "investigation," a double miscarriage of justice occurs: the wrongful conviction of an innocent person, and the avoidance of justice by the real perpetrator of the crime. It is more professional and more ethical to approach the case scientifically and with an open mind, and to gather information systematically. In order for an investigation conducted on this basis to be successful, it is essential that each step of the investigation should be documented (Crawshaw et al., 1998).

Investigative Thinking Styles

As Dean (2005) notes in police investigations, the experience of investigation begins for detectives when they are given a crime to solve. When handed a case, detectives apply methods they were trained in. Often, they follow a set of five basic procedural steps: collecting, checking, considering, connecting, and constructing.

As detectives conduct a series and/or a complex investigation, they become driven by the intensity of the challenge, which motivates them to do the best job they can for the victim(s) by catching the criminal(s) and solving the crime through the application of their investigative method.

In meeting this investigative challenge, detectives require skill to relate and communicate effectively with a variety of people to obtain information and establish a workable investigative focus. Such skill also requires detectives to be flexible in how they approach people and the case, while maintaining an appropriate level of emotional involvement toward victims, witnesses, informants, and suspects.

When exercising their investigative skill, detectives seek to maximize the possibilities of a good result by taking legally sanctioned and logically justifiable risks across a wide latitude of influence. Such justifiable risk-taking requires detectives to be proactive in applying creativity to how they seek new information and, if necessary, how they develop such information into evidence.

Many detectives are only trained in one way of investigative thinking, the method style. This style of investigative thinking is all about following the basic police procedural steps when doing investigation, which are the five C's above. However, there are three other levels or ways of thinking about the investigative process that experienced detectives use with serious and complex crimes. The three other levels are the challenge style, the skill style, and the risk style of investigative thinking.

The challenge level is all about what motivates detectives. At this level detectives think about the job, the victim, the crime, and the criminal. These four elements are the key sources of intensity that drive detectives to do the best they can do in a particular investigation.

At the skill level of investigative thinking, detectives are concerned with how they relate to people. Detectives must think about how they are going to relate to the victim, witnesses, possible suspects, the local community, and the wider general public in order to get the information they need to solve the case.

The risk style revolves around how detectives think through being proactively creative enough to discover new information and, if necessary, develop it into evidence that will stand up to testing in a court of law.

Although experienced detectives and investigators intuitively use these four levels of thinking in an investigation, it is rare that any one detective will give equal weight to all four styles of investigative thinking in a particular case, because detectives, like everyone else, have a preference for maybe one or two particular styles or ways of thinking.

Dean (2005) calls this phenomenon the cognitive psychology of police investigators—how police investigators (detectives) think when conducting a criminal investigation. The nature of the subject matter falls within the realm of the cognitive sciences, especially in relation to two branches of psychology: cognitive psychology, with its focus on the mental processes and complex behaviors involved in problem solving and decision making, and investigative psychology as a more generic term that subsumes many of the more specific areas associated with police psychology and the field of criminal or offender profiling.

Dean (2005) argues that investigation is essentially a mind game. When it comes to solving a crime a detective's ability to think as an investigator is everything. Four distinctly different ways of thinking are investigation as method, investigation as challenge, investigation as skill, and investigation as risk. All four ways of describing a criminal investigation can be seen as more or less partial understandings of the whole phenomenon of investigation.

Dean (1995, 2000, 2005) conducts empirical research in the overlapping domains of cognitive/investigative psychology in relation to a specific focus on investigative thinking. An example of one of the cases from this research is presented to illustrate the process of investigative thinking and the way in which various thinking styles come into play at critical points to achieve a successful outcome.

The case involved a 73-year-old man who was found bound with duct tape and murdered in his flat in a northern district of Singapore on August 21, 2002. A selection of mobile phones, jewelry, watches, and cash were stolen from the safe in his house. The informant was a 56-year-old female China national who worked as a part-time cleaner for the deceased. There were no witnesses to the crime and neighbors heard nothing unusual.

A state-action investigative chart was developed by Dean (2005) to assess the various states that a specific investigation goes through for a particular crime and the actions that investigators take as a result. In this murder case in Singapore, the topics on the state-action chart included interview friends, forensic evidence, public pressure, investigator motivation, interview cleaner, locate cleaner's son, and so forth. In this case, the state-action chart clearly represented how the method style of investigative thinking was carried out through the collection of forensic evidence at the scene, and gathered information from informal interviews with friends of the deceased indicated that the cleaner's son was most likely involved in some capacity. This speculation by the friends of the deceased was indicated on the chart based on the fact that the cleaner's son stayed over some nights in the house of the deceased.

The investigation stalled when all leads appeared to reach a dead end. Even the stolen mobile phones had not been used to make calls, so the service provider was not able to pinpoint their exact location.

However, the determination of the investigator exemplified the challenge style of investigative thinking, as he was being driven by the intensity of the job, the crime, and the victim to such an extent that he engaged in some proactive creative thinking (an example of the risk style) that kicked off the investigation again in an eventually positive direction.

The investigator approached the service provider to check whether any of the previous phone calls could reveal anything of use for the investigation. The service provider was able to give an estimated location of the missing mobile phones based on the signal picked up by their station. The investigator then made extensive enquiries at the local mobile phone shops in the estimated area and eventually located the second-hand dealer's shop where the suspect sold the mobile for ready cash. Such an attempt was unprecedented in any other homicide cases in Singapore.

As the case example illustrates, a number of changes in thinking style took place throughout this investigation. The investigation started, as all investigations do, with the application of the method style of investigative thinking, then moved to investigation as challenge, which helped spark the next change to investigation as skill, and finally the use of the 'risk style of investigative thinking was applied to the analysis of phone call details.

Dean's (2005) four distinctly different ways of thinking (styles) about the investigation process by detectives is illustrated in Figure 9.8.

As can be seen on Figure 9.8, there is a hierarchical structure to how investigators think. Not all cases will require the use of all four investigative thinking styles to solve them. However, as time marches on in an investigation without a result, then other styles of investigative thinking will need to come into play to increase the likelihood of a successful outcome. In essence, the more complex the crime, the higher the investigative thinking style required to solve it.

These four ways of thinking can be related to the codification versus the personalization strategy for knowledge management systems suggested by Hansen, Nohria, and Tierney(1999). Thinking styles one and three are

Figure 9.8. Ways of thinking about the investigation process

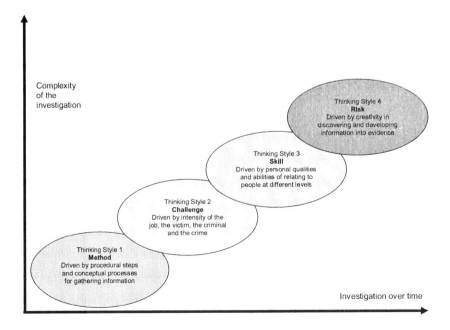

based more on explicit knowledge and are more suitable for codification than thinking styles two and four. Hence, the focus of our second research proposition in relation to how the thinking styles of method and skill may be more important to apply knowledge management systems to than the thinking styles of challenge and risk.

Stages of Knowledge Management Technology

The ambition level using knowledge management systems can again be defined in terms of stages of knowledge management technology, as illustrated in Figure 9.9.

Most criminal cases in Norway are never solved. An average of one third of all criminal cases that law enforcement agencies investigate are successful. There are, however, significant variations. For example, out of twenty murder cases each year, almost all of them are solved. In financial crime, such as money laundering, the success rate is not high. The causal loop diagram in Figure 9.10 illustrates how experience from successful investigations causes an accumulation in knowledge, thereby strengthening the competence of

Figure 9.9. Stages of growth model for police knowledge work

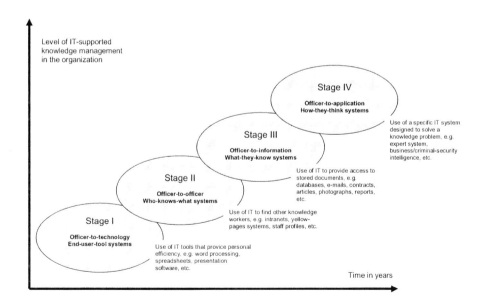

Figure 9.10. Causal loop diagram for the knowledge business of police investigations

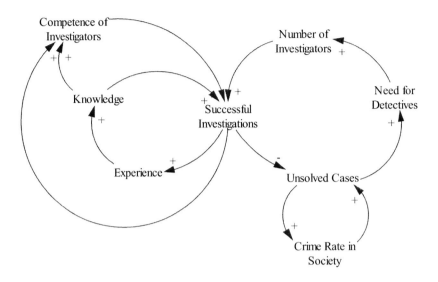

Figure 9.11. Reference mode for the knowledge business of police investigations

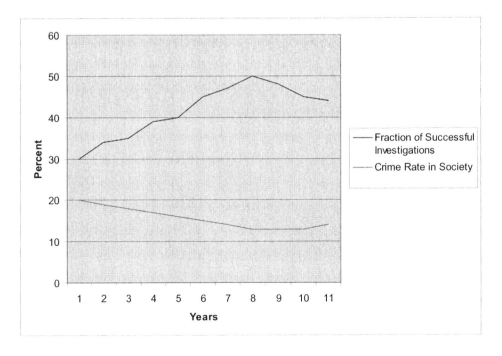

investigators and leading to further increase in the success rate for police investigations.

The causal loop diagram in Figure 9.10 might produce over time the behavior illustrated in Figure 9.11. Here we assume an improvement in the fraction of successful investigations from positive feedback loops. The positive feedback loops are both on the left side in Figure 9.10. Two positive loops on the left are the experience-knowledge loop and the knowledge-competence loop.

As the fraction of successful investigations increases, the number of unsolved cases decreases. When people experience this rise in the chance of being caught, crime rate in society decreases.

Police Leadership

In February 1994, William Bratton was appointed police commissioner of New York City. The odds were against him: The New York Police Department, with a $2 billion budget and a workforce of 35,000 police officers, was notoriously difficult to manage. Yet in less than 2 years, and without an increase in his budget, Bill Bratton turned New York into the safest large city of the nation.

Research conducted by Kim and Mauborgne (2003) led them to conclude that Bratton's turnaround was an example of tipping point leadership. The theory of tipping point, which has its roots in epidemiology, hinges on the insight that in any organization, once the beliefs and energies of a critical mass of people are engaged, conversion to a new idea will spread like an epidemic, bringing about fundamental change very quickly. The theory suggests that such a movement can be unleashed only by agents who make unforgettable and unarguable calls for change, who concentrate their resources on what really matters, who mobilize the commitment of the organization's key players, and who succeed in silencing the most vocal naysayers. Bratton did all of these things.

Kim and Mauborgne (2003) find that in many turnarounds, the hardest battle is simply getting people to agree on the causes of current problems and the need for change. Most CEOs try to make the case for change simply by pointing to the numbers and insisting that the company achieve better ones. But messages communicated through numbers seldom stick.

Tipping point leaders do not rely on numbers to break through the organization's cognitive hurdles. Instead, they put their key managers face-to-face with the operational problems so that the managers cannot evade reality. Poor performance becomes something they witness rather than hear about. Communicating in this way means that the message—performance is poor and needs to be fixed—sticks with people, which is essential if they are to be convinced not only that a turnaround is necessary but that it is something they can achieve.

Leaders like Bratton use a four-step process to bring about rapid, dramatic, and lasting change with limited resources. Tipping all four hurdles leads to rapid strategy reorientation and execution:

- **Cognitive hurdle:** Put managers face-to-face with problems and customers. Find new ways to communicate.

- **Resource hurdle:** Focus on the hot spots and bargain with partner organizations.

- **Motivational hurdle:** Put the stage lights on and frame the challenge to match the organization's various levels.

- **Political hurdle:** Identify and silence internal opponents; isolate external ones.

By addressing these hurdles to tipping point change, leaders will stand a chance of achieving the same kind of results as Bratton delivered to the citizens of New York. Between 1994 and 1996, felony crime fell 39%, murders 50%, and theft 35%. Gallup polls reported that public confidence in the NYPD jumped from 37% to 73% (Kim & Mauborgne, 2003).

Expert Systems

Expert systems can be seen as extreme knowledge management systems on a continuum representing the extent to which a system possesses reasoning capabilities. Expert systems are designed to be used by decision makers who do not possess expertise in the problem domain. The human expert's representation of the task domain provides the template for expert system design. The knowledge base and heuristic rules, which are used to systematically search a problem space, reflect the decision processes of the expert. A viable expert system is expected to perform this search as effectively and efficiently as a human expert. An expert system incorporates the reasoning capabilities of a domain expert and applies them in arriving at a decision. The system user needs little domain-specific knowledge in order for a decision or judgment to be made. The user's main decision is whether to accept the system's result (Dillard & Yuthas, 2001).

Decisions or judgments made by an expert system can be an intermediate component in a larger decision context. For example, an audit expert system may provide a judgment as to the adequacy of loan loss reserves that an auditor would use as input for making an audit opinion decision. The fact that the output supports or provides input for another decision does not make the system any less an expert system, according to Dillard and Yuthas (2001). The distinguishing feature of an expert system lies in its ability to arrive at a nonalgorithmic solution using processes consistent with those of a domain expert.

Curtis and Cobham (2002) define an expert system as a computerized system that performs the role of an expert or carries out a task that requires expertise. In order to understand what an expert system is, then, it is worth paying attention to the role of an expert and the nature of expertise. It is then important to ascertain what types of expert and expertise there are in business and what benefits will accrue to an organization when it develops an expert system.

For example, a doctor having a knowledge of diseases arrives at a diagnosis of an illness by reasoning from information given by the patient's symptoms and then prescribes medication on the basis of known characteristics of available drugs together with the patient's history. A lawyer advises a client on the likely outcome of litigation based on the facts of the particular case, an expert understanding of the law, and knowledge of the way the courts work and interpret this law in practice. An accountant looks at various characteristics of a company's performance and makes a judgment as to the likely state of health of that company.

All of these tasks involve some of the features for which computers traditionally have been noted—performing text and numeric processing quickly and efficiently—but they also involve one more ability: reasoning. Reasoning is the movement from details of a particular case and knowledge of the general subject area surrounding that case to the derivation of conclusions. Expert systems incorporate this reasoning by applying general rules in an information base to aspects of a particular case under consideration (Curtis & Cobham, 2002).

Expert systems are computer systems designed to make expert-level decisions within complex domains. The business applications of this advanced information technology has been varied and far-reaching, directed toward making operational, management, and strategic decisions.

Audit expert systems are systems applied in the auditing environment within the public accounting domain. Major public accounting firms have been quite active in developing such systems, and some argue that these tools and technologies will be increasingly important for survival as the firms strive to enhance their competitive position and to reduce their legal and business risk.

Dillard and Yuthas (2001) find that the implementation and use of these powerful systems raise a variety of significant ethical questions. As public accounting firms continue to devote substantial resources to the development of audit expert systems, dealing with the ethical risks and potential conse-quences to stakeholders takes on increasing significance. For example, when responsible behavior of an auditor is transferred to an audit expert system, the system is incapable of being held accountable for the consequences of decisions.

Expert systems can be used in all knowledge management processes described earlier. For knowledge retrieval, content management and information ex-traction technology represent a useful group of techniques. An example of an expert system for knowledge retrieval is the CORPORUM system. There are three essential aspects of this system (Wang, Hjelmervik, & Bremdal, 2001).

First, the CORPORUM system interprets text in the sense that it builds ontologies. Ontologies describe concepts and relationships between them. Ontologies can be seen as the building blocks of knowledge. The system captures ontologies that reflect world concepts as the user of the system sees and expresses them. The ontology produced constitutes a model of a person's interest or concern. Second, the interest model is applied as a knowledge base in order to determine contextual and thematic correspondence with documents available in the system. Finally, the interest model and the text interpretation process drive an information search and extraction process that character-izes hits in terms of both relevance and content. This new information can be stored in a database for future reference.

The CORPORUM software consists of a linguistic component, taking care of tasks such as lexical analysis and analysis at the syntactical level. At the semantic level the software performs word sense disambiguation by describing the context in which a particular word is being used. This is naturally closely related to knowledge representation issues. The system is able to augment meaning structures with concepts that are invented from the text. The core of the system is also able to extract information most pertinent to a specific text for summary creation, extract the so-called core concept area from a text, and represent results according to ranking based on specified interest for a specific contextual theme set by the user. In addition, the system generates explanations, which will allow the user to make an informed guess about which documents to look at and which to ignore. The system can point to exactly those parts of targeted documents that are most pertinent to a specific user's interest (Wang et al., 2001).

Like all software, CORPORUM is continuously improved and revised. The Content Management Suport (CMS) was introduced in 2005. It is based on technology that applies linguistics to characterize and index document content. The ontology-based approach focuses on semantics rather than shallow text patterns. The software can be applied for intelligent search and indexing, structure content in portals, annotating documents according to content, summarizing and compressing information, and extracting names and relations from text.

Another software in 2005, CORPORUM Best Practice, enables organizations to structure their business and work processes and improve value creation. It is a software tool and associated methodology to build organization-wide Best Practice. In operation, the Web part of the system is a work portal. It embraces an ontology-based set of templates that helps to publish work-related documentation. Company resources like check lists, control plans, Microsoft Word templates, images, and e-learning material that is relevant for any process or activity described can be linked in where it is useful and intuitive.

A final software to be mentioned is CORPORUM Intranet Search & Navigation (SLATEWeb), which is indexes and categorizes corporate information sources. Featuring language detection and find-related concept search, this tool lets companies find documents that would otherwise be hard to find. Categories are available to dynamically classify documents into a taxonomy or group structure. When different software packages from CORPORUM are evaluated for support of knowledge categories and levels, the result might look like Figure 9.12 for the knowledge management matrix.

Analysis and design necessary for building an expert system differ from a traditional data processing or information system. There are three major points of distinction that prevent expert systems development being subsumed under general frameworks of systems development (Curtis & Cobham, 2002):

Figure 9.12. Examples of CORPORUM software to support police work in the knowledge management matrix

Levels Categories	Core Knowledge	Advanced Knowledge	Innovative Knowledge
Administrative Knowledge	Knowledge Summarizer	Knowledge Server	Business Intelligence Portal
Policing Knowledge	Knowledge Factory	Knowledge Summarizer	Knowledge Server
Legal Knowledge	Knowledge Factory	Knowledge Factory	Business Intelligence Portal
Analytical Knowledge	Knowledge Server	SLATE	Knowledge Factory

1. **The subject matter is knowledge and reasoning as contrasted with data and processing:** Knowledge has both form and content, which need investigation. Form is connected with the mode of representation chosen—for instance, rules, semantic networks, or logic. Content needs careful attention as once the form is selected it is still a difficult task to translate the knowledge into the chosen representation form.

2. **Expert systems are expert/expertise oriented, whereas information systems are decision/function/organization-directed:** The expert system encapsulates the abilities of an expert or expertise and the aim is to provide a computerized replica of these facilities.

3. **Obtaining information for expert systems design presents different problems from those in traditional information systems design:** Many expert systems rely at least partly on incorporating expertise obtained from an expert. Few rely solely on the representation of textbook or rulebook knowledge. It is difficult generally to elicit this knowledge from an expert. In contrast, in designing an information system the analyst relies heavily on existing documentation as a guide to the amount, type, and content of formal information being passed around the system. In the development of an expert system the experts are regarded as repositories of knowledge.

Expert systems and traditional information systems have many significant differences. While processing in a traditional information system is primarily algorithmic, processing in an expert system includes symbolic conceptual-

izations. Input must be complete in a trad'
incomplete in an expert system. Search
frequently based on algorithms, whil
is frequently based on heuristics. F
traditional system. Data and info'
while knowledge is the focus ⌐

Expert systems can deliver the ս_
right time if it is known in advance ν.
right person to use or apply that informaս.
the right time when that specific information ν.
nonroutine and unstructured change in a business eս.
depend upon sense-making capabilities of knowledge ν.
the computational logic of the business and the data it proս
Gosain, & El Sawy, 2005).

Use of expert systems in law enforcement includes systems that atս
aid in information retrieval by drawing upon human heuristics or rules ս
procedures to investigate tasks. The AICAMS project is a knowledge-based
system for identifying suspects. AICAMS also includes a component to fulfill
the needs for a simple but effective facial identification procedure based on a
library of facial components. The system provides a capability for assembling
an infinite number of possible facial composites by varying the position and
size of the components. AICAMS also provides a geomapping component
by incorporating a map-based user interface (Chen et al., 2002).

Dynamics of E-Business Knowledge

This section documents some of the links between e-business and knowledge
management systems that might be explored in future empirical research.
The research propositions in this chapter illustrate the need for a contingent
approach to knowledge management systems that are to support e-business.
Knowledge management systems successfully supporting and improving
e-business performance have to satisfy several requirements. First, they
have to support the chosen e-business model(s). Second, they have to cause
improvements through redesign of e-business processes. Furthermore, a
more advanced stage of knowledge management technology in terms of
codification strategy will be more powerful and successful. These are some

...propositions presented in this chapter, which represents a rich
...se for future empirical studies.

...jective of a knowledge management system (KMS) is to support
...n, transfer, and application of knowledge in organizations (Feng,
...Liou, 2005). Electronic business (e-business) is marketing, buying,
...delivering, servicing, and paying for products, services, and informa-
...cross networks linking an enterprise and its prospects, customers, agents,
...liers, competitors, allies, and complementors (Weill & Vitale, 2002).

...veral researchers emphasize the important role of knowledge management
...ystems in e-business (e.g., El Sawy, 2001; Fahey, Srrivastava, Sharon, &
Smith, 2001; Holsapple & Singh, 2000; Malhotra, 2000, 2002; Plessis &
Boon, 2004; Singh, Iyer, & Salam, 2004; Tsai, Yu, & Lee, 2005). Garud and
Kumaraswany (2005) argue that knowledge has emerged as a strategically
significant resource for the firm. Accordingly, knowledge creation and transfer
becomes a key factor to gain and sustain a competitive advantage (Sambamurthy & Subramani, 2005). E-business processes can create additional customer
value through knowledge creation with customers (Kodama, 2005).

Plessis and Boon (2004) argue that the knowledge management value proposition with reference to e-business is not very different from the generic value
proposition of knowledge management. There are, however, subtle differences
in focus and areas of importance, such as the scale of knowledge-sharing
over geographical, divisional, and organizational boundaries, consolidation
of knowledge to provide one view of organizational knowledge, and the role
of technology in providing platforms for sharing knowledge internal and
external to the organization.

We are in an era of knowledge economy and knowledge-based competition.
In this era, an organization must be able to secure various types of knowledge assets and maximize their strategic value. To do so, many organizations
have begun to reexamine and rearrange their business strategies, processes,
information technologies, and organizational structures from a knowledge
perspective. This task has been complicated in the Internet-enabled business
environment. With the advances of Internet-related technologies, the intri-
cacy of the worldwide economy is fast changing. Lower cost, customized
products/service, and quick response have become the critical success factors
for most businesses. More and more competing firms are adopting collaborative work and knowledge management to create and maintain these critical
success factors. Collaborative works within an organization and between
organizations can not only share the work based on each member's expertise,

but also achieve a seamless information flow among the collaborative team members. Such sharing of knowledge has gone to improve productivity and decision quality of the participating organizations. In order to have effective collaborative work in electronic business, the management of knowledge is essential and critical (Li & Lai, 2005).

The purpose of this section is to discuss how knowledge management systems can support and improve e-business. Based on a review of the research literature, research propositions are developed in this chapter. Each proposition is concerned with relationships between knowledge management and e-business. Perspectives from the research literature applied in this chapter include drivers for digital transformation, evolving the e-business, e-business models, e-business process redesign, value configurations, knowledge transfer, knowledge management technology stages, and intangible assets.

This section makes an important contribution to the field, as there has been a missing link between know-what and know-how concerning cause and effect relationships between knowledge management systems and e-business. Know-what has stressed the importance of knowledge in e-business. This chapter makes a much-needed contribution to know-how, as it explores how knowledge management systems and e-business performance influence each other.

In the past, developing e-business systems were often given priority according to technical criteria rather than business imperatives. From the viewpoint of knowledge management, Tsai et al. (2005) found that e-business is an important process by which an enterprise wisely uses knowledge to create value. However, many companies use models of knowledge management that suit the industrial epoch. Far from benefiting these organizations, Malhotra (2000) found that these outdated models seriously undermine their information strategies. Their research findings make the following research propositions even more important to future successful support from knowledge management systems in e-business.

Knowledge Management as Key for E-Business Competitiveness

Allard and Holsapple (2002) argue that knowledge is the lifeblood of e-commerce. Processes and activities involved in e-commerce are technological means that contribute to managing knowledge.

There are several definitions of e-commerce depending on perspective or view. The trading view focuses on market-based activities such as buying and selling through utilization of computer-based technologies. The information exchange view holds that information itself may be a commodity that is bought and sold. The activity view acknowledges a wide range of business activities beyond trading that are accomplished with the use of technology. The effects view concentrates on the goals, reasons, and effects of e-commerce. The value chain view revolves around the value configuration of a value chain.

Because e-commerce involves knowledge-based organizations and because the manipulation of knowledge is the essence of what networked computer systems do, Allard and Holsapple (2002) argue that the definition of e-commerce should include knowledge as a basic concept, as well as noting the existence of technology that facilitates its manipulation. Therefore, they suggest the following definition:

An approach to achieving business goals in which technology for managing knowledge enables or facilitates execution of activities in and across value chains as well as supporting decision making underlying those activities. (p. 21)

This definition is presented both for e-commerce in a broad sense and for e-business. In this perspective, e-business refers to the way businesses are adapting to the new environment by utilizing electronic technologies in their activities as well as the mindset they adopt to make these changes.

Here, technology for managing knowledge lies in the core of the e-business definition. To systematically study, develop, and apply such technology for e-business, it is essential to adopt a perspective that gives a fairly comprehensive portrayal of KM. Several types of knowledge are involved in the conduct of e-business. Descriptive knowledge reflects know-what, because it describes the state of a specific domain including the items themselves, the relationships among those items, and the context in which they exist. Procedural knowledge refers to know-how, because it specifies the steps by which a task can be accomplished or a goal can be achieved. Reasoning knowledge focuses on know-why, because it identifies why things happen the way they do in specific situations and the conditions that allow certain conclusions to be drawn.

A practical example of the KM view of e-commerce is Ernie, an online consulting system from Ernst & Young. Organizations that cannot afford in-house experts or consultants on a topic can use the Ernie Web site to acquire needed knowledge. Ernie serves as a direct interface to Ernst & Young knowledge in such forms as proprietary databases, professional resources, and human knowledge providers (Holsapple & Singh, 2000).

When a client accesses Ernie to acquire knowledge, he/she is asked to formulate a question, assign it to a consultation category, and offer some background information as to how results are to be used. If a client has trouble formulating a question or simply does not know what to ask, he/she can access an extensive FAQ database for help. Based on the question submitted, Ernie selects relevant knowledge from knowledge repositories that may be human-based or computer-based. The knowledge selected could be descriptive (know-what), procedural (know-how), or reasoning (know-why), in the form of advice suggesting what to conclude about various circumstances. If needed knowledge is not in an available repository, Ernie may attempt to generate it (Holsapple & Singh, 2000).

Knowledge management as key for e-business competitiveness is not just a question of supplying knowledge to a client, as illustrated in the case of Ernie. Often, a consulting firm also has something to learn from its clients. Fosstenløkken, Løwendahl, & Revang (2003) studied knowledge development through client interaction. They identified several knowledge development processes. The process of professionals learning from clients occurs when sophisticated, knowledgeable clients are considered a key factor in knowledge development.

An interesting example of knowledge management as a key for e-business competitiveness is Web services for knowledge management in e-marketplaces, as discussed by Singh et al. (2004). A common strategic initiative of organizations engaged in e-business is the development of synergistic relations with collaborating value-chain partners to deliver their value proposition to customers. This requires the transparent flow of problem-specific knowledge to partner organizations over highly integrated information systems. Transparent exchange of information and knowledge across collaborating organizations requires technological foundations for integrating business processes using software architectures built upon industry standards. The unambiguously interpretable flow of knowledge to inform online business processes is a challenging task with significant competitive benefits for organizations that take technical initiative. Infomediary organizations can serve the e-business need for exchange of knowledge and information through value-added knowledge services to participating firms in the value chain through intelligent software systems integrated with Web service architecture.

In this context, Singh et al. (2004) define knowledge services as the exchange of problem domain-specific knowledge to inform decision activities of specific e-business processes, facilitated by an infomediary using intelligent software systems and a Web services architecture. Knowledge services are provided by the knowledge agent to users, through their agents, over heterogeneous information platforms using Web services as a foundation.

Malhotra (2002) studied ways of enabling knowledge exchanges for e-business communities, arguing that unsuccessful attempts of e-commerce models have increased interest in online communities as critical enablers of e-business success. Collaborate technologies need to account for the dual nature of knowledge management processes. The dual nature defines KM in terms of KM by design (such as corporate intranets) and KM by emergence (such as communities of practice). Applications of traditional collaborative systems such as group support systems, shared calendaring applications, and document management systems belong to KM by design.

Malhotra (2002) argues that there is a greater need for understanding how collaborative technology applications can support KM by emergence, which is necessary for business model innovation. Knowledge management by emergence is characterized by creation of cultural infrastructure for enabling continuous knowledge sharing, knowledge renewal, and knowledge creation.

Malhotra (2000) argues that advancing IT strategy to Internet time is needed. Strategic IT planning must focus on knowledge management for e-business performance. There is a need for synergy between capabilities of advanced information technologies and human creativity and innovation to realize the agility demanded by emerging business environments.

Knowledge in Drivers for Digital Transformation

The digital transformation of traditional businesses is occurring. New information technologies, such as broadband networks, mobile communications, and the Internet, have well known, but often unrealized, potential to transform businesses and industries. The key to success is understanding how and when to apply technologies. According to Andal-Ancion, Cartwright, and

Yip (2003), companies should look at 10 specific drivers to help determine their best strategy.

The ten drivers are electronic deliverability, information intensity, customizability, aggregation effects, search costs, real-time interface, contracting risk, network effects, standardization benefits, and missing competencies. These drivers determine the competitive advantage of deploying new information technology (Andal-Ancion et al., 2003):

1. **Electronic deliverability:** Some products have a large component that can be delivered electronically. Airline companies, for instance, enable customers to book reservations online, after which the confirmations and tickets can be delivered efficiently through e-mail.

2. **Information intensity:** Nearly all products have some information content, but the amount varies dramatically. Cars come with volumes of operating instructions; ice cream bought from a street vendor comes with no information except the name of its flavor.

3. **Customizability:** New information technologies allow many companies to tailor an overall offering to the specific needs and preferences of individual customers. In the past, newspapers were one-size-fits-all product. Today, online editions can be customized to include just the news and information that a particular subscriber is likely to want.

4. **Aggregation effects:** Products and services differ in the way they can be aggregated or combined. In the past, UK customers dealt with a bank for their savings and day-to-day transactions, a building society for their mortgages, an insurance agent for life and property policies, and an independent financial adviser for their investments. Thanks to new IT (and deregulation), institutions can offer customers bundled services (with attractive interest rates and better terms) to handle all those financial needs through one account.

5. **Search costs:** Before the advent of companies like Amazon.com, finding an out-of-print book could require considerable time and effort. Now, the Web provides people with vast amounts of information, regardless of their location or time zone, lowering the search costs for finding exactly the product or service they want.

6. **Real-time interface:** A real-time interface is necessary for companies and customers dealing with important information that changes suddenly and unpredictably. A good example is online trading, in which

rapid fluctuations in the stock market can be devastating for those who lack instantaneous access to that information.

7. **Contracting risk:** Buying new books online has little contracting risk for customers: Prices are relatively low specifying the exact titles is straightforward the physical quality of books varies little and merchants are motivated to fulfill each order efficiently to encourage customers to return. Buying cars online is a completely different matter: Prices are substantially higher specifying the exact product is difficult the physical quality of the vehicles can be different from the descriptions on a Web site and sellers do not typically expect repeat purchases, so they might be less motivated to deliver premium service.

8. **Network effects:** In many industries, the utility of a good or service increases with the number of people who are using it. A key benefit of using Microsoft Office, for instance, is that the suite of programs is ubiquitous in the business world, enabling people to share Word, PowerPoint, and Excel documents easily.

9. **Standardization benefits:** New IT has enabled companies to synchro-nize and standardize certain processes, resulting in greater efficiency in business-to-business transactions as well as increased convenience for customers. On the Web, the extensible markup language (XML) family of standards significantly increases a company's ability to broadcast a message to a wide audience in the most efficient and powerful way.

10. **Missing competencies:** New IT can facilitate company alliances in which partners use each other to fill in missing competencies.

We find that nine out of ten drivers, except contracting risk, derive from one of three knowledge processes: knowledge creation, storage and retrieval, and transfer. According to Alavi and Leidner (2001), organizations have four knowledge processes: creation, storage and retrieval, transfer, and application. Knowledge application is not included in the drivers for digital transformation because knowledge application represents the procedures that turn knowledge management processes into drivers of the digital transformation.

The remaining nine drivers are either about interaction between company and its external environment or about characteristics of products in terms of goods and services. For example, aggregation effects are only obtainable if a knowledge management system records the customer's demand for bundled services. Hence, we suggest that successful applications of drivers for digital transformation are dependent upon knowledge management systems.

Knowledge in Evolving the E-Business

For most firms, becoming an e-business is an evolutionary development (Porter, 2001). Earl (2000) has described a typical six-stage journey that corporations are likely to experience. The six stages are not necessarily definite periods of evolution, as companies may have activities at several neighboring stages at the same time. The six stages are illustrated in Figure 9.13.

While the early stages of evolution are concerned with simple applications of Internet technology for external and internal communication, later stages involve redesigning business processes and introducing new electronic business processes. Thus, we suggest that knowledge management systems are more important in later stages of evolving the e-business.

Figure 9.13. Stages of growth model for evolving the e-business

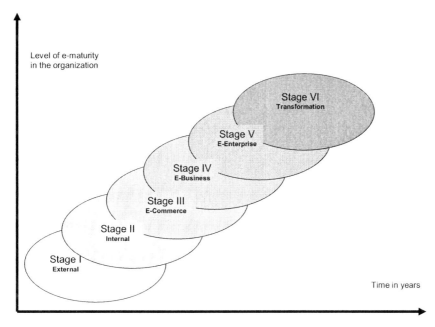

Knowledge in E-Business Models

A business model can be defined as the method by which a firm builds and uses its resources to offer its customers better value than its competitors and to take in money doing so. Weill and Vitale (2002) identified eight atomic e-business models, each of which describes the essence of conducting business electronically: direct to customer, full-service provider, whole of enterprise, intermediary, shared infrastructure, virtual community, value net integrator, and content provider.

In their discussion of IT infrastructure services needed for each e-business model, Weill and Vitale (2002) identified knowledge management system as the most critical service for content providers. A content provider is a firm that creates and provides content (information, products, or services) in digital form to customers. Thus, we suggest that knowledge management systems are more important in content providers than in other atomic e-business models.

A business model details how a firm makes money now and how it plans to do so in the long run. The model is what enables a firm to have a sustainable competitive advantage, to perform better than its rivals in the long term. A business model can be conceptualized as a system that is made up of components, linkages between the components, and dynamics. Weill and Vitale's (2001) eight atomic e-business models were presented earlier in this book.

Knowledge in E-Business Process Redesign

Business process redesign for e-business involves rethinking and redesigning business processes at both the enterprise and supply chain level to take advantage of Internet connectivity and new ways of creating value. El Sawy (2001) developed three principles for changing knowledge management around a process.

The first principle of "analyze and synthesize" emphasizes the interactive analysis and synthesis capabilities around a process to generate added value. A business process can be redesigned by adding analysis capabilities through software and intelligent information feeds that generate knowledge that can become a major part of the deliverable to the customer of the process. Both the executors and the customers of the process become more knowledgeable and enable better outcomes for the process. This tactic is especially applicable in knowledge-intensive processes where the value proposition to the customers of the process is increasingly based on providing good advice to customers and improving customer capacity to make intelligent decisions that they are comfortable with. This tactic is especially powerful in the provision of complex products and services.

The second principle of "connect, collect, and create" emphasizes growing intelligently reusable knowledge around the process through all who touch it. A business process can be redesigned by intelligently growing knowledge around it through all the people who take part in the process, whether they are the doers of the process or the customers of the process. Superior executions of the process are identified and best practices and tips shared so that subsequent executions are improved. Eventually, this learning can be used to further change the design of the process. A knowledge management infrastructure can be viewed as having three aspects: a connect aspect, a collect aspect, and a create aspect. The connect aspect includes ways of mapping connections to sources of expertise and specific knowledge. This is often done in a yellow pages format that lists sources of expertise around a process sorted by topic and issue rather than by job function or job title. The collect aspect includes ways of capturing and organizing knowledge so that it can be intelligently reused. This is done by setting up procedures through which knowledge can be captured, classified, filtered, and synthesized in meaningful ways that are directly relevant to the business process and can add value to its execution. The create aspect of knowledge management infrastructure involves setting up technological platforms, institutional forms, and physical or virtual spaces for shared knowledge creation. It allows the people who are involved with the process to exchange knowledge and jointly create it through informal conversations and ad hoc exchanges that contribute to expertise needed around a process, whether to execute it, reconfigure it, or improve it. A successful knowledge management infrastructure needs to have all three connect, collect, and create aspects.

The third and final knowledge principle, "personalize," emphasizes making the process intimate with the preferences and habits of participants. A business process can be redesigned by increasing its capabilities to learn about the preferences and habits of the customers and doers of the process. A knowledge base with customer profiles and preferences is built based on repeat executions of the process. The knowledge about preferences is then used in subsequent process executions to make the outcomes of the process more personalized to the customer or doer of the process. Taking advantage of this knowledge can add value to the process participants and speed up the process on subsequent executions. This knowledge can also be used to provide new process offerings and to redesign the process.

Three core business processes have to be redesigned for e-business: customer relationship management (CRM), supply chain management (SCM), and product development management (PDM). According to Fahey et al. (2001), the customer relationship management process is concerned with the creation and leveraging of linkages and relationships to external marketplace entities, especially channels and end users. Know-what needed for CRM includes answers to questions such as: What are your customers' wants and needs? Know-how needed includes answers to questions such as: How can you collect relevant information that can be used to accurately fulfill customer wants and needs? Know-why needed includes answers to questions such as: Why is the CRM process changing?

The supply chain management process is concerned with the acquisition of solution inputs and their transformation into desired customer benefits, while the product development management process is concerned with the development of new customer solutions and/or the invigoration of existing solutions. As for CRM, both SCM and PDM need answers to know-what, know-how, and know-why questions (Fahey et al., 2001). Know-what is describing current and future e-business change and its implications for strategy, operations, and competitive context. Know-how is what an organization does or must do to adapt and leverage e-business for strategic and operational purposes. Know-why is knowledge about why e-business is evolving as it is and what accounts for its impacts on competitive context, strategy, and operations.

Both El Sawy (2001) and Fahey et al. (2001) emphasize the importance of knowledge management systems in e-business process redesign. Hence, we suggest that successful redesign of business processes for e-business is dependent upon knowledge management systems.

Fahey et al. (2001) define e-business as an ability of a firm to electronically connect, in multiple ways, many organizations, both internal and external, for many different purposes. It allows an organization to execute electronic transactions with any individual entity along value creation processes. Along the value chain, for instance, among suppliers, logistics providers, wholesalers, distributors, service providers, and end customers, electronic transactions are executed. Managers can build pockets of know-what around specific domains of current, emerging, and potential change. Managers can learn from stories to identify critical know-how, such as how customers could interact electronically with various entities in the value creation. Considerations of know-what and know-why about a competitive context years into the future unavoidably gives rise to know-why issues, such as why customers are shifting from one form of electronic connection to another. Knowledge management emphasizes design and interaction among groups to enable the development and sharing of information, ideas, and perspectives on how e-business can transform processes.

Knowledge in Value Configurations

To comprehend the value that information technology provides to organizations, we must understand the way a particular organization conducts business and how information systems affect the performance of various component activities within the organization. A value configuration describes how value is created in a company for its customers. Value chain, value shop, and value network are alternative value configurations. Thus, we suggest that knowledge management systems are more important in value shops doing e-business than in value chains or value networks doing e-business.

The value shop is a company that creates value by solving unique problems for customers and clients (Stabell & Fjeldstad, 1998). Knowledge is the most important resource, and reputation is critical to firm success. A value shop is characterized by five primary activities: problem finding and acquisition, problem solving, choice, execution, and control and evaluation, as illustrated again in Figure 9.14.

Understanding how firms differ is a central challenge for both theory and practice of e-business. For a long time, the value chain was the only value configuration known to e-managers focusing on supply chain management. Recently, the problem-solving activities of value shops have emerged as more knowledge-intensive, and hence are in greater need of knowledge management systems.

One of the e-business models presented earlier, the content provider, has the value configuration of a value shop. It solves the knowledge needs of its customers by applying knowledge management systems such as data warehouses, electronic storage farms, case-based reasoning, and expert systems.

The value shop moves through the stages of growth for knowledge management systems to take advantage of end-user tools, communication networks, information sources, and intelligent applications. These systems are at the core

Figure 9.14. Value configuration of value shop

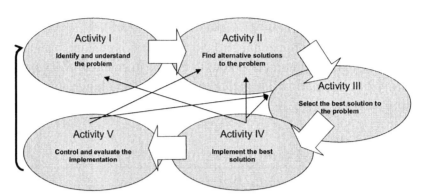

of the e-business in the value shop, while they are mostly only supporting and improving business processes in value chains and value networks.

Knowledge Transfer in E-Business

According to Alavi and Leidner (2001), organizations have four knowledge processes: creation, storage and retrieval, transfer, and application. In electronic business, the requirements on a KMS to support creation, storage and retrieval, and application of knowledge will not change dramatically. However, the requirements concerning support for knowledge transfer will change significantly. Thus, we suggest that knowledge transfer is the most important knowledge process in e-business.

The problem of knowledge transfer is often faced by individuals or groups once an appropriate source of knowledge is located (Sambamurthy & Subramani, 2005). The new challenge lies mostly in how to transfer knowledge between the vendor and the customer. The environment for communication in certain areas of a company will be drastically altered as a consequence of e-business. Knowledge, which earlier could be transferred between people in the same organization, now has to be transferred across two different organizations. Consequently, the channels for transferring knowledge will be more formal and impersonal. A KMS has to find a way to transfer all relevant information through more formal and impersonal channels, or to find a new creative way of making the communication channel less formal and/or impersonal.

According to Ko, Kirsch, and King (2005), some researchers have defined knowledge transfer as dyadic exchanges of organizational knowledge between a source and a recipient unit in which the identity of the recipient matters. Others also focus on the resulting changes to the recipient. For example, knowledge transfer can be seen as the process through which one unit (e.g., group, department, or division) is affected by the experience of another. Other researchers go further by arguing that knowledge transfer occurs when a contributor shares knowledge that is used by an adopter.

Knowledge is in the heads of individuals. Therefore, we have to understand knowledge transfer in terms of individual behavior (Liu & Chen, 2005). Wasko and Faraj (2005) examined social capital and knowledge contribution in electronic networks of practice. They found that reputation, centrality, and tenure were significant factors influencing the extent to which individuals are motivated to make knowledge contributions. Reputation is an important asset that an individual can leverage to achieve and maintain status within a collective. Centrality is the extent to which the individual is in regular contact with others; the more individuals are in regular contact with one another, the more likely they are to develop a habit of cooperation and act collectively. Individuals with longer tenure in the shared practice are likely to better understand how their expertise is relevant, and are thus better able to share knowledge with others.

Given the multiple objectives of knowledge transfer in e-business, only a sophisticated operationalization of the concept will suffice here. Since the literature suggests that key aspects of knowledge transfer are knowledge movement and the application of knowledge, Ko et al. (2005) captured both of these ideas by defining knowledge transfer as the communication of knowledge from a source so that it is learned and applied by a recipient. Knowledge is taken to be transferred when learning takes place and when the recipient understands the intricacies and implications associated with that knowledge so that he or she can apply it. For example, the vendor may transfer knowledge about testing procedures to the client who learns and applies this knowledge, as evidenced by clients developing test scripts, conducting tests of individual modules, and running integration tests to ascertain whether data are correctly passed between two or more modules.

Similarly, Inkpen and Tsang (2005) define knowledge transfer as a process through which one relationship partner is affected by the experience of another. Knowledge transfer manifests itself through changes in knowledge or performance of the recipient unit.

Stages of Knowledge Management Technology

The ambition level using knowledge management systems can be defined in terms of stages of knowledge management technology, as illustrated again in Figure 5.4.

Stage one is labeled end-user-tool systems or person-to-technology, as information technology provides people with tools that improve personal efficiency. Examples are word processing, spreadsheets, and presentation software. Stage two is labeled who-knows-what systems or person-to-person, as people use information technology to find other knowledge workers. Examples are yellow-page systems, CVs, and intranets. Stage three is labeled what-they-know systems or person-to-information, as information technology provides people with access to information that is typically stored in documents. Examples of documents are contracts, articles, drawings, blueprints, photographs, emails, presentations, and reports (Kankanhalli, Tan, & Wei, 2005). Stage four is labeled how-they-think systems or person-to-system, in which the system is intended to help solve a knowledge problem. Examples are expert systems and business intelligence.

In e-business, the electronic exchange of information requires that information is stored in electronic form. Therefore, we suggest that higher stages of knowledge management technology provide more effective support for electronic business.

In a different empirical setting, Ko et al. (2005) studied antecedents of knowledge transfer from consultants to clients in enterprise system implementations. They found that the greater the shared understanding between a consultant and a client, the greater the knowledge transfers. Furthermore, the greater the absorptive capacity of a client, the more intrinsically motivated the client and the consultant, the more credible the consultant, the greater a client's communication decoding competence, the greater a consultant's communication encoding competence, and the greater the knowledge transfer.

The stages of growth model can be interpreted as alternative strategies, where the alternative strategies are person-to-tools strategy, person-to-person strategy, person-to-information strategy, and person-to-system strategy. A comparison of these four alternatives can be made to the classification into personalization versus codification strategy by Hansen et al. (1999). In this comparison, stages one and two represent personalization, while stages three and four represent codification. Hence, we suggest that the codification strategy of knowledge management systems is more effective for e-business than the personalization strategy.

Stages of knowledge management technology is a relative concept concerned with IT's ability to process information for knowledge work. At later stages IT is more useful to knowledge work than IT at earlier stages. The relative concept implies that IT is more directly involved in knowledge work at higher stages, and that IT is able to support more advanced knowledge work at higher stages.

Some benchmark variables for the stages of growth model for knowledge management technology are listed in Figure 9.15.

In knowledge management technology, the intelligence continuum is an interesting concept. The intelligence continuum is a collection of key tools, techniques, and processes. Examples are data mining and business intelligence. Taken together, they represent a system for refining the data raw material stored in data marts and/or data warehouses, and maximizing the value and utility of these data assets for any organization. The first component at one end of the continuum is a generic information system, which generates data that is then captured in a data repository.

Figure 9.15. Characteristics of each stage of knowledge management technology

	Stage One **Tools**	**Stage Two** **Sources**	**Stage Three** **Contents**	**Stage Four** **Systems**
Trigger of IT for KM	Knowledge worker's need for end-user tools	Organization's need for information	Knowledge worker's need for information automation	Organization's need for work automation
Focus when applying IT to KM	Make IT available to knowledge workers	Enable knowledge sharing among knowledge workers	Enable sharing of electronic information among knowledge workers	Replace knowledge workers by information systems
Dominating strategy for KMT	Tool strategy	Flow strategy	Stock strategy	Growth strategy
Attitude toward IT in KM	Skeptics	Conservatives	Early adopters	Innovators

In order to maximize the value of the data and use it to improve processes, the techniques and tools of data mining, business intelligence, and analytics must be applied to the data warehouse. Once applied, the results become part of the data set that are reintroduced into the system and combined with the other inputs of people, processes, and technology to develop an improvement continuum. Thus, the intelligence continuum includes the generation of data, the analysis of these data to provide a diagnosis, and the reintroduction into the cycle as a prescriptive solution. In terms of the stages of growth model, a prescriptive solution from a system typically occurs at stage four.

An important application in the intelligence continuum is data mining, which occurs at stage three. Due to the immense size of the data sets in most organizations, computerized techniques are essential to help knowledge workers understand relationships and associations between data elements. Data mining is closely associated with databases and shares some common ground with statistics since both strive toward discovering structure in data. However, while statistical analysis starts with some kind of hypothesis about relationships in data, data mining does not. Data mining deals with heterogeneous databases, data sets, and data fields. Data mining, then, is the nontrivial process of identifying valid, novel, potentially useful, and ultimately understandable patterns from data.

Another technology-driven technique like data mining connected to knowledge management is the area of business intelligence and the now newer term business analytics. The business intelligence term has become synonymous with an umbrella description for a wide range of decision-support tools, some of which target specific user audiences. At the bottom of the business intelligence hierarchy are extractions and formatting tools, which are also known as data-extraction tools. The next level is known as warehouses and marts.

Human intelligence tools form the final level in the hierarchy and involve human expertise, opinions, and observations recorded to create a knowledge-based repository. These tools are the very top of business intelligence and represent business analytics specifically focused on analytic aspects. Here we find rule-based expert systems, fuzzy logic, and system dynamics modeling.

System dynamics modeling is an analytical tool to study business dynamics. The modeling process starts with sketching a model, then writing equations and specifying numerical quantities. Numerical quantities can be the result of data mining. Next, the model is simulated with simulation output automatically saved as a dataset. Finally, the simulation data can be examined with analysis tools to discover the dynamic behavior of variables in the model. Normal model construction follows a pattern of create, examine, and recreate, iterating until the model meets users' requirements. Debugging (making a model simulate properly) and model analysis (investigating output behavior) both play a part in refining the model. Reality check is another analytic to aid in the construction and refinement of a system dynamics model (Sterman, 2000).

Wickramasinghe and Silvers (2003) suggest that the orthopedic room represents an ideal environment for the application of a continuous improvement cycle that is dependent upon the intelligence continuum. For those patients with advanced degeneration of their hips and knees, arthroplasty of the knee and hip represent an opportunity to regain their function. Before the operation ever begins in the operating room, there are a large number of interdependent individual processes that must be completed. Each process requires data input and produces a data output such as patient history, diagnostic test, and consultations. The interaction between these data elements is not always maximized in terms of operating room scheduling and completion of the procedure.

The entire process of getting a patient to the operating room for a surgical procedure can be represented by three distinct phases: preoperative, intraoperative, and postoperative. The diagnostic evaluation of data and the reengineering of each of the potentially deficient processes will lead to increased efficiency. For example, many patients are allergic to the penicillin family of antibiotics that are often administered before surgery in order to minimize the risk of infection. For those patients who are allergic, a substitute drug requires a 45-minute monitored administration time as opposed to the much shorter administration time of the default agent. Since the antibiotic is only effective when administered prior to starting the procedure, this often means that a delay is experienced (Wickramasinghe & Silvers, 2003).

Intangible Assets in E-Business

Knowledge management systems support knowledge transfer within and between intangible assets. One approach to defining intangible assets in e-business is to distinguish among three families; the external structure, the internal structure, and the individual structure, as proposed by Sveiby (2001).

The external structure consists of the external environment. For the customer, the vendor is in the external environment. For the vendor, the customer is in the external environment. The internal structure consists of models, regulations, and information systems. The individual structure consists of staff competence. Knowledge transfer occurs within and among these three structures. Hence, we suggest that the external structure is the most important structure for successful knowledge transfer in e-business.

Knowledge transfer from individual to external structure concerns how the organization's employees transfer their knowledge to the organization's environment. The strategic question in relation to e-business would then be, how can employees use KMS to transfer knowledge and improve the competence of their customer? This is illustrated in Figure 5.6 by arrow 1.

Knowledge transfer from external structure to individuals occurs when employees learn from the customer, where the strategic question would be, how can the customer improve the competence of the employees using KMS? This is illustrated in Figure 9.16 by arrow 2.

Knowledge transfer within the external structure concerns what the customers tell each other about the service of an organization. For example, Kodama and Ohiro (2005) studied customer value creation through customer-as-innovator

Figure 9.16. Knowledge transfer within and among families of intangible assets

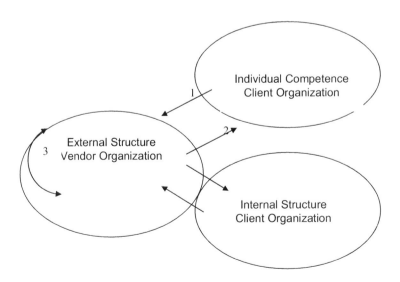

approach in the case of video processing LSI development. The strategic question would be, how can we secure and enable knowledge exchange between customers using KMS so our customers improve their competence?

Knowledge transfer from the external to internal structure concern what knowledge the organization can gain from the external environment and how the learning can be converted into action. The strategic question would be, how can competence from the customers improve the organization's systems, processes, and products, using KMS?

Knowledge transfer from internal to external structure is the counterpart from the above, and the strategic question would then be, how can the organization's systems, tools, and processes improve the competence of the customers using KMS?

One of the key authors in the area of intellectual capital is Sveiby (2001), who has developed a knowledge-based theory of the firm to guide in strategy formulation. He distinguished three families of intangible assets with the outsourcing vendor. The external structure family consists of relationships with customers and suppliers and the reputation (image) of the firm. Some of these relationships can be converted into legal property such as trademarks and brand names. The value of such assets in primarily influenced by how well the company solves its customers' problems, and there is always an element of uncertainty here.

The internal structure family consists of patents, concepts, models, and computer and administrative systems. These are created by the employees and are thus generally owned by the organization. The structure is partly independent of individuals and some of it remains even if a large number of the employees leave. The individual competence family consists of the competence of the professional staff, the experts, the research and development people, the factory workers, sales and marketing—in short, all those who have a direct contact with customers and whose work are within the business idea.

Competence is a term introduced here. Competence can be defined as the sum of knowledge, skills, and abilities at the individual level. With this definition, we say that knowledge is part of competence, and competence is part of intellectual capital.

These three families of intangible resources have slightly different definitions when compared to the capital elements. The external structure seems similar to relational capital, the internal structure seems similar to structural capital, and the individual competence seems similar to human capital.

To appreciate why a knowledge-based theory of the firm can be useful for strategy formulation, Sveiby (2001) considers some of the features that differentiate knowledge transfers from tangible goods transfers. In contrast to tangible goods, which tend to depreciate in value when they are used, knowledge grows when used and depreciates when not used. Competence in a language or a sport requires huge investments in training to build up, just as managerial competence takes a long time on –the job to learn. If one stops speaking the language it gradually dissipates.

Given three families of intangible assets, it is possible to identify nine knowledge transfers. These knowledge transfers can occur within a family and between families, as illustrated in Figure 9.17. Each of the nine knowledge transfers in Figure 9.17 can be explained as follows (Sveiby, 2001):

1. **Knowledge transfers between individuals** concern how to best enable the communication between employees within the organization. The strategic question is: How can we improve the transfer of competence between people in the organization? Activities for intellectual capital

Figure 9.17. Knowledge transfer within and between families of intangible assets

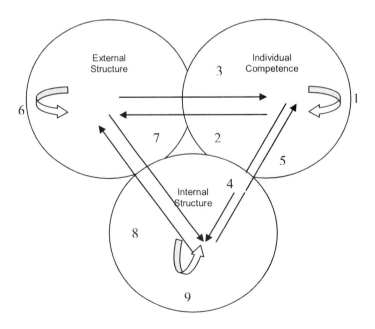

management focus on trust building, enabling team activities, induction programs, job rotation, and master/apprentice scheme.

2. **Knowledge transfers from individuals to external structure** concern how the organization's employees transfer their knowledge to the outer world. The strategic question is: How can the organization's employees improve the competence of customers, suppliers, and other stakeholders? Activities for intellectual capital management focus on enabling the employees to help customers learn about the products, getting rid of red tape, enabling job rotation with customers, holding product seminars, and providing customer education.

3. **Knowledge transfers from external structure to individuals** occur when employees learn from customers, suppliers, and community feedback through ideas, new experiences, and new technical knowledge. The strategic question is: How can the organization's customers, suppliers, and other stakeholders improve the competence of the employees? Activities for intellectual capital management focus on creating and maintaining good personal relationships among the organization's own people and the people outside the organization.

4. **Knowledge transfers from competence to internal structure** concern the transformation of human capital into more permanent structural capital through documented work routines, intranets, and data repositories. The strategic question is: How can we improve the conversion from individually held competence to systems, tools, and templates? Activities for intellectual capital management focus on tools, templates, processes, and systems so they can be shared more easily and efficiently.

5. **Knowledge transfers from internal structure to individual competence** is the counterpart of the above. Once competence is captured in a system it needs to be made available to other individuals in such a way that they improve their capacity to act. The strategic question is: How can we improve individuals' competence by using systems, tools, and templates? Activities for intellectual capital management focus on improving human-computer interface of systems, action-based learning processes, simulations, and interactive e-learning environments.

6. **Knowledge transfers within the external structure** concern what customers and others tell each other about the services of an organization. The strategic question is: How can we enable the conversations among the customers, suppliers, and other stakeholders so they improve their competence? Activities for intellectual capital management focus on

partnering and alliances, improving the image of the organization and the brand equity of its products and services, improving the quality of the offering, conducting product seminars and alumni programs.

7.   **Knowledge transfers from external to internal structure** concern what knowledge the organization can gain from the external world and how the learning can be converted into action. The strategic question is: How can competence from the customers, suppliers, and other stakeholders improve the organization's systems, tools and processes, and products? Activities for intellectual capital management focus on empowering call centers to interpret customer complaints, creating alliances to generate ideas for new products, and research and development alliances.

8.   **Knowledge transfers from internal to external structure** is the counterpart of the above. The strategic question is: How can the organization's systems, tools and processes and products improve the competence of the customers, suppliers, and other stakeholders? Activities for intellectual capital management focus on making the organization's systems, tools, and processes effective in servicing the customer, extranets, product tracking, help desks, and e-business.

9.   **Knowledge transfers within the internal structure** where the internal structure is the backbone of the organization. The strategic question is: How can the organization's systems, tools and processes, and products be effectively integrated? Activities for intellectual capital management focus on streamlining databases, building integrated information technology systems, and improving the office layout.

In addition to these nine knowledge-transfer mechanisms, the client has to retain several core capabilities. These ensure the elicitation and delivery of business requirements, the development of technical/business architecture, the managing of external supply, and the coordination and governance of these tasks.

The Case of Law Firms

Law firms are examples of content providers that lately have discovered the advantages of e-business. According to Weill and Vitale (2002), content providers must categorize and store their content in well-indexed modules so it can be combined and customized to meet client needs via a wide variety of channels. They argue that to succeed, a content provider must provide reliable, timely content in the right format and at the right price.

Legaliz is an example of a Norwegian law firm offering its services on the Internet as a content provider. It claims that it can offer legal advice faster, more cheaply, and with greater availability (24x7x54) than their traditional competitors. Even though there are important advantages for clients using the Internet for legal services, it is crucial that the clients are offered the same quality in content as in traditional law firms. The main difference from a KM perspective in e-business is how knowledge is transferred from the law firm to its clients.

According to Mountain (2001), legal Web advisors were pioneered in London in 1994 when the law firm Linklaters introduced a browser-based product called Blue Flag. Blue Flag is now a suite of products covering regulatory compliance, derivatives documentation, employee share plans, funds, share disclosure, and transaction management. Within months, another London law firm, Clifford Chance, followed with NextLaw, a Web-accessible online service that helps assess the legal and regulatory risks of e-commerce and reportedly required an investment of more than 1 million pounds sterling. Today, there are approximately a dozen online legal services in the UK, and the pace of their introduction is accelerating.

For a law firm, e-business is a new way to provide clients with the knowledge they possess and develop. Based on the client's problem, a solution can be delivered either by creating or by using existing knowledge. An example of a knowledge management system at stage four of the stage model is case-based reasoning. The client types in certain characteristics of the problem and answers questions from the knowledge management system. The system then searches similar cases in its database and develops a recommended solution to the problem based on earlier cases.

Generally, law firms belong to the industry of professional service firms. Knowledge development has been found to occur through client interaction in such firms (Fosstenløkken et al., 2003). The value-creation processes include both service-delivery processes, which create value directly for clients, and knowledge-development processes, which are indirectly value-creating, in that they enhance the value-creation potential of the firm, and thereby also the value of the firm itself to owners and other stakeholders. As value shops (Stabell & Fjeldstad, 1998) being content providers (Weill & Vitale, 2002), professional service firms can improve both business processes using the principles suggested by El Sawy (2001).

The Case of Supply Chains

The need for continual value innovation is driving supply chains to evolve from a purely transactional focus to leveraging interorganizational partnerships for sharing information, and ultimately, market knowledge creation. Supply chain partners are engaging in interlinked processes that enable rich (broad-ranging, high quality, and privileged) information sharing, and building information technology infrastructures that allow them to process information obtained from their partners to create new knowledge.

A study by Malhotra et al. (2005) uncovered and examined the variety of supply chain partnership configurations that exist based on differences in capability platforms, reflecting varying processes, and information systems. They identified five partnership configurations that were labeled collector, connector, cruncher, coercer, and collaborator.

The uncovering and characterization of supply chain configurations enabled Malhotra et al. (2005) to better understand how partner-enabled knowledge creation and operational efficiency can both be affected by shortcomings in organizational capability platforms and the nature of information exchanged.

Organizational capability platforms can be improved using two distinct types of partner interface-directed information systems that enable assimilation and transformation: memory systems for interorganizational activities and interpretation systems for interorganizational information.

Memory systems for interorganizational activities represent use of IT-based systems by an enterprise to store and retrieve information related to previous exchanges with its supply chain partners. Organizational memory is the means by which knowledge from the past can be utilized to understand and influence current activities. Information systems that support organizational memory store information from past activities and outcomes. Supporting organizational memory through information systems can play a significant role in the creation of new knowledge. Memory systems can manifest themselves as databases that store and enable retrieval of the history of events related to the formal interactions or informal information exchanges with business partners, both in terms of the processes that ensued as well as the outcomes. Such systems allow enterprises to bring previously stored information to bear on information received from external sources in order to create new knowledge and create operational efficiency. Memory systems are applications of information technology at stage three of the knowledge management technology stage model.

Interpretation systems for interorganization information represent use of IT-based systems by an enterprise to manipulate and interpret information received from its supply chain partners. Employees and teams within enterprises are conduits for knowledge creation and sharing. Their diverse cognitive needs require the use of information systems that are able to represent information in multiple ways—from global to minute—and allow dynamic configuration of interpretation. Use of IT-based interpretation systems enables information obtained from supply chain partners to be organized, rearranged, and processed to create new knowledge. A manifestation of such a system is data analysis and mining software that can help uncover patterns in data and enable insights to be generated by processing large quantities of raw data. Interpretation systems based on IT have been shown to enable more effective knowledge creation and generation of insights that lead to improved performance outcomes. Interpretation systems are applications of information technology at stage four of the knowledge management technology stage model.

Malhotra et al. (2005) conducted their research study in the context of the RosettaNet B2B initiative. RosettaNet is a consortium of major IT, electronic components, semiconductor manufacturing, telecommunications, and logistics enterprises working to create and implement industry-wide, open electronic business process standards for supply chain collaboration. RosettaNet helped the researchers identify their supply chain partners, restricted to three supply chain tiers: manufacturers, distributors, and retailers. This resulted in identifying 91 partnerships, which the researchers grouped into five partnership configurations.

Enterprises structuring their supply chain partnerships as collectors appeared to focus their resources on deploying standard electronic business interfaces with partners for supporting interorganizational process linkages and information exchange. In the second configuration, connector, the focus was structuring of interorganizational processes. Cruncher supply chain partnerships seem to be a polar opposite of connector configurations. While connector enterprises are externally focused (structuring their interorganizational processes), cruncher enterprises appear to focus on partner interface-directed information systems for storage and processing of information.

Coercive supply chain partnership was the fourth configuration identified. Here we typically find a very large enterprise with much power in the supply chain and a much smaller enterprise, where relative dependence determines the power that can be exerted by enterprises specifically for adoption of interorganizational information sharing systems. The fifth and final configuration was collaborator supply chain partnership. This configuration indicates advanced capabilities in the structuring of their interorganizational integrative processes.

The Case of Seven-Eleven in Japan

Seven-Eleven Japan is a company that has invested aggressively and successfully in information technology for many years. Tsai et al. (2005) argue that the company's strong performance rests on its information technology investments. The company developed an electronic ordering system (EOS) and a point-of-sales data-collection system (POS) to reduce the average turnover time of its stock and acquire information regarding the sales of its products. It used information technology to gain competitive advantage. Now, Seven-Eleven Japan is the largest and most profitable retailer in Japan. When it was designed, the POS system was able to gather customer information regarding age and gender, and was also able to make cross-comparisons in regard to the different types and quantities of products, as well as the time when they were bought.

In this way the enterprise was able to extend the knowledge level of knowing "which products sold well" to the level of knowing "who is buying these products." The POS comprises the design and implementation of the system's hardware and software. However, from the standpoint of knowledge management, the system is the construction of the knowledge about product sales analysis. After this enterprise determines the knowledge of product sales analysis as the enterprise's key ability (knowledge identification, selection, and acquisition), they translated this tacit knowledge that was formerly stored within the experienced sales specialists in the company's head office into the POS system (knowledge construction, which is also knowledge externalization).

This system is installed into each franchise, thereby allowing each franchise operator to learn how to use the system gathering and analyzing product sales (knowledge learning and culture, which is also knowledge externalization), thereby showing forth the effectiveness of implementing such a system. In other words, this enterprise, through building and implementing a POS system, has achieved knowledge of product sales analysis being disseminated throughout the whole of the enterprise, thus allowing this knowledge to be retained, used, and revised for the benefit of the whole organization (Tsai et al., 2005).

South African Case Study Findings

Plessis and Boon (2004) investigated the role of knowledge management in e-business in practice through questionnaires administered to selected South African corporations. They found that South African organizations understand the strategic importance of knowledge and knowledge management, but only apply knowledge management on an operational level. This is supported by the fact that knowledge management is not integrated into business, such as into the business process value chain, but is implemented as an administrative function.

E-business did not explode globally as anticipated in the years 1998-2000, and even less so in South Africa. The role that knowledge management played in e-business in South Africa will thus be smaller compared to other countries like the US and UK, simply because there is more e-business activity than in South Africa, according to Plessis and Boon (2004). Nevertheless, the survey showed that knowledge management was rated in as having an important role in e-business.

Plessis and Boon (2004) suggest that South African organizations should expose their knowledge workers to international knowledge management programs with an e-business focus where possible, such as through exchange programs to ensure they get adequate exposure to developments internationally.

E-Business Knowledge Dynamics

Businesses operate in a knowledge-driven economy and increasingly function as knowledge-based organizations. In such knowledge-rich environments, e-businesses must explicitly recognize knowledge and the processes and technologies for knowledge management and exchange across participants in the market place (Singh et al., 2004). To this end, Allard and Holsapple (2002) suggest KM audits. These give a way to assess and analyze effectiveness of e-business knowledge handling processes. Results of these audits can be a foundation for finding ways to enhance e-business competitiveness through KM improvements and to improve business innovation capability.

In this chapter, we have documented some of the links between e-business and KMS that need to be explored in future empirical research. With the growing importance of pooling knowledge resources, knowledge management will have to transcend organizational boundaries to include customers, vendors, and other partners using electronic information. However, the focus of previous research studies has mainly been on intraorganizational knowledge management. In this study, we have attempted to direct the attention of knowledge management researchers toward interorganizational interfaces.

In a different empirical setting, Malhotra et al. (2005) attempted to direct the attention of knowledge management researchers toward interorganizational interfaces. They studied absorptive capacity configurations in supply chains. Their study indicates that enterprises have to build requisite absorptive capacity to prepare for collaborative knowledge creation with their supply chain partners. Absorptive capacity in this context is the ability of enterprises to acquire and assimilate information from their supply chain partners and to transform and exploit this information to achieve superior operational and strategic outcomes.

Similarly, Allard and Holsapple (2002) attempted to direct the attention of knowledge management researchers toward interorganizational interfaces. They studied knowledge management as a key for e-business competitiveness. In their knowledge chain model, knowledge externalization describes the embedding of knowledge into organizational outputs that are then released into the external environment.

The research propositions in this chapter illustrate the need for a contingent approach to knowledge management systems that are to support e-business. We have seen different situations that require different KMS. For example, the business model of a content provider has knowledge at its core, while the business model of direct to customer is less dependent on knowledge management.

Implementation is an important issue for knowledge management systems in e-business. Critical success factors for KMS implementation will typically include resources for the implementation, user involvement in implementation, and management support for implementation. Such critical success factors can be studied in future research.

Knowledge management systems successfully supporting e-business and improving e-business performance have to satisfy several requirements. First, they have to support the chosen e-business model(s). Second, they have to cause improvements through redesign of e-business processes. Furthermore, more advanced stages of knowledge management technology in terms of codification strategy will be more powerful and successful. These are some of the research propositions presented in this chapter, which represents a rich knowledge base for future empirical studies. The avenue opened up through this chapter is for future research to look for situations, rather than general-izations, in terms of the contingent approach to management.

As a conclusion, some important causal influences between knowledge management and IT outsourcing relationships are mapped in the causal loop diagram in Figure 9.18. Causal loop diagramming is described by Sterman (2000) and presented as a tool by www.vensim.com.

More knowledge sharing will increase customer satisfaction, leading to higher e-business success. Learning from the success, new knowledge is created, causing modifications and extensions to the e-business model. The revised e-business model requires process redesign, and one important aspect of re-design will be more knowledge management technology. More technology for knowledge management improves knowledge sharing, leading to even higher customer satisfaction.

Figure 9.19 illustrates two positive feedback loops from Figure 9.18. When knowledge sharing increases, customer satisfaction increases, leading to greater e-business success, making it more attractive to continue the digital transformation, and leading to even more knowledge sharing. The other loop says that when knowledge sharing increases, more know-what, know-how, and know-why lead to greater process redesign, making new applications of knowledge management technology and leading to even more knowledge sharing.

Figure 9.18. Causal loop diagram for knowledge management in e-busi-ness

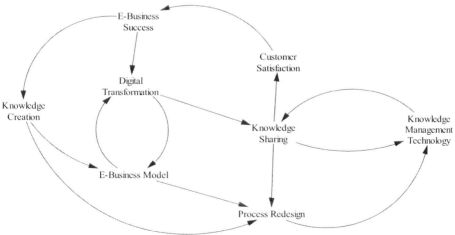

Figure 9.19. Positive feedback loops in the causal loop diagram

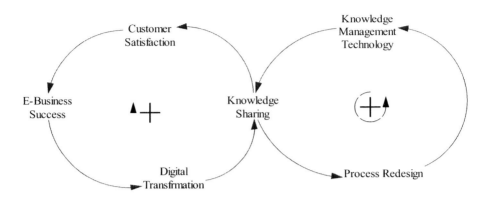

Effective knowledge management in electronic business is dependent on a knowledge-centered culture. Organizational culture is believed to be the most significant input to effective knowledge management and organizational learning, in that corporate culture determines values, beliefs, and work

Figure 9.20. Reference mode for knowledge management technology in electronic business

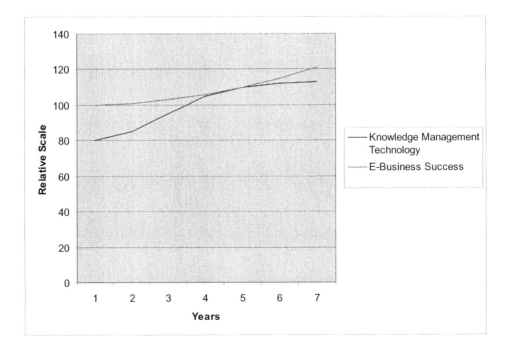

systems that could encourage or impede learning (knowledge creation) as well as knowledge sharing (Janz & Prasarnphanich, 2003). Therefore, an organization's culture should provide support and incentives as well as encourage knowledge-related activities by creating environments for knowledge exchange and accessibility.

The causal loops might produce a behavior of increasing e-business success caused by knowledge management technology, as illustrated in Figure 9.20.

Dynamics of Outsourcing Knowledge

With changing business environments, the locus of value creation is no longer within the boundaries of a single firm, but occurs instead at the nexus of relationships between parties. With the growing importance of pooling knowledge resources, knowledge management will have to transcend organizational boundaries. Based on current research literature, this chapter develops research propositions to study causal aspects of knowledge management systems supporting IT outsourcing relationships. Perspectives from the research literature applied in this chapter include knowledge transfer, strategic intent, knowledge management technology stages, intangible assets, resource-based theory, vendor value proposition, value shop, and knowledge strategy (Gottschalk & Solli-Sæther, 2006).

We suggest in this chapter that knowledge transfer is the most important knowledge process in an IT outsourcing relationship, that increase in knowledge transfer between vendor and client will improve partnership quality in IT outsourcing relationships, that a higher level of strategic intent for IT outsourcing requires a higher stage of knowledge management systems, and that vendor and client need to be at the same technological stage of growth to be able to successfully communicate with each other through knowledge management systems.

Furthermore, a codification strategy is more dependent on knowledge management systems than a personalization strategy in knowledge transfer between vendor and client in an IT outsourcing relationship; the external structure is the most important structure for successful knowledge transfer in IT outsourcing relationships; the need for knowledge management systems in an IT outsourcing relationship increases as vendor and client mobilize strategic resources in their relationship; and the need for knowledge management systems in an IT outsourcing relationship increases as the vendor increases his complementary competencies. Finally, vendor value shop performance in selecting and implementing the best solution for the client is dependent on the extent of client knowledge transfer, and knowledge management systems in outsourcing relationships are less important when the client is an expert-driven business.

With changing business environments, the locus of value creation is no longer within the boundaries of a single firm, but occurs instead at the nexus of relationships between parties (Malhotra et al., 2005). Enterprises have to rely on business partners to share knowledge and continually respond to change. With the growing importance of pooling knowledge resources, knowledge management will have to transcend organizational boundaries to include sourcing partners. However, the focus of previous research studies has mainly been on intraorganizational knowledge management. This chapter attempts to direct the attention of knowledge management researchers toward interorganizational interfaces.

As mentioned in the previous section, several researchers emphasize the important role of knowledge for interorganizational learning and innovation (e.g., Allard & Holsapple, 2002; Inkpen & Tsang, 2005; Ko et al., 2005; Malhotra et al., 2005; Wasko & Faraj, 2005). Garud and Kumaraswany (2005) argue that knowledge has emerged as a strategically significant resource for the firm. Accordingly, knowledge creation and transfer becomes a key factor to gain and sustain a competitive advantage (Sambamurthy & Subramani, 2005). The main objective of a knowledge management system is to support the creation, transfer, and application of knowledge in organizations (Feng et al., 2005).

An IT outsourcing relationship is an interorganizational arrangement for the exchange of IT services after the transfer of IT assets from the client to the vendor (Koh, Ang, & Straub, 2004). In an outsourcing setting, knowledge that earlier existed internally in an organization is moved to an external organization (Bahli & Rivard, 2005). Accordingly, changes in the knowledge transfer requirements are viewed as the single most important challenge to knowledge management systems in an outsourcing arrangement. Therefore, the focus of this chapter is how the requirements for knowledge management systems change when an organization has entered into an IT outsourcing relationship with another organization.

This section makes an important contribution to the field, as there has been a missing link between know-what and know-how concerning cause and effect relationships between knowledge management systems and IT outsourcing arrangement. Know-what has stressed the importance of knowledge in outsourcing relationships. Knowledge can be descriptive (know-what), procedural (know-how), or reasoning (know-why) (Fahey et al., 2001; Holsapple & Singh, 2000). This chapter makes a much-needed contribution to know-how, as it explores how knowledge management systems and IT outsourcing arrangements influence each other.

The outsourcing promise for the client is to explore and exploit the supplier's superior technical know-how (human capital), superior management practices (structural capital), economies of scale, and increasingly, access to strategic and business advice. This should enable the client to refocus on strategic, core capability, and knowledge areas. But Willcocks, Hindle, Feeny, and Lacity's (2004) research into IT outsourcing has shown consistently over the past decade that the prospects have been disappointing for meaningful knowledge management, and therefore value creation. Their research findings make the following research propositions even more important to future successful support from knowledge management systems in IT outsourcing relationships.

Outsourcing Management Competence

In the knowledge-based view of the firm, IT outsourcing can be seen as a mechanism to integrate IT knowledge from IT vendors. Further, IT outsourcing may encourage the generation of new ways to use IT for better organizational performance through positive interactions. Finally, some executives have concerns regarding the potential loss of internal know-how through IT outsourcing. Shi, Kunnathur, and Ragu-Nathan (2005) believe that a knowledge management-based perspective of IT outsourcing can help determine ways of avoiding loss of important knowledge and nurturing an organizational learning capability.

Shi et al. (2005) studied IT outsourcing management competence. They identified four IT outsourcing management competence dimensions:

- **Informed buying** is the capability of IT purchasing personnel to manage the IT outsourcing strategy that meet the interests of business.

- **Contract facilitation** is the mechanism through which IT services can be coordinated and synchronized, conflicts between users and suppliers be resolved in a collaborated fashion, lessons learned from one buyer-supplier relationship can be documented and applied to other situations, and both excessive user demands and cost overruns by vendors can be managed and limited.

- **Contract monitoring** is the capability of a firm to protect its business' contractual position over time.

- **Vendor development** is the capability of organizations looking beyond existing contractual arrangements to explore the long-term potentials for suppliers to create win-win situations in which the supplier increases revenues by providing services that increase business benefits.

In successful outsourcing management, Shi et al. (2005) found continuously interacting relationships among informed buying, contract management, and relationship management. They measured informed buying in terms of IT personnel having the capability to select the right IT sourcing strategy, making decisions based on business needs, and understanding the firm's technological criteria. Contract management was measured on items such as processes to ensure agreements, accountability, achievements, and meetings. Relationship management was measured on items such as single point of contact, confidence in conflict resolution, and coordination.

Knowledge Transfer in Outsourcing Relationships

In an IT outsourcing relationship, the requirements on a KMS to support creation, storage and retrieval, and application of knowledge will not change dramatically. However, the requirements concerning support for knowledge transfer will change significantly. Thus, we suggest that knowledge transfer is the most important knowledge process in an IT outsourcing relationship.

The problem of knowledge transfer is often faced by individuals or groups once an appropriate source of knowledge is located (Sambamurthy & Subramani, 2005). The new challenge lies mostly in how to transfer knowledge between the vendor and the client. The environment for communication in certain areas of a company will be drastically altered as a consequence of an outsourcing decision. Knowledge, which earlier could be transferred between people in the same organization, now has to be transferred across two different organizations. Consequently, the channels for transferring knowledge will be more formal and impersonal. A KMS has to find a way to transfer all relevant information through more formal and impersonal channels, or find a new creative way of making the communication channel less formal and/or impersonal.

According to Ko et al. (2005), some researchers have defined knowledge transfer as dyadic exchanges of organizational knowledge between a source and a recipient unit in which the identity of the recipient matters. Others also focus on the resulting changes to the recipient. For example, knowledge transfer can be seen as the process through which one unit (e.g., group, department, or division) is affected by the experience of another. Other researchers go further by arguing that knowledge transfer occurs when a contributor shares knowledge that is used by an adopter.

Knowledge is in the heads of individuals. Therefore, we have to understand knowledge transfer in terms of individual behavior. Wasko and Faraj (2005) examined social capital and knowledge contribution in electronic networks of practice. They found that reputation, centrality, and tenure were significant factors influencing the extent to which individuals are motivated to make knowledge contributions. Reputation is an important asset that an individual can leverage to achieve and maintain status within a collective. Centrality is the extent to which the individual is in regular contact with others—the more individuals are in regular contact with one another, the more likely they are to develop a habit of cooperation and act collectively. Individuals with longer tenure in the shared practice are likely to better understand how their expertise is relevant, and are thus better able to share knowledge with others.

Given the multiple objectives of knowledge transfer in IT outsourcing relationships, only a sophisticated operationalization of the concept will suffice here. Since the literature suggests that key aspects of knowledge transfer are knowledge movement and the application of knowledge, Ko et al. (2005) captured both of these ideas by defining knowledge transfer as the communication of knowledge from a source so that it is learned and applied by a recipient. Knowledge is taken to be transferred when learning takes place and when the recipient understands the intricacies and implications associated with that knowledge so that he or she can apply it. For example, the vendor may transfer knowledge about testing procedures to the client who learns and applies this knowledge, as evidenced by clients developing test scripts, conducting tests of individual modules, and running integration tests to ascertain whether data are correctly passed between two or more modules.

Similarly, Inkpen and Tsang (2005) define knowledge transfer as a process through which one relationship partner is affected by the experience of another. Knowledge transfer manifests itself through changes in knowledge or performance of the recipient unit.

Partnerships can create a competitive advantage through the strategic sharing of organizations' key information and knowledge. Close relationships result from more frequent and more relevant information and knowledge transferred between high-performance partners. By transferring knowledge between the client and vendor, they are able to sustain a more effective outsourcing relationship over time. Lee (2001) found that the association between the degree of knowledge sharing and outsourcing success is mediated by the quality of the partnership. Therefore, we suggest that an increase in knowledge transfer between vendor and client will improve the partnership quality in IT outsourcing relationships.

According to Lee and Kim (1999), there is a significant positive relationship between partnership quality and outsourcing success. In their research, they identified five factors that make up partnership quality: trust, business understanding, benefit-risk share, conflict avoidance, and commitment. A successful partnership enables participants to achieve organizational objectives and build a competitive advantage that each organization could not easily attain by itself.

The links and causalities are presented in Figure 9.21. First, the use of knowledge management systems to support knowledge transfer in IT outsourcing relationships has effects on the relationships. Next, these effects are determinants of partnership quality. Finally, partnership quality influences outsourcing effects.

For example, participation is important in a partnership. From a social perspective, participation is prescribed as a remedy when there is conflict, frustration, and vacillation in the group. Active participation of the partnership members plays a major part in enhancing the sustainability of their partnership over

Figure 9.21. Knowledge transfer influencing outsourcing success

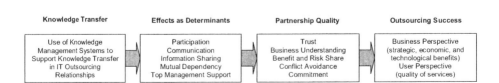

time (Lee & Kim, 1999). Knowledge transfer using knowledge management systems can be an enabler of easier and more comprehensive participation. Hence, participation is influenced by knowledge transfer, and participation influences partnership quality, as illustrated in Figure 6.1.

The shift to more distributed forms of organizations and the growth of interorganizational relationships such as outsourcing relationships have led to an increase in the transfer of knowledge between parties with asymmetric and incomplete information about each other. Because of this asymmetry and incompleteness, parties seeking knowledge may not be able to identify qualified knowledge providers, and the appropriate experts may fail to be motivated to engage in knowledge transfer.

Therefore, Lin, Geng, and Whinston (2005) proposed a sender-receiver framework for studying knowledge transfer under asymmetric and/or incomplete information. In developing the sender-receiver framework, they first introduced the market view of knowledge transfer, where knowledge is treated as a good that moves in a knowledge market where parties may have incomplete and asymmetric information about other participants and the knowledge itself.

A knowledge market exists within organizations when knowledge buyers and sellers within a firm expect to gain from a knowledge transaction (Davenport & Prusak, 1998). This market view is consistent with empirical studies, which show that an effective internal knowledge sharing and transfer system provides motivations to both the provider and the seeker. Knowledge markets also exist across organizations. Consulting firms are hired to provide strategic advice; companies sign licensing agreements and technology development contracts; services and business processes are outsourced to vendors (Lin et al., 2005).

There are two groups of participants in a knowledge transfer: senders who are knowledge sellers, and receivers who are knowledge buyers. The knowledge sender as well as the knowledge receiver can be an individual, a team, a firm, or a unit (subsidiary) within a firm. It can be assumed that each of them focuses on maximizing his/her own benefits, and their interests are generally not aligned. This applies to both the external knowledge market, where the sender and receiver belong to two different organizations, and the internal knowledge market, where they belong to the same organization but care primarily about their own interests.

Each sender is endowed with a piece of knowledge in which a receiver is interested. Specifically, the receiver hopes to derive benefits in terms of value from utilizing the knowledge. The value of knowledge is realized when the receiver has assimilated and used the knowledge, which has brought about outcomes attributable to the use of knowledge. Because knowledge transfer precedes knowledge utilization, the sender and the receiver cannot measure the realized value of knowledge when deciding on the transfer. Instead, the sender and the receiver form expectations of the value of knowledge based on their information.

The expected value of knowledge for the client in an outsourcing relationship is based on the client's information about available knowledge from the vendor. Ultimately, the value of knowledge can be realized when the client has assimilated and used the knowledge by achieving more efficient, more effective, and more competitive use of information technology in the organization. Such improved application of information technology based on knowledge transfer from vendor to client creates added value that the client might be willing to share with the vendor.

All of the information available to the sender and used by him to evaluate the knowledge is called the sender's information set. The receiver's information set is defined similarly. To derive the expected value of the knowledge transfer, the sender's and the receiver's information sets should contain at least the following five components (Lin et al., 2005):

1. The nature of the knowledge, such as the knowledge being tacit or explicit, proven or unproven.

2. The sender's knowledge capability, such as his area and level of expertise.

3. The context in which the knowledge is put to use (whether the context has idiosyncratic features).

4. The fit between the knowledge and the receiver based on the receiver's declared usage of the knowledge.

5. The ties between the sender and receiver, such as their frequency of interactions and trust. (p. 200)

Since we are interested in whether the vendor (sender) and the receiver (client) have sufficient information to estimate the value of the knowledge to be transferred, instead of studying the individual elements of a sender's or a receiver's information set, Lin et al. (2005) introduce the notion of completeness of an information set. One party's information set is considered complete if it contains sufficient information for its owner to reach the correct expected value of the knowledge transferred; otherwise, it is incomplete. The completeness or incompleteness of the sender's and the receiver's information sets is called the information structure of knowledge transfer.

Lin et al. (2005) identified four different information structures. Depending on the completeness or incompleteness of the sender's and the receiver's information sets, there are four possible combinations: symmetric complete information, sender-advantage asymmetric information, symmetric incomplete information, and receiver-advantage asymmetric information.

An outsourcing relationship typically starts with the third structure of symmetric incomplete information. Neither the potential knowledge sender (vendor) nor the knowledge receiver has complete information about the knowledge transfer. One challenge in this structure is for the sender and the receiver to find mechanisms to alleviate information incompleteness for both of them before knowledge transfer. One surprising aspect of this structure is that although no party holds information advantage over the other, strategic distortion in communication still happens (Lin et al., 2005).

Strategic Intent for IT Outsourcing

Research on IT outsourcing has identified several crucial ways in which clients relate to their IT outsourcing providers that influence outsourcing success (Lee, Miranda, & Kim, 2004). How can a KMS support knowledge transfer to make IT outsourcing successful in different IT outsourcing settings? In order to answer this question, we use the concept of strategic intent to identify different IT outsourcing arrangements. DiRomualdo and Gurbaxani (1998) discovered that besides information systems (IS) improvement that was purely driven by a singular focus on costs reduction and service improvement, there are two more kinds of strategic intent for IT outsourcing: business impact and commercial exploitation. Business impact refers to improving information technology's contribution to company performance within its existing lines of business, while commercial exploitation focuses on leveraging technology-related assets—applications, operations, infrastructure, and know-how—in the marketplace to generate new revenue and profit.

These three categories of strategic intent are cumulative, which means that focusing on business impact also incorporates a focus on IS improvement, and commercial exploitation encompasses both of the other elements. Therefore, we suggest that a higher level of strategic intent for IT outsourcing requires a higher stage of knowledge management systems.

The higher stage of knowledge management systems can be defined in terms of the stages of growth model for knowledge management technology, as described in the next section.

The findings of DiRomualdo and Gurbaxani (1998) establish the importance of understanding the different types of strategic intent for IT:

- **IS improvement:** Companies that want better performance from their core IS resources—the hardware, software, networks, people, and processes involved in managing and operating the technology and supporting users—have the strategic intent of IS improvement. Their objectives typically include cost reduction, service quality improvement, and acquisition of new technical skills and management competencies. They believe that outside specialists who are better able to keep pace with new technologies and skills, and who use superior processes and management methods, should manage some, if not all, of their IT services.

- **Business impact:** Many IS organizations are struggling to develop the right mix of technical and business skills to exploit technology. As a result, many companies are looking to the IT outsourcing market for help, on the premise that outsourcing vendors' state-of-the-art skills, capabilities, and proficiency at recruiting and managing technologists make them better than internal IS organizations at using IT to improve business results. This strategic intent is deploying IT to significantly improve critical aspects of business performance. Realizing this goal requires an understanding of the business and the link between IT and business processes, and the ability to implement new systems and business change simultaneously. This form of outsourcing brings new skills and capabilities that link IT to business results rather than those related purely to technology.

- **Commercial exploitation:** Outsourcing information technology with the strategic intent of commercial exploitation aims to improve the return on IT investment by generating new revenue and profit or by offsetting costs. The means by which IT assets can be leveraged commercially range from licensing systems and technologies developed initially for internal use through selling IS products and services to other firms, to launching new IT-based businesses. Companies pursuing commercial exploitation are often those with innovative information systems. Many come from technology-intensive industries, such as air transport and financial services, and have mission-critical systems that are expensive to maintain and enhance.

Based on the different types of strategic intent, DiRomualdo and Gurbaxani (1998), conclude that there is no "one size fits all" approach to IT outsourcing. Each type of strategic intent for IT outsourcing requires different approaches and tactics to be realized successfully. And last, but not least, each type re-quires different approaches to knowledge management to be successful.

Stages of Knowledge Management Technology

The ambition level using knowledge management systems can be defined in terms of stages of knowledge management technology, as described earlier in this book. The stage model was originally designed to describe to what extent a company has utilized knowledge management technology, while here we use these categories to describe at which level the KMS should be in order to meet the changes in requirements from various IT outsourcing relationships on knowledge management systems, as illustrated in Figure 9.22.

Figure 9.22. Contingent approach to knowledge management systems in IT outsourcing relationships

Strategic Intent Stage of KMS	IS Improvement	Business Impact	Commercial Exploitation
Person-to-Tools	End user tools to improve efficiency		
Person-to-Person	Efficient access to knowledge workers	Joint efforts for business process reengineering	Joint exploitation of assets
Person-to-Information	Efficient access to shared databases	Joint efforts for performance monitoring	Joint exploitation of resources
Person-to-System			

An IS improvement strategy requires KMS to provide each knowledge worker with appropriate and standardized tools such as Word, Excel, and e-mail at stage one. At stage two, an address book is needed, so that the client can find the updated information or the expert with the appropriate knowledge. At stage three, the client needs access to the vendor's technical database. In general, KMS in the IS improvement should use all the possible methods to facilitate the expertise from the vendor promptly flowing to the client when required.

A business impact strategy is to leverage the client's business processes. The challenge of the person-to-person systems is two-way communications between client and vendor. Joint contribution in the knowledge exchange is found a necessity. The KMS must enable both parties to interact through letting them share both explicit and tacit knowledge. Collaboration tools are a possible way to deal with this challenge, although as Alavi and Leidner (2001) see it, to make use of tacit knowledge through a KMS is a real challenge.

A commercial exploitation strategy has the purpose of making money on the organizations' IT assets. In addition to supporting knowledge transfer from vendor to client, the KMS has to effectively facilitate knowledge transfer from client to vendor. The vendor needs free access to the acquired IT assets to fully exploit it. This is also important to the client, as he will get better deals from selling his IT assets. In addition, the client needs continuous access to the IT assets that he has sold. This makes client and vendor mutually dependent on each other. A good KMS for this type of outsourcing arrangement has to include information about who knows what as well as what they know from vendor and client.

The stages model for knowledge management technology can be applied to develop another research proposition concerned with knowledge management in IT outsourcing relationships. As knowledge management systems to be applied in an outsourcing relationship involve two parties, both parties will have to be capable of using such applications. Thus, we suggest that vendor and client need to be at the same technological stage of growth to be able to successfully communicate with each other through knowledge management systems.

In a different empirical setting, Ko et al. (2005) studied antecedents of knowledge transfer from consultants to clients in enterprise system implementations. They found that the greater the shared understanding between a consultant and a client, the greater the knowledge transfers. Furthermore, the greater the absorptive capacity of a client, the more intrinsically motivated the client and the consultant, the more credible the consultant, the greater a client's communication decoding competence, the greater a consultant's communication encoding competence, and the greater the knowledge transfer.

The stages of growth model can be interpreted as alternative strategies, where the alternative strategies are person-to-tools strategy, person-to-person strategy, person-to-information strategy, and person-to-system strategy. A comparison of these four alternatives can be made to the classification into personalization versus codification strategy by Hansen et al. (1999). In this comparison, stages one and two represent personalization, while stages three and four represent codification. Therefore, it can be argued that the need for KMS is greater when the outsourcing relationship is supported by a codification strategy rather than a personalization strategy. Hence, we propose that a codification strategy is more dependent on knowledge management systems than a personalization strategy in knowledge transfer between vendor and client in an IT outsourcing relationship.

Intangible Assets in an Outsourcing Relationship

Knowledge management systems support knowledge transfer within and between intangible assets. One approach to defining intangible assets in an outsourcing relationship is to distinguish between three families: the external structure, the internal structure and the individual structure, as proposed by Sveiby (2001).

The external structure consists of the external environment. For the client, the vendor is in the external environment. For the vendor, the client is in the external environment. The internal structure consists of models, regulations, and information systems. The individual structure consists of staff competence. Knowledge transfer occurs within and between these three structures. Thus, we suggest that the external structure is the most important structure for successful knowledge transfer in IT outsourcing relationships.

Resource-Based Theory for Knowledge

We apply the knowledge-based view of the firm that has established itself as an important perspective in strategic management (Bock, Zmud, & Kim, 2005; Garud and Kumaraswamy, 2005). This perspective builds on the resource-based theory of the firm. According to the resource-based theory of the firm, performance differences across firms can be attributed to variances in the firms' resources and capabilities. Resources are considered strategic resources if they are (i) valuable, (ii) unique, (iii) inimitable, (iv) nontransferable, (v) nonsubstitutable, (vi) exploitable, and (vii) combinable. Thus, we suggest that the need for knowledge management systems in an IT outsourcing relationship increases as vendor and client mobilize strategic resources in their relationship.

The central tenet in resource-based theory is that unique organizational resources of both tangible and intangible nature are the real source of competitive advantage. With resource-based theory, organizations are viewed as a collection of resources that are heterogeneously distributed within and across industries. Accordingly, what makes the performance of an organization distinctive is the unique blend of the resources it possesses. A firm's resources include not only its physical assets such as plant and location but also its competencies. The ability to leverage distinctive internal and external competencies relative to environmental situations ultimately affects the performance of the business.

Exploring competencies in the context of the management of information technology is a relatively recent development in the evolution of the information systems discipline. The importance of developing competencies that allow organizations to successfully take advantage of information in their specific context has been noted. The concept of competence in the information systems literature is predominantly focused upon individual competence in the form of IT skill sets, rather than treated as an organizational construct. The focus has been on the technology supply side and individuals' skills, emphasizing the requirement for IT professionals to have not just technical skills but also business and interpersonal skills. More recently, change agentry as a skill for IT professionals has been proposed. The implication of this literature stream is that the solution to the problem of lacking benefits from IT is equipping IT specialists with additional skills. The inference is that the inability to deliver value from information arises from shortcomings in the IT function and among IT professionals.

Outsourcing gives a client organization access to resources in the vendor organization as the vendor handles IT functions for the client. Vendor resources can produce innovation, which is essential for long-term survival of the client. Quinn (2000) argues that the time is right for outsourcing innovation. Four powerful forces are currently driving the innovation revolution. First, demand is growing fast in the global economy, creating a host of new specialist markets sufficiently large to attract innovation. Second, the supply of scientists, technologists, and knowledge workers has skyrocketed, as have knowledge bases and the access to them. Third, interaction capabilities have grown. Fourth, new incentives have emerged.

Transformational outsourcing is an emerging practice to bring new capabilities to the organization. Resources are required to bring new capabilities, and resources bringing new capabilities can be found in an outsourcing vendor. In this context we apply the knowledge-based view of the firm that has established itself as an important perspective in strategic management. This perspective builds on the resource-based theory of the firm. According to the resource-based theory of the firm, performance differences across firms can be attributed to the variance in the firms' resources and capabilities. Resources that are valuable, unique, and difficult to imitate can provide the basis for firms' competitive advantages. In turn, these competitive advantages produce positive returns. According to Hitt et al. (2001), most of the few empirical tests of the resource-based theory that have been conducted have supported positive, direct effects of resources.

The essence of the resource-based theory of the firm lies in its emphasis on the internal resources available to the firm, rather than on the external opportunities and threats dictated by industry conditions. Firms are considered to be highly heterogeneous, and the bundles of resources available to each firm are different. This is both because firms have different initial resource endowments and because managerial decisions affect resource accumulation and the direction of firm growth as well as resource utilization (Løwendahl, 2000).

The resource-based theory of the firm holds that in order to generate sustainable competitive advantage a resource must provide economic value and must be presently scarce, difficult to imitate, nonsubstitutable, and not readily obtainable in factor markets. This theory rests on two key points—first, that resources are the determinants of firm performance, and second, that resources must be rare, valuable, difficult to imitate, and nonsubstitutable by other rare resources. When the latter occurs, a competitive advantage has been created. Resources can simultaneously be characterized as valuable, rare, nonsubstitutable, and inimitable. To the extent that an organization's physical assets, infrastructure, and workforce satisfy these criteria, they qualify as resources. A firm's performance depends fundamentally on its ability to have a distinctive, sustainable competitive advantage, which derives from the possession of firm-specific resources (Priem & Butler, 2001). The resource-based theory is a useful perspective in strategic management. Research on the competitive implications of such firm resources as knowledge, learning, culture, teamwork, and human capital, was given a significant boost by resource-based theory—a theory that indicated it was these kinds of resources that were most likely to be sources of sustainable competitive advantage for firms (Barney, 2001).

Firms' resource endowments, particularly intangible resources, are difficult to change except over the long term. For example, although human resources may be mobile to some extent, capabilities may not be valuable for all firms or even for their competitors. Some capabilities are based on firm-specific knowledge, and others are valuable when integrated with additional individual capabilities and specific firm resources. Therefore, intangible resources are more likely than tangible resources to produce a competitive advantage. In particular, intangible firm-specific resources such as knowledge allow firms to add value to incoming factors of production (Hitt et al., 2001). Resource-based theory attributes advantage in an industry to a firm's control over bundles of unique material, human, organizational, and locational resources and skills that enable unique value-creating strategies. A firm's resources are said to be a source of competitive advantage to the degree that they are scarce, specialized, appropriable, valuable, rare, and difficult to imitate or substitute.

Vendor Value Proposition

The value generation potential of an outsourcing relationship consists of three factors: client characteristics, the vendor-client relationship, and vendor characteristics. A key client characteristic is an understanding of how to manage resources that a firm does not own. A key in the vendor-client relationship is the formal (contractual) aspect of the relationship.

The third factor shaping the outsourcing value proposition is the vendor's own capabilities. According to Levina and Ross (2003), the concepts of complementarities and competencies explain that outsourcing vendors can increase productivity and reduce costs on client projects by applying a set of complementary application management competencies. This is the vendor value proposition. Thus, we suggest that the need for knowledge management systems in an IT outsourcing relationship increases as the vendor increases his complementary competencies.

The concept of complementarity posits that firms can improve productivity by engaging in complementary activities where benefits from doing more of one activity increase if the firm is also doing more of the other activity. This concept of complementarity has been used in studies of manufacturing to show that modern manufacturing approaches work as a system, rather than as a set of independent factors. Those firms that invest simultaneously in several complementary activities perform better than those firms that increase the level of some of these activities, but not others. In fact, literature on complementarity argues that firms that increase one factor without also increasing complementary factors may be worse off than firms that keep the factors at the same lower level.

An outsourcing vendor may develop different competencies. In the case study by Levina and Ross (2003), the vendor developed a set of three competencies to respond to client needs and market demands: IT personnel development, methodology development and dissemination, and customer relationship management:

- **IT personnel development** addressed existing IT labor market constraints by the vendor in ways that the client had not. The vendor replaced experienced, high-cost client staff with mostly lower-cost, junior programmers and then developed their skills through training, mentoring, and team-based project work. Junior staff valued the professional growth while their mentors often relished opportunities to watch somebody take off. As a professional services firm, the vendor viewed maintenance work as a first step in a career development path, which involved rotating professionals within engagements, assigning personnel development managers, and creating both technical and management hierarchies.

- **Methodology development and dissemination** was necessary for consistent delivery of best-of-breed solutions to client problems. Whereas the client's staff focused on addressing users' immediate needs, the vendor introduced methodologies that focused on overall operational improvements on projects. The vendor had a long history of methodology development. The methodologies not only specified processes, they also standardized project documentation through forms and templates such as change request forms, lost-time logs, and weekly status report forms to closely monitor project status.

- **Customer relationship management** was formalized through level of service agreements. Each agreement set a fixed price for agreed-upon services. The major philosophy of outsourcing was that the vendor is taking a risk. The vendor is responsible for whatever is defined in that client interface document as being the vendor's responsibility. While agreements might not lead to greater user satisfaction with the level of IT services, it did reduce uncertainty, thereby creating clearer expectations and an acceptance of limits. As users accepted these limits, they recognized and appreciated services that exceeded contract requirements.

These three competencies turned out to be complementary by being mutually reinforcing. Management practices targeted at one competency tended to enhance the other competencies as well. This reinforcing pattern was apparent in all three pairings of the competencies:

- **Personnel development and methodology development and dissemination are complementary competencies:** The methodology competency reinforced personnel development by helping junior staff learn quickly what they were expected to do. While methodologies were sometimes viewed as constraining individual initiative, one junior consultant argued that the methodology empowered her and others to challenge management directives that might be inconsistent with documented practices. In addition, standardization of practices around methodology facilitated staff rotations and scheduling. In the same way, personnel development practices, such as skill development, rotations, and promotion policies, provided training, encouragement, and incentives that led to consistent use and improvement of methodologies across the organization.

- **Methodology development and dissemination and customer relationship are complementary competencies:** When methodology delivered operational improvements, the vendor could sometimes increase service levels with no added cost to the client. In some cases, the vendor had been able to pull people off a project and had elected to share the savings with the client. These very visible improvements in IT service levels reinforced the customer relationship. Methodological approaches also improved customer relationship management practices by defining and standardizing best practices for creating and managing level of service agreements. The customer relationship management competence similarly reinforced the methodology competence. The vendor regularly communicated with the client to discuss issues and expectations, and one outcome was to help the client managers understand the methodologies so that they could facilitate, rather than hinder, the vendor's ability to meet expectations. Thus, client managers shared their knowledge of systems with the vendor and provided early warnings, where possible, when business or corporate IT changes might have an impact on the vendor's responsibilities.

- **Personnel development and customer relationship are complementary competencies:** Personnel development practices reinforced customer relationships by ensuring that staff understood and accepted accountability for meeting contractual obligations. Personnel development practices also developed communication skills to help staff establish customer expectations and build trust. At the same time, strong customer relationships led to better buy-in, on the customer's part, to personnel development policies that required release time or movement of personnel, such as training programs, mentoring, and job rotations.

The concepts of complementariness and core competencies explain that the vendor can increase productivity and reduce costs on client projects by applying this set of complementary application management competencies. Levina and Ross (2003) examined how the vendor delivers value to clients as a result of its ability to develop complementary competencies. First, they went beyond neoclassical economics theory to explain why potential clients are unlikely to develop these complementary competencies internally. They then explored the mechanisms that ensure that the benefits of the vendor's competencies are, in part, passed on to clients.

- **Why clients do not replicate and apply vendors' competencies:** Typically, clients have a different set of market structures and resource constraints than the IT services industry. Accordingly, clients have a different organization and different business processes. Clients have hired personnel to address the market conditions and customer demands of their industry. Clients can attempt to build IT application competencies rather than outsource to vendors, but, unlike vendors, they may find that optimizing the development and application of IT competencies will conflict with optimizing core business activities. Vendors, on the other hand, can shield themselves from these conflicts through the structure provided by contracts, which specify deliverables rather than levels of investment in competencies.

For example, to address labor market constraints, clients could increase the compensation of technical specialists, but non-IT workers might perceive the inflated IT salaries as unfair. Similarly, clients are typically not as well positioned as vendors to institute an IT personnel career development office or a practice of IT personnel rotation and promotion.

- **Why vendors share productivity gains with clients:** From the client perspective, the vendor's value proposition would not exist if the benefits of complementary competencies accrued solely to the vendor. Contract-based, interpersonal, and reputation-based mechanisms encourage vendors to share advantages with clients. Clients may deploy some contract-based mechanisms, including pilot projects, multiphase contracting with penalties, interpersonal relationship building, carrot-and-stick incentives and short-term contracts, and competent contract monitoring. All of these mechanisms increase client control and motivate vendors to demonstrate value to the client. Since the value of outsourcing to the client is very hard to measure, most researchers have focused on client satisfaction.

Reputation-based mechanisms provide vendors with a strong incentive to share productivity gains with clients. Vendors of IT service focus on reputation building in their relationships with clients. In addition to their current contracting structure, vendors care about their long-term market position. Thus, the vendor is inclined to share benefits with the client so that the information about the vendor's contribution enables it to win future contracts. Developing a solid industry reputation helps a vendor win new, and extend existing, engagements, which lead to the acquisition of, and control over, more projects.

Knowledge-intensive service firms like outsourcing vendors are typical value shops, and such firms depend on reputation for success, as reputation is a key driver of firm value creation. Reputation is a relational concept, in the sense that firms are judged by their stakeholders relative to their competitors. Reputation is what is generally said or believed about an entity, the net perception of a firm held by stakeholders judged relative to other firms. According to Sheehan (2002), there are four conditions, which must be present for reputation to work. First, rents earned from maintaining a good reputation must be greater than not. Second, there must be a minimum of contact among stakeholders to allow for the changes in reputation to be communicated. Third, there needs to be a possibility of repeat business. And lastly, there must be some uncertainty regarding the firm's type and/or behavior.

Reputation is related to the asymmetry of information, which is a typical feature of knowledge-intensive service firms. Asymmetry is present when clients believe the firm knows something that the clients do not and believe it is necessary to know to solve their problems.

Reputation can be classified as a strategic resource in knowledge-intensive firms. To be a strategic resource, it has to be valuable, rare, and costly to imitate, and possible to organize. Reputation is valuable, as it increases the value received by the client. Reputation is rare, as by definition only a few firms can be considered best in the industry. Reputation is costly to imitate, as it is difficult to build a reputation in the short run. Reputation is possible to organize in the general sense of controllability, which implies that a firm can be organized to take advantage of reputation as a resource.

Figure 9.23. Vendor's value proposition

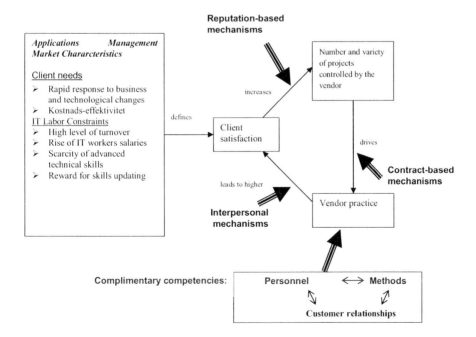

Client satisfaction is achieved in Figure 9.23 when the application of core competencies to projects is enabled by healthy client-vendor relationship, which is in part influenced by the vendor's expertise in managing client relationships. Competencies in turn grow through the vendor's firm-wide experience gained from controlling a large number and variety of projects, which in turn grow due to the reputation the vendor, and develops through its ability to satisfy customers. The model represents a set of positive feedback loops, which will result in negative outcomes if, for example, the competencies do not match client needs.

Erlingsson and Grødem (2005) conducted research to empirically test the vendor value proposition suggested by Levina and Ross (2003). Specifically, they formulated the following research question: What are the relationships among an IT outsourcing vendor's complementary core competencies and outsourcing success? In line with Levina and Ross (2003), their research proposed that the vendor has three core competencies, which are complementary to each other. The three core competencies are:

- Personnel development
- Methodology development and dissemination
- Customer relationship management

These arguably create more value as mutually reinforcing competencies than as individual, stand-alone competencies. Thus, benefits from doing more of one activity increases if the vendor is also doing more of another complementary competency. As Erlingsson and Grødem's (2005) research was attempting to empirically verify Levina and Ross's (2003) claims, the first six research propositions are made up from the competencies and the suggested complementary relationships between them as follows:

1. Will increased personnel development lead to more methodology development and dissemination?

2. Will increased methodology development and dissemination lead to more personnel development?

3. Will increased personnel development lead to more customer relationship management?

4. Will increased customer relationship management lead to more personnel development?

5. Will increased methodology development and dissemination lead to more customer relationship management?

6. Will increased customer relationship management lead to more methodology development and dissemination?

The final three propositions address the direct relationship between core competencies and outsourcing success. It can be reasoned that in order for the competencies to be complementary to each other and to have an effect on outsourcing success, both competencies must have an impact. If one competency does not have a relationship to outsourcing success, there is no mutuality. Therefore, the direct impact of each competency on outsourcing success contributes the last three propositions as follows:

7. Will more personnel development lead to increased IT outsourcing success?

8. Will more methodology development and dissemination lead to increased IT outsourcing success?

9. Will more customer relationship management lead to increased IT outsourcing success?

In Erlingsson and Grødem's (2005) research, outsourcing success was measured by customer benefits, customer satisfaction, and vendor benefits. Customer benefits are the extent of economical, technical, and strategic benefits attained. Customer satisfaction is the extent of overall satisfaction with the contract and desire to retain the outsourcing partner. Vendor benefits are the degree of economical, business development, and organizational benefits attained.

In their empirical study of outsourcing relationships, Erlingsson and Grødem (2005) tested the first six propositions using simple regression and found that all relationships between core competencies were statistically significant. This implies that the assumed complementarities between personnel development, methodology development and dissemination, and customer relationship management found initial support.

However, when applying multiple regression analysis, not all relationships were significant anymore. Relationships three to six were still statistically significant. The final complementary relationship, between customer relationship and methodology development, was not found to be present anymore. No statistical significance in either direction was shown. This contradicts the theory suggested by Levina and Ross (2003).

The last three propositions (seven, eight, and nine) did find support in the empirical research. Personnel development, customer relationship management, and methodology development and dissemination all influence outsourcing success. In our knowledge management perspective, such findings imply that improved knowledge management by the vendor in terms of personnel development, customer relationship management, and methodology development and dissemination will increase outsourcing success.

However, when applying multiple regression analysis, not all relationships were significant anymore. Based on their empirical research, Erlingsson and Grødem (2005) developed a new model of significant relationships

Figure 9.24. Empirical relationships for vendor competencies

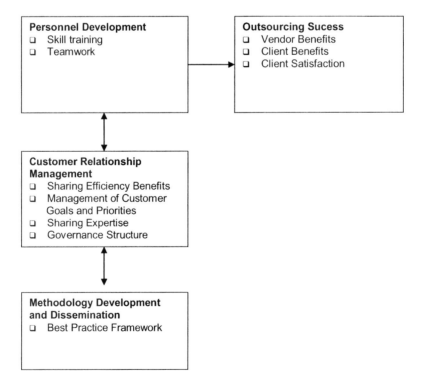

between vendor competencies and outsourcing success, as illustrated in Figure 9.24.

Personnel development in Figure 9.24 can be substituted with the more common term of human resource development. Human resource development is a process of developing and freeing up human potential and expertise through organizational development and personnel training and development in order to improve performance. Training is an important part of human resource development. There are two paths of skill training: formal and informal. Teamwork is another part of human resource development with an emphasis on cooperation rather than competition, on open disclosure of information, and on building loyalty to the firm as significant underpinnings of success. Norms of interaction for teamwork include willingness to value and respond to diversity, openness to criticism, and tolerance for failure.

Customer relationship management in Figure 6.4 is defined in terms of sharing efficiency benefits, management of customer goals and priorities, sharing expertise, and governance structure. Efficiency can be defined as the internal perspective to metrics like cost reduction and productivity enhancement. Management of customer goals and priorities is concerned with the vendor organization's ability to understand and satisfy the customer's needs and objectives by becoming better at meeting requirements. Sharing expertise with client's staff requires the vendor to have the right policies and procedures in order to transfer knowledge effectively to the client organization. Governance structure is the framework for assigning decision rights concerning principles, architecture, and infrastructure so that both vendor and customer have powers that match responsibilities.

Finally, methodology development and dissemination in Figure 6.4 is concerned with best practice framework. Best practice is the best of breed solutions to customer problems. For example, ITIL (Information Technology Infrastructure Library) provides a set of best practice guidelines and architectures to ensure that IT processes are closely aligned with business processes (Erlingsson & Grødem, 2005).

Value Shop as Vendor Value Configuration

When solving client problems, the vendor has the value configuration of value shop. The value shop is a company that creates value by solving unique problems for customers and clients (Stabell & Fjeldstad, 1998). Knowledge is the most important resource, and reputation is critical to firm success. A value shop is characterized by five primary activities: problem finding and acquisition, problem solving, choice, execution, and control and evaluation, as illustrated in Chapter one.

Problem finding and acquisition involves working with the customer to determine the exact nature of the problem or need. It involves deciding on the overall plan of approaching the problem. Problem solving is the actual generation of ideas and action (or treatment) plans. Choice represents the decision of choosing between alternatives. While the least important primary activity of the value shop in terms of time and effort, it is also the most important in terms of customer value. Execution represents communicating, organizing, and implementing the decision, or performing the treatment. Control and evaluation activities involve monitoring and measurement of how well the solution solved the original problem or met the original need. This may feed back into the first activity, problem finding and acquisition, for two reasons. First, if the proposed solution is inadequate or did not work, it feeds back into learning why it was inadequate and begins the problem-solving phase anew. Second, if the problem solution was successful, the firm might enlarge the scope of the problem-solving process to solve a bigger problem related to or dependent upon the first problem being solved. Thus, we suggest that vendor value shop performance in selecting and implementing the best solution for the client is dependent on the extent of client knowledge transfer.

Knowledge Strategy

Stock, flow, and growth strategies are alternative knowledge strategies (Hansen et al., 1999). Approaches to knowledge management are dependent on knowledge focus in the client organization. Distinctions can be made among expert-driven business, experience-driven business, and efficiency-driven business. An expert-driven business solves new problems with new methods. An experience-driven business solves new problems with experienced methods. An efficiency-driven business solves known problems with known methods.

The knowledge management strategy of an efficiency-driven business will be the stock strategy, while the flow strategy is more appropriate for the experience-driven business, and the growth strategy is more appropriate for the expert-driven business. Thus, we suggest that knowledge management systems in outsourcing relationships are less important when the client is an expert-driven business.

Approaches to knowledge management are dependent on knowledge focus in the organization. Distinctions can be made among expert-driven business, experience-driven business, and efficiency-driven business:

- **Expert-driven business** solves large, complex, risky, new, and unusual problems for customers. Competitive advantage is achieved through continuous improvisation and innovation. Knowledge workers apply general high-level knowledge to understand, solve, and learn. Learning from problem solving is important to be able to solve the next new and unknown problem for customers. An expert-driven business is characterized by both new problems and new methods for solution.

- **Experience-driven business** solves large and complicated problems for customers. The problems are new, but they can be solved with existing methods in a specific context every time. Competitive advantage is achieved through effective adaptation of existing problem-solving methodologies and techniques. Continuous improvement in effectiveness is important to be able to solve the next problem for customers. An experience-based business is characterized by new problems and existing methods for solution.

- **Efficiency-driven business** solves known problems. The quality of the solution is found in fast and inexpensive application to meet customer needs. Competitive advantage is achieved in the ability to make small adjustments in existing goods and services at a low price. An efficiency-driven business is characterized by known problems and known methods for solution.

Few knowledge-intensive firms are only active in one of these businesses. Most firms are active in several of these businesses. For example, medical doctors in a hospital are mainly in the experience-driven business of solving new problems with known methods. Sometimes, they are in the expert-driven business of solving new problems with new methods. Similarly, lawyers in a law firm are often in the expert-driven business, but most of the time in the experience-driven business. In some engineering firms, engineers are often in the efficiency-driven business, but most of the time in the experience-based business.

Knowledge focus will be different in expert-driven, experience-driven, and efficiency-driven businesses. In the expert-driven business, learning is important, while previous knowledge becomes obsolete. In the experience-driven business, know-how concerning problem solutions is important, while knowledge of previous problems becomes obsolete. In the efficiency-based business, all knowledge concerning both problems and solutions is important in an accumulation of knowledge to improve efficiency. These differences lead us to make distinctions between the following three knowledge management strategies of stock strategy, flow strategy, and growth strategy, as suggested by Hansen et al. (1999):

- **Stock strategy** is focused on collecting and storing all knowledge in information bases in the organization. Information is stored in databases and made available to knowledge workers in the organization and in knowledge networks. Knowledge workers use databases to stay updated on relevant problems, relevant methods, news, and opinions. Information on problems and methods accumulate over time in databases. This strategy can also be called person-to-knowledge strategy.

- **Flow strategy** is focused on collecting and storing knowledge in information bases in the organization as long as the information is used in knowledge work processes. If certain kinds of knowledge work disappear, then information for those work processes become obsolete and can be deleted from databases. This is a yellow-pages strategy where information on knowledge areas covered by individuals in the firm is registered. The link to knowledge sources in the form of individuals is made specific in the databases, so that the person source can be identified. When a knowledge worker starts on a new project, the person will search company databases to find colleagues who already have experience in solving these kinds of problems. This strategy can also be called person-to-person strategy.

- **Growth strategy** is focused on developing new knowledge. New knowledge is developed in innovative work processes taking place when knowledge workers have to solve new problems with new methods for customers. Often, several people are involved in the innovation, and together they have gone through a learning process. When a knowledge worker starts on a new project, the person will use the intraorganizational and interorganizational network to find information on work processes

Figure 9.25. Characteristics of knowledge management strategies

Characteristics	Stock strategy	Flow strategy	Growth strategy
Knowledge focus	Efficiency-driven business	Experience-driven business	Expert-driven business
Important persons	Chief knowledge officer Chief information officer Database engineers	Chief knowledge officer Experienced knowledge workers	Management Experts
Knowledge base	Databases and information systems	Information networks	Networks of experts, work processes and learning environments
Important elements	Access to databases and information systems	Access to knowledge space	Access to networks of experts and learning environments
Management task	Collecting information and making it available	Connecting persons to experienced knowledge workers	Providing access to networks
Learning	Efficiency training applying existing knowledge	Experience accumulation applying existing knowledge	Growth training developing new knowledge

and learning environments, which colleagues have used successfully in previous innovation processes.

There is a strong link between these three knowledge management strategies and the three alternatives of expert-driven, experience-driven, and efficiency-driven business. In Figure 9.25, characteristics of the three strategies are presented. Typically, efficiency-driven businesses will apply the stock strategy, while experience-driven businesses will apply the flow strategy, and expert-driven businesses will apply the growth strategy.

Maturity Model for IT Outsourcing Relationships

Stages of growth models have been used widely in both organizational research and information technology management research. According to King and Teo (1997), these models describe a wide variety of phenomena—the organizational life cycle, product life cycle, biological growth, and so forth. These models assume that predictable patterns (conceptualized in terms of stages) exist in the growth of organizations and in the growth of relationships among organizations.

In this section, a three-stage model for the evolution of an outsourcing relationship is proposed. The purpose of the model is both to understand the current situation in the relationship in terms of a specific stage and to develop strategies for moving to a higher stage in the future. The model is based on several management theories.

The first stage is the cost stage. This stage is based on transaction cost theory, neoclassical economic theory, contractual theory, theory of firm boundaries, and agency theory. The second stage is the resource stage. This stage is based on core competencies theory, resource-based theory, and relational exchange theory. The third and final stage is the partnership stage, which is based on partnership and alliance theory, stakeholder theory, and social exchange theory. Thus, we suggest that knowledge management systems are more important at higher stages of maturity in an outsourcing relationship.

Cost Stage

Initially, IT outsourcing is driven by cost concerns. According to neoclassical economic theory, firms outsource IT to attain cost advantages from assumed economies of scale and scope possessed by vendors (Ang & Straub, 1998). Neoclassical economic theory regards every business organization as a production function (Williamson, 2000), where their motivation is driven by profit maximization. This means that companies offer products and services to the market where they have a cost or production advantage. They rely on the marketplace where they have disadvantages. According to neoclassical economic theory, companies will justify their sourcing strategy based on evaluating possibilities for production cost savings. Thus, the question whether to outsource is a question of whether the marketplace can produce products and services at a lower price than internal production. In the context of IT outsourcing, a company will keep its IT function internally if this has production cost advantages, and it will outsource when the marketplace can offer production cost savings.

However, IT outsourcing causes additional costs to occur that are labeled transaction costs. Transaction costs occur in the exchange between client and vendor. According to transaction cost theory, transaction costs are positively associated with the necessity of investments in durable, specific assets; infrequency of transacting; task complexity and uncertainty; difficulty in measuring task performance; and independencies with other transactions.

Hancox and Hackney (2000) interviewed IT managers to find support for the transaction cost theory in IT outsourcing. Many of the features of transaction cost economics could be identified in the outsourcing arrangements.

When entering an IT outsourcing arrangement, vendor and client sign a contract. An outsourcing contract provides a legally binding, institutional framework in which each party's rights, duties, and responsibilities are codified and the goals, policies, and strategies underlying the arrangement are specified. Every outsourcing contract has the purpose of facilitating exchange and preventing opportunism.

Luo (2002) examined how contract, cooperation, and performance are associated with each other. He argues that contract and cooperation are not substitutes but complements in relation to performance. A contract alone is insufficient to guide outsourcing evolution and performance. Since outsourcing involves repeated interorganizational exchanges that become socially embedded over time, cooperation is an important safeguard mechanism mitigating external and internal hazards and overcoming adaptive limits of contracts, as we will see at higher levels of relationship maturity.

In an outsourcing relationship, the cooperating parties engage in an agency relationship defined as a contract under which one organization (the principal) engages another organization (the agent) to perform some service on its behalf which involves delegating some decision-making authority to the agent. Agency theory describes the relationship between the two parties.

According to Eisenhardt (1985), agency theory is concerned with resolving two problems that can occur in agency relationships. The first is the agency problem that arises when the desires or goals of the principal and agent conflict, and it is difficult or expensive for the principal to verify what the agent is actually doing. The second is the problem of risk sharing that arises when the principal and agent have different risk preferences. These problems are well known in IT outsourcing. An example might be that the client organization wants to reduce its costs, while the vendor organization wants to maximize profits.

A final theory for the cost stage is the theory of firm boundaries. Firm boundaries, defined as the scope of revenue-sharing arrangements across individuals, reflect trade-offs associated with referral problems, which are problems of matching economic opportunities to individuals' efficiency (Garicano & Hubbard, 2003). A large theoretical literature focuses on the question, "What determines firms' boundaries?" In our case of IT outsourcing, firms' boundaries are determined by the extent to which there are large markets for specialization. If there are large markets for IT services available from vendors, then a client company will tend to outsource more of its internal IT function.

When an outsourcing relationship has solved all problems at the cost stage, the parties are ready for resource stage. Solving all problems implies that the client achieves intended cost savings, transaction costs are at an acceptable level, the contract is successful in preventing opportunistic behavior, principal and agent avoid conflicts, and the division of labor between client and vendor works satisfactorily.

Resource Stage

The central tenet in resource-based theory is that unique organizational resources of both tangible and intangible nature are the real source of competitive advantage. With resource-based theory, organizations are viewed as a collection of resources that are heterogeneously distributed within and across industries.

Outsourcing gives a client organization access to resources in the vendor organization as the vendor handles IT functions for the client. Vendor resources can produce innovation, which is essential for long-term survival of the client. Quinn (2000) argues that the time is right for outsourcing innovation, because demand is growing fast in the global economy, creating a host of new specialist markets sufficiently large to attract innovation.

The value generation potential of an outsourcing relationship consists of three factors: client characteristics, the vendor-client relationship, and vendor characteristics. A key client characteristic is an understanding of how to manage resources that a firm does not own. A key in the vendor-client relationship is the formal (contractual) aspect of the relationship. The third factor shaping the outsourcing value proposition is the vendor's own capabilities. From an outsourcing vendor's perspective, there are many potential opportunities and benefits for the client. These opportunities and benefits can be derived from the IT outsourcing vendor's value proposition. Important vendor characteristics include capabilities such as technical competence, understanding the customer's business, and relationship management.

Levina and Ross (2003) stressed the importance of vendor characteristics in terms of the vendor value proposition. The concepts of complementariness and competencies explain that outsourcing vendors can increase productivity and reduce costs on client projects by applying a set of complementary application management competencies. They identified three complementary vendor competencies: IT personnel development, methodology development and dissemination, and customer relationship management.

The value generation potential from vendor resources can be significant for the client. If the vendor has strategic resources, applications of these resources for the client can provide the client organization with sustained competitive advantage. Strategic resources are characterized by being valuable, rare, inimitable, nontransferable, nonsubstitutable, combinable, and exploitable (Barney, 2002).

The resource stage is not only characterized by access to vendor resources. Also, the client will focus on internal resources at this stage. Those resources are typically concerned with core competencies. After outsourcing, the client organization will typically focus on and strengthen its core competencies. Core competencies can be defined as the skills that are the determinant resources for a firm's competitive advantage. Quinn (1999) argues that core competencies are not products or "those things we do relatively well." They are those activities—usually intellectually based service activities or systems—that the company performs better than any other enterprise. They are the set of skills and systems that a company does at best-in-the-world levels and through which a company creates uniquely high value for customers.

According to the theory of core competencies, developing best-in-the-world capabilities is crucial in designing a core competency strategy. Long-term advantage will depend on identifying the next unique combination no one else is exploiting in the marketplace; however, sustainable competitive advantage is strongest if tied to firm-specific capabilities.

When the vendor value proposition is working in terms of successful application of vendor resources for the client organization, and when the client organization is able to work on its core competencies, then the relationship is ready to move from the resource stage to the partnership stage.

Partnership Stage

Partnership appears to be a less rigorously defined analytical framework than other theories such as transaction costs, agency, and core competencies. Indeed, the very word "partnership" has a more everyday ring to it and is associated with the readily understood characteristics that may be found in a relationship between two or more parties in a particular context. Partnership's treatment in the IS literature seems largely nontheoretical, perhaps reflecting a wide diversity of practical arrangements and the absence of a single commonly recognized theory. Although the sharing of risk and reward is sometimes mentioned in the IS literature, often the emphasis is on intangibles, such as trust, comfort, understanding, flexibility, cooperation, shared values, goals, problem solving, good interpersonal relation, and regular communication (Hancox & Hackney, 2000).

Partnership, often referred to as an alliance, has frequently been noted as a major feature of IT outsourcing. Alliances are broadly defined as collaborative efforts between two or more firms in which the firms cooperate in an effort to achieve mutually compatible goals that they could not achieve easily alone.

According to relational exchange theory, a partnership is dependent on relational norms. Norms are expectations about behavior that are at least partially shared by a group of decision makers. Norms are important in relational exchange because they provide the governance rules of the game. Relational norms are based on the expectation of mutuality of interest, essentially prescribing stewardship behavior, and are designed to enhance the wellbeing of the relationship as a whole (Lambe, Spekman, & Hunt, 2000).

Social exchange theory suggests that each party in an exchange relationship compares the social and economic outcomes from these interactions to those that are available from exchange alternatives, which determines their dependence on the exchange relationship. Positive economic and social outcomes over time increase the partners' trust of each other and commitment to maintaining the exchange relationship (Lambe, Whitman, & Spekman, 2001).

A final theory that can illustrate the partnership stage is stakeholder theory. Stakeholder theory is concerned with balancing the interests of the stakeholders in an outsourcing relationship. According to Lacity and Willcocks (2000), there are four distinct client IT stakeholder groups and three distinct supplier IT stakeholder groups. The groups identified are customer senior business managers, customer senior IT managers, customer IT staff, customer IT users, and supplier senior managers, supplier account managers, and supplier IT staff.

Comparison of Stages

As illustrated in Figure 9.26, the cost stage is concerned with high economic benefits, low transaction costs, effective contracts, good principal-agent cooperation, and efficient division of labor from firm boundaries.

The resource stage is concerned with access to vendor resources, resources for innovation, strategic resources, and development of core competencies in the client organization in terms of skills and capabilities. The third and final partnership stage is concerned with alliance work, economic exchanges, mutual relational norms, social exchanges, and balancing stakeholder interests. Characteristics of each stage are listed in Figure 9.27.

As an outsourcing relationship matures, the maturity model suggests that performance measures develop beyond cost minimization and operational efficiency into business productivity and technology innovation, and further

Figure 9.26. Critical issues in each stage of maturity in outsourcing relationships

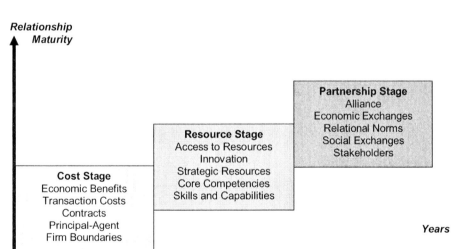

Figure 9.27. Characteristics of stages in outsourcing relationships

	Stage 1 Cost Stage	Stage 2 Resource Stage	Stage 3 Partnership Stage
Performance measures	Cost minimization Operational efficiency	Business productivity Technology innovation	Business benefits Mutual goals
Contract focus	Specified obligations Service level agreements	Key competence Critical projects	Profit sharing People exchanges
Relationship	Division of labor Service exchanges	Resource transactions Economic exchanges	Joint projects Social exchanges
Vendor management	Account manager	Operations manager	Business manager
Client management	IT manager	Division manager	Business manager
Vendor role	Supplier Contractual partner	Agent Strategic resource	Partner
Client role	Buyer Define technology requirements	Principal Define business needs	Partner Codeveloping business processes
Transplant role	Excellent operations	Technology initiatives	Complementary capabilities, skills, competences, and methods
Control mechanism	Service-level agreement Costs	Project performance Service quality	Strategy implementation
Governance arrangement	Duopoly IT infrastructure	Federation Applications	Monarchy Investments
Knowledge management	Information	Explicit knowledge	Tacit knowledge
Transactions	Scheduled	On demand	Continuous
Client dependency	Low	Medium	High
Vendor involvement	Low	Medium	High
Service improvements	Procurement	Innovation projects	Continuous innovation

into business benefits and achievement of mutual goals for client and vendor. The outsourcing contract changes focus from specified obligations and service-level agreements, to availability of strategic resources, management of key competence and critical projects, to arrangements for profit sharing and personnel exchanges between vendor and client.

Figure 9.28. Knowledge management issues depending on relationship maturity

	Stage 1 Cost Stage	Stage 2 Resource Stage	Stage 3 Partnership Stage
Know-what *Descriptive* *knowledge*	Financial transactions Service transactions	Resources and competences needed in business process redesign	Partner goals and strategies Partner culture
Know-how *Procedural* *knowledge*	Transaction processes Exchange processes	Business process redesign	Contributions to partner performance
Know-why *Reasoning* *knowledge*	Incidents in financial transactions Incidents in service transactions	Effects of business process redesign	Partner behavior in the relationship

Knowledge Needs

Knowledge needs will vary from stage to stage. At the cost stage, accounting and financial information is important. At the resource stage, resource information is needed. Finally, at the partnership stage, relationship support is needed. Examples of knowledge needs are listed in Figure 9.28.

Outsourcing Knowledge Dynamics

With the growing importance of pooling knowledge resources, knowledge management will have to transcend organizational boundaries to include sourcing partners. However, the focus of previous research studies has mainly been on intraorganizational knowledge management. In this study, we have attempted to direct the attention of knowledge management researchers toward interorganizational interfaces.

In a different empirical setting, Malhotra et al. (2005) attempted to direct the attention of knowledge management researchers toward interorganizational interfaces. They studied absorptive capacity configurations in supply chains. Their study indicates that enterprises have to build requisite absorptive capacity to prepare for collaborative knowledge creation with their supply chain partners. Absorptive capacity in this context is the ability of enterprises to acquire and assimilate information from their supply chain partners and to transform and exploit this information to achieve superior operational and strategic outcomes.

Similarly, Allard and Holsapple (2002) attempted to direct the attention of knowledge management researchers toward interorganizational interfaces. They studied knowledge management as a key for e-business competitiveness. In their knowledge chain model, knowledge externalization describes the embedding of knowledge into organizational outputs that are then released into the external environment.

The extent of interorganizational knowledge transfer between vendor and client in an IT outsourcing relationship will depend on the extent of outsourcing. Total IT outsourcing will typically require a greater extent of interorganizational knowledge transfer (Barthélemy & Geyer, 2004). This can be explored in future research, as outsourcing choices represent alternate ways for organizations to leverage available resources to increase the value of IT in meeting corporate objectives (Lee et al., 2004).

Knowledge management systems successfully supporting IT outsourcing relationships have to satisfy several requirements. First, they have to enable knowledge transfer between vendor and client. Second, they have to match strategic intent and knowledge management strategy. Furthermore, vendor and client need to be at the same technological stage of growth to be able to successfully communicate with each other through knowledge management systems. These are some of the research propositions presented in this chapter, which represents a rich knowledge base for future empirical studies.

In this chapter, we have learned that:

- Knowledge transfer is the most important and most relevant knowledge management mechanism in an IT outsourcing relationship.
- Vendor and client need to be at the same technological stage of growth to be able to successfully communicate with each other through knowledge management systems.
- Strategic intent influences knowledge needs.

Furthermore, we have developed several causal links from knowledge management systems to IT. Important concepts in these links are innovation, shared understanding, cost efficiency, social interaction, partnership quality, and access to vendor's intellectual capital.

Some of the important causal influences between knowledge management and IT outsourcing relationships are mapped in the causal loop diagram in Figure 9.29. Causal loop diagramming is described by Sterman (2000) and presented as a tool by www.vensim.com.

Figure 9.29 illustrates that knowledge transfer is the most important and most relevant knowledge management mechanism in an IT outsourcing relationship. Knowledge transfer is supported by knowledge management technology. More knowledge transfer increases the extent of social interaction between vendor and client, thereby improving partnership quality. Increased knowledge transfer also improved shared understanding, which leads to higher cost efficiency in tasks that have to be performed and services that are to be delivered.

Figure 9.30 illustrates one positive feedback loop from Figure 9.29. When knowledge transfer increases, shared understanding increases, causing improved cost efficiency, leading to more investments in knowledge management technology, and causing even more knowledge transfer between the IT outsourcing partners.

Figure 9.29. Causal loop diagram for knowledge management in outsourcing relationships

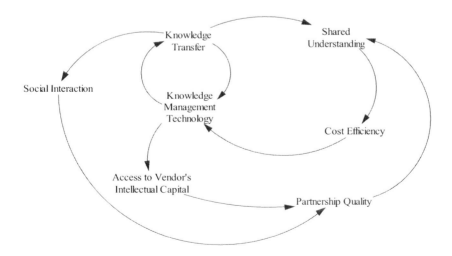

Figure 9.30. Positive feedback loop in the causal loop diagram

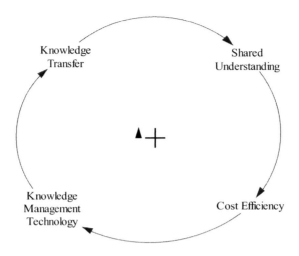

Figure 9.31. Reference mode for knowledge management technology in IT outsourcing

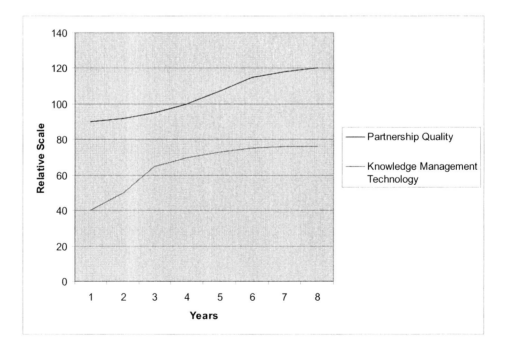

Figure 9.31 illustrates how causal loops can be translated into business dynamics. Partnership quality is influenced by the extent of knowledge management technology.

References

Alavi, M., & Leidner, D. E. (2001). Knowledge management and knowledge management systems: Conceptual foundations and research issues. *MIS Quarterly, 25*(1), 107-136.

Allard, S., & Holsapple, C. W. (2002). Knowledge management as a key for e-business competitiveness: From the knowledge chain to KM audits. *Journal of Computer Information Systems (JCIS), 42*(5), 19-25.

Andal-Ancion, A., Cartwright, P. A., & Yip, G. S. (2003). The digital transformation of traditional businesses. *Sloan Management Review,* Summer, 34-41.

Ang, S., & Straub, D. W. (1998). Production and transaction economics and IS outsourcing: A study of the U.S. banking industry. *MIS Quarterly, 22*(4), 535-552.

Artz, K. W., & Brush, T. H. (2000). Asset specificity, uncertainty and relational norms: An examination of coordination costs in collaborative strategic alliances. *Journal of Economic Behavior & Organization, 41*(4), 337-362.

Bahli, B., & Rivard, S. (2005). Validating measures of information technology outsourcing risk factors. *Omega, 22,* 175-187.

Barney, J. B. (2001). Is the resource-based 'view' a useful perspective for strategic management research? Yes. *Academy of Management Review, 26*(1), 41-56.

Barney, J. B. (2002). *Gaining and sustaining competitive advantage.* Upper Saddle River NJ: Prentice Hall.

Becker, W. M., Herman, M. F., Samuelson, P. A., & Webb, A. P. (2001). Lawyers get down to business. *The McKinsey Quarterly, 2001*(2), 45-55.

Bock, G. W., Zmud, R. W., & Kim, Y. G. (2005). Behavioral intention formation in knowledge sharing: Examining the roles of extrinsic motivators, social-psychological forces, and organizational climate. *MIS Quarterly, 29*(1), 87-111.

Chandra, C., & Kumar, S. (2000). Supply chain management in theory and practice: A passing fad or a fundamental change? *Industrial Management & Data Systems, 100*(3), 100-113.

Chen, H., Schroeder, J., Hauck, R. V., Ridgeway, L., Atabakhsh, H., Gupta, H., Boarman, C., Rasmussen, K., & Clements, A. W. (2002). COPLINK connect: Information and knowledge management for law enforcement. *Decision Support Systems, 34,* 271-285.

Curtis, G., & Cobham, D. (2002). *Business information systems: Analysis, design and practice.* Prentice Hall.

Crawshaw, R., Devlin, B., & Williamson, T. (1998). *Human rights and policing.* Netherlands: Kluwer Law International.

Das, T. K., & Teng, B. S. (2002). Alliance constellations: A social exchange perspective. *Academy of Management Review, 27*(3), 445-456.

Davenport, T. H., & Prusak, L. (1998). *Working knowledge.* Boston: Harvard Business School Press.

Dean, G. (1995). Police reform: Rethinking operational policing. *American Journal of Criminal Justice, 23*(4), 337-347.

Dean, G. (2000). The experience of investigation for detectives. Unpublished doctoral dissertation, Queensland University of Technology, Brisbane, Australia.

Dean, G. (2005). *The cognitive psychology of police investigators.* Paper presented at School of Justice Studies, Faculty of Law, Queensland University of Technology, Brisbane, Australia.

Dillard, J. F., & Yuthas, K. (2001). Responsibility ethic for audit expert systems. *Journal of Business Ethics, 30,* 337-359.

DiRomualdo, A., & Gurbaxani, V. (1998). Strategic intent for IT outsourcing. *Sloan Management Review, 39*(4), 67-80.

Druckman, M. (1998). Social exchange theory: Premises and prospects. *International Negotiation, 3*(2), 253-266.

Earl, M. J. (2000). Evolving the e-business. *Business Strategy Review, 11*(2), 33-38.

Edum-Fotwe, F. T., & McCaffer, R. (2000). Developing project management competency: Perspectives from the construction industry. *International Journal of Project Management, 18*(2), 111-124.

Edwards, D. L., & Mahling, D. E. (1997). Toward knowledge management systems in the legal domain. *Proceedings of the International ACM SIGGROUP Conference on Supporting Group Work Group*, The Association of Computing Machinery ACM, 158-166.

Eisenhardt, K. M. (1985). Control: Organizational and economic approaches. *Management Science, 31*(2), 134-149.

El Sawy, O. A. (2001). *Redesigning enterprise processes for e-business*. Boston: McGraw-Hill.

Erlingsson, O. G., & Grødem, E. (2005). *Vendor's complementary core competences and IT outsourcing success: An empirical investigation*. Unpublished master's thesis, Norwegian School of Management, Oslo, Norway.

Fahey, L., Srrivastava, R., Sharon, J. S., & Smith, D. E. (2001). Linking e-business and operating processes: The role of knowledge management. *IBM Systems Journal, 40*(4), 889-907.

Feng, K., Chen, E. T., & Liou, W. (2005). Implementation of knowledge management systems and firm performance: An empirical investigation. *Journal of Computer Information Systems (JCIS), 45*(2), 92-104.

Fielding, N. (1984). Police socialization and police competence. *The British Journal of Sociology, 35*(4), 568-590.

Foltz, C. B., Cronan, T. P., & Jones, T. W. (2005). Have you met your organization's computer usage policy? *Industrial Management & Data Systems, 105*(2), 137-146.

Frame, J. D. (1995). *Managing projects in organizations*. San Francisco: Jossey-Bass Publishers.

Fosstenløkken, S. W., Løwendahl, B. R., & Revang, Ø. (2003). Knowledge development through client interaction: A comparative study. *Organization Studies, 24*(6), 859-879.

Galanter, M., & Palay, T. (1991). *Tournament of lawyers: The transformation of the big law firms*. Chicago: The University of Chicago Press.

Garicano, L., & Hubbard, T. N. (2003). Firms' boundaries and the division of labor: Empirical strategies. *Journal of the European Economic Association, 1*(2/3), 495-502.

Garud, R., & Kumaraswamy, A. (2005). Vicious and virtuous circles in the management of knowledge: The case of Infosys Technologies. *MIS Quarterly, 29*(1), 9-33.

Gilley, M. K., & Rasheed, A. (2000). Making more by doing less: An analysis of outsourcing and its effects on firm performance. *Journal of Management, 26*(4), 763-790.

Gonzales, R., Gasco, J., & Llopis, J. (2005). Information systems outsourcing risks: A study of large firms. *Industrial Management & Data Systems, 105*(1), 45-62.

Gottschalk, P., & Karlsen, J. T. (2002). Management roles for successful IT projects. *Project Management, 8*(1), 7-13.

Gottschalk, P., & Solli-Sæther, H. (2006). *Managing successful IT outsourcing relationships*. Hershey, PA: Idea Group Publishing.

Grover, V., & Davenport, T. H. (2001). General perspectives on knowledge management: Fostering a research agenda. *Journal of Management Information Systems, 18*(1), 5-21.

Grover, V., Jeong, S. R., Kettinger, W. J., & Lee, C. C. (1993). The chief information officer: A study of managerial roles. *Journal of Management Information Systems, 10*(2), 107-130.

Grover, V., Teng, T. C., & Cheon, M. J. (1998). Towards a theoretically-based contingency model of information systems outsourcing. In L. P. Willcocks & M. C. Lacity (Eds.), *Strategic sourcing of information systems: Perspectives and practices*. Chichester, UK: John Wiley & Sons.

Hancox, M., & Hackney, R. (2000). IT outsourcing: Frameworks for conceptualizing practice and perception. *Information Systems Journal, 10*(3), 217-237.

Hansen, M. T., Nohria, N., & Tierney, T. (1999, March-April). What's your strategy for managing knowledge? *Harvard Business Review*, 106-116.

Hitt, M. A., Bierman, L., Shumizu, K., & Kochhar, R. (2001). Direct and moderating effects of human capital on strategy and performance in professional service firms: A resourced-based perspective. *Academy of Management Journal, 44*(1), 13-28.

Holsapple, C. W., & Singh, M. (2000). Electronic commerce: From a definitional taxonomy toward a knowledge-management view. *Journal of Organizational Computing and Electronic Commerce, 10*(3), 149-170.

Inkpen, A. C., & Tsang, E. W. K. (2005). Social capital, networks, and knowledge transfer. *Academy of Management Review, 30*(1), 146-165.

Janz, B. D., & Prasarnphanich, P. (2003). Understanding the antecedents of effective knowledge management: The importance of a knowledge-centered culture. *Decision Sciences, 34*(2), 351-384.

Jones, E. (2000). Remaking the firm: How KM is changing legal practice. *Knowledge Management Magazine,* www.kmmag.com

Kankanhalli, A., Tan, B. C. Y., & Wei, K. K. (2005). Contributing knowledge to electronic knowledge repositories: An empirical investigation. *MIS Quarterly, 29*(1), 113-143.

Karlsen, J. T., & Gottschalk, P. (2002). External or internal focus? A comparison of IT executive and IT project manager roles. *Engineering Management Journal, 14*(2), 5-11.

Kern, T., & Blois, K. (2002). Norm development in outsourcing relationship. *Journal of Information Technology, 17,* 32-42.

Kern, T., & Willcocks, L. P. (2000). Contract, control and presentation in IT outsourcing: Research in thirteen UK organizations. *Journal of Global Information Management, 8*(4), 15-29.

Kern, T., & Willcocks, L. P. (2002). Exploring relationships in information technology outsourcing: The interaction approach. *European Journal of Information Systems, 11,* 3-19.

Kim, C. W., & Mauborgne, R. (2003). Tipping point leadership. *Harvard Business Review,* April, 61-69.

King, W. R., & Teo, T. S. H. (1997). Integration between business planning and information systems planning: Validating a stage hypothesis. *Decision Sciences, 28*(2), 279-307.

Ko, D. G., Kirsch, L. J., & King, W. R. (2005). Antecedents of knowledge transfer from consultants to clients in enterprise system implementations. *MIS Quarterly, 29*(1), 59-85.

Koh, C., Ang, S., & Straub, D. W. (2004). IT outsourcing success: A psychological contract perspective. *Information Systems Research, 15*(4), 356-373.

Kodama, M. (2005). Customer value creation through knowledge creation with customers: Case studies of IT and multimedia businesses in Japan. *International Journal of Innovation and Learning, 2*(4), 357-385.

Kodama, M., & Ohira, H. (2005). Customer value creation through customer-as-innovator approach: A case study of video processing LSI development. *International Journal of Innovation and Learning, 2*(2), 175-185.

Lacity, M. C., & Willcocks, L. P. (2000). Relationships in IT outsourcing: A stakeholder perspective. In R. W. Zmud (Ed.), *Framing the domains of IT management: Projecting the future through the past*. Cincinnati, OH: Pinnaflex Educational Resources.

Lambe, C. J., Spekman, R. E., & Hunt, S. D. (2000). Interimistic relational exchange: Conceptualization and propositional development. *Journal of the Academy of Marketing Science, 28*(2), 212-225.

Lambe, C. J., Spekman, R. E., & Hunt, S. D. (2002). Alliance competence, resources, and alliance success: Conceptualization, measurement, and initial test. *Journal of the Academy of Marketing Science, 30*(2), 141-158.

Lambe, C. J., Wittmann, C. M., & Spekman, R. E. (2001). Social exchange theory and research on business-to-business relational exchange. *Journal of Business-to-Business Marketing, 8*(3), 1-36.

Lee, J. N. (2001). The impact of knowledge sharing, organizational capability and partnership quality on IS outsourcing success. *Information & Management, 38*(5), 323-335.

Lee, J. N., & Kim, Y. G. (1999). Effect of partnership quality on IS outsourcing success: Conceptual framework and empirical validation. *Journal of Management Information Systems, 15*(4), 29-61.

Lee, J. N., Miranda, S. M., & Kim, Y. G. (2004). IT outsourcing strategies: Universalistic, contingency, and configurational explanations of success. *Information Systems Research, 15*(2), 110-131.

Lee, M. K. O. (1996). IT outsourcing contracts: Practical issues for management. *Industrial Management & Data Systems, 96*(1), 15-20.

Levina, N., & Ross, J. W. (2003). From the vendor's perspective: Exploring the value proposition in information technology outsourcing. *MIS Quarterly, 27*(3), 331-364.

Li, E., & Lai, H. (2005). Collaborative work and knowledge management in electronic business. *Decision Support Systems, 39*, 545-547.

Lin, L., Geng, X., & Whinston, A. B. (2005). A sender-receiver framework for knowledge transfer. *MIS Quarterly, 29*(2), 197-219.

Liu, C. C., & Chen, S. Y. (2005). Determinants of knowledge sharing of e-learners. *International Journal of Innovation and Learning, 2*(4), 434-445.

Lonsdale, C., & Cox, A. (2000). The historical development of outsourcing: The latest fad? *Industrial Management & Data Systems, 100*(9), 444-450.

Luen, T. W., & Al-Hawamdeh, S. (2001). Knowledge management in the public sector: Principles and practices in police work. *Journal of Information Science, 27*(5), 311-318.

Luo, Y. (2002). Contract, cooperation, and performance in international joint ventures. *Strategic Management Journal, 23,* 903-991.

Løwendahl, B. R. (2000). *Strategic management of professional service firms.* Copenhagen, Denmark: Copenhagen Business School Press.

Malhotra, Y. (2000). Knowledge management for e-business performance: Advancing information strategy to "Internet Time." *Information Strategy: The Executive's Journal,* Summer, 5-16.

Malhotra, Y. (2002). Enabling knowledge exchanges for e-business communities. *Information Strategy: The Executive's Journal,* Spring, 26-31.

Malhotra, A., Gosain, S., & El Sawy, O. A. (2005). Absorptive capacity configurations in supply chains: Gearing for partner-enabled market knowledge creation. *MIS Quarterly, 2*(1), 145-187.

May, T. Y., Korczynski, M., & Frenkel, S. J. (2002). Organizational and occupational commitment: Knowledge workers in large corporations. *Journal of Management Studies, 39*(6), 775-801.

Mintzberg, H. (1990). The manager's job: Folklore and fact. *Harvard Business Review, 68*(2), 163-177.

Mintzberg, H. (1994). Rounding out the manager's job. *Sloan Management Review, 36*(1), 11-26.

Mountain, D. (2001). Could new technologies cause great law firms to fail? *Journal of Information, Law and Technology,* issue 1, 9 pages. http://elj.warwick.ac.uk/jilt/

Murch, R. (2000). *Project management: Best practices for IT professionals.* New York: Prentice Hall.

Nahapiet, J., & Ghoshal, S. (1998). Social capital, intellectual capital, and the organizational advantage. *Academy of Management Review, 23*(2), 242-266.

O'Connor, K. (2000). How to overcome the cultural barriers that can blockade knowledge management. *Law Technology News,* May, www.lawtechnews.com

Perrons, R. K., & Platts, K. (2004). The role of clockspeed in outsourcing decisions for new technologies: Insights from the prisoner's dilemma. *Industrial Management & Data Systems, 104*(7), 624-632.

Pettus, M. L. (2001). The resourced-based view as a development growth process: Evidence from the deregulated trucking industry. *Academy of Management Journal, 44*(4), 878-896.

Plessis, M., & Boon, J. A. (2004). Knowledge management in e-business and customer relationship management: South African case study findings. *International Journal of Information Management, 24,* 73-86.

Porter, M. E. (2001), Strategy and the Internet. *Harvard Business Review,* March, 63-78.

Quinn, J. B. (1999). Strategic outsourcing: Leveraging knowledge capabilities. *Sloan Management Review,* Summer, 9-21.

Quinn, J. B. (2000). Outsourcing innovation: The new engine of growth. *Sloan Management Review,* Summer, 13-28.

Priem, R. L., & Butler, J. E. (2001). Is the resourced-based view a useful perspective for strategic management research? *Academy of Management Review, 26*(1), 22-40.

Sambamurthy, V., & Subramani, M. (2005). Special issue on information technologies and knowledge management. *MIS Quarterly, 29*(1), 1-7.

Singh, R., Iyer, L., & Salam, A. F. (2004). Web service for knowledge management in e-marketplaces. *E-Service Journal,* 32-52.

Shankman, N. A. (1999). Reframing the debate between agency and stakeholder theories of the firm. *Journal of Business Ethics, 19*(4), 319-334.

Sheehan, N. T. (2002). *Reputation as a driver in knowledge-intensive service firms.* Series of doctoral dissertations, Norwegian School of Management, Sandvika, Norway.

Shi, Z., Kunnathur, A. S., & Ragu-Nathan, T. S. (2005). IS outsourcing management competence dimensions: Instrument development and relationship exploration. *Information & Management, 42,* 901-919.

Stabell, C. B., & Fjeldstad , Ø. D. (1998). Configuring value for competitive advantage: On chains, shops, and networks. *Strategic Management Journal, 19,* 413-437.

Stake, R. E. (1994). Case studies. In N. K. Denzin & Y. S. Lincoln (Eds.), *Handbook of qualitative research* (pp. 236-247). Thousand Oaks, CA: Sage Publications,.

Sterman, J. D. (2000). *Business dynamics: Systems thinking and modeling for a complex world.* Boston: McGraw-Hill.

Susskind, R. (2000). *Transforming the law.* UK: Oxford University Press.

Sveiby, K. E. (2001). A knowledge-based theory of the firm to guide in strategy formulation. *Journal of Intellectual Capital, 2*(4), 344-358.

Tsai, M. T., Yu, M. C., & Lee, K. W. (2005). Developing e-business systems based on KM process perspective: A case study of Seven-Eleven Japan. *The Journal of American Academy of Business,* March, 285-289.

Wang, K., Hjelmervik, O. R., & Bremdal, B. (2001). *Introduction to knowledge management.* Trondheim, Norway: Tapir Academic Press.

Wasko, M. M., & Faraj, S. (2005). Why should I share? Examining social capital and knowledge contribution in electronic networks of practice. *MIS Quarterly, 29*(1), 35-57.

Weill, P., & Vitale, M. R. (2001). *Place to space, migrating to e-business models.* Boston: Harvard Business School Press.

Weill, P., & Vitale, M. R. (2002). What IT infrastructure capabilities are needed to implement e-business models? *MIS Quarterly Executive, 1*(1), 17-34.

Wickramasinghe, N., & Silvers, J. B. (2003). IS/IT prescription to enable medical group practices to manage managed care. *Health Care Management Science, 6,* 75-86.

Willcocks, L. P., Hindle, J. L., Feeny, D. F., & Lacity, M. C. (2004). IT and business process outsourcing: The knowledge potential. *Information Systems Management,* Summer, 7-15.

Williamson, O. E. (2000). The new institutional economics: Taking stock, looking ahead. *Journal of Economic Literature, 38,* 595-613.

Chapter X

Conclusion

This conclusion chapter will summarize and tie all of the information in this book together by focusing on the business dynamics in information technology. System dynamics for the entire IT organization in an enterprise, as well as the entire IT industry, is of importance to enable alignment between business needs and information technology capabilities.

Interactions between organizational performance and information technology create dynamics over time. Some of these dynamics are counterintuitive and surprising to management. Some of these dynamics have a spiraling effect of information technology that can cause not only exponential growth and prosperity, but also decline and collapse. Understanding the dynamics is essential to successful information technology management.

Many examples of such phenomena were presented in this book. For example, in IT governance, infrastructure congestion may increase as a consequence of infrastructure investment. The positive feedback loop illustrated in Figure 3 in chapter 3 goes like this: Higher infrastructure congestion leads to more infrastructure investment, more infrastructure investment leads to better infrastructure capability, better infrastructure capability leads to more infrastructure visits, and more infrastructure visits leads to even higher infrastructure congestion.

This example is similar to traffic congestion in cities such as Oslo, Norway. After having improved the highway around the city of Oslo some years ago, traffic congestion is now higher than ever before on this highway. One of the major reasons for this result is the increasing distance between living location and working location. As the highway improved, people selected housing in nicer neighborhoods that were often further away from work. As the highway improved, people did not move when the office location moved to a location farther away. This analogy to infrastructure congestion is interesting in light of service-oriented architecture for infrastructure that was popular in 2006.

Another example in this book is concerned with dynamics of outsourcing relationships. Based on Lee and Kim's (1999) static study of partnership quality, this book developed a dynamic model of partnership quality. In Lee and Kim's (1999) study, partnership was found to be one of the significant determinants of partnership quality. In the system dynamics model, participation is part of a positive feedback loop consisting of agency quality, participation, and partnership quality. If agency quality deteriorates, for example because of alliance management experience, then participation will decrease and partnership quality will deteriorate, leading to further deterioration in agency quality.

This is illustrated in Figure 2 in hapter 6. The point is that a positive feedback loop is self-enforcing in both negative and positive directions. Depending on the starting point, such a feedback loop might cause fast deterioration in partnership quality. As illustrated, if the starting point is deterioration in agency quality, then partnership quality will go down as a consequence of lower participation.

An interesting aspect of system dynamics that was not included in this book is the effect of delays on business dynamics. Often, delays cause fluctuations over time. For example, if the IT organization experiences fluctuations in performance over time, this might have been caused by the CIO's decision making rather than external factors.

System dynamics modeling involves much more than presented in this book. It is a computer simulation tool, enabling computer simulations of business dynamics in information technology based on different assumptions and scenarios. The interested reader might find what he or she is looking for in Sterman's (2000) book on business dynamics.

Perhaps the most important dynamics described in this book are concerned with knowledge management. According to the resource-based theory of the firm (Garud & Kumaraswamy, 2005), organizational resources are the real source of competitive advantage. In the knowledge economy, the most important resource—sometimes the only resource in an enterprise—is knowledge. While knowledge is stored in the heads of people, the raw material in terms of information is stored in computers. The dynamic interactions between information in computers and knowledge in heads of employees determine success or failure for the enterprise.

In this perspective, information technology must have the capability to enable knowledge work and to support development of strategic knowledge resources. Strategic knowledge resources are characterized by being valuable, rare, inimitable, nonsubstitutable, nontransferable, combinable, and exploitable. Dynamic interactions between information and knowledge should enable more knowledge resources to become strategic over time.

In the information technology community, top management involvement is often stressed. However, I will not conclude this book by writing that top management should understand and manage business dynamics in information technology. Rather, I suggest that the emerging army of knowledge workers in most organizations should do it themselves in their knowledge management organization.

In a company with 10,000 employees, there is 1 CEO and 9,999 other employees. The only way 9,999 people can get their job done is by not involving the CEO in all of it. Business dynamics in information technology is an example. As I document in another book, the CEO does not control much in an enterprise (Gottschalk, 2006): "Being a CEO means bearing full responsibility for a company's success or failure, but being unable to control most of what will determine it." (p.13)

References

Garud, R., & Kumaraswamy, A. (2005). Vicious and virtuous circles in the management of knowledge: The case of Infosys technologies. *MIS Quarterly, 29*(1), 9-33.

Gottschalk, P. (2006). *CIO and corporate strategic management: Changing role of CIO to CEO*. Hershey, PA: Idea Group Publishing.

Lee, J.-N., & Kim, Y.-G. (1999). Effect of partnership quality on IS outsourcing success: Conceptual framework and empirical validation. *Journal of Management Information Systems, 15*(4), 29-61.

Sterman, J.D. (2000). *Business dynamics: Systems thinking and modeling for a complex world*. Boston: McGraw-Hill.

About the Authors

Petter Gottschalk is professor of information and knowledge management at the Norwegian School of Management in Oslo, Norway. He teaches at the Arab Academy in Alexandria, Fudan University in Shanghai, and Nanyang University in Singapore. Dr. Gottschalk has written several books published by Idea Group: *Strategic Knowledge Management Technology Managing Successful IT Outsourcing Relationships* with Hans Solli-Sæther, *E-Business Strategy, Sourcing and Governance*, *Knowledge Management Systems in Law Enforcement: Technologies and Techniques*, *CIO and Corporate Strategic Management: Changing Role of CIO to CEO*, and *Knowledge Management Systems: Value Shop Creation*. Petter Gottschalk earned his MBA at the Technical University of Berlin, Germany, his MSc at Thayer School of Engineering, Dartmouth College, and the Sloan School of Management at Massachusetts Institute of Technology, and his DBA at Henley Management College at Brunel University, UK. For more than 15 years, Dr. Gottschalk was an executive in business organizations. He was the CIO of ABB Norway, the CEO of ABB Datacables, and the CEO of the Norwegian Computing Center.

FOREWORD AUTHORS:

Stefan Holgersson earned his PhD in information systems development at the University of Linköping in Sweden. The aim and direction of his research is policing, and he works part-time as a patrolling officer. Besides being a patrolling officer, he is part of the Swedish negotiator team and works in a special group that strives to communicate with participants in riot situations on the street. He is involved in information system projects in the Swedish police force, which focus on providing useable systems for the users at the street level.

Rob Tweehuysen, Msc, has a background in applied mathematics from the Technical University of Delft in the Netherlands. His professional career involves positions at different levels, ranging from R&D to business development: researcher at Philips Physics Laboratory (Eindhoven, the Netherlands); Visiting Research Fellow at the System Dynamics Group at Dartmouth College (USA); Business Development, Financial Planning and Corporate Strategy of the Océ Group (Venlo, the Netherlands), Deputy Director of Marketing and Strategy at TNO; consultant of RAND Europe (Leiden, the Netherlands). Since 1998 he has directed his own company, Tweehuysen B.V., which specializes in identifying, selecting, and developing new business, particularly in ife sciences. He is cofounder and shareholder of the high-tech companies Chiralix BV, Spinnovation BV, Sensor Sense BV, Encapson BV, NovioMetrix BV.

Index

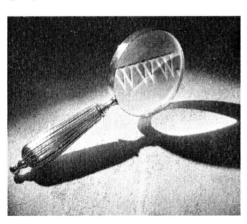